THE FATHERS OF THE CHURCH

A NEW TRANSLATION

VOLUME 42

THE FATHERS OF THE CHURCH

A NEW TRANSLATION

SAINT AMBROSE

HEXAMERON, PARADISE, AND CAIN AND ABEL

Translated by

JOHN J. SAVAGE

The Catholic University of America Press
Washington, D. C.

NIHIL OBSTAT:

JOHN A. GOODWINE

Censor Librorum

IMPRIMATUR:

✠ FRANCIS CARDINAL SPELLMAN

Archbishop of New York

June 17, 1961

The *nihil obstat* and *imprimatur* are official declarations that a book or pamphlet is free of doctrinal or moral error. No implication is contained therein that those who have granted the *nihil obstat* and *imprimatur* agree with the content, opinions, or statements expressed.

Library of Congress Catalog Card No. 77-081354
ISBN-13: 978-0-8132-1383-5 (pbk.)

Reprinted 1977
Reprinted 1985
First paperback reprint 2003

INTRODUCTION

THE CIRCUMSTANCES of the life of St. Ambrose up to 374, when he became bishop of Milan, are well known. The date of his birth is usually given as either 333 or 340. His father was *praefectus praetorio Galliarum,* with headquarters at Trier. After her husband's early death, the widowed mother brought her three children to Rome. There, Ambrose, the youngest of the children, attended the rhetorical schools in preparation for a public career. He attained the office of consul about 370, with two northern provinces under his control. His election as bishop of Milan on the death of the Arian bishop Auxentius followed a few years later. His affability, his sense of justice, and his accessibility endeared him to everyone, emperors and commoners alike. His days were spent in administrative work. Still, by diligent application he was able to advance in learning, like many a busy priest or professor today, as he prepared himself for his frequent public appearances.[1]

In the intervening period between his advancement to the office of bishop and the delivery of the nine homilies on

1 See *De officiis ministrorum* 1.1.4: *Discendum igitur mihi simul et docendum est, quoniam non vacavit ante discere.*

The Six Days of Creation,[2] probably during Holy Week in 387,[3] Ambrose devoted himself to such preliminary studies as *Paradise* and *Cain and Abel*. The precise date of the sermons on creation is still a matter of dispute. Bardenhewer[4] because of a reference in *Hexameron* (3.1.3) to a complete victory over Arianism, places the work in a period not before 389.

For the homilies on the creation Ambrose is much indebted to the celebrated work on the same subject by his Greek contemporary, St. Basil, who also rose to the office of bishop. Basil's sermons were delivered about seventeen years previous to those given by his Latin admirer and, like those of Ambrose, in the course of one week in Lent. Ambrose does not actually mention Basil's name in the text of his work, but he refers in one passage (4.11) to the authority of one 'who preceded him in time and in ability.' It would be a mistake to assume that Ambrose's work is merely a translation. It is, in fact, a free adaptation in a Latin dress, filled with reminiscences from Ambrose's wide reading in the Latin classics which he seems to have harbored in his memory since his student days in Rome. The concluding part of his book on the work of the sixth day owed much to the author's reading in medical writers such as Galen. Ambrose's remarks on the symbolism of the struc-

---

2 Manuscript tradition favors the spelling 'Exameron' rather than the usual 'Hexameron' (cf. C. Schenkl, CSEL 32.1.1). Each of the six books is concerned with the special work of creation completed on each of the six days. St. Ambrose devoted two homilies each to the work of the first, third, and fifth days, making a total of nine homilies altogether.

3 It is interesting to note that this date coincides with the dates given for St. Augustine's baptism at the hands of St. Ambrose. See F. D. Dudden, *The Life and Times of St. Ambrose* II (Oxford 1935) 713, for support of this date for *Hexameron*.

4 O. Bardenhewer, *Geschichte der altkirchlichen Literatur* III (2nd ed., Freiburg B. 1923) 498-510. Cf. B. Altaner, *Patrologie* (2nd ed. Freiburg i. B.) 333.

ture of the human body have a striking pertinence even today. Ambrose's dependence on Basil for most of his exposition should not cause us to shut our eyes to the importance of his achievement in this one of his major works. Here we are introduced to the great tradition of hexameron literature in the West. To say with Robbins that this work of St. Ambrose 'has little independent value' is to overlook its significance as a literary masterpiece.[5]

Following in the footsteps of his great model, Ambrose has made these sermons into a series of Christian and humanistic observations on nature and man in their relations to their Creator, who formed them out of no pre-existing material. In elaborating this thought from the manifold body of evidence presented by the Scriptures, Ambrose has in addition resorted to over a hundred reminiscences from his beloved Latin poet. Virgil's theocentric philosophy as expressed especially in his *Georgics* became an object of fascination to his fellow countryman—one might almost say his fellow townsman, for Virgil spent part of his boyhood as a student in Milan. Ambrose has something of the spirit of the Roman poet who also marveled at the wonders of the created world in language that is often full of charm, 'All the charm of all the Muses often flowering in a lonely word.' Many of these 'lonely words' Ambrose embedded in his mosaic on creation. Of 103 reminiscences of Virgil, about one-half are reflections of passages in the *Georgics;* the *Aeneid* supplied over forty; and there are eight passages that suggest that Ambrose held the *Eclogues* in some esteem.[6]

As we might suspect from his *De officiis ministrorum,* modeled on Cicero's well-known work, the most popular

5 F. E. Robbins, *The Hexaemeral Literature* (Chicago 1912) n. 58.
6 Cf. Sister Mary D. Diederich, *Vergil in the Works of St. Ambrose* Washington 1931); Sister M. Theresa of the Cross Springer, *Nature Imagery in the Works of St. Ambrose* (Washington 1931).

prose author with Ambrose was Cicero. One is not surprised, therefore, that there are about twenty reflections from Cicero in *Hexameron,* taken largely from the commendation given to agricultural pursuits in *De senectute.* The Lucretian phrases which appear here and there in *Hexameron* seem to be part of the common stock of scientific terms to which the Roman poet gave currency. We are somewhat taken by surprise to see how Ambrose has stored in his mind some half-score of Horace's happy phrases. Sallust, so popular in the Christian schools for his moral maxims, furnishes three clear reflections. Of course, the majority of citations or reminiscences are from the Old and New Testaments, being in *Hexameron* at the ratio of five or six to one of the non-Christian authors. Nevertheless, this proportion is a striking one. Here we find ourselves firmly entrenched in the great tradition of Christian humanism. We are reminded of the *suavitas* or charm which Augustine felt was the characteristic of the homilies of Ambrose.[7]

This and the following two minor works of St. Ambrose have never before been translated into English. There is no question that a work such as *Hexameron,* because of its intrinsic worth and because of its unusual influence on later literature and art, deserves to appear in an English dress.[8] This book, with its many poetic overtones, is a challenge to any translator. The precious bits which the late E. K. Rand rendered into choice English in his *Founders* make us wish that he had applied his skill to the work as a whole. Some of the strikingly poetic passages in *Hexameron* overflowed

7 See the brief but penetrating statements on the humanism of St. Ambrose in Gerald Groveland Walsh, *Medieval Humanism* (New York 1942) 27-28.

8 Cf. Pierre de Labriolle, *Histoire de la littérature latine chrétienne* (Paris 1947) 409. Ambrose, notwithstanding his ties with classical prose style, has set the pattern for the future, if not in prose, at least in verse; see M. P. Cunningham, *Studies in Philology* 52 (1955) 509-514.

into Ambrose's famous hymns, especially the famous '*Aeterne rerum Conditor*.' This hymn can be looked upon as either a prelude or a postlude to his prose work on creation.

The two minor works, the translation of which appears in this volume, reflect Ambrose's wide reading in the allegorical interpretation of much of the Old Testament, found especially in several volumes by Philo Judaeus of Alexandria.[9] The rhetorical style of these two works suggest that, like the homilies on creation, they were delivered orally and, perhaps, also recorded by a *notarius*.[10]

The homily *Paradise* is an early work of St. Ambrose. This is clear from a statement he makes in a letter addressed to Sabinus.[11] In this letter, which was written soon after the publication of *Hexameron* (*c.* 389), Ambrose refers to *Paradise* in terms that are somewhat derogatory, stating that it was written many years ago before he had acquired experience as a bishop. Since he became bishop of Milan in 374, it may be conjectured that *Paradise* was written a year or two later, that is, about 375. It would be difficult to determine what changes or modifications, if any, the author would have made in the treatment of this subject at a time when, presumably, his judgment was more mature. Ambrose, in the course of his letter to Sabinus, seems to emphasize what he has already discussed in his homily (3.13 and 11.57) that Paradise should not be regarded as a place, but as an aspect of the higher part of our nature. Ambrose was well acquainted with the allegorical interpretation of the Old Testament found in the works of Philo Judæus, although he mentions the name of this influential writer but once (4.25).

St. Ambrose seems to have planned *Cain and Abel* as a

9 *Philo* with an English translation by F. H. Colson and G. H. Whitaker I-VIII (London and New York 1929).

10 See *Hexameron* 5.12.36.

11 Letter 43; it is translated as Letter 25 by Sister Mary Beyenka (Fathers of the Church 26) 129-134.

continuation of *Paradise*. If the date 375 is accepted for the latter work, then *Cain and Abel* was written soon after. Both of these minor works follow a rhetorical pattern characteristic of the 'homily.' St. Ambrose is committed to the allegorical mode of interpretation laid down by Philo, especially in *De sacrificiis Abelis et Caini.*[12] Although he is thus not the first to introduce this method of interpretation in the West, he has set upon it his imposing stamp—a stamp which is conspicuous in medieval art and literature.

The translation has been based principally on the critical edition of C. Schenkl, CSEL 32.1, for *Hexameron* (3-261), for the *De Paradiso* (267-336) and for *De Cain et Abel* (339-409). The valuable Benedictine edition of 1686-90 as reprinted in Migne, *PL* 14 (123-274; 275-314; 315-341), has been consulted. For the sake of arousing the interest of the reader the translator has ventured to break up the longer paragraphs.

The citations from Scripture conform for the most part to Challoner's revision of the Rheims-Douay translation for the Old Testament. For the New Testament and for Genesis, except where St. Ambrose's quotations represent a definite departure from the Vulgate, the new translations undertaken under the auspices of the Confraternity of Christian Doctrine have been used. The *Hexameron,* since it presupposed the text and Scriptural quotation of St. Basil's work on the same subject, presented a special problem. So many departures from the Vulgate appeared in these citations of St. Ambrose that is seemed unnecessary to refer to the Septuagint version in so many individual cases.

---

12 *Philonis Alexandrini opera quae supersunt* I, ed. L. Cohn (Berlin 1896) 202-257. The extent of Ambrose's dependence on Philo can be gauged by consulting the extensive list of parallels cited by C. Schenkl in his critical edition, CSEL 32.1 3-261, 339-409.

SELECT BIBLIOGRAPHY

Editions and Translations:

Cohn, L., and P. Wendland, *Philonis Alexandrini opera quae supersunt* (Berlin 1896) I 1-60 (*De opificio mundi*); 61-169 (*Legum allegoriae*).

Colson, F. H., and G. H. Whitaker, *Philo,* text with translation into English (London and New York 1929) I (*De opificio mundi; Legum allegoriae*); supplementary Vol. I. ed. R. Marcus (Cambridge, Mass. 1953) (*Quaestiones in Genesim*).

Frisch, J. du, et N. le Nourry, *Sancti Ambrosii episcopi opera,* 2 v. (Paris 1686-1690).

Giet, S., *Basile de Césaree, homélies sur l'Hexaeméron,* Greek text with French translations (Paris 1949).

Migne, J. P., *Patrologiae Latinae cursus completus* (3rd reprint of Benedictine edition), (Paris 1845) 14.123-274; 275-314; 315-341.

Niederhuber. J. E., *Ambrosius von Mailand Exameron,* trans. into German, Bibliothek der Kirchenväter I (Kempten and Munich 1914).

Pasteris, E., *San Ambrogio, L'esamerone ossia dell' origine e natura delle cose,* text with translation. into Italian, Corona Patrum Salesiana ser. Lat. 4 (Turin 1937).

Schenkl, C., *Sancti Ambrosii Opera,* Corpus Scriptorum Ecclesia sticorum Latinorum 32.1 (Vienna 1896) 3-261; 267-336; 339-409.

BIBLIOGRAPHY

Secondary Works:

Altaner, B., *Patrologie* (2nd ed., Freiburg i. B. 1950).

Bardenhewer, O., *Geschichte der altkirchlichen Literatur* III (2nd ed, Freiburg i. B. 1923).

Breiher, E., "Philo Judaeus," *Catholic Encyclopedia* XII (New York 1911) 23-25.

Diederich, Sister Mary D., *Vergil in the Works of St. Ambrose* (Washington 1931).

Dudden, F. H., *The Life and Times of St. Ambrose,* 2 v. (Oxford 1935).

Labriolle, Pierre de, *Histoire de la littérature latine chrétienne* (3rd ed., Paris 1947).

Rand, E. K., *Founders of the Middle Ages* (Cambridge, Mass. 1928).

Springer, Sister M. Theresa of the Cross, *Nature Imagery in the Works of St. Ambrose* (Washington 1931).

Walpole, A. S., *Early Latin Hymns* (Cambridge 1922) 16-114.

Wolfson, H. A., *Philo* I (Cambridge, Mass. 1947) 295-324, (*Creation*); 424-462 (*Free Will*).

SAINT AMBROSE

HEXAMERON, PARADISE, AND CAIN AND ABEL

Translated by

JOHN J. SAVAGE

Professor Emeritus of Classics

Fordham University

THE SIX DAYS OF CREATION

BOOK ONE: THE FIRST DAY

THE FIRST HOMILY

Chapter 1

To such an extent have men's opinions varied that some, like Plato and his pupils, have established three principles for all things; that is, God, Idea, and Matter. The same philosophers hold that these principles are uncreated, incorruptible, and without a beginning. They maintain that God, acting not as a creator of matter but as a craftsman who reproduced a model, that is, an Idea, made the world out of matter. This matter, which they call ὕλη, is considered to have given the power of creation to all things. The world, too, they regard as incorruptible, not created or made. Still others hold opinions such as those which Aristotle considered worthy of being discussed with his pupils. These postulate two principles, matter and form, and along with these a third principle which is called 'efficient,' which Aristotle considered to be sufficient to bring effectively into existence what in his opinion should be initiated.

(2) What, therefore, is more absurd than to link the eternity of the work of creation with the eternity of God the omnipotent? Or to identify the creation itself with God so as to confer divine honors on the sky, the earth, and the sea? From this opinion there proceeds the belief that parts of the world are gods. Yet on the constitution of the world itself there is no small difference of opinion among philosophers.

(3) Pythagoras maintains that there is one world. Others say that the number of worlds is countless, as was stated by Democritus, whose treatment of the natural sciences has been granted the highest authority by the ancients.[1] That the world always was and always will be is the claim of Aristotle. On the other hand, Plato ventures to assert that the world did not always exist, but that it will always exist. A great many writers, however, give us evidence from their works that they believe that the world did not always exist and that it will not exist forever.

(4) How is it possible to arrive at an estimate of the truth amid such warring opinions? Some, indeed, state that the world itself is God, inasmuch as they consider that a divine mind seems to be within it, while others maintain that God is in parts of the world; others still, that He is in both—in which case it would be impossible to determine what is the appearance of God, or what is His number, position, life, or activity. If this evaluation of the world be followed, we have to understand God to be without sense, something which rotates, is round, is aflame, and impelled

1 Cf. Cicero, *De natura deorum* 1.120.

by certain movements—something driven, not by its own force, but by something external to it.[2]

Chapter 2

(5) Under the inspiration of the Holy Spirit, Moses, a holy man, foresaw that these errors would appear among men and perhaps had already appeared. At the opening of his work he speaks thus: 'In the beginning God created heaven and earth.'[1] He linked together the beginnings of things, the Creator of the world, and the creation of matter in order that you might understand that God existed before the beginning of the world or that He was Himself the beginning of all things. So in the Gospel, in answer to those who were inquiring of Him 'Who art thou?' He replied: 'I am the beginning, I who speak with you.'[2] All this was that you might know that He gave to all created things their beginnings and that He is the Creator of the world—not one who imitates matter under the guidance of some Idea, from which He formed His work, not in accordance with His will, but in compliance with a self-proposed model. Fittingly, too, Moses says: 'In the beginning He created,' in order that, where He had made clear the effect of the operation already completed, before giving an indication of its having been begun, He might thus express the incomprehensible speed of the work.

(6) Our attention should be drawn to the person who uttered this statement. He was, of course, Moses, a man learned in all the science of the Egyptians. He was rescued

2 *Ibid.* 2.46.

1 Gen. 1.1.
2 John 8.25 (Clementine Vulgate).

from the river by the daughter of Pharao, who cherished him as if he were her own son and desired that he be trained and instructed in all phases of secular learning with aid furnished from the royal treasury. Although he received his name from water,[3] he did not consider as true the hypothesis held by Thales, that all things are derived from water. And although he had been educated in the royal palace, he preferred, because of his love of justice, to undergo voluntary exile rather than, because of his love of justice, to be a servant of sin in the midst of pleasure as a high official at a tyrant's court. Finally, before he was called to the task of liberating his people, he fell into disgrace, urged on, as he was, by his natural zeal for what is right to the extent of avenging the wrong done to his fellow countrymen. Wherefore, he tore himself away from pleasure and, shunning all the excitement of the royal palace, retired to a secluded spot in Ethiopia. There, removed from all other cares, he gave himself wholly to divine contemplation, in order that he might behold the glory of God face to face. This is in accord with the testimony of Scripture, that 'there arose no greater prophet in Israel like unto Moses, whom the Lord knew face to face.'[4] He spoke to God the highest, not in a vision nor in dreams, but mouth to mouth. Plainly and clearly, not by figures nor by riddles,[5] there was bestowed on him the gift of the divine presence.

(7) And so Moses opened his mouth and uttered what the Lord spoke within him, according to the promise He made to him when He directed him to go to King Pharao: 'Go therefore and I will open thy mouth and instruct thee what thou shouldst speak.'[6] For, if he had already accepted from God what he should say concerning the liberation of the

3 Cf. Exod. 2.10.
4 Deut. 34.10.
5 Cf. Num. 12.6-8.
6 Exod. 4.12.

people, how much more should you accept what He should say concerning heaven? Therefore, 'not in the persuasive words of wisdom,' not in philosophical fallacies, 'but in the demonstration of the Spirit and power,'[7] he has ventured to say as if he were a witness of the divine work: 'In the beginning God created heaven and earth.' He did not look forward to a late and leisurely creation of the world out of a concourse of atoms. He did not await a pupil, so to speak, of matter, who, by contemplating it, could fashion a world. Rather, he thought that God should be declared to be its Author. Being a man full of wisdom, he noticed that the substances and the causes of things visible and invisible were contained in the divine mind. He did not hold, as the philosophers teach, that a stronger conjunction of atoms furnished the cause of their continuous duration. He pointed out that those who give such tiny and unsubstantial first principles to heaven and earth were just weaving a web like a spider's. How could these be joined together by chance as well as being dissolved in the same planless way, without a firm basis in the divine power of their Ruler? No wonder that they know not their Ruler who know not their God, by whom all things are ruled and governed. Let us follow him who knew both the Author and the Ruler, and let us not be led astray by vain opinions.

Chapter 3

(8) 'In the beginning,' he said. What a good arrangement that he should first assert what these men are accustomed to deny, that they may realize, too, that there was a beginning to the world, lest men be of the opinion that the

---

7 1 Cor. 2.4.

world was without a beginning. For this reason David, too, in speaking of 'heaven, earth, and sea,' says: 'Thou hast made all things in wisdom.'[1] He [Moses] gave, therefore, a beginning to the world; he gave also to the creature infirmity, lest we believe him to be without a beginning, uncreated, and still partaking in the divine essence. And fittingly he added: 'He created, lest it be thought there was a delay in creation. Furthermore, men would see also how incomparable the Creator was who completed such a great work in the briefest moment of His creative act, so much so that the effect of His will anticipated the perception of time. No one saw Him in the act of creation; they saw only the created work before them. Where, therefore, was there a delay, since you may read: 'For He spoke and they were made; He commanded and they were created'?[2] He who in a momentary exercise of His will completed such a majestic work employed no art or skill so that those things which were not were so quickly brought into existence; the will did not outrun the creation nor the creation, the will.

(9) You admire the work, you seek for a Creator who granted a beginning to such a great work, who so speedily made it? He [Moses] gives us the information immediately, saying that 'God created heaven and earth.' You have the name of the Creator; you ought not to have any doubts. He it is in whose name Melchisedech blessed Abraham, the forefather of many peoples, saying: 'Blessed be Abram by the most high God, creator of heaven and earth.'[3] And Abraham believed God and said: 'I raise my hand to the Lord God most high, creator of heaven and earth.'[4] You see that this was not an invention made by man, but an

1 Ps. 103.24.
2 Ps. 32.9; 148.5.
3 Gen. 14.19.
4 Gen. 14.22.

announcement made by God. For God is Melchisedech, that is, 'He is king of peace and justice, having neither the beginning of days nor end of life.'[5] No wonder, therefore, that God, who is without end, gave a beginning to all things, so that what was not began to exist. No wonder that God, who contains all things in His power and incomprehensible majesty, created the things that are visible, since He also created those things that are not visible. Who would assert that the visible is more significant than the invisible, 'for the things that are seen are temporal, but the things that are not seen are eternal'?[6] Who can doubt that God, who spoke by the Prophets, created these things, saying: 'Who hath measured the waters in the hollow of his hand and weighed the heavens with his palm? Who hath poised with three fingers the bulk of the earth and weighed the mountains in scales and the hills in a balance? Who hath understood the sense of the Lord? Or who hath been his counsellor; or who hath taught him?'[7] Of Him we also read elsewhere: 'For he holds the circuit of the earth and made the earth as nothing.'[8] And Jeremias says: 'The gods that have not made heaven and earth will perish from the earth and from among those places that are under heaven. He that made the earth by his power and prepared the world by his wisdom and stretched out the heavens at his knowledge and a multitude of waters in the heaven.' And he added: 'Man is become a fool for knowledge.'[9] How can one who pursues the corruptible things of the world and thinks that from these things he can comprehend the truth of divine nature not become a fool as he makes use of the artifices of sophistry?

5 Heb. 7.2,3.
6 2 Cor. 4.18.
7 Isa. 40.12,13.
8 Isa. 40.22,23.
9 Jer. 10.11-14.

(10) Since, therefore, so many oracles are heard in which God gives testimony that He made the world, do not then believe that it was without a beginning because the world is said to be, as it were, a sphere in which there would appear to be no beginning. And when it thunders, everything is stirred around about us as if in a whirling movement, so that one cannot easily comprehend either where the vortex begins or where it ends. The reason is this: To perceive by one's senses the beginning of a circle is considered to be impossible. You cannot discover the beginning of a sphere or from what point the round disk of the moon begins or where it ends in its monthly wanings. Not even if you do not understand it yourself does this phenomenon cease to begin or in any way to come to an end. If you were to draw a circle with ink or pencil or with a compass, you could not easily detect with your eyes or mentally recall after an interval of time the point where you began or where you completed your circle. Yet you are conscious that you made a beginning and also came to an end. The reason is this: What has escaped the senses has not caused the truth to be undermined.

Again, what has a beginning also has an end; it is obvious that which has an end also has a beginning. The Saviour Himself tells us in the Gospel that there is to be an end of the world, saying: 'For this world as we see it is passing away'; and 'Heaven and earth will pass away, but my words will not pass away'; and further on: 'Behold I am with you all days, even unto the consummation of the world.'[10]

(11) How, then, can philosophers maintain that the world is co-eternal with God and make the created equal with the Creator of all things? How can they hold that the material body of the world should be linked with the

10 1 Cor. 7.31; Matt. 24.35; 28.20.

invisible and unapproachable divine nature?—so much the more, since, according to their own teachings, they cannot deny that an object whose parts are subject to corruption and mutability must as a whole be subject to the same influences which its own separate parts undergo.

Chapter 4

Therefore, He who uttered these words, 'In the beginning God created heaven and earth,' teaches us that there is a beginning. (12) The term 'beginning' has reference either to time or to number or to foundation. We see that this is true in the construction of a house: the foundation is the beginning. We know, too, from the authority of Scripture that one can speak of a beginning of a conversion or of a falling away.[1] The beginning of a work of art lies in the craft itself, which is the source of the individual skills of a series of craftsmen. There is also a beginning to good works. This consists in a most commendable purpose or end, as, for example, acts of charity have their source in deeds which are done to do honor to God, for we are especially urged to come to the aid of our fellow men. The term 'beginning' is applied also to the power of God. It is concerned with the category of time when we deal with the question of the time when God made heaven and earth, that is, at the commencement of the world, when it began to come into being, in the words of Wisdom: 'When he prepared the heaven I was present.'[2] If we apply the term to number, then it is right that you understand that at first He created heaven and earth; next, hills, regions, and the boundaries of the inhabitable world. Or we may understand that before He created the rest of

1 Wisd. 14.12-14.
2 Prov. 8.27.

visible creatures, day, night, fruit-bearing trees, and the various kinds of animals He created heaven and earth. But, if you apply the term to foundation, you will see, if you read the words of Wisdom, that the beginning is the foundation: 'When he made the foundations of the earth, I was with him forming all things.'[3]

There is also the beginning of good instruction, as it is said: 'The fear of the Lord is the beginning of wisdom,'[4] since he who fears the Lord departs from error and directs his ways to the path of virtue. Except a man fear the Lord, he is unable to renounce sin.

(13) In like manner, also, we can understand this statement: 'This month shall be to you the beginning of months.'[5] although that statement is to be interpreted merely of time, because there is reference to the Pasch of the Lord, which is celebrated at the beginning of spring. Therefore, He created heaven and earth at the time when the months began, from which time it is fitting that the world took its rise. Then there was the mild temperature of spring, a season suitable for all things.

Consequently, the year, too, has the stamp of a world coming to birth, as the splendor of the springtime shines forth all the more clearly because of the winter's ice and darkness now past. The shape of the circles of years to come has been given form by the first dawn of the world. Based on that precedent, the succession of years would tend to arise, and at the commencement of each year new seedlings would be produced, as the Lord God has said: 'Let the earth bring forth the green herb and such as may seed, and the fruit tree, yielding fruit after its kind. And immediately the earth produced the green herb and the fruit-bearing

3 Prov. 8.29,30.
4 Prov. 1.7.
5 Exod. 12.2.

tree.'[6] By this very fact both the constant mildness of divine Providence and the speed in which the earth germinates favor for us the hypothesis of a vernal period. For, although it was in the power of God to ordain creation at any time whatsoever and for earthly nature to obey, so that amid winter's ice and frost earth might bear and produce fruits under the fostering hand of His celestial power, He refrained. It was not in His eternal plan that the land held fast in the rigid bonds of frost should suddenly be released to bear fruits and that blooming plants should mingle with frosts unsightly.[7]

Wherefore, in order to show that the creation of the world took place in the spring, Scripture says: 'This month shall be to you the beginning of months, it is for you the first in the months of the year,'[8] calling the first month the springtime. It was fitting that the beginning of the year be the beginning of generation and that generation itself be fostered by the gentler breezes. The tender germs of matter would be unable to endure exposure to the bitter cold of winter or to the torrid heat of summer.[9]

(14) At the same time, one may note, since it belongs here by right, that the entrance into this generation and into this way of life seems to have occurred at the time when the regular transition from this generation to regeneration takes place.

The sons of Israel left Egypt in the season of spring and passed through the sea, being baptized in the cloud and in the sea, as the Apostle said.[10] At that time each year the Pasch of Jesus Christ is celebrated, that is to say, the passing over from vices to virtues, from the desires of the flesh to

6 Gen. 1.11.
7 Cf. Virgil, *Georgics* 2.330-345; Lucretius 5.783-792.
8 Exod. 12.2.
9 Cf. Virgil, *Georgics* 2.343-345.
10 Cf. 1 Cor. 10.1.

grace and sobriety of mind, from the unleavened bread of malice and wickedness to truth and sincerity.[11] Accordingly, the regenerated are thus addressed: 'This month shall be to you the beginning of months; it is for you the first in the months of the year.'

The person who is baptized leaves behind and abandons in a spiritual sense that prince of the world, Pharao, when he says: 'I renounce thee, devil, both thy works and thy power.'[12] No longer will he serve him, either by the earthly passions of his body or by the errors of a corrupt mind. On this occasion every evil deed of his sinks to the bottom like lead. Protected as he is by good works on his right and his left, he endeavors to cross over the waters of this life with step untainted.

Scripture also says in the book called Numbers: 'Amalec, the beginning of nations, whose seed will be destroyed.'[13] And, of course, Amalec is not the first of all nations. Amalec, in fact, is interpreted to mean the king of the wicked and by the wicked it is intended to mean the Gentiles. There is no reason why we should not accept him as one whose seed shall perish. His seed are the wicked and the unfaithful, to whom the Lord says: 'You are the voice of your father the devil.'[14]

(15) A beginning in a mystical sense is denoted by the statement: 'I am the first and last, the beginning and the end.'[15] The words of the Gospel are significant in this connection, especially wherein the Lord, when asked who He was, replied: 'I am the beginning, I who speak with you.'[16] In truth, He who is the beginning of all things by virtue of

11 Cf. 1 Cor. 5.8.
12 John 14.30.
13 Num. 24.20.
14 Cf. John 8.44.
15 Apoc. 1.8.
16 John 8.25 (Clementine Vulgate).

His divinity is also the end, because there is no one after Him. According to the Gospel, the beginning of the ways of God is in His work, so that the race of men might learn by Him to follow the ways of the Lord and to perform the works of God.[17]

Therefore, in this beginning, that is, in Christ, God created heaven and earth, because 'All things were made through him and without him was made nothing that was made.'[18] Again: 'In him all things hold together and he is the firstborn of every creature.'[19] Moreover, He was before every creature because He is holy. The firstborn indeed are holy, as 'the firstborn of Israel,'[20] not in the sense of being before all, but because the firstborn are holier than the rest. The Lord is holy above all creatures for the very reason that He assumed a body. He alone is without sin and without vanity, while all 'creation was made subject to vanity.'[21]

(16) We can also understand that the statement, 'In the beginning God created heaven and earth,' has reference to a period. The beginning of a journey is not yet a completion, nor is the beginning of a building yet the finished house.

Finally, others have interpreted the Greek phrase ἐν κεφαλαίῳ as if *in capite,* by which is meant that in a brief moment the sum of the operation was completed. Then there are also those who interpret the beginning not in a temporal sense, but as something before time. Hence, they use the Greek word κεφάλαιον in the sense of its Latin equivalent, *caput,* indicating by this the sum of the work. Heaven and earth, in fact, are the sum of the invisible things which appear not only as the adornment of this world, but also as a testimony of invisible things and as 'an evidence of things

17 Cf. Prov. 8.22.
18 John 1.3.
19 Col. 1.15.
20 Exod. 4.22.
21 Rom. 8.20.

that are not seen,'[22] according to the prophecy: 'The heavens show forth the glory of God and the firmament declareth the work of his hands.'[23] The Apostle, inspired by the above, expresses in other words the same thought when he says: 'For his invisible attributes are understood through the things that are made.'[24] We can find it easy to understand, then, that the Creator of Angels, Dominations, and Powers is He who in a moment of His power made this great beauty of the world out of nothing, which did not itself have existence and gave substance to things or causes that did not themselves exist.

Chapter 5

(17) This world is an example of the workings of God, because, while we observe the work, the Worker is brought before us. The arts may be considered in various aspects. There are those which are practical. These relate to the movement of the body or to the sound of the voice. When the movement or the sound has passed away, there is nothing that survives or remains for the spectators or the hearers. Other arts are theoretical. These display the vigor of the mind. There are other arts of such a nature that, even when the processes of operation cease, the handiwork remains visible. As an example of this we have buildings or woven material which, even when the craftsman is silent, still exhibit his skill, so that testimony is presented of the craftsman's own work. In a similar way, this work is a distinctive mark of divine majesty from which the wisdom of God is made manifest. On beholding this, raising the eyes of his mind at the same time to the things invisible, the Psalmist

22 Heb. 11.1.
23 Ps. 18.1.
24 Rom. 1.20.

says: 'How great are thy works, O Lord; Thou hast made all things in wisdom.'[1]

(18) Certainly not without reason do we read that the world was made, for many of the Gentiles who maintain that the world is co-eternal with God, as if it were a shadow of divine power, affirm also that it subsists of itself. Although they admit that the cause of it is God, they assert that the cause does not proceed from His own will and rule. Rather, they make it to be analogous to the shadow in respect to the body. For the shadow stays close to the body and a flash follows the light more by natural association than by exercise of free will.

Therefore, Moses says most commendably that 'God created heaven and earth.' He did not say that He made it subsist or that He provided a cause for the world to exist. Rather, He created it as a good man makes what would be of use, as a philosopher propounding his best thoughts, as one all-powerful foreseeing what is to be the most magnificent. Again, how can one imagine a shadow where a body did not exist, since there cannot be a corporeal shadow where a body did not exist, since there cannot be a corporeal shadow of an incorporeal God? Also, how can the brilliance of incorporeal light be corporeal?

(19) If you are seeking after the splendor of God, the Son is the image of the invisible God. As God is, so is the image. God is invisible; then the image also is invisible. It is 'the brightness of the glory of His Father and an image of His substance.'[2] 'In the beginning,' we are told, 'God created heaven and earth.' And the world was therefore created and that which was not began to exist. And the word of God was in the beginning and always was.[3]

---

1 Ps. 103.24.
2 Heb. 1.3.
3 John 1.1.

The Angels, Dominations, and Powers, although they began to exist at some time, were already in existence when the world was created. For all things 'were created, things visible and things invisible, whether Thrones or Dominations or Principalities or Powers. All things,' we are told, 'have been created through and unto him.'[4]

What is meant by 'created unto him'? Because He is the heir of the Father, from the fact that inheritance passed from the Father unto Him, as the Father says: 'Ask of me and I will give thee the Gentiles for thine inheritance.'[5] This inheritance nevertheless passed to the Son and returns from the Son to the Father. And so in notable fashion the Apostle said in this place that the Son was the Author of all things, one who holds all things by His majesty. Addressing the Romans, he says concerning the Father: 'For from him and through him and unto him are all things.'[6] 'From him' means the beginning and origin of the substance of the universe, that is, by His will and power. For all things began by His will, because one only is the Father, from whom all things come. By this is meant that He created through Himself, who created from what source He desired. 'Through him' means the continuation of the universe; 'unto him' means its end.

'From him,' therefore, is the material; 'through him,' the operation by which the universe is bound and linked together; 'unto him,' because as long as He wishes all things remain and endure by His power and the end of all things is directed toward the will of God, by whose free act all things are resolved.

---

4 Col. 1.16.
5 Ps. 2.8.
6 Rom. 11.36.

Chapter 6

(20) In the beginning of time, therefore, God created heaven and earth. Time proceeds from this world, not before the world. And the day is a division of time, not its beginning.

In the course of our account we may affirm that the Lord created day and night, which constitute time changes. And on the second day He created the firmament by which He divided the water which was under the heaven from the water above the heaven. Nevertheless, for our present purposes it is sufficient to assert that in the beginning He created the heaven, from which proceeds the preliminary cause of generation, and created the earth, in which existed the substance of generation.

In fact, with heaven and earth were created those four elements from which are generated everything in the world. The elements are four in number: heaven, fire, water, and earth—elements which are found mingled in all things. You may find fire also in earth, for it frequently arises from stones and iron; you may find it also in the heavens, since it may take fire and the skies may gleam with brilliant stars. In the heavens, too, we can perceive the presence of water, which is either above the heavens or from that high position falls frequently to earth in heavy rainstorms.

We can in many ways demonstrate this, if we observe that these elements are of advantage in the building of a church. But, since it is not profitable to be concerned with this, let us rather turn our attention to those matters which may be fruitful for eternal life.

(21) It is sufficient, therefore, to set forth what we find in the writings of Isaias concerning the nature and the substance of the heavens. In modest and familiar language he described the nature of the heavens when he said that God

'hath fixed the heavens like smoke,'[1] desiring to declare it to be not of solid but of subtle nature.

As to its form, what Isaias has said about the firmament of the heavens makes it more than clear that God created 'heaven like a vault,' because within the range of heaven all things which move in the sea and land are enclosed. This is the implication, too, of what we read that 'God stretched out the heavens.'[2] He stretched it out as you would stretch skins over tents, the dwelling places of the saints, or as a scroll, that the names of many be inscribed therein who merited the grace of Christ by their faith and devotion. To all such it is said: 'Rejoice in this that your names are written in heaven.'[3]

(22) On the nature and position of the earth there should be no need to enter into discussion at this point with respect to what is to come. It is sufficient for our information to state what the text of the Holy Scriptures establishes, namely, that, 'he hangeth the earth upon nothing.'[4]

What need is there to discuss whether the earth hangs in the air or rests on the water? From this would arise a controversy as to whether the nature of the air which is slight and yielding is such as to sustain a mass of earth; also, the question would arise, if the earth rested on the waters, would not the earth by its weight fall and sink into the waters? Or would not the waters of the sea give way to the earth and, moved from its accustomed place, would not the sea pour itself over the borders of the land?

There are many, too, who have maintained that the earth, placed in the midst of the air, remains motionless there by its own weight, because it extends itself equally on all

1 Isa. 51.6.
2 Isa. 40.22.
3 Luke 10.20.
4 Job 26.7.

sides. As to this subject, let us reflect on what was said by the Lord to His servant Job when He spoke through the clouds: 'Where wast thou when I laid the foundations of the earth? Tell me if thou hast understanding. Who hath laid the measures thereof, if thou knowest? Or who hath stretched the line upon it? Or upon what are the circles grounded? And further on: 'I shut up the sea with doors, and I said: Hitherto thou shalt come and shalt go no further, but in thee shall be broken thy waves.'[5] Does not God clearly show that all things are established by His majesty, not by number, weight, and measures? For the creature has not given the law; rather, he accepts it or abides by that which has been accepted.

The earth is therefore not suspended in the middle of the universe like a balance hung in equilibrium, but the majesty of God holds it together by the law of His own will, so that what is steadfast should prevail over the void and unstable. The Prophet David also bears witness to this when he says: 'He has founded the earth upon its own bases: it shall not be moved for ever and ever.'[6] There, certainly, God is asserted to be not merely an artist, but one who is omnipotent, as one who suspended the earth, not from some central point, but from the firmament according to His command, and did not allow it to sway. We ought not to accept the measurement as coming from the center, but as the result of a divine decree, because the measurement is not that of an art, but that of power, of justice and of knowledge. All things do not escape His wisdom as if they were immeasurable, but underlie His knowledge as if they were already measured. When we read: 'I have established the pillars thereof,'[7] we cannot believe that the world was supported

5 Job. 38.4-6,8,11.
6 Ps. 103.5.
7 Ps. 74.4.

actually by columns, but rather by that power that props up the substance of the earth and sustains it.

How the disposition of the earth therefore depends upon the power of God, you may learn also where it is written: 'He looketh upon the earth and maketh it tremble,'[8] and elsewhere: 'One again I move the earth.'[9] Therefore, the earth remains immovable not by its balances, but is moved frequently by the nod and free will of God, as Job, too, says: 'The Lord shaketh it from its foundations, and the pillars thereof tremble.' And elsewhere: 'Hell is naked before him and there is no covering for death. He stretched out the north over the empty space and hangeth the earth upon nothing. He bindeth up the waters in his clouds. The pillars of heaven fled away and are in dread at his rebuke. By his power the seas are calmed, by his wisdom is struck down the sea-monster, and the gates of heaven fear him.'[10]

By the will of God, therefore, the earth remains immovable. 'The earth standeth for ever,' according to Ecclesiastes,[11] yet is moved and nods according to the will of God. It does not therefore continue to exist because based on its own foundations. It does not stay stable because of its own props. The Lord established it by the support of His will, because 'in his hand are all the ends of the earth.'[12] The simplicity of this faith is worth all the proffered proofs.

Let others hold approvingly that the earth never will fall, because it keeps its position in the midst of the world in accordance with nature. They maintain that it is from necessity that the earth remains in its place and is not inclined in another direction, as long as it does not move contrary to nature but in accordance with it. Let them take occasion to

8 Ps. 103.32.
9 Agg. 2.7.
10 Job 9.6; 26.6-11.
11 Eccle. 1.4.
12 Ps. 94.4.

magnify the excellence of their divine Artist and eternal Craftsman. What artist is not indebted to Him? 'Who gave to women the knowledge of weaving or the understanding of embroidery?'[13] However, I who am unable to comprehend the excellence of His majesty and His art do not entrust myself to theoretical weights and measures. Rather, I believe that all things depend on His will, which is the foundation of the universe and because of which the world endures up to the present.

For this belief one may find authority also in the words of the Apostle. It is written: 'For creation was made subject to vanity—not by its own will, but by reason of him who made it subject—in hope,' because creation itself will also be delivered from its slavery to corruption when the grace of divine reward will shine forth.[14]

(23) Why should I enumerate the theories which philosophers in their discussions have woven concerning the nature and composition of the substance of the heavens? While some maintain that the heavens are composed of the four elements, others assign the formation of the heavens to what is called a fifth nature of a new body. They conceive this body to be ethereal and unmixed with fire, air, water or earth, whereas the elements of this world have their own special course and customary motion according to nature, the heavier elements sinking downward; the light and rare elements rising upwards. Each of these elements has, in fact, its own proper motion. However, in the circular quality of a sphere these elements are confused and lose the impulse of their course, inasmuch as a sphere is turned around in its orb and hence the elements above change place with the elements beneath and vice-versa. And where these movements have undergone change in accordance with

13 Cf. Job 38.36 (Septuagint).
14 Rom. 8.20; cf. 8.21.

nature, they state that by necessity the quality of the substances therein usually suffers a corresponding change. Well, then, should we defend the theory of an ethereal body, lest the heavens appear subject to corruption?

What is composed of corruptible elements, for example, must of necessity undergo dissolution. This is seen from the fact that these elements are of different nature and cannot have a simple and unalterable motion, since a diverse movement of the elements leads to discord. There cannot be, in fact, one motion appropriate to and in accord with elements that are opposite; what is suitable to the lighter elements does not befit the weightier one. Accordingly, where there is a necessary motion of the heavens upwards, this is weighed down by the terrestial elements. On the other hand, when there is an impulse to a downward motion, there is fiery opposition from the fiery element, for it is being forced downward contrary to its usual course. Everything which is impelled in a contrary direction does not comply with its nature. Rather, it is quickly dissolved by necessity and is broken up into those parts out of which it seems to be composed, each part returning respectively to its own peculiar place. For this reason, other philosophers, noting that these elements are unstable, have been led to believe that the substance of the heavens and of the stars is ethereal. They introduced what they called a fifth corporeal nature, which they thought was sufficient to give an enduring permanency to the substance of the heavens.[15]

(24) But this opinion could not withstand the words of the Prophet, which the divine majesty of our Lord Jesus Christ, our God, has confirmed in the Gospel. For David has said: 'In the beginning, O Lord, thou foundest the earth and the heavens are the work of thy hands. They shall perish but thou remainest, and all of them shall grow old as a

15 See W. Turner, *History of Philosophy* (Boston 1903) 145.

garment. And as vesture thou shalt change them and they shall be changed. But thou art always the selfsame and thy years shall not fail.'[16] To such a degree did the Lord confirm this that He said: 'Heaven and earth will pass away, but my words will not pass away.'[17]

They labor to no purpose who, in order to claim perpetuity for the heavens, have thought it best to introduce the so-called fifth ethereal body, although they can see, as well as I can, that, if an entirely dissimilar part is attached to a body, it usually gives that body a defect rather than otherwise. At the same time, take note that the Prophet David, in mentioning the earth first and after that the heavens, believed that the work of the Lord should be made manifest. When he said: 'He spoke and they were made,'[18] it is of no consequence what you assert first, since both were done at the same time, in order to preclude the idea that the heavens may appear to have been given the priority in the divine substance, so as to be considered of more importance by right of primogeniture in the order of created things.

Accordingly, let us leave these men to their contentions, men who contradict themselves by their mutual disputes. Sufficient for our salvation is not disputatious controversy but doctrine—not the cleverness of argumentation, but fidelity of the mind—that we may serve, not a creature, but our Creator, who is God, blessed for all ages.

16 Ps. 101.26-28.
17 Matt. 24.35.
18 Ps. 148.5.

THE SECOND HOMILY

Chapter 7

(25) 'And the earth was void and without forms.'[1] The good architect lays the foundation first, and afterwards, when the foundation has been laid, plots the various parts of the building, one after the other, and then adds thereto the ornamentation. When the foundation of the earth has been laid and the substance of the heavens stabilized—these two are, as it were, the hinges of the universe—he added: 'And the earth was void and without form.' What is the meaning of the word 'was'? Perhaps that men may not extend their hypothesis to refer to something without end and without beginning and say: See how matter, the so-called ὕλη of the philosophers, did not have a beginning according even to the divine Scriptures. However, to those who hold this belief you will reply that it is written: 'And Cain was a husbandman.' And concerning him who was called Jubal, Scripture states: 'He was father of them who played upon the psalter and the cithern.'[2] Also: 'There was a man in the land of Austide whose name was Job.'[3] Let them cease, therefore, to raise questions on the meaning of the word, especially since Moses had already asserted: 'God created the earth.' It 'was' therefore from the fact that it was 'created.'

If they say that it was without beginning, maintaining that not only God, but also ὕλη, had no beginning, let them give a clear answer to the question: Where, indeed, was it? If it was in some place, then the place, too, is asserted to

1 Gen. 1.2.
2 Gen. 4.2,21.
3 Job 1.1. (Septuagint).

have been without a beginning, in which place was the material of the universe, which according to them had no beginning. But, if it seems absurd to think of a place, then perhaps we ought to imagine a flying earth, which, lacking a foundation, was suspended 'by the oarage of its wings.'[4] Whence, therefore, can we lay hold of wings for it, unless, perchance, we were to interpret and apply thereto the words of the Prophet: 'From the wings of the earth we have heard prodigies,' and 'Woe to the land to the oarage of ships.'[5]

But, following this interpretation, in what air did the earth fly? It could not fly without air. Yet air could not yet have existed, because without material for the world no distinction of the elements had been made, since up to this point the elements had not been created. Where, then, was this material supported 'by the oarage of wings'? It was not in the air, because the air is a body of the world. The Scriptures teach us that air is a body, because 'when an arrow is shot at a mark,' aimed at by the bowman, 'the air presently cometh together again.'[6]

Where, therefore, was the ὕλη [material]? Are you to suppose by some notion that it was God? God, a spirit most pure and incomprehensible, with a nature that is invisible and incorruptible, who 'dwells in light inaccessible,'[7] was therefore the place of the material of the world? And was God a part of this world, of which not even the meanest of the servants of God have a part, as we are told in the Scriptures: 'They are not of this world, even as I am not of the world.'[8]

(26) How, then, have things visible associated themselves with the invisible and how has that which is disorganized

4 Virgil, *Aeneid* 1.301.
5 Isa. 24.16; 18.1 (Septuagint).
6 Wisd. 5.12.
7 1 Tim. 6.16.
8 John 17.16.

been linked with Him who has bestowed order and beauty on all things? Unless, perchance, they believe that the earth was invisible of itself in its substance, because it had been said: 'And the earth was invisible.' Or they might hold that the earth was invisible for the reason that when covered by water it could not be seen by mortal eyes, just as much as that which lies in deep water escapes the notice of our sharpest eyes. Nothing, in fact, is invisible to God, but something created in this world has, in this instance, been thought to be invisible to him by one who, too, is created.

Invisible, also, was the earth, because the light which illumined the world did not as yet exist, nor did the sun. The luminaries of the sky were, in fact, created later. But, if the rays of the sun frequently illuminate even that which is covered by water and reveal by the brilliance of its light things immersed in the depths, who would doubt that He can see what is invisible in the deep? Unless, perchance, we are to hold that the earth was invisible, because the earth was not yet visited by the Word and protection of God—the earth which did not yet contain man, for whose sake the Lord looked down upon the earth, as it is written: 'The Lord hath looked down upon the children of men, to see if there be any that understand and seek God.' And elsewhere He says: 'Thou hast caused judgment to be hurled from heaven: the earth trembled and was still.'[9] And justly is the earth called invisible, because it was without order, not having as yet received from its Creator its appropriate form and beauty.

(27) And perhaps they may say: Why did not God, in accordance with the words, 'He spoke and they were made,'[10] grant to the elements at the same time as they arose their appropriate adornments, as if He, at the moment

---

9 Ps. 13.2; 75.9.
10 Ps. 148.5.

of creation, were unable to cause the heavens immediately to gleam with studded stars and the earth to be clothed with flowers and fruit? That could very well have happened. Yet Scripture points out that things were first created and afterwards put in order, lest it be supposed that they were not actually created and that they had no beginning, just as if the nature of things had been, as it were, generated from the beginning and did not appear to be something added afterwards. 'And the earth was without form,' we read, yet these same philosophers accord to it the privileges of immortality which they grant God. What would they say if its beauty shone forth from the beginning? The earth is described as immersed in water, condemned, as it were, to a shipwreck in its own first principles. Yet, some do not believe that the earth was made. What, then, if it lay claim to ornament from the moment of its creation?

Add to this the fact that God willed it that we be imitators of Himself, so that we first make something and afterwards beautify it. We would run the danger of attempting two projects at one time and accomplishing neither. And our faith grows strong step by step. For that reason, God created first and afterwards beautified, in order that we may believe that He who made and He who adorned were one and the same person. Otherwise, we might suppose that one adorned and that another performed the act of creation, whereas the same person achieved both, creating first and afterwards adorning, in order that one act might be believed as a result of the other.

You find in the Gospel clear testimony on this subject. For the Lord, when proposing to raise Lazarus to life, first ordered the Jews to remove the stone from the sepulcher, in order that, on seeing him dead, they might believe afterwards that he had risen from the dead. Next, He called Lazarus by name, and he arose and came forth with his hands and feet bound.[11] Could not He who was able to restore the dead to life also remove the stone? And could not He who was able to restore the dead man to life also set him free from his bonds? Could not He who granted Lazarus power to walk with his feet still bound also render it possible for him to come forth with his fetters already broken? Of course, we see that He wished to point out first that the man was dead, so that they might believe with their own eyes. The next step was to raise him from the dead and the third to bid them unbind with their own hands the mortuary bands. By this process faith might be engendered in the hearts of the incredulous and belief come to life gradually, step by step.

Chapter 8

(28) God created first, therefore, heaven and earth, but He did not will them to be perpetual; rather, they subserve the final end of our corruptible nature. Hence, in the book of Isaias He says: 'Lift up your eyes to heaven and look down on the earth beneath: for the heavens have the compactness of smoke and the earth shall be worn away like a garment.'[1] This is the earth which before was unformed. The seas were not yet confined within their limits and the earth was inundated by a deep flood. Observe that even now the earth has become unsightly with marshy mire and is not subject to the plough[2] where water has everywhere covered the land. The land was, therefore, unformed, since it was as yet unploughed by the industrious attentions of the farmer,

---

11 Cf. John 11.39-44.

---

1 Isa. 51.6.
2 Cf. Virgil, *Georgics* 2.223.

for the cultivator had still to appear. It was unformed because it was devoid of growing plants. The banks of streams lacked their grassy slopes; the land was not shady with groves or productive in fruits of the earth. The overhanging brows of the mountains did not produce shade; flowers did not as yet give forth odors; still unknown were the delights of the vineyard. Correctly, then, was the land called unformed which was devoid of ornament and which did not present to view the linked rows of budding vine shoots. God wished to show us that the world itself would have no attraction unless a husbandman had improved it with varied culture. The very heavens, when seen covered with clouds, often inspire men with dread fear and with sadness of heart. The earth, when saturated with rain, arouses our aversion. Who is not moved to fright by the sight of stormy seas? Most admirable is the aspect of created things. But what would they have been without light, what would they have been without heat and without the gathering together of waters, in which element some have supposed that this universe of ours, when once immersed, had its primal origin. Take away the sun from the earth; take away the round spheres of stars from the sky—every object is then shrouded in dread darkness. Thus it was before the Lord poured light into this world.

And for that reason Scripture says: 'Darkness was over the abyss.'[3] There was darkness because the brilliance of light was absent; there was darkness because the air itself was dark. Water itself beneath a cloud is dark because 'dark are the waters in the clouds of air.'[4] There was, therefore, darkness over the abyss of waters. I am not of the opinion that by darkness are to be understood the powers of evil, in that their wickedness was brought about by God. The reason is, of

3 Gen. 1.2.
4 Ps. 17.12.

course, that evil is not a substance, but an accident and that it is a deviation from the goodness of nature.

(29) Accordingly, a discussion of the question of evil in the constitution of the world should be laid aside for the moment, lest we seem to mingle that which is depraved with the work that is divine and with the beauty of the created. Especially should this be so for the reason that Scripture adds: 'And the spirit of God moved over the waters.'[5] Although some consider this spirit as air, others think of it as the vital breath of the air which we take in and emit. However, in agreement with the saints and the faithful we consider this to be the Holy Spirit, so that the operation of the Holy Trinity clearly shines forth in the constitution of the world. Preceded by the statement that 'In the beginning God created heaven and earth,' that is, God created it in Christ or the Son of God had, as God, created it or God created it through the Son, since 'all things were made through him and without him was made nothing that was made.'[6] There was still to come the plenitude of the operation in the Spirit, as it is written: 'By the word of the Lord the heavens were established and all the power of them by the spirit of his mouth.'[7] As we are instructed in the psalm concerning the work of the Word, which is the work of God, and on the power which the Holy Spirit bestowed, so is echoed here the prophetic oracle, namely, that 'God spoke' and 'God created' and 'the Spirit of God moved over the waters.' While adorning the firmament of the heavens, the Spirit fittingly moved over the earth, destined to bear fruit, because by the aid of the Spirit it held the seeds of new birth which were to germinate according to the words of the Prophet: 'Send forth thy Spirit and they shall be created

5 Gen. 1.2.
6 John 1.3.
7 Ps. 32.6.

and thou shalt renew the face of the earth.'[8] Finally, the Syriac text, which is close to the Hebrew and agrees with it in word for the most part, expresses it in this fashion: 'And the Spirit of God brooded over the waters,' that is, gave life, in order to help the birth of new creatures and by cherishing them give them the breath of life. For the Holy Spirit, too, is called Creator, as we read in Job: 'The divine Spirit which made me.'[9]

If, therefore, the Holy Spirit moved over the waters, there could not exist, just where the Spirit claimed such honor, the darkness of forces which are contrary to it. But if, as some would have it, we are to interpret 'Spirit' as 'air,' let these people answer the question: How did the Scripture speak of the 'Spirit of God,' when it would have been sufficient to mention simply 'Spirit'?

(30) These would have it, then, that first the four elements were generated by the Lord our God—that is, heaven, earth, sea, and air—for the reason that fire and air are the causes of things, while earth and water furnish the material from which are derived the beauty and form of the world. Where, therefore, could the darkness of the spirits of evil find a place, when the world has vested itself with the beauty of this august figure? Are we to hold that God at the same time created evil? But evil arose from us, and was not made by a Creator God. It is produced by the lightness of our morals; it has no prior right over any created thing, nor has it the dignity of a natural substance. It is a fault due to our mutability and is an error due to our fall. God desires it to be eradicated from the souls of each and everyone. How, then, could He have generated it? The Prophet cries out: 'Cease to do perversely.'[10] And

8 Ps. 103.30.
9 Job 33.4.
10 Isa. 1.16.

holy David has stated it with definiteness: 'Turn away from evil and do good.'[11] How, then, can we assign to God the beginning of evil?

But this is the fatal theory of those who thought the Church should be thrown into confusion. From this are derived the sect of Marcio, of Valentinus;[12] hence, too, that deadly pest of the Manichaeans which attempted to bring contagion to the minds of the faithful. Why do we search of ourselves to see in the light of life the darkness of death? Divine Scripture confers salvation on us and is fragrant with the perfume of life, so that he who reads may acquire sweetness and not rush into danger to his own destruction. Read with simplicity, man; I would not encourage you, a misdirected interpreter, to dig up meanings for yourself. The language is simple: 'God created heaven and earth.' He created what was not, not what was. And the earth was invisible, because water flowed over it and covered it. Darkness was diffused over it, because there was not yet the light of day, or the rays of the sun which can reveal even what lies hid beneath the waters.

Why, then, do they say that God created evil, although from principles contrary and opposed nothing whatsoever is generated? Light does not generate death nor does light give birth to darkness. And the processes of generation are not like the mutability of human emotions. The latter change from one opposite principle to another according to the various questions at issue. The former are not deflected from one point to its opposite, but, being created either by their authors or by causes of the same nature, they stand in a similar relationship to their Creator.

(31) What, then, are we to say? If evil has no beginning,

---

11 Ps. 33.15.

12 See P. de Labriolle, *Histoire de la littérature latine chrétienne* (Paris 1920) 120.

as if uncreated or not made by God, from what source did nature derive it? Because no rational being has denied that evil exists in a world like this in which accident and death are so frequent. Yet from what we have already said we can gather that evil is not a living substance, but is a deviation of mind and soul away from the path of true virtue, a deviation which frequently steals upon the souls of the unaware. The greater danger is not, therefore, from what is external to us, but from our own selves. Our adversary is within us, within us is the author of error, locked, I say, within our very selves. Look closely on your intentions; explore the disposition of your mind; set up guards to watch over the thoughts of your mind and the cupidities of your heart. You yourself are the cause of your wickedness; you yourself are the leader of your own crimes and the instigator of your own misdeeds. Why do you summon an alien nature to furnish an excuse for your sins?

Would that you did not give rein to yourself; would that you did not rush recklessly on; would that neither by immoderate desires nor through wrath or cupidity you involved yourself in bonds which trap us like so many nets. And surely it is in our power to moderate our desires; to curb our anger; to check our evil passions. It is also within our power to give ourselves up to luxurious living; to add fire to our lusts; to stir up the fires of our anger or lend our ears to one who ministers to them; to be unduly puffed up by pride; to allow ourselves to be carried away by acts of cruelty rather than that we should bend ourselves to humble deeds and find delight in acts of kindliness.

Why, then, man, do you accuse nature? Nature has old age and illness which serve as so many impediments to our lives. But old age becomes sweeter and more useful by its wise counsels and characters. It becomes more ready to face inevitable death with constancy and becomes more heroic in quelling lusts of the flesh.[13] Infirmity of the body, too, is conducive to sobriety of mind. Hence the Apostle says: 'When I am weak, then am I strong.' Accordingly, he gloried not in his virtues but in his infirmities. A divine saying also flashes forth from that salutary oracle: 'Strength is made perfect in weakness.'[14] We ought to guard ourselves against the 'sins of youth'[15] which arise from free acts of our will, and we should avoid the irrational passions of the body. Let us not search outside of ourselves or attribute to others the causes of that of which we ourselves are sole masters. Let us, rather, recognize these causes as belonging to us alone. We ought to attribute to ourselves the choice of an evil which we are unable to do without consent of the will rather than ascribe the same to others. In the courts of the world guilt so is imputed and punishment meted out, not to those compelled to crime by necessity, but to those who have acted voluntarily. It is true that the person who in a rage slays another is subject to the penalty of death. Why, even according to the decree of the divine law itself, a person who inadvertently kills another may expect impunity by accepting the possibility of exile, if he wishes to escape punishment.[16]

This, then, may be stated on the question of what in the real sense of the word seems to be evil. Wrong does not exist except when the mind and conscience are implicated and bound up with the guilt. Moreover, no intelligent person would call poverty, disgrace, or death an evil. He would not list them in the category of evils, because they are not the opposite of those goods held in the highest esteem—goods which seem to fall to our lot either from causes which stem from nature or from the favorable circumstance of our lives.

---

13 Cf. Cicero, *De senectute* 14.47.
14 2 Cor. 12.10,9.
15 Ps. 24.7.
16 Cf. Num. 35.22-25.

(32) Not without a purpose have we introduced this digression in order to prove that the phrase 'darkness and the abyss' should be taken in literal sense. In fact, the darkness under discussion comes especially from the shadow cast from the heavens, since every body produces a shadow by which it casts a shade either on what is near by or on what is beneath it, and above it casts a shadow on those objects which it seems to cover or include. The firmament of the heavens does include the earth, because, as we have shown above, heaven stretches itself out like a vault. Therefore, darkness was not an original substance, but the mist of darkness accompanied like a shadow the body of the world. Accordingly, at the instant that the world arose at the divine command there was enclosed within it a shadow. Just as if a person in the midst of a plain illumined by the midday sun were, at the spur of the moment, to hedge some spot and cover it with thick leafy branches, would not his hut with its rude, stage-like background become rather all the more obscure within in contrast to the exterior, so brilliantly illuminated?[17] Or why was a place closed on all sides called a cave unless it is that it is a place obscured by darkness and forbidding because of its blackness?[18]

This darkness then was over the abyss of waters. For the Gospel teaches us that the abyss is a mass of deep waters, where, in fact, the demons entreated the Saviour 'not to command them to depart into the abyss.' But He who taught that the will of the demons should not be obeyed caused them to enter into the bodies of swine. And the herd of swine rushed down the cliff into the pool, so that the demons did not escape what they rebelled against, but were, as they

17 Cf. Virgil, *Aeneid* 1.164,165, and the note of Servius (*editio Harvardiana* 1946, 95) on *scaena* ('stage').

18 *Antrum—atro situ.*

deserved, submerged in the depths.[19] Unformed, therefore, was the appearance and shape of this world.

Chapter 9

(33) 'And the Spirit of God,' he said, 'moved over the waters. And God said: Be light made.'[1] Rightly, therefore, was the Spirit of God sent forth where the divine operation was to begin. He said: 'Be light made.' Whence should the voice of God in Scripture begin, if not with light? Whence should the adornment of the world take its beginning, if not from light?

There would be no purpose in the world if it were not seen. In fact, God Himself was in the light, because He 'dwells in light inaccessible,' and He 'was the true light that enlightens every man who comes into this world.'[2] But He wishes the light to be such as might be perceived by mortal eyes. The person who desires to erect a house as a fitting habitation for the head of a family determines first how it may receive light abundantly before he lays the foundation. This is the first requisite. If this is lacking, the whole house is without beauty and is uninhabitable. It is light which sets off the other beautiful objects in the house.

'Let light be made,' He said. When the word 'light' is used, it is not intended to mean merely the preparation for performance; rather, it is the splendor of the operation itself in action. The Fabricator of nature uttered the word 'light' and also created it. The Word of God is His will; the work of God is nature. He created light and illumined the dark-

19 Cf. Luke 8.31,32.

1 Gen. 1.2,3.
2 1 Tim. 6.16; John 1.9.

ness. 'And God said, be light made, and light was made.'[3] He did not speak in order that action should follow; rather, the action was completed with the Word. Hence, David appropriately uttered the statement, 'He spoke and they were made,'[4] because the fulfillment of the act accompanied the Word.

God, therefore, is the Author of light and the place and cause of darkness is the world. But the good Author uttered the word 'light' so that He might reveal the world by infusing brightness therein and thus make its aspect beautiful. Suddenly, then, the air became bright and darkness shrank in terror from the brilliance of the novel brightness. The brilliance of the light which suddenly permeated the whole universe overwhelmed the darkness and, as it were, plunged it into the abyss. Fittingly, therefore, and appropriately was it said: 'Light was made.' For, just as light quickly illuminated the heavens, the earth, and the seas, and in a moment, without our being aware of it, when the land is unveiled at the splendor of dawn, this light is perceived as it encompasses us, in such a manner should its birth be explained. Why do we marvel at the fact that God simply said 'light' and flashed forth brilliance on a darkling world, when we know that, if a person immersed in water should emit oil from his mouth, all that which is hidden in the deep is made clearer?

God did not speak as one would utter a sound through the vocal organs or as a movement of the tongue might produce an exhortation from heaven or as a sound of words might strike this air of ours. His purpose was to reveal the knowledge of His will by the effects of His work.

3 Gen. 1.3.
4 Ps. 148.5.

(34) 'And He divided the light from the darkness and God saw the light that it was good.'[5] He spoke, and no one heard the sound of His voice. He divided, and no one noticed the effort expended in His work. He saw, and no one observed the glance of His eyes. 'And God saw,' he says, 'the light that it was good.' He did not see that of which He had no knowledge, nor did He approve what He before had neither known nor seen. It is a fitting quality of good works that they need no one to applaud them outside of oneself, but when they are seen give evidence of their own intrinsic value. It is more important that one be approved in the sight of men rather than be lauded in their conversation, since such a person relies on his own testimony and not on the recommendations of others.

But if in our own experience we are able to perceive by means of our eyes, by the aid of which the beauty of natural objects is immediately appreciated, how much more is this true in the case of God! He sees all things which He approves and approves of all things which He sees, according to the Scriptures: 'The eyes of the Lord are upon the just.'[6] The nature of light is of such a kind that its value does not rest in number or measurement or weight as is the case with other things. Its whole value comes from its appearance. Accordingly, Scripture fittingly described the nature of light, which pleases us when seen, inasmuch as it furnishes us with the ability to see. Not undeservingly was light able to find as its eulogist one who first justly praised it, since it was also responsible for making the other objects in the world worthy of commendation. God, therefore, saw the light and illumined it with His countenance and saw that it was good. And this is a conviction not only on the part of God, but of all mankind. And so the value of light

5 Gen. 1.4.
6 Ps. 33.16.

is conceded to be great, not only because of its splendor, but also on account of its usefulness. For this reason there was a division made between light and darkness, so that, when separated, there would seem to be no grounds for confusing the nature of light and the nature of darkness.

(35) 'And God called the light, day, and the darkness, night,'[7] in order that day and night might be distinguished even in name. For this reason we notice that the rising of light rather than that of the sun seems to open the day. The beginning of day closes up night's exit and a definite time limit and an established boundary seem to have been prescribed for night and day. The sun gives the day its brilliance; the light, its existence. The sky is often overlaid with clouds, so that the sun is hidden and its rays are not seen. Still, the presence of light points to the fact that it is day and that darkness has vanished.

Chapter 10

(36) 'And there was made evening and morning, one day.'[1] Some inquire why Scripture first mentions evening and after that, morning? Would not this appear to mean that night came before day? They do not notice that this is preceded by a reference to day: 'And God called light, day, and the darkness, night,' and then, again, because the evening is the termination of day and morning is the termination of night.

Therefore, in order to give preference and primacy to the day of creation, Scripture first indicated the end of a day, which night was soon to follow, and then it added the

---

7 Gen. 1.5.

---

1 Gen. 1.5.

termination of night. There is a further reason why Scripture could not prefer night to day: It included in the term 'day' the space of time for both day and night and bestowed on that term the prestige, as it were, of a principal name. And this usage is found in Scripture to confer a name on the more important element. This is proved by numerous examples, for Jacob has said also: 'The days of my life have been short and wretched.'[2] And again: 'All the days of my life.'[3] And David set down: 'The days of my years';[4] he did not say also 'the night.' Hence we note that those events which are now recorded in the form of history have established for themselves a precedent for the relation of future events.

The beginning of the day rests on God's word: 'Be light made, and light was made.'[5] The end of day is the evening. Now, the succeeding day follows after the termination of night. The thought of God is clear. First He called light 'day' and next He called darkness 'night.'

(37) In notable fashion has Scripture spoken of a 'day,' not the 'first day.' Because a second, then a third, day, and finally the remaining days were to follow, a 'first day' could have been mentioned, following in this way the natural order.[6] But Scripture established a law that twenty-four hours, including both day and night, should be given the name of day only, as if one were to say the length of one day is twenty-four hours in extent. In such fashion, also, is the generation of men reckoned which is understood to include that of women, also. Because what is secondary is bound up with what is primary, the nights in this reckoning are considered to be component parts of the days that are counted.

2 Gen. 47.9.
3 Ps. 22.6.
4 Ps. 89.10.
5 Gen. 1.5.
6 Cf. Philo, *De opificio mundi* 5 (*Philonis opera*, ed. L. Cohn, I).

Therefore, just as there is a single revolution of time, so there is but one day. There are many who call even a week one day, because it returns to itself, just as one days does, and one might say seven times revolves back on itself. This is the form of a circle, to begin with itself and to return to itself. Hence, Scripture speaks at times of an age of the world. Although in other passages there is a mention of an age, there Scripture seems to mean the diversities in public and private affairs: 'For the day of the Lord is great and glorious.'[7] And elsewhere: 'What avail is it to you to seek the day of the Lord.'[8] And here is meant darkness and not light, for it is clear that that day when innocence will gleam forth and guilt be tormented is dark to those who are conscious of evil deeds and unworthy acts. Moreover, Scripture teaches us that the everlasting day of eternal reward is to be one in which there is no interchange or intermission of day and night.

(38) Fittingly, then, in calling one day the interchange of both times Scripture closes this period with morning, so that we are taught that day begins with light and in light comes to an end. This is true because day and night could not be considered as a unit of time unless that time has been completely traversed. Hence, 'let us walk becomingly as in the day' and 'let us lay aside the works of darkness.'[9] We know that night is passed in sleep and forgetfulness so that the body may find rest. Night is not designed for the performance of any task or of any transaction. Let us not be sharers in feasting and drunkenness, in chambering and immodesty. Let us not say: Darkness and walls cover us and who knows if the Most High will see us.[10] But let there be

7 Joel 2.11.
8 Amos 5.18.
9 Rom. 13.12,13.
10 Cf. Eccli. 23.26.

in us a love of light and an esteem of goodness, so that, as if walking in daylight, we may desire that our works shine in the presence of God. To Him be honor, praise, glory, and power, together with our Lord Jesus Christ and with the Holy Spirit, from eternity and now and always, for ever and ever. Amen.[11]

11 Cf. Matt. 5.16.

BOOK TWO: THE SECOND DAY

THE THIRD HOMILY

Chapter 1

We have finished as best we could our discussion of the first day—or, rather, of one day, in order to keep to the phrase preferred by the inspired book. On this day, by the work of the omnipotent God, and the Lord Jesus Christ, together with the Holy Spirit, we know that the heavens were founded, the earth was created, the waters and the air were sent forth around us, and a separation was made between light and darkness.

Who, therefore, does not marvel at the fact that a world formed of dissimilar elements should rise to the level of unity in one body, that this body should combine by indissoluble laws of concord and love to link together and form a union of such discordant elements? Furthermore, who does not marvel that these elements so naturally separate should be tied together in the bonds of unity and peace as if by an indivisible compact? Or who in a moment of weakness would, on beholding this, question the possibilities of order or plans? All these elements a divine power incomprehensible to human minds and incapable of being expressed in our language has by the might of His will woven closely together.

(2) God, therefore, created the heavens and the earth and those things which He as Author has ordained to exist, not just as a designer of their form but as a Creator of their nature. How, in fact, can the creative power of God which is impassive and the nature of matter which is passive form an agreement together, as if one borrowed from the other what was lacking in each? If matter is uncreated, then God is without the power to create matter and must borrow from matter what is a conditional basis for His work. If, however, matter is unformed, it surely is remarkable that such material, co-eternal with God, which has not received from the Creator its substance, but has itself possessed it in timeless existence, has been unable to bestow beauty on itself. The Creator of all things, therefore, would have found ready for His work more things than He contributed to it. He would have found material on which to work and would have merely bestowed the form which would confer beauty on what has already been found.

Hence, such a day should be distinguished from the others as 'one day,' and should not be compared with other days as 'the first day,' for on it the foundations of all things were laid and there began to come into existence the causes of all things on which the substance of this world and of the entire visible creation is based. Wherefore, our discourse can now proceed to the wonderful works of the second day. The importance of these works should not be rated by what we have achieved in our discussion, but should, in accordance with Scripture, be referred to the praise of the Creator.

(3) I bid you, therefore, be considerate enough to regard

in a natural sense our plausible discourse and to weigh our statements in simplicity of mind and with attentive intellect, not following the traditions of philosophy nor those who gather the semblance of truth in the 'vain deceit'[1] of the arts of persuasion, but in accordance with the rule of truth, which is set forth in the inspired words of God and is poured into the hearts of the faithful by the contemplation of such sublimity. For it is written: 'Strengthen thou me in thy words.' 'The wicked have told me fables but not as thy law, O Lord. All thy statutes are truth.'[2] Therefore, not the nature of the elements, but Christ Himself, who created the world in the abundance and plenitude of His divinity, should be our standard in the examination of what was created and in the question as to what natural power is able to achieve. The people who beheld with their own eyes the miracles related in the Gospel of the healing of the leper and that of giving sight to the blind did not regard these as a medical process, but rather, marveling at the power of the Lord, 'gave praise to God,' as it is written.[3] Moses did not follow the calculations of the Egyptians and the conjunctions of the stars and the relations of the elements when he stretched out his hand to divide the Red Sea, but was complying with the commands of divine power. Hence, he says himself: 'Thy right hand, O Lord, is magnified in strength. Thy right hand, O Lord, hath broken the enemy.'[4] To Him, therefore, ye faithful people, lift up your mind and bring to Him all your heart. God does not see as man does: God sees with His mind; man sees with his countenance. Therefore, man does not see as God does. Give ear to what God saw and what He praised. Do not, therefore, estimate

1 Col. 2.8; Eph. 5.6.
2 Ps. 118.28,85,86.
3 Matt. 8.2; 9.30; Luke 18.43.
4 Exod. 15.6.

with your eyes nor weigh with your mind the problem of creation. Rather, you should not regard as a subject for debate what God saw and approved of.

Chapter 2

(4) And God said: 'Let there be a firmament made amidst the waters and let it divide the waters from the waters, and it was so.'[1] Listen to the words of God: 'Let there be,' He said. This is the word of a commander, not of an adviser. He gives orders to nature and does not comply with its power. He does not regard its measurements, nor does He examine its weight. His will is the measure of things and His word is the completion of the work. 'Let there be a firmament made amidst the waters,' He said. Firm is everything which God has established. Appropriately enough has He stated: 'Let there be a firmament made' before He added 'amidst the waters,' in order that you might first believe that the firmament was made by God's command before you would begin to doubt about the problem of the fluid nature of water. If the nature of the elements is taken into consideration, how it is possible for the firmament to be stable between the waters? The one is liquid, the other solid; one is active, the other, passive. 'And let it divide the waters from the waters,' He said. But water usually mingles, not separates. How, then, does He command what He knows to be a contradiction in terms of the first principles of the elements? But, since His word is nature's birth, justly therefore does He who gave nature its origin presume to give nature its law.

1 Gen. 1.6.

(5) But first let us discuss the problem of the nature of the firmament, whether it is the same as what God previously called heaven or something different? The question also arises whether there are two heavens or more. There are some who say that there is but one heaven. Moreover, they maintain, since there was only one ὕλη, as they call it, that there could not be at hand material for making a second heaven. Moreover, since this material had been already consumed in the first heaven, there would be nothing left over in their opinion which would furnish material for a second or third heaven. On the other hand, an opinion that there are countless heavens is held by others,[2] who thereby furnish an occasion for laughter to some members of their own school (contending among themselves even more than they do with us), who pretend to prove by mathematical means and the law of necessity that another heaven could not exist. Again, they maintain that nature could not allow that a second or a third such entity should exist and it would not be a fitting exercise of power for a Creator to bring into existence many heavens.

And who would not find the crafty and eloquent phrases of these men a subject of ridicule? They would not deny the human capacity of making more objects of the same kind from one and the same material, yet they doubt whether the Creator of all things can make more heavens, of whom it is written: 'But the Lord made the heavens,' and elsewhere: 'He hath done all things whatsoever he would.'[3] Why is it difficult for one whose wishes are acts? Their theory that this impossibility exists is, therefore, unsubstantial when they treat of God, of whom in truth it is said: 'Nothing is impossible to thee.'[4]

---

2 Cf. Cicero, *Academica* 2.55 (Democritus).
3 Ps. 95.5; 113.3.
4 Mark 14.36.

(6) Accordingly, we cannot deny the existence of not only a second heaven, but also of a third, since the Apostle attests in his writings that he 'was caught up to the third heaven.'[5] David, too, introduced 'Heaven of heavens' into the chorus of those who give praise to God. In imitation of him philosophers introduced the harmonious movement of five constellations along with the sun and moon, to whose spheres or, rather, round bodies they state that all things are connected.[6] They consider that these bodies, bound together and, as it were, linked one with the other, are borne in a backward motion and one contrary to the rest of things. By the impact and motion of these spheres there is produced a tone full of sweetness, the fruit of consummate art and of most delightful modulation, inasmuch as the air, torn apart by such artful motion, combines in even and melodious fashion high and low notes to such a degree that it surpasses in sweetness any other musical composition.

(7) If you should inquire into the truth of this phenomenon and demand that proof be presented to our senses and to our hearing, these philosophers are embarrassed. For, if what they say were true, how is it possible that we who are accustomed to hear lesser sounds do not perceive the impact of the movement of the sphere? This takes place, according to their theory, when in the course of the sphere's motion the celestial sphere, to which the course of the constellations is uninterruptedly attached, produces by its swifter motion a high tone, while the lunar sphere gives us a deeper tone. If, then, we demand a proof of that hypothesis from the evidence of our sense of hearing, they report that our ears have become deafened and our sense of hearing has become dulled because we have become accustomed to that sound from the first moment of our birth. And they present an illustration from the river Nile, the mightiest of rivers. In that

---

5 2 Cor. 12.2.

6 Pythagoras and his school; cf. Cicero, *Somnium Scipionis* 6.17.

place where that river flows precipitously from the highest mountains into the Cataracts, the noise of the waterfall is so great that the ears of the natives are affected to the extent that they are said to be deaf.

But experience itself presents us an easy rebuttal to their arguments. We are able to hear thunderbolts produced by the collision of clouds; how, then, are we unable to hear the revolution of such mighty spheres which, in proportion surely to their swifter motion, should produce sounds all the more resounding? They maintain, furthermore, that such music does not reach the earth. Otherwise, men, captivated by the sweetness and charm which that exceedingly swift motion of the heavens produces, would from the regions of the east as far as the west have abandoned all their occupations and labors. Thus, everything here would be in a state of inactivity as a result of what might be called the rapture of men at the sound of celestial music. But subjects which are alien to our purpose and to divine testimony should be left to those 'who are outside.'[7] We should adhere closely to the doctrine laid down by the celestial Scriptures.

Chapter 3

(8) Our argument, then, is based on the word of God: 'Let there be a firmament made amidst the waters and let it divide the waters from the waters.'[1] And from this arises the question whether He calls the firmament the heaven which He had already created, concerning which it is written: 'In the beginning God created heaven and earth.'[2] I am not unaware of the interpretation which some have held on this

7 1 Cor. 5.12,13; Col. 4.5; 1 Tim. 3.7.

1 Gen. 1.6.
2 Gen. 1.1.

subject, namely, that as the creation at the hands of God and the foundation of heaven has been before expressly stated by Scripture, so a clearer exposition of the work of creation is here given. Whereas in one place a summary of the work, as it were, is briefly stated, in the other, the nature of the operation is depicted according to the specific aspect of things as they appear at the same moment of creation. But there is something which needs our consideration: there is question of another word for heaven, 'firmament,' and there emerges an aspect and condition of more solid character, to which is added the person of a co-operating agent. For it is written: 'And God divided the waters that were under the firmament from those that were above the firmament.'[3]

(9) And first of all these interpreters wish to destroy the profound impressions which frequent reading of the Scriptures have made in our mind, maintaining that waters cannot exist above the heavens. That heavenly sphere, they say, is round, with the earth in the middle of it; hence, water cannot stay on that circular surface, from which it needs must flow easily away, falling from a higher to a lower position. For how, they say, can water remain on a sphere when the sphere itself revolves?

This is one of those sophistical arguments of the subtlest kind. Grant me an opportunity to reply. If it is not granted, there need be no further room for discussion.

They ask us to concede to them that heaven turns on its axis with a swift motion, while the sphere of the earth remains motionless, so as to conclude that waters cannot stay above the heavens, because the axis of heaven as it revolved would cause these to flow off. They wish, in fact, that we grant them their premise and that our reply be based on their beliefs. In this way they would avoid the question

3 Gen. 1.7.

of the existence of length and breadth in that height and depth,[4] a fact which no one can comprehend except Him who is filled 'with the fullness of the Godhead,'[5] as the Apostle says. For who can easily set himself up to be a judge of God's work? There exists, therefore, breadth in the very heights of heaven.

To speak of matters within our knowledge, there are a great many buildings which are round in the exterior but are square-shaped within, and vice-versa. These buildings have level places on top, where water usually collects. We are led to mention these matters in order to draw the attention of these interpreters to the fact that their opinions can be confuted by other opinions closer to the truth and that they may cease measuring such a mighty work of God in terms of human work and merely on an estimate of our own capacities.

(10) We follow the tradition of the Scriptures and we value the work by our esteem of the Author, as to what was said, who said it, and to whom it was said. 'Let there be a firmament made,' He said, 'amidst the waters and let it divide the waters from the waters.'[6] From this I learn that the firmament is made by a command by which the water was to be separated and the water above be divided from the water below. What is clearer than this?

He who commanded the waters to be separated by the interposition of the firmament lying between them provided also the manner of their remaining in position, once they were divided and separated. The word of God gives nature its power and an enduring quality to its matter, as long as He who established it wishes it to be so, as it is written: 'He hath established them forever and for ages of ages. He hath made a decree and it shall not pass away.' And that you may

4 Cf. Eph. 3.18.
5 Col. 2.9.

know that He said this concerning these waters which you say cannot exist in the higher parts of the heavens, listen to the words which precede: 'Praise him, ye heaven of heavens, and let all the waters above the heavens praise the name of the Lord.'[7]

Did He not speak to you in such a way as to answer your objections? 'For he spoke and they were made. He commanded and they were created. He hath established them forever and for ages of ages. He hath made a decree and it shall not pass away.'[8] Does He not seem to you to be one who is fitted to give a law to His work? Here speaks to you a God venerable by nature, inestimable in magnitude, in rewards immeasurable, in His works incomprehensible, the depth of whose wisdom who can ever strive to measure?[9] But He speaks to His Son, that is, to His arm; He speaks to His power; He speaks to His wisdom, to His justice. And the Son acts as one who is powerful; He acts as the power of God; He acts as the wisdom of God, as divine justice. When you hear this, why do you marvel if, by the operation of such majesty, water can be held suspended above the celestial firmament?

(11) Reflect on this when dealing with other matters, with what is seen by the eyes of men—reflect on this if you look for an explanation of how the sea divided at the crossing of the Jews. This is not a customary act of nature that water should separate itself from water and that the waters intermingling in the midst of the earth should be divided. The waves became solid, we are told, and like the waters in the firmament they checked their course when they reached their unusual boundaries.[10] Could not the Lord have set

6 Gen. 1.6.
7 Ps. 148.6,4.
8 Ps. 148.5,6.
9 Cf. Rom. 11.33.
10 Cf. Exod. 15.8.

free the Hebrew people in a quite different manner? But He wished to show that by taking note of such a spectacle you might come to think that what is not even visible to your eyes ought to inspire belief. The Jordan, too, inverting its course, returned to its source.[11] That water in its course should stand still is considered to be unusual. That it should flow upwards without any external aid is considered to be impossible. But why is it impossible for Him who gave strength to the weak, so that they could say: 'I can do all things in him who strengthens me.'[12]

Let them tell us whether, when 'the air thickens into cloud,'[13] rain is then produced by clouds or whether it is collected in the lap of the clouds? We so frequently see clouds issuing from the mountains. I ask you: Does the water rise from the earth or does the water which is over the heavens fall in copious rain? If water rises, it surely is against nature that the element which is heavier should be borne to a higher place and that it should be carried there by air, although this is a lighter element. Or if water is whirled by the rapid motion of the entire world system, in that case it is absorbed from the lowest sphere and, likewise, it is poured forth from the highest. If it does not cease to be poured forth, as they claim, surely it does not cease to be absorbed, because, if the axis of the heavens is ever in movement, the water, too, is always being absorbed. If water descends, then it is clear that it is continuously above the heavens in a position from which it can flow downwards.

What prevents us, then, from admitting that water is suspended above the heavens? How can they say that the earth, although it is certainly heavier than water, stays suspended and immobile in the middle? Following the same

11 Cf. Ps. 113.3.
12 Phil. 4.13.
13 Virgil, *Aeneid* 5.20.

principle, they can admit the water which is above the heavens does not descend because of the rotation of that celestial sphere. Just as the earth is suspended in the void and stays immobile in position, its weight being balanced on every side,[14] in like manner the water, too, is balanced by weights either equal to or greater than that of the earth. For the same reason, the sea does not tend to inundate the land without a special command to do so.

(12) When they state again that the glittering sphere of heaven revolves with its fiery stars, did not Divine Providence necessarily forsee that water more than sufficient to temper the heat of the burning axis should exist within the sphere of heaven and above it? For the reason that fire makes its presence felt everywhere, for the same reason, too, water abounded on the earth, lest it be parched by the heat of the burning sun and of the twinkling stars and thus delicate things be injured at their birth by an unfamiliar warmth.[15] How great a number of springs, rivers, and lakes irrigate the earth, parched, as it is, by some fire within![16] If, too, that interior fire does not give life to them, how could the trees or grain germinate or seedling burst forth or, when they have sprouted, be brought to maturity? Fire, also, frequently issues forth from rocks and from wood itself when a tree is being cut down. Fire, therefore, is a necessary element in the work of creation in order that things remain in due order and arrangement and that the clemency of the sky may temper the rigidity of water. In like manner even excessive quantities of water are not superfluous, where there is danger of one element being consumed by another; unless the proportion of both elements is a suitable one, then

14 Cf. Ovid, *Metamorphoses* 1.12.
15 Cf. Virgil, *Eclogues* 6.33-36; *vapor* for 'warmth' is Lucretian (3.126).
16 Cf. Lucretius 5.457-466.

fire may dry up the water, just as water, too, extinguishes fire.

Accordingly, God balanced the universe with weights and measures. He has measured even the drops of rain, as we read in the book of Job.[17] Knowing that either there would be a tendency toward a failure or a dissolution of the universe, if one element preponderated over the other, He controlled for that reason the extent of each, so that fire would not supply more heat, or water more moisture, than would lead to the diminution of either under His guidance, by which the superfluous was drained off and a sufficiency was held in reserve.

Such great streams of mighty rivers still burst forth from the earth. We have the Nile that inundates Egypt with its overflowing waters; the Danube which divides the barbarians of the eastern regions from the Roman people, until it hides itself in the Black Sea; the Rhine which directs its course from a defile in the Alps until it reaches the depths of the ocean—a notable barricade for the Roman empire against savage nations; the Po, a trusty conveyor of maritime produce for the support of Italy; the Rhone, which with its rapid current cuts the waters of the Tyrrhenian sea, thereby adding to the perils of sailors, according to report, because of the struggle for mastery between the river currents and the sea waves; and, rising in the northern regions and combining in the Caucasus Mountains with many other streams, the Phasis River rushes headlong to the sea. It would be tedious to enumerate the names of each and every river which either flows into our sea or empties itself into the ocean. Notwithstanding such an abundance of water in the world, the soil in the southern zone for the most part is still scorched and reduced to dust by excessive heat. The toil of the unhappy farmer is spent in vain, so

17 Cf. Job 36.27.

much so that, when the wells and streams are dried up, he frequently fails to find enough water to sustain life. And there will be a time when He will say to the deep: 'Be thou desolate and I will dry up all the rivers,'[18] as through Isaias He announced the future. But before that day established by the divine will shall come, no little conflict among themselves is presented by the specific natures of the elements. Hence, the world is frequently affected by violent inundations or is afflicted by the extremes of heat and aridity.

(13) Be not concerned, therefore, with the extraordinary excess of water in the world; take note, rather, of the force exercised by heat and you will not be incredulous. Fire is able to absorb much, a fact which ought to be clear to us from an experiment. When physicians burn a small candle and attach it to the inside of certain types of vases, narrow in the spout, rather flat on top and hollow within, how does it happen that this heat attracts to itself all the moisture? Who, therefore, doubts that the burning æther, glowing with mighty heat, would cause everything to be consumed by fire if it were not held in check by a law laid down by its Author, so that neither rivers nor lakes nor the seas themselves could subdue its strength? And so, water falling from above gushes forth generally in such storms of rain that rivers and lakes suddenly are filled and the very seas overflow. Hence, we often see the sun, too, veiled in vaporous exhalations. This is clear proof that the sun, in order to temper its heat, has appropriated to itself the element of water.

(14) So great is their zeal in assailing truth that they go as far as to assert that the sun itself is devoid of heat by nature, for the reason that it is white and not ruddy or red as fire is. And so they say it is not fiery by nature and, if

18 Isa. 44.27.

it has some heat, they maintain that this is the result of the unusual speed of its revolutions. This theory ought to be accepted, they claim, for the reason that the sun does not seem to consume any moisture, because it does not have a natural heat by means of which moisture is either diminished or very often drained off. Notwithstanding these arguments they do not succeed in their purpose, because it makes no difference whether heat is natural or acquired or proceeds from some other cause, since every fire is a consumer of moisture or of any material such as can be burned by the application of fire. For, if you touch leaves with a spark obtained, not from wood which is already partly burned, but from one produced by the friction of sticks, such a flame increases its strength, just as if you were to light a torch from a fire. But if you should kindle a light from a flame or another lighted object, these two have a fire of the same appearance and character as if the fire were produced, not by nature, but by accident.[19] These men should, from the point of view, at least, of the heat of the sun, take note that God has set different times and places for the sun's courses, lest, if it should linger always in the same places, it might burn them up with its daily heat. Concerning the reasons for the bitter and salty nature of sea water, the same people relate that so much water is absorbed by heat as it is obtained from the confluent rivers, and that so much water is evaporated each day by the heat as is furnished by the daily inflow from the various rivers. This phenomenon is held to take place by a certain power of selection on the part of the sun, which takes to itself what is pure and light and leaves what is heavy and earthy. As a result, there is left that salty and dry quality in the water, unsuited to man's consumption and enjoyment.

19 Cf. Lucretius 2.1115.

Chapter 4

(15) But let us return to our theme: 'Let there be a firmament made amidst the water.'[1] Let it not disturb you, as I have already said, that above He speaks of heaven and here of a firmament, since David also says: 'The heavens narrate the glory of God and the firmament declareth the work of his hands.'[2] That is to say, the created world, when one beholds it, praises its own Author, for His invisible majesty is recognized through the things that are visible.[3] It seems to me that the word 'heaven' is a generic term, because Scripture testifies to the existence of very many heavens. The word 'firmament' is more specific, since here also we read: 'And he called the firmament, heaven.'[4] In a general way, He would seem to have said above that heaven was made in the beginning so as to take in the entire fabric of celestial creation, and that here the specific solidity of this exterior firmament is meant. This is called the firmament of heaven, as we read in the prophetic hymn, 'Blessed are thou in the firmament of heaven.'[5]

For heaven, which in Greek is called οὐρανός, in Latin, *caelum,* is connected with the word 'stamped' [*caelatum*], because the heavens have the lights of the stars impressed on them like embossed work, just as silver plate is said to be 'stamped' when it glitters with figures in relief. The word οὐρανός seems to be derived from the Greek verb 'to be seen' [ὁρᾶσθαι]. In distinction, therefore, to the earth, which is darker, the sky is called οὐρανός, because it is bright, that is to say, visible. Hence, I believe, is the origin

1 Gen. 1.6.
2 Ps. 18.2.
3 Cf.. Rom. 1.20.
4 Gen. 1.8.
5 Dan. 3.56.

of that expression: 'The winged ones of heaven always behold the face of my Father, who is in heaven.'[6] And again: 'The winged fowl above the firmament of heaven.'[7] The powers which exist in that visible place behold all these things and have them subject to their observation.

(16) Therefore, the heavens were closed in the times of Elias when godlessness reigned with Achab and Jezabel,[8] since the people were made responsible for the sacrilege of their kings. For that reason, no one attempted to raise his eyes to heaven, no one paid reverence to his Creator, but, rather, worshiped sticks and stones. How do we come to this conclusion? Because in His maledictions against the people of Israel God said: 'The heaven that is over thee will be of brass and your soil of iron,'[9] when paying the price of godlessness, the people of Juda were punished by the inclemency of heaven and the sterility of earth—for heaven is the source of fertility. Therefore, Moses, too, granted this blessing to the tribe of Joseph: 'From the confines of heaven and from the dew and from the deep that lieth beneath and from the course of the sun in accordance with the season and from the months that meet and from the tops of the mountains and the eternal hills.'[10] For it is true that the fruitfulness of the earth is sustained by heavenly guidance.

Hence, the sky which gives forth no moisture at a time when no showers break through the clouds has the appearance of iron. The sky is also of 'iron' when the air is dark and dense, with clouds of the color of iron rust, at a time when the earth is held in bonds by the rigidity of cold. Then moisture seems to be suspended over our heads and to be ready to fall at any moment. Frequently, too, water is

6 Matt. 18.10.
7 Gen. 1.20.
8 Cf. 3 Kings 17.1.
10 Deut. 33.13-15.

solidified in the form of snow when subjected to icy winds at a time when snow falls through the cleft air.

This firmament cannot be broken, you see, without a noise. It also is called a firmament because it is not weak nor without resistance. Hence, in dealing with thunderbolts, which give forth a tremendous crash when currents of air on the point of arising in the midst of the clouds meet together in collision, the Scripture speaks of strengthening the thunderbolt.[11] Therefore, the firmament is called because of its firmness or because it has been made firm by divine power, just as Scripture teaches us, saying: 'Praise ye him in the firmament of his power.'[12]

(17) And I am not unaware that some refer 'the heaven of heavens' to the intelligible powers, the firmament to the efficient powers and that the heavens praise and 'shine forth the glory of God and the firmament declareth it'[13]—yet, as we have said above, they declare them not as spiritual powers, but as things of the world. Others also interpret the waters to mean the purificatory powers. We accept this interpretation as a simple adornment to our treatise. To us, however, it does not appear to be inappropriate nor absurd, if we are to understand these to be real waters for the reasons given above. According to the hymn of the Prophet, dew, frost, cold and heat bless the Lord, the earth, too, blesses Him.[14] Furthermore, we do not understand the stars to be unseen powers of nature, but as having real existence. Even dragons give praise to the Lord, because their nature and aspect, if one examines them closely, are not without presenting a certain modicum of beauty and design.

---

11 Cf. Amos 4.13.
12 Ps. 150. 1.
13 Ps. 148.4.
14 Cf. Dan. 3.64,65.

Chapter 5

(18) 'And God saw that it was good.'[1] The Son does what the Father desires. No degeneration of nature is found in Him whose work does not degenerate from the will of the Father. He saw, it is certain, but not with corporeal eyes. He designated that the limit of vision should conform to the plenitude of His grace,[2] by which means His judgment may be made known to us, for we in fact often dispute even on subjects which are divine.

What wonder is it, then, if those men who are able to turn their attention to the work of creation also raise questions on the generation of the Creator Himself. Him they call to judgment; Him they dare refer to as unjust and unworthy of His descent. And so you read both 'God spoke' and 'God created,' in which both Father and Son are honored with the same name of majesty. 'And God saw that it was good.' He spoke as if speaking to one who knew all the wishes of His Father. He saw as if He knew all that His Son had accomplished, acting with Him in community of operation.

(19) 'He saw that it was good.' He did not, of course, recognize that of which He was ignorant. Rather, His approval was given to what gave Him pleasure. The work did not please Him as something unknown, just as the Father, who was pleased with the Son, was not like one unknown, as it is written: 'This is my beloved Son, in whom I am well pleased.'[3] The Son always knows the will of the Father and the Father that of the Son. And the Son listens to the Father and the Father hears the Son through the unity of nature, will, and substance. The Son, therefore, bears witness to this

1 Gen. 1.10.
2 Cf. John 1.14.
3 Matt. 3.17.

in the Gospel, speaking to the Father: 'I know that thou always hearest me.'[4]

The Son is 'the image of the invisible God.'[5] All that the Father is, the Son sets forth as an image. The Father illumines and makes Him manifest for us all as 'the brightness of his glory.'[6] The Son, too, beholds the work of the Father and the Father that of the Son, as the Lord Himself has declared: 'The Son can do nothing of himself but only what he sees the Father doing.'[7] He sees, therefore, the Father doing and sees and hears Him in like manner through the hidden power of His invisible nature. Therefore, He says: As I hear, so do I judge, and 'my judgment is true, because I am not alone, but with me is he who sent me, the Father.'[8]

(20) This is the mystic sense. The moral sense is this: 'He saw' for me; 'He approved' for me. What God has approved, do not consider worthy of blame, since you recall that the statement, 'What God has cleansed, do not thou call common,'[9] has been written for you. Hence, let no one blaspheme what is good before God! If the firmament is good, how much more so is its Creator, even if the Arians would not admit it and the followers of Eunomianus should object, the no less corrupt fruit of a degenerate root!

(21) 'God saw that it was good.' Artists usually work first on individual parts and afterwards join them together with skill. Those who start to carve out of marble the features or bodies of men or mould them in bronze or wax[10] do not know exactly how the individual components will blend together, nor the beauty which will be the result of the final

4 John 11.42.
5 2 Cor. 4.4.
6 Heb. 1.3.
7 John 5.19.
8 John 8.16.
9 Acts 10.15.
10 Cf. Virgil, *Aeneid* 6.847,848.

work. And so they dare not praise fully, but praise only in part.

God, however, as judge of the whole work, forseeing what is going to happen as something completed, commends that part of His work which is still in its initial stages, being already cognizant of its terminaton. This is not to be wondered at, since in His case the completion of a thing does not depend on the termination of the actual work. It rests, rather, on the predetermination of His will. He praises each individual part as befitting what is to come. He praises the total work, which is compounded of the elegance of each part. True beauty, in fact, consists of a fitting adjustment in each part and in the whole, so that the charm in each part and the full appropriateness of the form in the completed work are worthy of commendation.[11]

(22) But now let us put an end to the second day, lest, while we are attending to the work of the firmament, we may cause our hearers to languish because of the prolixity of our discourse—in a discourse which, prolonged into a night which is still devoid of the light of a moon and stars, may bring obscurity to those who are returning home. For the luminaries of the heavens have not as yet been created. Our purpose is also to allow our hearers to refresh themselves with food and drink, so that, while their minds have banqueted, the frailty of their flesh may not find cause to complain of a fast lasting even until nightfall.

---

11 Ancient literary criticism followed this pattern; cf. Pliny, *Epistola* 8.4; 2.5; 3.15.

BOOK THREE: THE THIRD DAY

THE FOURTH HOMILY

Chapter 1

IN OUR DISCOURSE today, the third day rises, as it is recorded in Scripture, a notable day which freed the earth from inundation at the bidding of God: 'Let the waters that are under the heaven be gathered together into one place.'[1] With this fact it is my wish to begin my preface.

'Let the waters be gathered together.' These words were spoken, and the waters gathered together. It has often been said, 'let the people be gathered together,' and there was no gathering. It brings no slight blush of shame to see that the elements which are without sensibility are obedient to the command of God, whereas men to whom their Author has bestowed sensibility fail to obey His injunction. And perhaps it is the same blush of shame which has brought you here today in greater numbers. It would hardly appear right for the people to fail to congregate in the church of the Lord on the day in which water is congregated in one body.

(2) This is not the only example of the obedience of water available to us, for elsewhere we find it written: 'The waters

1 Gen. 1.6.

saw thee, O God, the waters saw thee and they were afraid.'[2] What is said here of the waters does not seem to be without a semblance of truth, since elsewhere the Prophet also speaks in the same manner: 'The sea saw and fled: Jordan was turned back.[3] Who does not know how in actual fact the sea fled at the crossing of the Hebrews? When the waters were divided, the people crossed over, believing because of the dust under their feet that the sea had fled, and that the waters had vanished. Therefore, the Egyptian believed what he saw and entered in, but the waters which had fled returned for him. The waters, then, know how to congregate, how to fear, and how to flee, when commanded to do so by God. Let us imitate these waters and let us recognize one congregation of the Lord, one Church.

(3) There once were gathered here waters from every valley, from every marsh, from every lake. The valley signifies heresy; the valley means the people of the Gentiles, because 'The Lord is God of the hills, but is not God of the valleys.'[4] Therefore, in the Church there is exultation; among the heretics and Gentiles, there is grief and weeping. Hence Scripture says: 'In the valley he set up tears.'[5] Accordingly, the Catholic people have congregated from every valley. Now, there are not many congregations; rather, there is one congregation, one Church. Here, too, was it said: 'Let waters be congregated from every valley,' and there came into existence a spiritual congregation, one people. Out of heretics and Gentiles has the Church become filled.

The valley is a theater, the valley is a circus where runs the horse who 'is useless for safety,'[6] where there is vile and

2 Ps. 76.17.
3 Ps. 113.3.
4 3 Kings 20.28.
5 Ps. 83.7.
6 Ps. 32.17.

abject contention, where there is the ignoble strife of litigants. From these, then, who used to cleave to the circus has faith grown in the Church, and daily attendance is increasing.

(4) The marsh is self-indulgence, the marsh is intemperance, the marsh is incontinence, where are found wallowing places for lusts, the grunts of beasts, and the lairs of passions. Whoever falls therein is dragged down and does not emerge. Here men's feet find no foothold, but waver uncertainly. Here water fowls are begrimed when they bathe, and above us are heard the mournful cries of doves. Here the sluggish turtle buries himself in the muddy waters. Therefore we have the sayings: 'A boar in the marsh,' 'a stag at the fountains.'[7] And so from every marsh, where like frogs they have sung their ancient chant of complaint, has congregated here faith; here, too, have congregated purity of heart and simplicity of mind.

(5) Waters have gathered from every lake and from every pit, so that no one prepares a pit for his brother wherein he himself may fall.[8] Rather, all love each other in mutual love, all cherish one the other, and support themselves as one body, although of diverse members.[9] They find delight not in the baleful songs sung by theatrical performers, songs which lead to sensual love, but in the chants of the Church. Here we hear the voice of the people singing in harmony the praises of God. The sight of their piety gives us pleasure. Here are people who find no delight in tapestries of purple or costly stage curtains. Their pleasure lies rather in their admiration of this most beautiful fabric of the world, this accord of unlike elements, this heaven that is 'spread out like a tent to dwell in'[10] to protect those who inhabit this

---

7 Cf. Ps. 79.14; 41.2.
8 Cf. Prov. 26.27.
9 Cf. Rom. 12.4.
10 Isa. 40.22.

world. They find their pleasure in the earth allotted to them for their labors, in the ambient air, in the seas here enclosed in their bounds. In the people who are the instruments of the operations of God they hear music which echoes from melodious sound of God's word, within which the Spirit of God works. They see this temple here, the holy place of the Trinity, the habitation of sanctity, the holy Church, in which gleam those celestial curtains of which it is said: 'Enlarge the place of thy tents and of thy curtains; fasten, spare not, lengthen thy cords and strengthen thy stakes; stretch further on the right and on the left; and thy seed shall inherit the Gentiles and thou shalt inhabit the desolate cities.'[11] The Church, therefore, has its curtains, by which it raises aloft the good life, shields the sinner, and overshadows the fault.

(6) This is the Church, which is founded upon the seas and is prepared upon the rivers.[12] For the Church is made strong and is prepared above you, who flow down as rivers do from that pure source into the fountain of the world, of whom it has been said: 'The floods have lifted up, O Lord: the floods have lifted up their voices with the voice of many waters.' And the Psalmist added: 'Wonderful are the surges of the sea; wonderful is the Lord on high.'[13] Beneficent are the woods; you have drunk from that perennial and full spring, whither you are flowing, which says to you: 'He who believes in me' (as the Scripture says), 'from within him shall flow rivers of living water.'[14] He said this, however, of the Spirit, whom they who believed in him were to receive. But, like the waters of the good Jordan, return with me to the beginning.

11 Isa. 54.2,3.
12 Cf. Ps. 23.2.
13 Ps. 92.3,4.
14 John 7.38.

Chapter 2

(7) 'Let the waters,' Scripture says, 'that are under the heaven be gathered together into one place and let the dry land appear. And it was so done.'[1]

Perhaps one may not at all believe in our preceding discussion, where we have argued that the earth was invisible for the reason that it was covered with water, so that it could not be seen by corporeal eyes, for his own point of view, that is, from our condition here, did the Prophet speak—not from that of the majesty of divine nature, which, of course, sees all things. In order to point out to you that we have undertaken this laborious task, not for the sake of displaying our talents, but for your instruction, we bring as witnesses for our cause texts from Scriptures. These clearly prove that, after the gathering of the water above the earth and its later falling down into the seas, the dry land appeared. Let them cease, therefore, as far as we are concerned, to stir up contentious disputes by saying: How is the earth invisible when form and color are naturally attached to every body and every color presupposes a form?

The voice of God cries out: 'Let the waters be gathered together and let the dry land appear.' And again Scripture says: 'The waters are gathered together in one place and the dry land appeared.'[2] Why was there need to repeat this, if the Prophet had not thought it necessary to forestall disputes? Does he not seem to say: 'I have not said the earth was invisible according to nature, but in respect to the inundation of waters?' Hence, he added that the dry land, which before was not seen, showed itself when this covering was removed.

(8) Again, they sow the seeds of other disputes by saying:

1 Gen. 1.9.
2 *Ibid.*

If the waters were in different masses, how came it about, if these masses were in the upper regions, that the waters did not flow down to that place where, after the command given by God, they eventually arrived? For they say it is natural that waters flow of themselves into lower regions. Moreover, if these masses were below, how did it come to pass that they rose up to higher regions, a movement contrary to the nature of water? Accordingly, either this natural course did not need God's command or, notwithstanding this command, it could not succeed because it is contrary to nature.

I will gladly respond to this question, if they will first reply to me and show me that before God's command this was the nature of water, namely, flowing and falling downward. It does not have this quality from association with the other elements; it is, rather, a special quality, peculiar to itself. It is not the result of some natural propensity, but issues from the will and operation of the most high God. The waters listen to the command of God and the voice of God is the efficient cause of nature. This voice coincides with the completion of the effect of its operation. The water began to flow downwards so as to form one mass—water which before this had been spread over all the earth and had settled in numerous lurking places. I had not read of its course before, of its movements I had been uninformed: my eye had not seen, nor had my ear heard. The water stood still in diverse places; at the voice of God it was moved. Does it not seem that the voice of God gave it this natural tendency? The creature followed the injunction of its Creator and from the law proceeded custom, the law of its first constitution left its imprint for future ages.

Hence, God created day and night at the same time. Since that time, day and night continue their daily succession and renewal. The water was ordered to run together in a mass. From that moment, water runs. Springs flow down to form rivers, rivers run into larger bodies of water;[3] lakes find an outlet in the seas; wave precedes wave, presses on it, and follows. There is but one way, one mass. Althought the depths differ, the surface remains, however, at an equal level. Hence, too, I believe it is called *'aequor'* [level] because its surface is level.

(9) I have made my reply according to the point of view of my adversaries. Let them now answer my question: Have they ever seen springs shoot up from below? Or water rise out of the ground? Who compels it to do so? Whence does it issue forth? How is it that it does not fall? How does it happen that such deep openings spill forth water? These phenomena are in accordance with the mysterious secrets of nature. Moreover, who does not know that water frequently falls to a very low depth with a great rush and then rises up to a higher position, even to the summit of a mountain? Also, that in canals made by a craftsman's hands, the water often subsides as much as it previously had been uplifted? Accordingly, if either by its own force or by the skill of an engineer water is conducted and raised contrary to its own nature, do we wonder if by the operation of divine command it has acquired some disposition in its nature which it did not have before?

They may say now to me how God 'gathered the waters of the sea as in a vessel,' as Scripture has it, and how 'he brought forth water out of the rocks.' Could not He who brought forth water, which did not exist, out of a rock, also not guide water which already existed? 'He struck the rock,' cried David, 'and the streams overflowed,' and elsewhere, 'above the mountains shall the waters stand.'[4] In the Gospel we read that when there was a severe storm and the sea

3 Cf. Virgil, *Aeneid* 1.607.
4 Ps. 32.7; cf. 77.16; Ps. 77.20; 103.6.

was in violent motion, so much so that the Apostles feared the dangers of shipwreck and aroused the Lord Jesus who was asleep in the stern, He arose and rebuked the wind and the sea and the tempest was abated and calm was restored.[5] Could not He who was able to calm the whole sea at His bidding also move the waters by His command? Well, in the account of the flood it is related that 'the fountains of the great deep were broken up' and that God afterwards caused the wind to blow over the deep so as to dry up the waters.[6] If these men do not wish to concede that nature obeyed and that the habitual character of an element was changed by God's command, at least they can concede this: the waters could have been moved by the force of the wind, a phenomenon to be seen every day on the sea, when the waters flow in the direction of the movement of the wind. If the sea was dried up by the force of a strong south wind in the time of Moses,[7] could not a body of water be dried up in the same manner? Did not the waters, too, have the power of flowing into the sea, water which later on was actually severed from the bed of the sea? Let them learn that nature can be changed, after water burst forth from a rock and iron floated on water,[8] a marvel which Eliseus succeeded in doing by the power of prayer and not by command.

If, therefore, Eliseus caused iron, contrary to nature, to lose its weight in water, could not Christ put the water in motion? But He had the power of moving the waters who was able to say, 'Lazarus, come forth'[9] and bring the dead back to life, since God always brings to pass what He ordains. In like manner understand the words: 'Let the waters be gathered together in one place,' and they were

5 Cf. Matt. 8.24,26.
6 Gen. 7.11; cf. 8.1.
7 Cf. Exod. 14.27.
8 Cf. Exod. 17.6; 4 Kings 6.6.
9 John 11.43.

gathered. By saying: 'Let them be gathered,' He not only moved the waters from their place, but He also set them down in a place, so that they would not flow away, but stand still.

(10) The following is on this account a greater marvel: how all the bodies of water flowed into one body and how that one body was not full to overflowing. Scripture, too, reckoned this among extraordinary happenings by stating: 'All the rivers run into the sea, yet the sea doth not overflow.'[10] By the command of God, therefore, two things are accomplished: the waters flow, yet do not overflow. A boundary is set up by which the seas are circumscribed and confined, lest the waters inundate everything by pouring over the earth and lest the earth, devoid of cultivation, may prevent the soil from fulfilling its natural function of producing in abundance.

Let them recognize the fact, therefore, that this is the result of divine precept and of celestial operation, for the Lord addresses Job from the clouds, saying, among other things, this, also, about the barrier of the sea: 'I set my bounds around it and made it bars and doors, and I said: "hitherto thou come and shalt go no further, but on thyself shall be broken thine own waves." '[11] Do we not ourselves often see the sea billowing so that its waves rise up 'like a sheer mountain of water,'[12] when it breaks its force in foam against the shore, beaten back by what might be called the barriers of the low-lying sandy beach, according to what the Scripture says: 'Will you not then fear me, saith the Lord, who has set the sand a bound for the sea?'[13] Thus the violent onslaught of the sea is held in check by the most

---

10 Eccle. 1.7.
11 Job 38.10,11.
12 Virgil, *Aeneid* 1.105.
13 Jer. 5.22.

unstable of all things, ordinary coarse sand of the seashore. The waves recoil and are guided to their prescribed bounds by a command from heaven, and the violent movement of the water is broken by meeting itself. It then departs in receding ripples.[14]

(11) Moreover, unless the force of a celestial decree did not serve as a check, who would prevent the Red Sea from pouring over the plains of Egypt (which is claimed to be flat and low-lying with very deep valleys) and from mingling its waters with the Egyptian Sea? The men who wished to connect these two seas and to make them one have made us aware of the fact. The Egyptian Sesostris of an older period and Darius the Mede, in virtue of his greater power, wanted to put into effect what had been attempted before their time by a native of the country. This fact is substantial evidence that the Indian Ocean, which includes the Red Sea, is of higher elevation than the Egyptian Sea, the level of whose waters is lower. And it may well have been that both kings relinquished their projects lest the sea, in headlong rush from a higher to a lower level, should inundate their land.

Chapter 3

(12) And now, on the statement: 'Let the waters be gathered together in one place,' the question would arise: How could one body of water be formed from what is scattered over lakes, marshes and swamps, also waters which inundate valleys, plains and level lands, stemming from springs and from rivers? Moreover, how could these waters form one mass, whereas today waters are scattered in diverse seas? For we speak of such varied seas as these: the ocean,

---

14 Cf. Virgil, *Aeneid* 1.161.

the Tyrrhenian, Adriatic, Indian, Egyptian, and Pontic seas, the Propontic, the Hellespont, Euxine, Aegean, Ionian, and Atlantic seas. Many also speak of a Cretic Sea and of a Northern Caspian. Let us therefore consider the meaning of the words of Scripture and weigh them with exactitude.

(13) 'Let the waters,' He said, 'be gathered together in one place.' The mass of water is continuous and unbroken, yet there are different coastal bays, as a profane writer states.[1] For the Pontus is a very large bay of our sea [the Mediterranean] to which different names are given in different places. Rightly so, because the regions adjacent to these bodies of water give them special names, yet there is but one mass of water, because one continuous and unbroken body of water extends from the Indian sea up the shores of Cadiz and from there extends to the Red Sea, to the extreme limit of the world, which is enclosed by the circumambient Ocean. Within this circle the Adriatic mingles with the Tyrrhenian Sea, while other seas form a union with the Adriatic—seas distinguished from it by name, but not by a difference of water mass.

Hence, God has fittingly said: 'The getting together of waters he called seas.'[2] And so there is one general mass which is called a sea and many bodies of water which are called seas after the regions where they are situated. Just as there are many lands, such as Africa, Spain, Thrace, Macedonia, Syria, Egypt, Gaul, and Italy, which are given names from their respective regions, so there is but one earth. In a similar manner, there are many seas named after their locations, but there is but one actual sea, as the Prophet says: 'Thine are the heavens and thine is the earth, the world and the fulness thereof Thou hast founded; the north

1 Cicero, in *Timaeus,* now a fragment.
2 Gen. 1.10.

and the sea thou hast created.'[3] And the Lord Himself says to Job: 'I have shut up the sea with doors.'[4]

(14) Now that we have spoken of one mass, the question arises how a single body of water could drain the land of water, although that water had previously possessed all the land, poured into the hollow places in the mountains, plains, and valleys—water which lay stagnant in an universal inundation. For, if everything was covered in this way—for He would not have said: 'The earth appeared,' unless He wished to indicate that it was uncovered everywhere—if the flood in the time of Noe hid even the mountains when there already was a separation of the waters above the heavens and those below the firmament—if this were so, then how can one doubt that the tops of the mountains were hidden in the inundation we speak of? Whence, then, came that overabundant supply of water? What reservoirs were there, so continuous and unbroken as to hold all the water in place?

(15) On this subject there is much at hand for the formulation of reply. First of all, the Creator of all things had the power of enlarging space—a power which some before us have in their private opinion laid down as a possibility. And I am not overlooking in this case the potency of God; but what He actually has done, which I have not learned from the clear testimony of Scripture, I pass over as a mystery, lest, perchance, that stir up other questions starting even from this point. Nevertheless, I maintain in accord with the Scriptures that God can extend the low-lying regions and the open plains, as He has said: 'I will go before thee and make level the mountains.'[5] The very force of water can also make its bed deeper by the violent movements of the waves and by the impact of the surf of that wild

3 Ps. 88.12,13.
4 Job 38.8.
5 Isa. 45.2.

element which day by day stirs up the bottom of the sea, drawing forth sands from its very depths.

Who, then, knows how far that mighty sea pours its waters which, unapproachable even to daring navigators, encloses the British Isles with its innumerable bays and extends even to remote regions, unknown and unrecorded even in legendary tales? Who is not aware of the mass of water from the sea which has seeped into the numerous lakes, such as the Lucrine and Lake Avernus in Italy, Lake Tiberias, too, in Palestine, not to mention that lake that lies in the desert region of Arabia between Palestine and Egypt,[6] and the water which has seeped into the several ports made by Augustus and by Trajan, as well as into many similar ones throughout the entire world?

(16) Still, there are some lakes and standing waters which are not connected with other waters, such as Lake Como, Lake Garda, the Alban lake—and many others. How then can one speak of one mass of water? But, just as God made two luminaries, the sun and the moon—although there still exist, to be sure, the lights of the stars—in like manner, we speak also of one mass of water, although there are very many such. The reason is that what has not been taken in consideration in any enumeration is not reckoned in the sum total.

Chapter 4

(17) But it seems that, while I was speaking of the sea, I exceeded my bounds a little. Let us return to our theme and let us reflect on the words of the Lord: 'Let the waters be gathered together into one place and let the dry land

6 The Dead Sea.

appear,'[1] He did not say: 'Let the land appear.' Who does not note the appropriateness of this statement? For the earth could be a composite of mud and water, and thus its appearance would be concealed by the inundating water. The term 'dry" applies not only to the general nature of the earth, but can also be used in a specific way, so that the earth may be useful, firm, suitable, and ready for cultivation. At the same time, it was provided that the earth would, to all appearance, have been dry by the hand of God rather than by the sun, for the earth actually became dry before the sun was created. Wherefore, David, too, distinguished the sea from the land, referring to the Lord God: 'For the sea is his and he made it, and his hands made the dry land.'[2]

The word 'dry' is the expression of a natural characteristic; the word 'earth' is a simple name of a thing which has in itself that same characteristic. Just as the word 'animal' is a generic term which includes within it a certain notable property, and as man has his special characteristic which is reason, in like manner the word 'earth' can be used indifferently of what is saturated with water or of a place 'in a desert land and where there is no way and no water.'[3] Therefore, the land saturated with water has within it elements of dryness, as it has been written: 'He hath turned rivers into a wilderness and the sources of waters into dry ground,'[4] that is to say, He made dry the land that was before filled with water.

(18) The earth, therefore, has its own peculiar property, just as the individual elements have, for each has its own characteristic: the air is humid, water is cold, and fire is warm. That these are the chief qualities of each of the

1 Gen. 1.9.
2 Ps. 94.5.
3 Ps. 62.3.
4 Ps. 106.33.

elements can be determined by our observation. If we should desire to make a test of these elements with our bodily senses we find that their qualities exist in a certain combination. For example, we discover earth to be dry and cold; water, cold and humid; air, warm and humid; fire, warm and dry. Thus, each and every one of the elements is bound together by qualities shared in common with some other element.

Since earth has a quality both dry and cold, it is connected with water by association of its cold quality, and through water it is related to the air because the air is humid. Hence, water seems to embrace with its two arms, as it were, cold and humidity, on the one side, the earth, on the other, air—the earth with its quality of coldness, the air with its quality of humidity. Air, by its nature, also forms an intermediary between two opposing elements, that is, between water and fire, for it binds both elements together. It shares with water the quality of humidity and with fire the quality of warmth. Fire, too, since it is by nature warm and dry, is bound to air by its quality of warmth, and, because of its dry quality, is turned back to form an association and a union with earth. In this manner these elements, by a circuitous process, meet together in a dance measure of concord and association. Hence, the Latin *elementa* is found in Greek as στοιχεῖα, denoting agreement and harmony.

(19) We have come to this point because Scripture says that God called the earth 'dry,' that is to say, He denominated by its natural quality that which is its prime characteristic. The natural characteristic for earth is dryness. This is a quality reserved for it. Its prime quality, therefore, is dryness. A secondary quality is that of coldness, but this does not take precedence over its primary trait. The fact that it is humid is also derived from its kinship with water. Hence, the former characteristic is peculiar to the earth, the other is alien: dryness belongs to earth; humidity is alien to it. The Author

of nature accordingly adhered to what He had first granted to the earth, for one quality is founded on nature; the other comes from an [external] cause. The peculiar qualities of the earth, therefore, ought to be determined from the primary qualities, not from what is accidental, in order that our knowledge might be formed from an observation of the preferred characteristic.

Chapter 5

(20) 'And God saw that it was good.' We do not fail to record the fact that some do not believe that either in the Hebrew or in other versions it is said: 'The waters were gathered together into their places and dry land appeared. And God called the dry land Earth and the gathering together of the waters he called Seas.'[1] Also, when God said: 'And it was so done,'[2] they are generally of the opinion that there we have the words of the Creator signifying the fulfillment of the work. But, because in regard also to other created things there is found first the formula of a command and afterwards the repeated indication or execution of a work, for that reason we do not think that which is considered an addition to be in the nature of an absurdity, even if by other interpreters sufficient proof may be presented for either its truth or its authenticity. Much that was added or attached to the Hebrew version by the writers of the Septuagint we have discovered not to be superfluous.

(21) God saw, then, that the sea was good. The aspect of this element is beautiful, either when the sea foams with its

1 Gen. 1.10.

2 Gen. 1.9; thus the Vulgate may be translated. The most recent version, 'And so it was,' follows the Hebrews and Septuagint more closely.

surging white caps and mountings billows, or when it bedews the rocks with its snowy spray, or even when under a balmy breeze it shimmers, often in this case presenting itself to the beholder from afar in colors of purple, suggesting serene tranquillity. Such is the aspect of the sea when it does not beat the nearby shores with the onrush of its waves, but when the waters greet it, as it were, in a fond embrace of peace. How gentle is the sound, how pleasing the splash of the water, how pleasant and rhythmic the wave-beats! Notwithstanding all this, I am of the opinion that the beauty of such a creation is not to be estimated by the standard of our own eyes, but is to be gauged in the design of the work as a whole by its conformity and agreement with the intention of its Creator.

(22) The sea, therefore, is good; first, because it supplies the moisture necessary for the earth, to which it furnishes, so to speak, a sustaining fluid through the hidden apertures of its veins. The sea is good in its functions as a biding-place for the rivers, as a source of rainfall, as a place for the reception of alluvial deposits, as a carrier of merchandise, thereby linking distant people together. Furthermore, the sea defends us from the perils of warfare; by the sea, the fury of the barbarian is hedged in; the sea provides support in times of necessity, a refuge in times of danger, a delightful place for seekers after pleasure; it is a source of health for the sick,[3] it joins together the separated; to voyagers it is a time-saver, to men in trouble a place of escape, to tax-payers it is an aid, and to the farmer in distress it is a means of livelihood. From the sea we obtain rain for the earth, since water is drawn from the sea which is deprived of its moisture by the sun's rays. Then, the higher it reaches, the colder it becomes by reason of the shadowy coolness of the clouds. As a result, we have rainfall, which not only relieves the earth

3 See Mullach, *Fragmenta phil. Graec.* I 518a *vs* 15.

of its dryness, but also provides nourishment to the famishing fields.

(23) Why need I enumerate the islands, which often adorn the sea with their jewelled necklaces? Men who hide themselves there seek to escape from the world with all its inducements to intemperate living with a firm purpose to live in continence and thereby avoid the dubious conflicts of this life. The sea, then, is a hiding-place for the temperate, an abode for those who wish to practice continency, a refuge for those in distress, a haven for the secure, a place of tranquillity for the unworldy and a place in this world for the prudent and moderate. Moreover, it provides an incentive to devout living for the faithful, so that they may rival the gentle sound of lapping waters with the songs of the psalms. Thus, the islands voice their approval with their tranquil chorus of blessed waters and with the singing of pious hymns resound.

How is it possible for me to comprehend all the beauty of the sea—a beauty beheld by the Creator? Why say more? What else is that melodic sound of the waves if not the melody of the people? Hence, the sea is often well compared to a church which 'disgorges a tide' through all its vestibules at the first array of the approaching congregation;[4] then, as the whole people unite in prayer, there is a hiss of receding waves; the echo of the psalms when sung in responsive harmony by men and women, maidens and children is like the sound of breaking waves. Wherefore, what need I say of this water other than it washes away sin and that the salutary breath of the Holy Spirit is found in it?

(24) May God grant us our prayer: to sail on a swift ship under a favorable breeze and finally reach a haven of safety; that we may not be exposed to spiritual obstacles too great to overcome; that we may not meet with ship-

4 Virgil, *Georgics* 2.462.

wreck to our faith. We pray, also, for a peace profound and, if there be anything that may arouse the storms of this world against us, that we may have as our ever-watchful pilot our Lord Jesus, who by His command can calm the tempest and restore once more the sea's tranquillity.[5] To Him be honor and glory in perpetuity, both now and forever, and for all ages to come. Amen.

5 Matt. 8.26; Luke 8.24.

THE FIFTH HOMILY

Chapter 6

(25) When the waters receded, it was proper that a special aspect and charm be bestowed on the earth so that it would cease 'to be invisible and without form.'[1] For many maintain that a thing is invisible because it has no special aspect. For that reason they hold that the earth was invisible —not because it could not be seen by the most high God or by His angels, but because it was without a special aspect. It could not be seen by men or even beasts because they had not yet been created. What provides this aspect for the earth is the soil's verdure and vegetation. Hence, in order to bestow visibility and form on the earth, God says: 'Let the earth bring forth the green herb and such as may seed and the fruit tree yielding fruit after its kind, which may have seed in itself upon the earth.'[2]

(26) Let us pay heed to the words of truth! Their content is the salvation of those who hear! For that first declaration of God is a law of nature which requires that every creature be born. This law has continued in force for all ages, with the intent to prescribe how a continuous succession of plants may experience in time to come modes of generation and fructification.[3] And so, first there is germination, when the seeds seem to burst forth newly born; next, when the sprout has burst forth and becomes a green shoot; when the green shoot has grown a little it becomes the green herb. How serviceable, how effective, is the speech: 'Let the earth bring forth the green herb,' that is so say, let the earth bring

1 Gen. 1.2.
2 Gen. 1.11.
3 Cf. Virgil, *Georgics* 2.122-134.

forth of itself, let it not seek the aid of another, let it not be needful of any other ministrations.

(27) Many, it is true, are accustomed to state that the earth could not have germinated without the warmth of the sun's temperate heat and in some way by its fostering rays. Hence, the Gentiles bestow divine honors on the sun, because it penetrates the bowels of the earth with the power of its heat and in that way cherishes the scattered seed or frees from the bonds of frost the sap of the trees. Listen, then, to God who utters words like these: Let the foolish speech of men be silent for future time, let their baseless opinions cease to be! Before the light of the sun shall appear, let the green herb be born, let its light be prior to that of the sun. Let the earth germinate before its receives the fostering care of the sun, lest there be an occasion for human error to grow. Let everyone be informed that the sun is not the author of vegetation. The earth is freed through the clemency of God; the fruit of the earth emerges therefrom through His indulgence. How can the sun give the faculty of life to growing plants, when these have already been brought forth by the life-giving creative power of God before the sun entered into such a life as this? The sun in younger than the green shoot, younger than the green plant!

Chapter 7

(28) And perhaps some may wonder why sustenance for animals was provided before food for man was created. In this matter we ought to take note of the depths of God's wisdom,[1] in that He does not neglect the least of things. For, the divine Wisdom utters these words in the Gospel: 'Look at the birds of the air, they do not sow or reap or

1 Cf. Rom. 11.33.

gather into barns, yet your heavenly Father feeds them. Are you of much more value than they?'[2] If these have their food through the kindness of God, then no one ought to pride himself on his own industry and natural ability. And no one ought to give simple and natural food precedence over the rest. The former is the food of the temperate; the rest of foods contribute to delight and luxury. One is common to all living things; the other, to a few. Hence, such a fact furnishes us with an example for frugal living, and is a wise injunction that we ought to be content to live on simple herbs, on cheap vegetables and fruits such as nature has presented to us and the generosity of God has offered to us. This sort of food is wholesome and useful, too, in that it wards off disease and prevents indigestion. No human labor has provided it; it is, rather, the bounteous gift of God. Vegetables are at hand which were not sown; there is fruit that needed no seed—all so sweet and pleasant that they furnish enjoyment even to those who have already sated themselves. In a word, the food that was used for the first course continued to be used for the second.

(29) What more need I add to the theme of the marvels of this creation and to the proof of the existence of a Creative Wisdom? For, in the appearance of a bud on the one hand, and in the provision of a green herb, on the other, there lies an image of the life of man and what may be termed a clear indication and mirror of our nature and of our condition. That green herb and flower of the field are a figure of the flesh of man, as the true interpreter of divinity has expressed in organ tones: 'Cry! What shall I cry? All flesh is grass and all the glory of man is as the flower of the field. The grass is withered and the flower is fallen, but the word of the Lord endureth forever.'[3] This is the thought of God

2 Matt. 6.26.
3 Isa. 40.6-9; 1 Peter 1.24.

though uttered by the voice of man. God says: 'Cry,' but He speaks in the person of Isaias, who answered: 'What shall I cry?' and, as he had heard what he should say, added: 'All flesh is grass.' And with truth, for the glory of man waxes green in his flesh like grass, and what is considered to be sublime is actually a lowly green herb. Blooming early as a flower and briefly as the green herb, it has the outward appearance of vigor, but its fruit has no lasting quality. It displays like a flower the joys of a happy existence, but is destined to pass away in all too brief a moment like the green herb, 'which withereth before it be plucked up.'[4] For what strength can there be in flesh, what enduring quality can there be in health?

Today you may behold a youth who is strong and vigorous in the flower of his age, pleasing in aspect and with the fine glow of health.[5] Tomorrow you meet the same youth, but how changed are his form and features![6] The young man who the previous day appeared to luxuriate in health and beauty is now an object of pity, prostrate and weakened by the inroads of some illness. Toil or want take their toll of health: some suffer from stomach ills; others from abuse of wine. Still others are enfeebled by old age; others are emasculated and disfigured by overindulgence in pleasure. Is it not true that 'the grass is withered and that the flower has fallen?'[7]

Another man, who claims nobility from his grandfather and great-grandfather[8] and has been made illustrious by the insignia of offices held by his ancestors, a man renowned by the trappings of his noble birth, abounding in friends, surrounded on both sides by a crowd of clients

4 Ps. 128.6.
5 Cf. Virgil, *Aeneid* 1.168.
6 Cf. Virgil, *Aeneid* 2.274.
7 Isa. 40.7.
8 Cf. Virgil, *Aeneid* 7.56.

who accompany him like a troop of slaves to and from his house[9]—should this man suddenly find himself faced with some passing peril, he is abandoned by all, he is shunned by his friends and assailed by his relatives. Consider how true it is that the life of man is like the grass of the field, 'which withereth before it is plucked up.'

There is also the man who for a long time has had abundance of wealth, the fame of whose generosity has flitted over the lips of every man,[10] a man renowned for his honors, outstanding in power, with a lofty seat in the tribunals, enthroned aloft and regarded as happy by the populace while he is being announced by the cries of the heralds. By a sudden change of fortune he is dragged away into the same prison into which he himself had cast others. Among his own victims he bewails in anguish his impending punishment. What crowds of sycophants and what a invidious procession of throngs of people had formerly conducted him from his home! Just one night put an end to the splendor of that triumphal pomp! Human glory of this kind is like a flower of the field which, even when it is taken away, contributes nothing to the labor. From it no fruit is obtained and, when it is allowed to fall, it fades away, depriving man of the protective covering by which he is shaded from above and animated within.

(31) Would that we could imitate the green herb concerning which the Lord speaks: 'Let the earth bring forth the green herb and such as may seed and the fruit tree yielding fruit after its kind of a like nature.'[11] Let us sow, therefore, the seed after its kind. What that kind is, hear the Apostle who says that we ought to seek after that divine seed, if we would succeed in any way in finding the divine:

---

9 Cf. Sallust, *Bellum Jug.* 85.10.
10 Cf. Ennius, cited by Cicero, *Tusculan Disputations* 1.34.
11 Gen. 1.11.

'Though he is not far from any one of us. For in him we live and move and have our being as some of you,' he adds, 'have said: "For we are also his offering." '[12]

Following this principle, let us sow the seed, not in the flesh, but in the spirit. For we ought not to sow carnal seeds, but spiritual ones,[13] if we desire to attain eternal life. And what that 'likeness' is you are not unaware, you who have been made to the 'image and likeness' of God. The green herb corresponds to its kind. You do not correspond to your kind. When a grain of wheat is scattered over the soil it returns the gift of its kind; but you degenerate. Grain does not dishonor the true character of its seed; you dishonor the purity of your soul, the vigor of your mind, the chastity of your body.

(32) Do you recognize the fact that you are the work of Christ? With His own hands He formed you, as we read, yet you, Manichaean, you assume for yourself another author. God the Father says to His Son: 'Let us make man to our image and likeness,'[14] yet you, adherent of Photinus, say that in the construction of the world there was no Christ.[15] And you, follower of Eunomius, say the Son is unlike the Father. For if He is His image, then He is in no wise dissimilar; rather, He reflects entirely His Father, who impressed on Him the unity of His substance. The Father says: 'Let us make'; yet you refuse to co-operate. The Son carried out what the Father spoke, yet you deny the equality in Him in whom the Father was well pleased.[16]

12 Acts 17.27,28.
13 Cf. 1 Cor. 9.11.
14 Gen. 1.26; cf. 1.27.
15 See Vol. 22 of this series, p. 329.
16 Cf. Matt. 3.17.

Chapter 8

(33) 'Let the earth,' He said, 'bring forth the green herb after its kind.'[1] All things which are referred to as growing in the earth begin with a seed. When it has emerged a little it becomes a green shoot, then a stalk, and finally bears fruit. There are growing plants which spring from the root, such as trees which are not sown from seed, but grow from the roots of other trees. We see in the case of a reed how at its base there emerges from its side a sort of bulb from which other seeds germinate. There is in the root, therefore, something which has the potency of a seed. There are grafted plants, too, which germinate higher up. Hence, some plants reproduce themselves from the root; others are reproduced in diverse ways. For in every growing thing there is either a seed or something which has the power of a seed. These plants follow their kind, so that what emerges from them is similar to what has been sown or like those from whose roots they germinate. As examples we can point to the fact that wheat produces wheat and that from millet comes millet; again, the pear tree with its white flowers[2] produces pears, and the chestnut trees springs from the root of the chestnut.

(34) 'Let the earth,' He said, 'bring forth the green herb after its kind.' And forthwith the earth in labor brought forth new plants; girding herself with the garments of verdure, she luxuriated in fecundity, and decked in diverse seedlings, she claimed them as her own fitting adornments. We marvel at the speed of that productivity. How many more wonders appear, if you examine each plant, noticing how the seed when laid in the earth decays and, if it did not die, would bear no fruit; but when it decays, by that

1 Gen. 1.11.

2 Cf. Virgil, *Georgics* 2.71,72.

very act of death, arises to bear fruit in greater abundance.[3] The pliable sod receives, then, a grain of wheat;[4] the scattered seed is controlled by the use of the hoe and mother earth cherishes it in firm embraces to her breast. When that grain decays, there comes the pleasing aspect of the green burgeoning shoot, which immediately reveals its kind from its similarity to its own seed, so that you may discover the nature of the plant even in the very beginning of its growth, and its fruit, too, is made evident to you. Gradually, it grows so as eventually to attain full maturity and height. At the point when the jointed stalk emerges, sheaths for the grain to come are being prepared. Within these the grain is being formed, so that cold may not cause injury to the plant in its tender beginnings, or the heat of the sun burn it, or the cruel violence of the wind and rain beat it to the ground. In addition, the ear of wheat has wonderfully formed rows both pleasing in appearance and made for the protection of the plant, resulting from their naturally interwoven texture which is the creation of divine Providence. Moreover, in order to serve as a support for and to offset the weight of a more abundant number of ears, the stalk itself is enclosed in what may be termed sheaths, so that by its reinforced strength it can sustain manifold grains of wheat and that it may not be bent towards the earth because of its inability to bear its burden. Then, over the ear is erected a rampart in the form of a beard, so that a line of defense may be extended to protect the ear from injury from the attacks of little birds, by which means the wheat grain is keep intact from the devastion of their claws.[5]

(35) What shall I say of the kindness of God in providing things useful for the human race? The earth returned with

3 Cf. John 12.24.
4 Cf. Virgil, *Georgics* 1.44.
5 Cf. Cicero, *De senectute* 15.51, for language and thought.

interest what it had received, even with compound interest! Men often deceive and often defraud the money-lender of his just due. But the earth remains faithful to promises and, if at time it does not pay back, if, perchance, severe cold or extraordinary dry weather or tremendous rain storms bring disaster, the losses of a single year are counterbalanced by the year which follows. And so, when the harvest belies the hopes of the farmer, in no way does the earth forsake him. Again, when she smiles on him, fertile Mother Earth pours forth her offspring, so that she never incurs a loss to her creditors.

(36) When the land, in fact, is completely stocked, how can we, if we are to rely on our tongue, satisfactorily describe the pleasant sights and scents and the joys of the countryman? But we have the testimony of the Scripture, wherein we note that the delights of the countryside are compared to the blessing and grace of the saints, for Isaac, a holy man, says: 'The smell of my son is the smell of a plentiful field.'[6]

How can I describe the violets with their shades of purple, the lilies of brilliant white, and the roses with their shades of red? How describe the landscape painted with flowers, sometimes of a golden hue or of varied colors or of bright yellow, among which you cannot decide whether their beauty or their fragrant scent gives more delight.[7] Our eyes revel in this pleasant spectacle as that fragrance which fills us with its sweetness is spread far and wide. Whence the Lord has justly said: 'And with me is the beauty of the field.'[8] This beauty is with Him because He has created it. What other artist could so depict such charm in each and every object? 'Consider the lilies of the field,' what brilliance in their

6 Gen. 27.27.
7 Cf. Virgil, *Georgics* 2.132.
8 Ps. 49.11.

petals, how they appear to arise in packed rows all the way to the top so as to form a goblet! Note how within it gleams like gold, and, furthermore, how around its edge as a defense against any injury a kind of rampart is constructed! If any one were to pluck this flower and take each petal apart, what craftsman's hand is so expert as to be able to restore the form of the lily? Who is such an effective imitator of nature as to presume to reconstruct this flower, to which the Lord has so borne testimony as to say: 'Not even Solomon in all his glory was so arrayed like one of these'?[9] A king so rich and wise was deemed inferior to the beauty of this flower!

(3) Why should I enumerate the health-giving juices of herbs or the remedies provided by shrubs and leaves? When a stag is sick, he eats the branches of the olive tree and becomes well. The leaves of the olive, too, cure the locusts of illness. The application of the leaves of a bramble to a serpent bring about his death. Gnats will not trouble you if you anoint yourself with wormwood which has been cooked in oil.

Chapter 9

(38) But some perhaps may say: How do you account for the fact that deadly poisonous plants grow along with those that are of use, for example, there is found along with wheat the poisonous hemlock, a plant discoverable among those that support life. Unless you are on your guard against it, this plant can injure your health. Found growing among other plants that help to sustain life are hellebore and monk's hood, which too often delude and deceive the gatherer.[1] But would you find fault with the earth because

9 Matt. 6.28,29.

1 Cf. Virgil, *Georgics* 2.152.

not all men are good? What is of more consequence, you should realize that not all the angels of heaven were good. The sun itself by its excessive heat parches the ears of wheat and causes the young growing plants to wither, whereas the moon shows voyagers the way and reveals the lurking places of robbers.[2] Is it right, therefore, that we disregard the bounty of the Founder in furnishing us useful things and, just because of certain noxious plants, detract from the forethought of the Creator? Some people act as if everything had to be created for our gourmandizing or as if there was just a trifling amount left by the kindness of God to minister to our appetites. Definite foods have been allotted to us which are known to all, foods which provide us with both pleasure and physical health.

(39) Each and every thing which is produced from the earth has its own reason for existence, which, as far as it can, fulfills the general plan of creation. Some things, therefore, are created for our consumption; other things serve for other uses. There is nothing without a purpose; there is nothing superfluous in what germinates from the earth. What you consider as useless has use for others; as a matter of fact, it often is useful to you in another way. That which does not serve for food has medical qualities, and it often happens that what is harmful to you provides harmless food for birds or wild beasts. Thus, starlings feed on the hemlock without any ill effects, since by their physical nature they are immune to its deadly and poisonous sap. Such sap, in fact, is cold by nature, which, when conducted through fine pores into the region of the heart, by a process of premature digestion is prevented from reaching the vital organs themselves. Those who are expert on the nature of hellebore say that it provides food and sustenance to quails and that through a certain natural composition of their

2 Cf. St. Ambrose, *Hymns* 2.7 (*nocturna lux viantibus*).

bodies these animals become immune to its harmful effects. The fact is that through medical science this plant frequently serves to preserve the health of the human body, to which it seems to be adverse. As a consequence, what the doctor's hand converts to the preservation of our health becomes even to a greater degree, through its natural qualities, a means for providing food for others. Slumber is often induced, too, by the use of the mandrake, whenever the sick are troubled by their inability to sleep. Why need I speak of opium which has come to be used almost daily, inasmuch as severe intestinal pains are allayed by its use? And it has not escaped our notice that the ravings of the sensual passions frequently have been stayed by hemlock and that with hellebore the prolonged sufferings of a sick body have found relief.

(40) The Creator, therefore, is not liable to blame in these matters; actually, His bounty is increased thereby, inasmuch as what you believed was created to bring danger to you is designed to bring to you health-giving remedies. That which leads to danger is directed otherwise by Providence and what is conducive to our health is not lost through our own prudence and industry.

Is it true that, following a mysterious urge of nature, sheep and goats have learned to shun what is harmful to them and for this purpose are able to make use of smell alone, since they are devoid of reason? Do they not go so far as to recognize a way of avoiding danger and of protecting their health? Do they not distinguish between what is likely to be noxious and what will be beneficial? So true is this that they are said frequently to look for herbs known to them and to apply these as a remedy to a wound when they sense that they have been hit with poisoned weapons. Food, therefore, becomes for them a medicine. As a result, you may behold arrows in the act of falling from a wound, the poison actually vanishing and not adhering. Furthermore, poison is a food for stags. The snake flees a stag and slays a lion. The dragon winds himself around an elephant, whose downfall brings death to the victor. Thus, they both strive with their utmost strength, one to bind fast the other's foot so that the fall of the vanquished cannot harm him; the other, so that he may not be surprised in a narrow passageway when trailing the herd and thus be caught by a hind leg. In such a situation the elephant would be unable to turn around and crush the dragon with his heavy foot or have the assistance of another elephant at his rear.

(41) Therefore, if irrational animals know what herbs may serve as medicine or what methods may bring assistance to them, can man, who is born with the faculty of reason, be ignorant of this? Or is he such a stranger to truth that he cannot at all perceive what are the uses especially designed for everything? Or is he so ungrateful for the good things provided by nature that, because a draught of bull's blood is deadly to man, this laborious animal ought not for that reason be born or ought to be created without blood? Yet, he possesses a quality which is useful in the cultivation of the fields, adaptable for the service of ploughing and for sustenance, a precious possession. By his manifold uses he in a sound prop to farmers, for whom—should they come to know their own blessings[3]—God has created all things with the words: 'Let the earth bring forth the green herb and such as may seed after its kind.'[4] For He has included in this statement not only what contributes to the farmers' support from herbs, roots, trees and other plants which grow without seed, but He also includes such produce as is acquired by the industrious skill of the toiler of the fields.

(42) How fitting is it that He did not command the earth

3 Cf. Virgil, *Georgics* 2.458.
4 Gen. 1.11.

generously to give forth seed and fruits, but ordained that the fields should first germinate and then bring forth plants. Next He bade the seed to grow according to the specific nature of its kind, so that at no time would the landscape be without its charm; first, the verdure of spring for our pleasure, and later the heaped-up piles of harvest for our use.

Chapter 10

(43) Perhaps someone might say: How does the earth produce seed according to its kind, when often the seed sown degenerates and, although good wheat was sown, the result is a wheat plant of a quality inferior in color and in form? If this ever happens, one should not attribute this deterioration to a change of species, but rather, it seems, to to some inferiority or some disease in the seed. It does not cease to be wheat if it has been blighted by frost or mildewed by rain. It has been changed in appearance rather than in kind, and also in color as a result of the corruption it has undergone. Hence, it frequently happens that mildewed grain returns to the appearance of its stock, if it is exposed to the heat of the sun or of fire, or if it is entrusted to careful cultivators, who cherish it by protecting it from inclemencies of climate and foster it in soil that is fertile. In this way, what has suffered degeneration in the parent stock is restored in the next generation. Hence, there is no danger that the precept of God, to which nature has accustomed itself, may become void in future time by a failure of propagation, since today the integrity of the stock is still preserved in the seeds.

(44) We know that cockle and the other alien seeds which often are interspersed among fruits of the earth are called 'weeds' in the Gospel. These, however, belong to a special

species and have not degenerated into another species by a process of mutation from the seed of the wheat plant. The Lord told us that this is so when He said: 'The kingdom of heaven is like a man who sowed good seed in his field, but while men were asleep, his enemy came and sowed weeds among the wheat.' We gather from this that weeds and wheat certainly seem to be distinct both in name and in kind. Hence, the servants, too, said to the householder: 'Sir, didst thou not sow good seed in thy field? How then does it have weeds? He said to them: "An enemy has done this." '[1] One is the seed of the Devil; the other, that of Christ which is sown in accordance with justice. Therefore, the Son of Man sowed one and the Devil sowed the other. For that reason the nature of each is distinct, since the sowers are opposed. Christ sows the kingdom of God, whereas the Devil sows sin. How, therefore, can this kingdom be of one and the same race as sin? 'This is the kingdom of God,' He says, 'as though a man should cast seed into the earth.'[2]

(45) There is a Man who sows the word, of whom it is written: 'The sower sows the word.'[3] This Man sowed the word over the earth when He said: 'Let the earth bring forth the green herb,' and immediately the seeds came to birth and diverse were the species of things which shone forth in brilliance. At this point the fields in their beautiful green color furnished abundance of food; the yellowing ears of wheat in the fields suggested an image of the billowing sea in the waving of that rich harvest in the breeze. Of itself the earth brought forth profusely all kinds of fruits. Although it could not be ploughed in the absence of a cultivator—for the farmer had not yet been created—the earth, though unplowed, teemed with rich harvests, inasmuch as an in-

---

1 Cf. Matt. 3.24-27.
2 Mark 4.26.
3 Mark 4.14.

dolent husbandman did not have occasion to defraud the earth of its abundance. For each plant attains fertility according to the merits of the labor involved in the cultivation of the fields. Punishment is meted out for our neglect or remissness if the soil be deprived of its rich abundance either by flood or aridity, the fall of hailstones or by some other misfortune. Then, too, the earth everywhere brought forth spontaneously fruits of the soil, because He who is the fullness of the universe had so ordained it.[4] The word of God fructified on the earth and the earth had not, because of any curse, suffered condemnation. The origins and birth of the world are more remote than our sins and more recent than our error, because of which we have been condemned 'to eat bread in the sweat of our face,'[5] and without sweat to be incapable of sustaining life.

(46) Even today the fertility of the earth carries into effect its age-old fecundity by exercise of spontaneous growth, for you see how many plants are still grown without being sown. But even in much that is gathered by the labor of our hands there still remains a large part of our produce which, by the kindness of Providence, comes without effort to us while we are at rest. This we are taught by the reading of the Gospel before us, wherein the Lord says: 'This is the kingdom of God, as though a man should cast seed into the earth, then sleep and rise night and day and the seed should sprout and grow without his knowing it. For of itself the earth bears the crop, first the blade, then the ear, then the full grain in the ear. But when the fruit is ripe, immediately he puts in the sickle because the harvest has come.'[6] Therefore, while you are asleep, man, and without your knowing it, the earth of itself produces its fruits. You fall asleep and

4 Cf. Col. 1.19.
5 Gen. 3.19.
6 Mark 4.26-29.

then rise, marveling how the grain has increased in the course of one night.

Chapter 11

(47) We have often spoken concerning the green herb; now let us discuss the plant that bears fruit according to its kind, 'which may have seed in itself.'[1] 'He spoke and they were made,'[2] and immediately the earth was adorned with groves as formerly it had been decked with flowers and with the verdure of the grass of the fields. The trees were assembled; the forests arose and the peaks of the hills were clothed with leaves. Here the pine and there the cypress raised aloft their towering heads; the cedars and the pitch-pines gathered in groups. The fir tree also advanced in procession, a tree which was not satisfied to have its roots in the earth and its head on high, but was destined, while mariners are safe, to undergo perils from wind and wave on the sea. The laurel, too, gave forth its scent as it rose, a shrub never to be denuded of its foliage. There arose, also, the shady evergreen oak, destined to preserve its shimmering even in winter time. For nature maintained in every case through future ages the prerogatives which had been impressed on it at the moment of Creation. Hence, the evergreen oak and the cypress adhere to these prerogatives, so that no wind may despoil them of the adornment of their locks.

(48) Mingling formerly with the flowers of the earth and without thorns, the rose, most beautiful of all flowers, displayed its beauty without guile; afterwards, the thorn fenced around this charming flower, presenting, as it were,

1 Gen. 1.11.
2 Ps. 32.9.

an image of human life in which what is pleasing in our activities is often acccompanied with the stings of anxieties which everywhere surround us. In fact, the elegance of our life is entrenched and hedged about by certain cares, so that sadness is close neighbor to beauty. Hence, when each one of us find joys either in the pleasing exercise of our reason or in the attainment of more than usual success in life, it is fitting that we should call to mind this sin of ours, by means of which there was imposed upon us by rightful condemnation the mind's thorns and the spirit's brambles, when we were happily sojourning amid the delights of paradise. Although you may shine, man, with the splendor of nobility or by reason of your superior power or by the brilliance of your virtue, the thorn is ever close to you, the bramble is ever near you. Ever be mindful of what is beneath you. You blossom into life above a thorn and this beauty does not last for long. In a brief passage of time each and every one of us withers in the flower of his age.

Chapter 12

(49) In truth, while you realize that you possess frailty in common with the flowers, you know that you have access to delight in the use of the vine, from which is produced wine, wherein the heart of man finds cheer.[1] Would that, man, you could imitate the example of this species of plant, so that you may bear fruit for your own joy and delight. In yourself lies the sweetness of your charm, from you does it blossom, in you it sojourns, within you it rests, in your own self you must search for the jubilant quality of your

1 Cf. Ps. 103.15.

conscience. For that reason He says: 'Drink water out of thine own cistern and the streams of thine own well.'[2]

First of all, there is nothing more pleasing than the scent of a blossoming vine. Furthermore, the juice when extracted from the flower of this vine produces a drink which is pleasureable and health-giving. Again, who does not marvel at the fact that from the seed of the grape springs forth a vine that climbs even as high as the top of a tree? The vine fondles the tree by embracing and binding it with the tentacles of its hands and arms, clothes it with vine leaves, and crowns it with garlands of grapes. In imitation of our life, the vine first plants deep its living roots; then, because its nature is flexible and likely to fall, it uses its tendrils like arms in order to hold tight whatever it seizes. By this means it raises itself and lifts itself on high.[3]

(50) Similar to this vine are the members of the Church, who are planted with the root of faith and are held in check by the vine-shoots of humility. On this subject the Prophet beautifully says: 'Thou hast brought a vineyard out of Egypt: thou plantest the roots thereof and it filled the land. The shadow of it covered the hills and the branches thereof the cedars of God. It stretched forth its branches unto the sea and its boughs unto the river.'[4] And the Lord Himself spoke through Isaias, saying: 'My beloved had a vineyard on a hill in a fruitful place. And I fenced it in and dug around the vine of Sorech and I built a tower in the midst thereof.'[5] He fenced it in with a rampart, as it were of heavenly precepts and with the angels standing guard, for 'the angel of the lord shall encamp round about them that fear him.'[6] He placed in the Church a tower, so to speak,

2 Prov. 5.15.
3 For the entire passage, cf. Cicero, *De senectute* 15.52.
4 Ps. 79.9-12.
5 Isa. 5.1,2.
6 Ps. 33.8.

of Apostles, Prophets, and Doctors, ready to defend the peace of the Church. He dug around it, when He had freed it from the burden of earthly anxieties. For nothing burdens the mind more than solicitude for the world and cupidity either for wealth or for power.

There occurs an example of this in the Gospel, where we can read the story of the woman 'who had sickness caused by a spirit, and she was bent over, so that she was unable to look upwards.'[7] Bent over, in fact, was her soul, which inclined to terrestrial rewards and possessed not heavenly grace. Jesus beheld her and addressed her; immediately she laid aside her earthly burdens. These people also were burdened with these cupidities to whom He addressed these words: 'Come to me, all you who labor and are burdened and I will give you rest.'[8] And so the soul of that woman breathed once more and stood erect like a vine around which the soil has been dug and cleared.

(51) But the same vine, after the soil has been cleared around it, is raised up and bound, so that it may not bend back towards the ground. Some of the shoots are pruned; others are allowed to grow. Those branches which grow in aimless profusion are pruned; those which the good cultivator reckons to be productive are permitted to grow. What need is there to describe the rows of stakes and the orderly process of binding the vine shoots? These operations teach us truly and clearly that equality should be observed in the Church, so that no man of wealth and high position should exalt himself and that no one who is poor and lowly should despair. Liberty is one and the same for all members of the Church; all men possess justice and favor in an impartial manner.

For that reason the tower is placed in the middle, to serve

7 Luke 13.11.
8 Matt. 11.28.

all around as an example of those countrymen and those fishermen who deserved to hold fast the fort of virtue. By their example our courage is aroused and is not permitted to lie mean and despised on the ground. Rather, each and every one of us has his mind raised aloft to higher things so that he dares to say: 'But our citizenship is in heaven.'[9] Hence, to prevent it from being bent and battered by the storms and tempests of the world, the vine holds in the embrace of love, by means of those tendrils and bonds of which we spoke, all that are near and finds rest in being joined with them. That is love, therefore, which binds us with things on high and plants us in heaven. Because 'he who abides in love, God abides in him.' Hence the Lord also says: 'Abide in me and I in you. As the branch cannot bear fruit of itself unless it remain on the vine, so neither can you unless you abide in me. I am the vine, you are the branches.'[10]

(52) It seems clear, therefore, that the example of the vine is designed, as this passage indicates, for the instruction of our lives. It is observed to bud in the mild warmth of early spring and next to produce fruit from the joints of the shoots, from which a grape is formed. This gradually increases in size, but it still retains its bitter taste. When, however, it is ripened and mellowed by the sun, it acquires its sweetness. Meanwhile, the vine is decked in green leaves by which it is protected in no slight manner from frosts and other injuries and is defended from the sun's heat. Is there any spectacle which is more pleasing or any fruit that is sweeter?[11] What a joy to behold the rows of hanging grapes like so many jewels of a beautiful countryside, to pluck those grapes gleaming in colors of gold or purple!

9 Phil. 3.20.
10 John 4.16; 9.15.
11 Cf. Cicero, *De senectute* 15.53.

You may notice that hyacinths and other gems are brilliant in color, how indigo gleams and how beautifully the pearl shines; still, you do not derive a warning from this, man, that your last day on earth should not find your fruit unripened or that the completion of your time of life should show but slight achievement. Unripened fruit is often bitter in taste. It cannot be sweet until it has grown to perfect maturity. A man perfect in this manner will not ordinarily be harmed by the cold of dread death nor by the heat of the sun of iniquity, because a spiritual grace overshadows him, quelling the fires of cupidity for the things of this world and defending him from the lusts and the burning desires of the flesh.

Let them praise you who behold you and let them admire the marshaled bands of the Church like the serried rows of vine branches, let everyone among the faithful gaze upon the gems of the soul, let them find delight in the maturity of prudence, in the splendor of faith, in the charm of Christian affirmation, in the beauty of justice, in the fecundity of pity, so that it may be said of you: 'Thy wife is a fruitful vine on the sides of thy house,'[12] for the reason that you imitate by the exercise of your abundant and generous giving the plenteous return of a fruit-bearing vine.

Chapter 13

(53) But why do I linger in describing just the vine, when all species of trees have their utility? Some are created to provide fruit; others are granted for our use. Those which are not overproductive of fruit are nevertheless more valuable for the uses they serve. The cedar is suitable for constructing the roof of a house, because its material is of such a kind as

12 Ps. 127.3.

to furnish both spacious length for the roof and a quality of lightness for the walls. For the construction of rafters and the adornment of the pediments the most adaptable wood is that of the cypress. Hence, the Church, too, tells us in the Canticles: 'The beams of our houses are of cedar, our rafters of cypress trees.'[1] These words point to the beautiful adornments of its pedimental structure, which, as beams do, uphold by their excellent qualities the superstructure of the Church and give charm to its façade.

The laurel and the palm are emblems of victory. The heads of victors are crowned with laurel; the palm adorns the victor's hand. Hence, the Church, too, says: 'I said: I will go up into the palm tree, I will take hold of the heights thereof.'[2] Seeing the sublimity of the Word and hoping to be able to ascend to its height and to the summit of knowledge, he says: 'I will go up into the palm tree,' that he may abandon all things that are low and strive after things that are higher, to the prize of Christ, in order that he may pluck its fruit and taste it, for sweet is the fruit of virtue.

Again, what shall we say of the poplar, a tree that provides shade for victorious crowns and for binding vines a flexible shoot.[3] What other mystical meaning has this, if not to stand for the goodness of the bonds of Christ? These bonds do not hurt—they are the bonds of grace and of love, so that every person should glory in his bonds as Paul gloried in them when he said: 'Paul, a prisoner of Jesus Christ.'[4] When bound in these same bonds, those of self-denial and of love, he said: 'Who shall separate us from the love of Jesus Christ?'[5] When bound also by these same bonds,

1 Cant. 1.16.
2 Cant. 7.8.
3 Cf. Virgil, *Eclogues* 3.83.
4 Philem. 1.
5 Rom. 8.35.

David has said: 'On the willows in the midst thereof we hung up our instruments.'[6]

The box-wood tree, because of its light material, trains the child's hand when it is used for forming the outlines of the letters of the alphabet. Hence Scripture says: 'Write upon box,'[7] in order that you may be admonished by the wood itself (which is an evergreen and is never devoid of foliage) never to be deprived of the support of your hope, but rather that the hope of salvation may be generated by faith.

(54) Why should I enumerate the great variety of trees, their particular diversities and beauties? Why speak of the wide-spreading beech tree, the slender fir, the leafy pine tree, the shady evergreen oak, the two-colored poplar,[8] the chestnut that loves the groves and ever tends to sprout again as soon as it is cut down? Why relate how in the trees themselves one can determine whether the tree is old or young? In the younger trees the branches are rather slender; in the older they are strong and gnarled; in the former, the leaves are smoother and are far apart; in the latter the leaves are rougher and more shriveled. There are trees which, because their roots are old and completely dead, are unable, if perchance they are cut down, to reproduce themselves; others show a vigorous youth and a more productive nature; a thorough pruning is conducive to profit rather than to harm, so much so that they shoot forth anew and renew themselves in so many offshoots for generations.

(55) There is another occasion for us to marvel at the fact that there is sex even in fruit and distinction of sex in trees. You may notice how the palm tree which produces dates often reaches towards and bends beneath that tree

6 Ps. 136.2.
7 Isa. 30.8.
8 Cf. Virgil, *Aeneid* 8.276.

which country children call the male palm, presenting in this act a spectacle of one eager for an embrace. That palm tree is female and betrays her sex by her appearance of subjection. Hence, cultivators of groves inject into its branches the seed of dates or of male palm trees, by which is infused into that tree what may be called a sense of its function and sweetness of a desired marital embrace. After the performance of this rite it once more rises up and lifts its branches and elevates its foliage into their former state and condition.

There is similar belief regarding the fig tree. For this reason many are said to plant the wild fig tree beside the cultivated and productive tree, because the fruit of the prolific cultivated fig tree, due either to wind or to heat, is said to fall to the ground. Hence, those acquainted with this method remedy this weakness on the part of the productive fig tree by binding it to the fruit of the wild fig, so that the cultivated tree is able to retain its own fruit, which would at any moment be likely to fall if this remedial procedure were not followed.

From this mystery of nature we are admonished not to shun those who have been separated from our faith and from association with us. And so a Gentile who was converted can be all the more a passionate defender of the faith as he was formerly strong in upholding his error. And if one is a convert from heresy, he can be a stout supporter of that new faith to which he has turned after a change in his convictions. Especially will this be true if he has been gifted by nature to give vivid expression to his opinions and if he finds support in his own moral tendencies toward temperance and chastity. Be lavish, therefore, in your attentions to him, in order that you may, like the productive fig tree, strengthen your own virtue as a result of the presence and juxtaposition of that other uncultivated tree. For in this way your moral purpose may not be weakened and the fruit of your zeal and grace will be preserved.

(56) How many examples there are of phenomena wherein a natural hardness can be controlled by careful attention to detail in the art of cultivation. Frequently, pomegranates blossom quickly, but are unable to bear fruit without the careful application of remedial methods in the hands of experts, when, as often happens, the juice disappears within the fruit, although it presents a healthy appearance externally. This phenomenon can not without reason be compared to the Church, to which it is applied in the words of the Canticle: 'Thy cheeks are as a piece of a pomegranate,' and further on: 'If the vineyard flourish, if the pomegranates flourish.'[9] For the Church presents to our eyes the brilliance of faith and man's adherence to it—the Church, enhanced by the blood of so many martyrs and by what is more valuable still, by the blood of Christ; at the same time, in the possession of this pomegranate she preserves and includes in one protecting shell plenteous fruit within, involving manifold acts of virtue: the wise man conceals in his heart the good work he performs.[10]

It is said also that fruit growers apply remedial methods of this sort to the almond tree so as to render sweet the bitterness of its fruit. They bore a hole in the root of the tree and insert in the middle of it a shoot of that tree which the Greeks call πεύκη and which we call the pitch-pine. When this is done, the bitter taste of its juice disappears.

Accordingly, if the qualities of plants are changed by the process of agriculture, is it not possible to allay any sort of infirmity of the passions by a striving after knowledge and learning? Let no one, then, who is allured by youthful intemperance despair of his conversion. Wood frequently is turned

9 Cant. 4.3; 7.12.
10 Cf. Prov. 11.13.

to better uses; cannot the hearts of men be likewise changed?

(57) We have shown that there exist different species of fruit among trees of diverse nature and likewise that the same kind of tree often produces fruit of a dissimilar character. The male species produces one kind, while the female furnishes us with another—facts which we have already discussed in a preceding chapter in connection with dates.

Who can comprehend the variety, the appearance, and the delightful qualities of fruits, the usefulness of each and every product of the soil, and the peculiar sap which seems appropriate to each one; furthermore, how fruits of a rather bitter taste serve as medicine to heal our ailing stomachs by allaying swelling and rawness within; again, how the unhealthy humors of the body are modified by the sweet quality inherent in fruits?

Hence, that art of medicine is older which can cure by the use of herbs and juices. No condition of health is founded on a firmer basis than that which is acquired by the aid of health-giving nourishment. Wherefore, following the guidance of nature we are led to believe that food is our sole medicine. It is certain that open sores are closed by the use of herbs; our internal ills are cured by herbs. For this reason physicians need to know the efficacy of herbs, for from this source the practice of medicine took its rise.

Chapter 14

(58) But to return to a discussion of the ordinary fruit: some there are which are ripened directly by the sun; others reach maturity enclosed in a shell and hull. Apples, pears, and the various species of grape are all exposed naked to the sun. Walnuts and hazelnuts as well as the kernel of the pine-

nut, although covered with a shell and hull, are nourished by the heat of the sun. However deeply the kernel of the pine-nut lies buried, it still is nourished by the sun's heat.

(59) Such, then, is the providence of the Lord that, wherever the fruit is of a softer quality, there the thickness of the leaf presents in defense of the fruit a stouter protective covering, as we see, for example, in the fruit of the fig tree. The more delicate fruits, therefore, need a stronger defense, as the Lord Himself teaches us, speaking through the mouth of Jeremias: 'Like these good figs, so will I regard the captives of Juda, whom I have sent forth out of this place into the land of the Chaldeans for their good. And I will set my eyes upon them for their good.'[1] For He surrounded His precious ones, as it were, with a stouter covering of His mercy, lest the tender fruit should perish before its time. And so, too, He says of them in a later passage: 'My delicate ones have walked rough ways.' To these He speaks further on: 'Be constant, my children, and cry to the Lord.'[2] Against all storms and injuries this is the sole and inviolable protection and impenetrable defense.

Where, therefore, there is tender fruit, there is found a thicker covering and protection furnished by the leaves. On the other hand, where the fruit is sturdier, there the leaves are more delicate, as we see in the case of the apple tree. In the case of the sturdier apple there is not much need for protection to aid it, for the very thickness of the protective shade would serve rather to bring injury to its fruit.

(60) Then, again, the beauty of nature and the profound mysteries of divine wisdom are manifested to us by the leaf of the vine. We note that it is so divided into parts as to present the appearance of three leaves. The middle part is so distinct that it seems to the onlooker to be a separate

1 Jer. 24.5,6.
2 Bar. 4.26.27.

piece, were it not for the fact that it forms a juncture with the lower parts. This seems to follow a natural principle in that it both admits the sunlight more easily and furnishes shade. Then, the middle part of the leaf extends itself and becomes more narrow at the top as it grows, so that it offers more natural beauty than protection. For this reason it seems to present the form of the prize of a victor at the games, indicating that the grape holds the first place among the other species of hanging fruit. By the silent judgment of nature and, furthermore, by its clear decision the grape comes into being as the natural form and emblem of victory. The vine leaf, therefore, carries its prize with it, inasmuch as it furnishes defense for itself against the inclemencies of the air and the violence of storms, while at the same time it presents no obstacle to the reception of the sun's heat from which the grape receives warmth and coloring, growth, and increase.

The fig leaf, too, not unlike the vine leaf, is divided into four parts. This fact appears all the more clearly because of its larger leaf, although its extremities have not the pointed character of the vine leaf. Whereas the leaf of the fig is stronger and thicker, that of the vine presents a more elegant form. The thickness of the fig leaf serves to ward off injury due to storms, while its cleft nature permits the fruit to profit from warmth. Again, this species of fruit feels the force of hail storms less, but reaches maturity quicker, because it seems to hide away from injuries and at the same time to lie open to fostering influences.

(61) Why should I describe the different kinds of leaves, how some are round and others, longer; how some are flexible and others, more rigid; how some leaves do not fall readily, no matter how strong the wind, and how others are shaken off even by a slight motion of the wind?

Chapter 15

(62) It would be an endless task to inquire into the properties of each and every thing, either to distinguish diversities by presenting clear evidence for such or to reveal by unfailing proof concealed and hidden causes. For example, water is one and the same substance, yet it often changes into various forms. Water assumes a yellow color in sand; it becomes foamy amid rocks. It has a green aspect in the midst of groves and presents various colors in a region of flowers, becoming brighter among lilies and ruddier amid roses. Water in a grassy region is clearer, but more turbid in marshy places. At its source a stream is more limpid, while sea water is darker. We see, therefore, that water assumes the color of the places through which it flows.

In like manner, too, water undergoes changes due to temperature: in heated places it becomes hot, in shady regions it becomes cool; when exposed to the sun, water acquires excess of heat; when snow falls, it assumes a white color in the form of ice. And what a change takes place in its very taste; at one time it is somewhat sharp, at another somewhat bitter; at times it is rather harsh, at times somewhat tart, and then again rather sweet. These variations are due to the qualities of the substance with which water has been mixed. It becomes bitter because of the infusion of immature juices, as when the shells of nuts are pounded and when leaves are disintegrated. Water becomes bitter by the infusion of wormwood, becomes stronger from an admixture of wine and more tart when garlic is added; it becomes heavy or sweet as the result of the addition of poison or honey. In fact, if the mastick tree and the fruit of the turpentine tree or the kernel of nuts are infused with water, the resulting mixture can readily take on the filmy nature of oil.

While water supplies nourishment to all plants, it contributes in diverse ways its useful quality to each. If it waters the roots or rains on them from the clouds, it confers distinct strength to all: the root grows in size, the trunk is enlarged, the branches are extended, the leaves become green, the seeds are nourished, and the fruit is likely to increase in number. And so, although water is the nurse of all things, the sap of some species of tree as a result its activity is made somewhat bitter; another becomes sweeter; still others become either sluggish or quick in action. In their quality of sweetness, too, plants manifest differences one with the other. The vine has one type of sweetness, the olive, another; there is a difference between the cherry and the fig; the apple has a distinctive quality and the date is different from the rest.

(63) Even to the touch waters appear at one time smooth, at another, rough. They often give the impression of having oil on their surfaces. Water differs, too, in weight as frequently as in appearance, for in many places it is considered somewhat heavy; in other places, light. No wonder, therefore, if water, while it presents differences in itself, varies also in respect to the quality of the gum of the trees which is generated by the intake of the same water.

The gum of the cherry tree differs in quality from that which exudes from the mastick tree. Also, it is known that the sweet-smelling woods of the Orient distil a drop of balsam of unlike nature. The twigs of the fennel in Egypt and in Libya exude also by some secret process of nature a distinct kind of gum. Why should I relate to you, without burdening you with my discourse, the fact that amber is something which exudes from a shrub and that the gum hardens to form a solid mass of such precious material? This account is supported by evidence of no inconsiderable value, since leaves or very small fragments of twigs or certain tiny species of insects are often found in amber. The drop of amber while still in a more fluid state seems to have laid hold of these objects and to have retained them when the material had solidified.[1]

(64) But why do I with my indifferent discourse vie with the high and priceless principles of nature, since this discourse springs from the human intellect, whereas divine Providence has created the nature of all things? Hence, the reins of my diffuse discourse should, as it were, be checked,[2] lest I may seem to usurp the wisdom divinely conferred on Solomon in the Scriptures in expounding the 'diversities of plants and the virtues of roots and all such things as are hid and not foreseen.'[3] Yet, these things were not revealed by him in a clear light. In my opinion he would very likely have been able to discourse on the various species of plants,[4] yet he would not have been able to expound fully the nature of all created things.

Chapter 16

(65) But if the harvests are often more joyous as a result of a plentiful supply of water,[1] if the leguminous plants become green and the manifold beauty of gardens is roused and revivified; if the banks of overflowing rivers become resplendent with their verdant cushions,[2] how much more effective is the Word of God than any water course in causing every plant suddenly to burst into flower! Then the plains hastened to bring forth fruit not entrusted to them, gardens were supplied with all manner of vegetables hitherto unknown, and flowers began to germinate in a marvelous

1 Cf. Pliny, *Historia naturalis* 27.43,46.
2 Cf. Virgil, *Georgics* 2.541,542.
3 Wisd. 7.20,21.
4 Cf. 3 Kings 4.33.

1 Cf. Virgil, *Georgics* 1.1.
2 Cf. Virgil, *Aeneid* 6.674.

manner. The banks of streams began to vest themselves in myrtle. The trees made haste to rise; quickly they clothed themselves in flower,[3] furnishing sustenance for men and food for animals. Fruit became the common property of all; its enjoyment is offered to all. A twofold gift is presented by trees: at one and the same time we are granted nourishment for our bodies and a means of warding off the sun's rays in the cool of their shade; the fruit provides food and the leaves give us occasion for enjoyable living.

However, because the providence of the Creator foresaw that man in his greed would claim the fruit especially for himself, He took care that the rest of living creatures would be given their special nourishment. And so food of no inconsiderable amount was provided for them from the leaves and bark of forest trees. What would avail for medical purposes was provided for both equally: that is, the sap, gum, and young shoots of plants. Hence, the Creator has commanded from the beginning to come forth from the bowels of the earth by the might of His providence those plants which we have later by experiment, use, and example found to be useful, for God destined them for the purpose for which they were adapted.

(66) And the Lord commanded: 'Let the earth bring forth the green herb and the fruit tree yielding fruit after its kind, whose seed is in it,'[4] lest someone may say that neither fruit nor seed appears in many trees and lest a person may think that the divine command is faulty in some respect, by which, in fact, truth may be called into question. Let such a person take note that it can never happen that all things that grow should not eventually spring up out of seeds or possess some qualities which seem to be in keeping with the vital power of seeds. If we pay particular attention

3 Cf. Virgil, *Georgics* 1.187.
4 Gen. 1.1.

to this matter, our understanding of the facts will be aided by the clarity of the evidence. For example, willow trees do not seem to have seeds, but they have in their leaves a kind of kernel which has the efficasy of a seed. When this is committed to the earth, there arises a tree as if it came from a planted sucker. It comes to life as if from a seed. From that kernel a root is truly formed. From the root not only is the willow developed, but there grows a forest of other trees of like kind. The root, too, has the generative quality of a seed; hence, many have propagated their groves by such a process as this.

(67) The power of God is great in everything. Let no one wonder if I have stated that the power of God is great in plants, since He has said that His power was great in the locusts and in the bruchus,[5] for the reason that by the affliction of sterility and famine they punished the offenses to His divine majesty. For great is the power of His patience; great, too, of His providence. Unworthy were they who had injured the Creator of the earth to enjoy earth's fruitfulness! And He is truly great in avenging such great impiety with misery and famine. Hence, if the earth brought forth the sterile bruchus by the mighty power of God, how much greater is the power which brings into being that which is fertile!

(68) Who on seeing a pine cone would not marvel at the art that is indelibly impressed on nature by the command of God and at the fact that, although extended at unequal lengths, the sheath arises from the center core in homogeneous fashion, whereby it protects its own fruit. Hence it preserves the same appearance and arrangement all around. And in every place there is a surplus of kernels and in the circle of the year there comes the blessing of the fruit. Therefore, in this pine cone nature seems to express an image of itself; it preserves its peculiar properties which it received

5 A kind of locust without wings.

from that divine and celestial command and it repeats in the succession and order of the years its generation until the end of time is fulfilled.

(69) But as in this fruit nature imprints a pleasing representation of itself, so, too, in the tamarisk, that is, in the humble plants,[6] nature has impressed an image of its unrelenting artfulness. For, just as there are men everywhere who are double-dealers at heart, who, while they show themselves to be gracious and unaffected in the presence of good men, cleave to those who are most vicious—so in a similar way these plants have a contrary tendency to spring up in both well-watered regions and in desert lands. That is why Jeremias compared dubious and insincere characters to tamarisks.[7]

Chapter 17

(70) 'Let the earth bring forth,' God said, and immediately the whole earth was filled with growing vegetation. And to man it was said: 'Love the Lord thy God,'[1] yet the love of God is not instilled in the hearts of all. Deafer are the hearts of men than the hardest rock. The earth, in compliance with its Author, furnishes us with fruit which is not owed to us; we deny the debt when we do not give homage to the Author.

(71) Behold the providence of God in little things and, because you are unable to comprehend it, marvel at the fact that He has kept some plants always in foliage while He desired that others undergo changes by being deprived of their vesture. The earth preserves its verdure amid the

6 Cf. Virgil, *Eclogues* 4.2.
7 Jer. 17.6.

1 Deut. 6.5; Matt. 22.37.

white snow and the cold hoar frost,[2] and, although hidden in ice, its offspring still preserve no slight trace of their viridity.

Those species of trees, also, which are clothed in evergreen foliage have not inconsiderable differences. The olive and the pine always preserve their vesture. Nevertheless, they change their leaves frequently, displaying them, not as something permanent, but as successive adornments of their tree. The apparentely unbroken nature of their garb they thus dissimulate by such an interchange. Again, the palm remains always green by reason of the retentive and enduring qualities of its foliage, not because of any change. For the leaves which it first produced continue to perpetuate themselves without recourse to substitution.

Imitate the palm, man, so that it may be said also to you: 'Thy stature is like a palm tree.'[3] Preserve the verdure of your childhood and of that natural innocence of youth which you have received from the beginning, and may you possess the fruits, prepared in due time, of what was planted along the course of the waters—and may there be no fall to your leaf!

To this verdure of grace everflourishing in Christ the Church refers in saying: 'I sat down under his shadow whom I desired.'[4] The Apostles received this privileged gift of verdure, whose leaves could never fall, so as to provide shade for the healing of the sick.[5] Their fidelity of heart and the superabundance of their merits provided shade for bodily infirmities. Remain, therefore, planted in the house of the Lord so as to flourish like a palm in His halls, whence the grace of the Church may ascend for you and 'the odor of

2 Cf. Virgil, *Georgics* 2.376.
3 Cant 7.7.
4 Cant. 2.3.
5 Cf. Acts 5.15.

thy mouth may be like apples and thy throat like the best wine,' so that you may be inebriated in Christ.[6]

(72) This verse serves to remind us that we should take up once more our subject wherein it was stated that the vine, too, blossomed forth by the command of God. This vine, we know, was planted by Noe after the flood. We read, in fact, that 'Noe, a husbandman, began to till the ground and planted a vineyard and drank of his wine and slept.'[7] Noe, therefore, was not the author of the vine, but of its planting, for he could not have planted it unless he had already found it fully grown. He is just the cultivator, therefore, of the vine. Its Author, God, who knew that wine fostered health and sharpened wits when taken sparingly, but led to vice if used immoderately, has given us this plant in the act of creation. Excess of wine He set aside as an exercise for man's will to the extent that nature's parsimony might inculcate in him the lesson of sobriety and that man might ascribe to himself the harm due to excess and the sin of intoxication. In fact, Noe himself was intoxicated and slept under the influence of wine,[8] so we see that he who attained to such glory through the flood exposed himself to unsightliness because of his misuse of wine. But the Lord has retained in the vine the privileges due to His creation, so that He converted its fruit for our salvation and made it possible that remission of our sins should emerge from this plant.[9]

Hence, Isaac spoke reverently when he said: 'The smell of Jacob is the smell of a plentiful field,'[10] that is, a natural odor. For what is sweeter than a plentiful field, what is more delightful than the perfume of the vine, what is more pleasing

6 Cant. 7.8.9; 5.1.
7 Gen. 9.20,21.
8 *Ibid.*
9 Matt. 26.28.
10 Gen. 27.27.

than the blossom of the bean? Hence, before us a certain writer[11] has ingeniously said: 'The patriarch did not perceive the odor of vine or fig or fruit, but he breathed the perfume of virtue.' I for my part hold to the following interpretation: the odor of the land, unmixed and pure, infused not with guile, but with the truth of celestial indulgence, stands for the beauty of a prayer which blesses. Hence, what the Lord confers on us from the dew of heaven so as to give strength to the vine, to the olive and to the grain may be reckoned among our most precious benedictions.

To Him be honor, praise, and glory everlasting, from the beginning of time, now, always, and for ever. Amen.

---

11 Perhaps Hippolytus or Origen; cf. Philo, *Quaestiones in Gen.* 4.214.

BOOK IV: THE FOURTH DAY

THE SIXTH HOMILY

Chapter 1

To PREVENT DETERIORATION of wine it is customary for those who gather in the vintage to first clean the vessels before the wine is poured in. For of what avail is it 'to plant the vine in rows,'[1] to loosen the earth each year or to make furrows with a plough, to prune or to tie back the shoots and join them in marriage, as it were, to the elms,[2] if after such toil the wine stored away in the vessels becomes sour? In like manner, if a person desires to behold the sun rising in the morning, he proceeds to cleanse his eyes, lest there be within any speck of dust or dirt which would dull the observer's eyesight or prevent any misty darkness from obscuring the vision of the spectator.

In our reading of the Scripture passage, the sun, which before this did not exist, has now to arise. We have now passed the first day without a sun, and the second and the

1 Virgil. *Eclogues* 1.74.
2 Cf. Virgil, *Georgics* 1.2.

third days we have completed still without a sun. On the fourth day God bade the luminaries of the heavens to be created: the sun, the moon and stars. The sun begins to arise. Cleanse, now, the eyes of your mind and the inward gaze of your soul, lest any mote of sin dull the keenness of your mind and disturb the aspect of your pure heart. Cleanse your ear, in order that you may receive the clear flow of holy Scripture in a clean receptacle, so that no impurity may enter therein. With its great splendor the sun precedes the day, filling the world with its great light, encompassing it with warm exhalations.

Be on your guard against stressing merely the magnitude of the sun. Its excessive brilliance may blind the eyes of your mind, as happens in the case of one who directs his sight directly at its beams. Because of the deflection of light, such a person is suddenly bereft of his sight and, if he does not turn his face and eyes in another direction, he is led to believe that nothing is visible and that he is deprived of his powers of vision. However, if he turns his eyes aside, their functional operation remains unimpaired.

See, therefore that the rays of the rising sun do not trouble your sight. For that reason, look first upon the firmament of heaven which was made before the sun; look first upon the earth which began to be visible and was already formed before the sun put in its appearance; look at the plants of the earth which preceded in time the light of the sun. The bramble preceded the sun; the blade of grass is older than the moon. Therefore, do not believe that object to be a god to which the gifts of God are seen to be preferred. Three days have passed. No one, meanwhile, has looked for the sun, yet the brilliance of light has been in evidence everywhere. For the day, too, has its light which is itself the precursor of the sun.

(2) Do not, therefore, without due consideration put your trust in the sun. It is true that it is the eye of the world,[3] the joy of the day, the beauty of the heavens, the charm of nature and the most conspicuous object in creation.[4] When you behold it, reflect on its Author. When you admire it, give praise to its Creator.

If the sun as consort of and participant in nature is so pleasing, how much goodness is there to be found in that 'Sun of Justice'?[5] If the sun is so swift that in its rapid course by day and night it is able to traverse all things, how great is He who is always and everywhere and fills all things with His majesty![6] If that which is bidden to come forth is deemed worthy of our admiration, how much more does He surpass our admiration of whom we read: 'Who commandeth the sun and it riseth not'![7] If the sun which the succession of the seasons advances or recedes[8] is mighty, how mighty must He be, also, who, 'when he emptied himself'[9] that we might be able to see Him who 'was the true light that enlightens every man who comes into this world'![10] If the sun which from the interposition of the earth often undergoes eclipses is an extraordinary object, how surpassing is the majesty of Him who says: 'Yet one little while and I will move the heaven and the earth'![11] The former is hidden by the earth, which in its turn cannot sustain the influence of the Lord except when it is supported by the reality of His will. If the blind suffer loss by being deprived of beholding the beauty of the sun, how great is the loss of the sinner who, despoiled of the

3 Cf. Ovid, *Metamorphoses* 4.197,228.
4 Cf. Mullach, *Frag. phil. graec.* I 518 *vs.* 25 and 513 *vs.* 12 (*secundus*).
5 Mal. 3.4.
6 Ps. 71.19.
7 Job 9.7.
8 See Dante, *Paradiso* 10.28-30.
9 Phil. 2.7.
10 John 1.9.
11 Agg. 2.7.

gift of the true light, is subject to the darkness of night eternal!

(3) When, therefore, you see the sun, take note, too, of the green earth which was formed before it; take note of the green herb which holds priority in rank; take note of the woods which nod their approval, because they came into being before the light of heaven. Do you think for a moment that the herb is greater than the sun or that the woods hold a position of preference? Far be it from us to prefer things that have no feeling to Him who is the provider of such a spectacle! What else, therefore, does 'the depth of the wisdom and the knowledge of God'[12] have in view when the woods came into being before these two luminaries of the world[13] (those eyes, as it were, of the celestial firmament), unless it is that all might recognize by the testimony of holy Scripture that without the aid of the sun the earth can be productive? The earth which could cause the first seeds of things to germinate without the aid of the sun can surely nourish the seeds provided for it and can, without the heat of the sun, bring forth offspring by its own fostering care.

(4) With the voice, so to speak, of her gifts does Nature cry out: Good, indeed, is the sun, but good only in respect of service, not of command; good, too, as one who assists at my fecundity, not as one who creates; good, also, as the nourisher of my fruits, not as one who is the author of them. At times the sun burns up my produce and often is the cause of injury to me, leaving me in many places without provision. I am not ungrateful to my fellow servant, one who is granted to me for my use, subject like me to toil, to vanity, and to the service of corruption! With me he groans, with me he is in travail, in order that there may come the adoption of sons and the redemption of the human race by

12 Rom. 11.33.
13 See Virgil, *Georgics* 1.5,6.

which we, too, may be freed from servitude.[14] By my side he praises the Author; along with me he sings a hymn to the Lord God. Where his beauty is most pronounced, there I have common cause with him. Where the sun blesses, there the earth blesses, also;[15] with me share their blessings the fruit-bearing trees, the flocks and birds. At sea the sailor reproaches the sun and longs for me. In the hills the shepherd shuns him and hastens to my foliage, to my trees, under whose shadow he may find comfort in the heat, and hastens to my springs when he is thirsty and fatigued.

Chapter 2

(5) But in case the evidence presented to your eyes may appear to be scanty, cleanse your ear and apply it to the heavenly oracles: 'On the word of two or three witnesses every word is confirmed.'[1] Hear God speaking: 'Let there be lights made in the firmament of heaven to give light upon the earth.'[2]

Who says this? God says it. And to whom is He speaking, if not to His Son? Therefore, God the Father says: 'Let the Sun be made,' and the Son made the sun, for it was fitting that the 'Sun of Justice' should make the sun of the world.[3] He, therefore, brought it to light. He illuminated it and granted it the power of light. Therefore the sun was made; for this reason it is also a subject, since it has been said: 'Thou hast foundeth the earth and it continueth. By thy ordinance the day goeth on: for all things serve thee.'[4]

14 Cf. Rom. 8.21,22.
15 Cf. Ps. 148.3; Dan. 3.62.

1 Matt. 18.16.
2 Gen. 1.14.
3 Cf. Mal. 4.2.
4 Ps. 118.90,91.

In truth, since day serves, wherefore does not the sun which was made in the presence of the day also serve? Wherefore do not they serve, too, the moon and the stars which were made in the power of the night?[5] Surely the greater the beauty which the Creator has granted to them—as, for instance, an unusual brightness is bestowed on the air by the brilliance of the sun, the day has a serener light, and the darkness of night is illuminated by the flashing rays of the sun and stars, the sky twinkles with its ignited lamps as if crowned with flowers, reminding one of a paradise in bloom, resplendent with living garlands of sweet-smelling roses—the greater the beauty, then, which seems to have been granted to these, the greater is the debt they owe: 'To whom much is given, much is required.'[6] And so the sun has been well called by many the adornment of the sky, the precious jewels of which are the stars.

(6) Furthermore, that we may know that the fertility of the earth is not to be ascribed to the heat of the sun, but should be assigned to the goodness of God, the Prophet says: 'They all look to you to give them food in due time. When you give it to them, they gather it; when you open your hand, they are filled with good things.' And further on: 'When you send forth your spirit, they are created and you renew the face of the earth.'[7] And in the Gospels: 'Look at the birds of the sky: they do not sow or reap; yet your heavenly Father feeds them.'[8] The sun and moon are not, therefore, authors of fecundity, but God the Father through the Lord Jesus bestows on all things the gift of freedom of fertility.

(7) The Prophet has beautifully expounded the meaning of those words of his: 'God made the sun to rule the day

5 Cf. Ps. 135.8,9.
6 Luke 12.48.
7 Ps. 103.27,28.
8 Matt. 6.26.

and the moon to rule the night.'[9] For in the same Psalm 103 mentioned above he wrote: 'You made the moon to mark the season; the sun knows the hour of its setting.'[10] When the day begins to complete its hours, the sun recognizes that its setting is due. The sun is, therefore, in the power of the day and the moon is in the power of the night, which must accommodate itself to the changes of time; now it is filled with light, and again is devoid of it.

Most authors seem, indeed, to interpret this passage  mystically of Christ and the Church, maintaining that Christ had knowledge of His passion in the body when He said: 'Father, the hour has come! Glorify thy Son,'[11] so that by this His setting He might grant eternal life to all men who were threatened with eternal death, and that the Church may have her seasons, namely, of persecution and of peace. The Church, like the moon, seems to lose light, but she does not. She can be cast in shadow, but she cannot lose her light. For example, the Church is weakened by the desertion of some in time of persecution, but is replenished by the witness of her martyrs. Wherefore, glorified by the victories of blood shed for Christ, she may pour forth all the more abundantly over the entire world the light of her devotedness and her faith.

In fact, the moon undergoes a diminution of its light, not, however, of its mass, at the time when it seems to give up its light in the course of the month, so that it may borrow from the sun. This phenomenon can be easily observed when the atmosphere is pure and transparent and no cloud passes before the moon, rendering it obscure. The orb of the moon remains intact, although the whole of it does not shine as does a part of it. Its size is the same as it usually appears when it is filled with light. A certain shadow makes it appear that the moon

9 Ps. 135.8.
10 Ps. 103.19.
11 John 17.1.

is bereft of light. Hence, it is only the horns that shine. The moon's form is circular: this fact reveals itself, even if its light is partly diminished.

Chapter 3

(8) This statement can give us occasion for thought: 'Let there be lights in the firmament of the heavens to separate day from night,'[1] because it had already been said, when God created the light, that 'God separated the light from the darkness and there was evening and morning, the first day.'[2]

But let us reflect on the fact that the light of day is one thing and the light of the sun and moon and stars another, for the reason that the sun itself with its rays appears to add to its brilliance to the light of day. This can be seen at the dawn of day or at its setting. There is daylight, in fact, before the rising of the sun, but it is far from being brilliant. The light gleams forth more resplendently, of course, when the sun is at noon. This is pointed out by the Prophet when he says: 'And he will bring forth thy justice as the light and thy judgment as the noonday.'[3] He compares the justice of the saint not merely to light: he means the light of midday.

(9) Therefore, God ordained that there should not be just one indication by which to distinguish day from night. He established two signs by which light should be divided: one at the rising of the sun and another at its setting. Likewise, the rising of the stars would mark the division between the setting of the sun and the beginning of night. When the

1 Gen. 1.14,15.
2 Gen. 1.4,5.
3 Ps. 36.6.

sun has set, there still remains some remnant of daylight until darkness covers the earth. Then the moon rises and the stars. It is very evident that the extent of the night is measured by the illumination of the moon and stars, since the sun on its rising causes the glitter of the moon and of all the stars to be invisible by day. As to the day, even the burning rays of the sun can inform us that daylight and sunlight differ both in their nature and in their aspect. The aspect of daylight is uncompounded: it merely furnishes light. The sun, on the other hand, not merely has the power of illuminating; it has also the power of heating. The sun is fiery, and fire both illuminates and burns.

Hence, when God wished to show to Moses His marvelous power for the purpose of stirring him to greater zeal in His service and of inflaming his heart to belief, He appeared to Moses in a flaming bush.[4] But the bush was not afire; it appeared merely to shine with the appearance of fire. One function of fire, therefore, was void, the other was in operation. The power of kindling was lacking, though the power of illumination was functioning. And so Moses marveled that fire, contrary to its nature, did not burn the bush, since this was an element which usually consumes materials of a more solid nature. The fire of the Lord illuminates, not consumes.

(10) Still, you perhaps may say, wherefore is it written: 'I am a consuming fire'?[5] Your suggestion is a good one. God usually consumes only the sinful. Even in the retributions dispensed to men in accordance with their merits we perceive the nature of divine fire. It illuminates some and consumes others. It illuminates the just and consumes the wicked. It does not illuminate the same people which it consumes.

---

4 Cf. Exod. 3.2.
5 Deut. 4.24.

Rather, its illumination is inextinguishable in the direction of its performance toward the good, whereas its power of consumption is mighty to punish the sinner.

(11) But let us return to the division between day and night. At the coming of daylight, night is put to flight. At the departure of daylight, night appears everywhere. There is no association between light and darkness, since the Lord set this down as a principle at the beginning of His work. When He made the light, He made a distinction between light and darkness. Accordingly, in clear daylight, when the sun has sprinkled its rays upon the earth,[6] we see how the shadow of an object, man, or plant is separated from the light. We note how in the morning this shadow falls toward the west, while in the evening it turns toward the east and in midday toward the north. Nevertheless, the shadow is a thing apart and has nothing in common with the light. In a similar way, night seems to yield to daylight and to verge away from its light. In fact, as has been pointed out by more expert authors who have precedence over us whether in time or in ability, night is a shadow of the earth.

The shadow adheres and stays close to the body in accordance with nature, so much so that artists strive to depict the shadows of objects in their paintings. They maintain that it is the province of art not to ignore a quality inherent in nature. An artist whose painting does not represent the requisite shadows may be likened to one who contravenes the natural law. When, then, an object in daylight happens to face the sun, there arises a shadow of that part from which the sunlight is deflected. In the same way, at sunset, when the earth stands in the way of the light of day or of the sunlight, there is an effect of shadow. Hence it is clear that night is caused by the shadow of the earth.

6 Cf. Virgil, *Aeneid* 9.461.

Chapter 4

(12) God made the sun, moon, and stars, and allotted to them the measurement of time, the sun for the daytime and the moon and stars for night. The former augments the beauty of the day; the latter illumine the shadow and the darkness: 'Let them serve as signs and for the fixing of seasons, days and years.'[1] The sun, moon, and stars divide time in diverse fashion, but in an equal manner in respect to changes based on months, and 'they serve as signs' for them, also. We cannot deny that some signs are formed from the sun and moon together. The Lord said: 'And there will be signs in the sun, moon and stars.'[2] And when the Apostles asked for a sign of His coming, He replied: 'The sun will be darkened and the moon will not give her light and the stars will fall from heaven.'[3] These, He said, were to be the signs of a fulfillment in the future, but for us in our anxiety these should serve as an appropriate measure of time.

(13) In fact, some men have attempted to set down the characteristics of birth days and the future state of each newborn child. Yet a prognostication of this sort is both vain and useless to those who seek it and is an impossibility for those who promise it. What is so inane as to suppose that everyone should be convinced that he is what his birth has made him? No one, then, ought to change his condition of life and his habits or strive to become better, but, rather, remain in that conviction. In which case you cannot commend the good nor condemn the wicked, since each seems to comply with the destiny of his birth. And wherefore has the Lord laid down rewards for the good or punishment for the wicked if their habits are prescribed by fate and their

1 Gen. 1.14.
2 Luke 21.25.
3 Matt. 24.29.

social behavior depends on the course of the stars? And what else does this lead to other than to deprive man of his humanity,[4] if no room is left for character, no outlet for education or for freedom of action?

How many do we see snatched from amid their vices and sins to be converted to a better life? It was certainly not the circumstances of their birth which freed and called the Apostles from the company of sinners. Rather, the coming of Christ sanctified them and the hour of His Passion redeemed them from death. The condemned thief who was crucified with our Lord passed over into everlasting paradise, not because of a favorable nativity, but because of his confession of faith.[5] It was not the influence of his natal star, but the offense of having neglected the divine prophecy which cast Jonas into the sea. A whale which received him and after three days vomited him forth,[6] as a symbol of future mystery, and preserved him for the service of prophecy. Peter was rescued from impending death in prison by the angel of Christ,[7] not by the disposition of the stars. Blindness converted Paul to grace when he was struck by a viper.[8] When he was a victim of shipwreck he was saved, not by his natal star, but by the merits of his piety.[9]

What shall we say of those who by the prayers of the Apostles arose from the dead?[10] Was it their natal star or the grace of the Apostles that restored them? What need was there for them to restort to fasting and expose themselves to danger, if they could obtain what they desired simply by virtue of their natal star? If they had put their trust in that, they would never, while awaiting the destinies

4 Cf. Cicero, *De finibus* 5.35.
5 Cf. Luke 23.42.
6 Jonas 1.2-15; 2.11.
7 Cf. Acts 12.7.
8 Cf. Acts 9.8,18.
9 Cf. Acts 28.3.
10 Cf. Acts 9.40.

meted out to them by fate, have reached such perfection of grace.

(14) What about the impossibility of all this? In fact, if we allow some force to their arguments for the sake of refuting them and not for the sake of proof, they say that the time of our birth is of great importance. This time should be determined strictly within the limits of moments of the smallest extent, because, if no heed is paid to exactness, the greatest differences do ensue. Only the tiniest moment separates the nativity of the helpless from that of the powerful, of the needy from the rich, of the innocent from the guilty. It often happens that at the same hour is born one who is destined to a long life and one who will die in early childhood, if other circumstances turn out to be dissimilar and if there is just one single point of difference.

Let them reconstruct the following if they would. Suppose a woman is giving birth to a child. As a matter of course the midwife first observes the child. She looks for his cry as giving evidence of life and notes whether the child is a male or a female. How many moments will you allow for all these acts? Suppose that there is an astrologer near at hand. Can a man be present at a childbirth? While the midwife is giving information and while the Chaldean is listening and setting up the horoscope, the fates of the new-born child have already entered the space of the lot belonging to another person. It follows that while an investigation is being made regarding the fate of one person, the nativity of another is in the process of being established.

Even suppose that what they maintain concerning fate and nativity is true, their conclusions connot, however, be true. A moment passes away: 'Time is flying beyond recall.'[11] There is no doubt that time is made up of moments and of 'a twinkling of an eye.' I am led to believe that assumption

---

11 Virgil, *Georgics* 3.284.

since we shall all arise, as the Apostle testifies, in a moment, in the twinkling of an eye: 'Behold I tell you a mystery: we shall all indeed rise, but we shall not all be changed—in a moment, in the twinkling of an eye, at the last trumpet and the dead shall rise incorruptible and we shall be changed.'[12] Between the time when the child was born, taken up, and laid down again; between the time of his cry and the report of it, how many moments do you think have elapsed!

So far I have only touched the surface of this question. The upholders of this system divide that well-known circle of twelve signs, which has such vital importance for them, into twelve parts. Furthermore, as the sun travels over the twelfth part of that indescribable sphere—it completes its course in this way in the period of a year—they divide each one of these twelve parts into thirty smaller divisions which the Greeks call μοῖραι, and each of these smaller divisions they separate in turn into sixty other individual parts. How incomprehensible all this is! To think that the moment of a nativity is made up of a sixtieth of a sixtieth part and that such is exactly the motion and the aspect of each sign occurring at the actual moment of a nativity! Wherefore, since it is impossible to take such tenuous moments of time into account and since the slightest variation introduces an enormous error, the whole affair is based on mere phantasy. Its advocates are ignorant of their own destiny. How, then, can they know that of other men? They do not know what is in store for themselves. Can they announce the future of others? It is ridiculous to believe this, because if they were able to do so, they would inevitably foresee what the future held for themselves.

(15) Now how stupid it is to think that if a person were to say that he was born under the sign of Aries and should suppose that, just because such an animal is pre-eminent in

12 1 Cor. 15.51.

his own herd, he himself would turn out to be conspicuous for his wisdom! Or that he would become quite rich for the reason that the Ram possesses by nature a raiment and every year puts on a new and costly garment. Wherefore this man would appear to be one who is destined to be no stranger to profit and gain. In a similar way they form their conclusions regarding the signs of the Bull and the Fishes. From the nature of ordinary animals they consider that the significance of the movements of the heavens and of the signs can be interpreted. And so our food and our sustenance have established for us the destines of our lives, that is to say, the Ram, the Bull, and the Fish imprint on us the norms of our character! Wherefore, then, do they summon from heaven the causes for material things and the basis for this life of ours, when at the same time they share the causes of their own motion with the celestial signs, arguing from the very qualities of ordinary human food? They maintain that a person born under the Ram is generous because the ram yields its wool without resistance. They prefer to ascribe that kind of virtue to the nature of an ordinary animal than to heaven, from which comes to us the gleam of sunshine, and often, too, a downfall of rain. They assert that those who at their birth fall under the aspect of the Bull will be subject to toil and will endure servitude,[13] because that laborious animal willingly submits his neck to the yoke. They say, too, that those whom at their birth the Scorpion has encircled will turn out to be assassins[14] and that they will spit out the venom of wickedness—a venom which is in essence poisonous.

Why, therefore, do you pretend on the basis of the significance of celestial signs to give an authoritative standard for living? Why do you present certain nonsensical facts as proof

13 Cf. Manilius, *Astronomica* 4.143.
14 Cf. Petronius, *Cena Trim.* 39.

of your assertion? If the movements of the heavens take their character from the moral qualities typical of such animals, then heaven itself seems to be subject to the influences of bestial natures, since from these natures it supposedly has received a substantial and vital force which it would communicate to men. But if this is a far cry from what is the truth, so much the more ridiculous is it to think that these men, deprived as they are of any solid basis of fact, should have recourse to this assumption in order to give credence to their arguments.

(16) Next let us consider the fact that they give the name of 'planet' to those signs which by their movements determine the destinies of our lives. Either, as the name indicates, the planets wander for all time, or, if we follow their own statements, they move along in rapid motion. We are told that the planets in innumerable circular movements change their positions ten thousand times, or, if this seems incredible, show manifold aspects each day. Whatever may be the case, it cannot be accepted that such a wandering course and such a swift motion can be the means of establishing a fixed and immovable lot as a basis for our lives. Again, they maintain that the movements of the planets are not all equal. Some move around with more speed, others are slower in motion, so that they often at the same time gaze upon and hide from each other in the course of their transits.

(17) They say that it makes considerable difference whether favorable or unfavorable and harmful signs look at the inception of a birth and the difference in birth lies in the fact that the aspect of a favorable sign confers very great benefits, while that of an unfavorable sign brings with it considerable harm. Such are the terms which they use of these very signs that they hold in veneration. I feel it necessary to make use of the vocabulary of those whose assertions I discuss, lest they proceed to remind me that their argu-

ments have been ignored rather than utterly refuted. For example, that wandering and swift movement to which I have made reference escapes their comprehension in their attempt to establish to a nicety as an aspect of a favorable sign a point or moment of incomprehensible time. It frequently happens, in fact, that the threat of an unfavorable sign enters as a disturbing factor in the midst of their calculations.

What wonder, then, if men are deceived when favorable signs are defamed? If the very nature of these signs is believed to be unfavorable, then God, who is supreme, is accused of being the creator of evil and responsible for wickedness. If, in fact, the signs are considered to have taken on by their own volition the power of harming the innocent and injuring those who are conscious of not having up to that time done any vile deed for which a punishment is assigned even before the fault is committed, what, I repeat, is so irrational, exceeding in that respect even the irrationality of of beasts, as to attribute the practice of deceit or of good will, not to the merits of men, but to the movements of the signs? He was in no way guilty, it is said, but an unfavorable sign looked upon him! He came in contact with the star of Saturn. On the other hand, by a very slight deviation, according to their calculations, bad omens are shunned and wrong-doing avoided.

(18) This wisdom of theirs is similar to that encountered in a spider's web from which a gnat or fly cannot extricate itself once it has become entangled therein.[15] However, if an animal more robust by nature is seen to enter the web, right away it passes through, breaks the feeble strands, and destroys the useless snares. Such are the nets of the Chaldeans. In these nets the weak are trapped, but those of a more robust nature find no obstacle there. You who have more

15 See A. J. Festugière. *TAPA* 85 (1954) 67.

strength of character say to the astrologers when you see them: You weave spider's webs which cannot have any use or binding force when a person strikes against them, not in a moment of weakness like a gnat or a fly, but like a sparrow or a dove, rending their meshes in the swiftness of their winged flight.

In fact, what sensible man would believe that signs, which frequently change from day to day and so many times return on themselves, can by their movements denote what are the indications of future power? If such were the case, what combinations indicating royal birth would be announced day after day! As a consequence, kings would be born every day. Succession to the throne would not be transmitted to sons. Rather, at all time men of diverse social conditions would arise who would lay claim to the rights of imperial power. What king, therefore, would care to think under these circumstances of the birth of a son to succeed him, if the royal power is destined for someone else and if it is not within his own power to hand down to his own children the imperial succession?

We read, of course, that 'Abia begot Asaph, Asaph begot Josaphat, Josophat begat Joram, Joram begat Ozias,'[16] and so up to the time of the captivity every succession took place through a line of kings of equal rank and honor. Do you think that, because they were kings, they had the power actually to govern their own movements—movements which were committed to the control of the celestial signs? What human being can have dominion over these?

(19) Again, if all our acts and deeds depend on the fates acquired at our birth and not on principles of morality, why are laws established and statutes promulgated by which punishment is meted out to the wicked and security bestowed

16 Matt. 1.7,8.

on the innocent? Why is pardon not granted to the accused, since, to be sure, they fell into crime by reason, as is maintained, of necessity and not by an act of their own will? Why does the farmer toil and not rather wait until it is time to convey into his storehouses the produce for which he has not labored, relying on the prerogatives of his birth? If he was destined by birth to be endowed with wealth without the expenditure of labor, he should undoubtedly wait until the earth brings forth fruit spontaneously without seed. If such were the case he should not sink his ploughshare into the earth or put his hands on the curved scythe or undergo the expense of harvesting the grapes. Rather, the wine would without effort flow plenteously into his stock of jars. Without effort, too, he would let the wild olive berry exude its oil without the labor of grafting upon the trunk of the olive tree. In the same way a merchant who travels over the wide seas would not be in dread of the perils that threaten his own life, for it is within his power, because of a certain destiny allotted to him at birth, to come without labor into a wealth of treasure.

But this is far from the accepted opinion. As a matter of fact, the farmer cleaves the earth 'with deep-driven plough'; 'stripped he ploughs, stripped he sows'; stripped in the glowing 'heat he thrashes on the floor the parched ears.'[17] The merchant, impatient when the east winds are blowing, ploughs the sea often when the course is unsafe. Insolent and rash men such as these are condemned by the Prophet, who says:[18] 'Be thou ashamed, O Sidon, the sea speaketh,' that is to say, if dangers do not move you, then shame can check and modesty confound you. 'Be thou ashamed, O Sidon,' in which there is no place for virtue, no care for safety, no young men exercised in arms and ready to fight in defense of

17 Virgil, *Georgics* 1.45,298,299.
18 Isa. 23.4,3.

their country. They are anxiously and entirely preoccupied with gain and the benefits derived from commerce. 'What the merchant sows, so does he reap.'

What reward is there for a Christian, if in his activities and labors he follows the dictates of necessity, not those of his own free will? There, where destiny decides, personal initiative is held in no esteem.

Chapter 5

(20) We have spoken at length on this subject and do not desire to say any more, lest some people may form the opinion that what was taken up merely for the purpose of refutation has been presented for the purpose of publicizing it. As a matter of fact, how can these subjects which as children we held in ridicule now seriously enter our thoughts in our declining years? Therefore, let us now direct our pen to what remains of our reading of Scripture.

(21) 'Let there be lights to serve as signs and for the fixing of seasons, days and years,'[1] He said. We have already discussed the subject of 'signs.'

What are seasons but successive changes, that is, winter, spring, summer, and autumn? During these seasons the passage of the sun is either swift or slow, scarcely touching us at one time with its rays; at another, burning us with its heat. And so we have winter when the sun lingers in the southern regions. When the sun is somewhat far away, the earth grows rigid with frost and is stiffened by cold. The earth is covered by all-pervading nocturnal shadows, so that the nights are much longer in extent than are the days. From this fact it happens that during the storms of winter a great amount of snow and rain is precipitated. When, how-

1 Gen. 1.14.

ever, the sun, leaving the southern regions, returns to its position over the earth, the duration of day and night becomes equal. Then, the more it prolongs its sojourn, the more it gradually tempers the air with its heat and with the clemency of its atmosphere, which fosters all things and forces them once more to reproduction. The result is that the earth germinates and the seeds released from the furrows come to life again, the trees sprout and in their effort to perpetuate their kind successively each year all species of terrestial and marine life propagate themselves. But when the sun rises toward the summer solstice in the north, the daytime is lengthened, thereby narrowing and restricting the period of night. And so, the more assiduously the sun links itself and mingles with our atmosphere, the more completely does it furnish heat to the air and at the same time dry up the moisture of the earth, thus causing the seeds to sprout forth and the offspring of the forests to ripen, as it were, into manhood. At the time when the sun becomes warmer, the shadows at noon become shorter, inasmuch as the sun in this region shines from a position high above us.

(22) Since the Synagogue says in the Canticle of Canticles: 'Show me, O thou whom my soul has loved, where thou feedest, where thou liest at midday, lest perchance I begin to wander after the flocks of thy companions,'[2] that is: Announce to me, O Christ, whom has my soul loved. Why not rather whom [my soul] loves? The Synagogue loved, but the Church loves and never changes her affection for Christ. 'Where thou feedest,' we read, 'where thou liest at midday.' I desire to follow you into those places like a foster-child, to whom I once held fast as if in wedlock and I wish to search for your flock because I have lost mine. You feed at midday in the Church's pasture where Justice

2 Cant. 1.6.
3 Cf. Ps. 36.6.

shines, where Judgment gleams like the noonday,[3] where no shadow is seen, where the days are longer, because the Sun of Justice dwells therein for a longer time just as in the months of summer. The day of the Lord is, therefore, not brief. It is long because it has been written: 'Before the great day of the Lord doth come.'[4] Hence Jacob says: 'All the days of my life are brief and evil,'[5] for a dubious light is evil. Brief days are, therefore, of dubious light and are not luminous. The contrary is true of the long days, as many people who live in warm countries realize from experience. Accordingly, the Synagogue in its brief and evil days was in very deep shade. Its type is often expressed in the person of Jacob or of his people. It did not behold the Sun of Justice shining from overhead, but, rather, since winter was at hand, shining from the direction of the south. But this is said to the Church: 'The winter is now past, is over and gone. The flowers have appeared in our land, the time of the harvest has come.'[6] Winter existed before the coming of Christ; after His coming, the flowers of the spring and summer's harvest appear. Since it faces the light shining from the south and from the region of the converted Gentiles, the Synagogue lies in shadow. The Gentiles 'who sat in darkness'—the Gentiles, the people of the nations, a confused people—'have seen a great light; to them that sat in the region and shadow of death, a light has arisen.'[7] This is a great and divine light which is not darkened by any shadow of death. So it shines from above, because through the voice of Zachary it is written: 'Wherewith the Orient from on high has visited us, to shine on those who sit in darkness and in the shadow of death.'[8] There is, of course, a shadow of salvation, not of

4 Joel 2.31.
5 Gen. 47.9.
6 Cant. 2.11.
7 Matt. 4.16; Isa. 9.2.
8 Luke 1.78.

death, as has been said: 'Thou shalt protect me under the shadow of thy wings'[9]—'shadow,' in fact, because it is of the body; 'shadow,' too, because it is of the cross. It is the shadow of salvation, because in it was the remission of sins and the resurrection of the dead.

(23) We can state the problem succinctly in the following way: winter days are short while their shadows are long; summer days are long, whereas their shadows are short. In the middle of the day a shadow is shorter than it is at its beginning or end. This is the situation with us who live in the west. However, there are people living in the southern regions who for two days in the year are without shadows, since the sun's rays strike from a position directly overhead, thus illuminating everything on all sides. Hence, these are called in Greek 'Ascii.'[10] Many also report the fact that in that region the sun is so perpendicularly situated above that water can be seen gleaming deep down through the narrow openings of a well. In the south there is report of a people who are called 'Amphiscii'[11] because they cast a shadow on each side.

The person, in fact, who travels in the direction of the sun casts his shadow behind him. This happens when he advances toward the east in the morning hours or toward the south at midday or toward the west at sunset. From three directions, therefore, may the sun strike a person; from the east, the south, and the west. Our shadows are behind us in the morning and in the evening, and at noon the situation is similar. Moreover, the sun does not reach us from the north. For that reason, if you face northward in the morning or in the evening or at midday you cast no shadow behind you. Only those people who live in the southern regions of this world which we inhabit are able, it appears, to cast their

9 Ps. 16.8.
10 Men without a shadow.
11 Men with double shadows.

shadows in a southerly direction. This is said to happen in the height of summer when the sun is advancing toward the north.

For us there is the relief of autumn. At its coming the excessive heat of summer is broken. Autumn, relaxing its warmth and moderating its temperature to what is equable, hands us over without malice or harm to the breezes of winter.

(24) 'Let there be [lights] for the fixing of days,'[12] says the Scripture—not that they may make the days, but that they may have a principal part in their making, so that the sun may illuminate the dawn with more generous gifts and with its light can designate the course of the entire day. In such a sense some interpret the words of the Prophet: 'The sun to rule the day, the moon and the stars to rule the night,'[13] as they cast their lights around.

The sun and the moon, too, were designed 'to fix the years.' The moon in twelve times thirty days, according to the Hebrews, completes the year with the addition of a few days, and according to the Romans with an intercalary day added every fourth year. The solstitial year is that portion of time which corresponds to the completion of a period in which the sun makes a circuit through all the signs and then returns to the point of its departure.[14]

Chapter 6

(25) God made, therefore, these two great luminaries. We may assume that by their own right they are great and not merely by comparison with other objects such as the broad

12 Gen. 1.14.
13 Ps. 135.8,9.
14 Cf. Isidore, *Etymol.* 5.36.3.

heavens and the mighty sea. We must admit the mightiness of that sun which fills with its heat the entire earth as the moon, too, fills not only the earth with its light, but also this atmosphere of ours, the sea, and the firmament. In whatevery part of the heavens these lights may be, they illuminate everything and are observed equally by all. So much is this true that people of every race believe that these luminaries delight in lingering in their respective native countries. They believe that they are present there only, furnishing light to them alone, whereas these lights shine on all without distinction. Everyone is convinced, moreover, that he is nearer these luminaries than any other individual.

As a proof of its great size one may note that the orb of the moon seems to all men to be of the same dimensions. Although at times its light may increase or diminish, its appearance on any one night is the same for me as it is for all men. If it were to appear smaller to distant people and if to people living nearer it would seem to shine more brilliantly, we would then have clear indications of the narrow compass of its range and its extent. The reason is that all objects are considered by us to be smaller when we are some distance away from them, while other objects are regarded as larger if seen closer at hand. The size of an object increases in proportion as the beholder comes nearer. The sun's rays are neither nearer to any one individual nor more remote. In like manner, the sphere of the moon has for all men the same size. The sun when it rises appears at the same instant alike to the people of India and of Britain. When it sets, the sun does not appear to be smaller to the inhabitants of the east than it does to those of the west. When the sun rises it does not seem to the people of the west to be smaller than it does to the people of the east. As Scripture says: 'As far as the east is from the west.'[1] These points are distant

1 Ps. 102.12.

one from the other but that is not true in regard to the sun. It does not lie nearer any other object nor more remote from it.

(26) Do not be disturbed by the fact that the sun on rising seems to be about a cubit in extent. Rather, consider that between the sun and the earth there lies a space which our vision, because of its weakness, cannot penetrate without a loss of effectiveness. Our vision is clouded. Are we to conclude that the sun or moon is clouded, also? Our vision is limited. Does that make more limited the things that we see? The apparent size of an object is diminished, not the real. We ought not to ascribe to the luminaries a weakness which is due merely to our senses.

Our sight deceives us. Therefore, do not put trust in its testimony. The heavenly bodies present the appearance of smallness, but their form is actually not so. If from the top of a mountain you wish to view a plain before your eyes with cattle feeding therein, will they not take on the appearance of ants?[2] If you should look far out to sea from some point on shore, will not the largest ships with their sails flashing amid the blue of the sea appear to you in the distance like doves in flight? More than that, even the islands with their extensive areas which deck the sea seem circumscribed in a narrow space, taking on a smooth appearance instead of a rough one, a look of density instead of its contrary! Take account, therefore, of the weakness of your eyesight and like a just judge rely on yourself, putting trust as the same time in those things which we affirm to be true.[3]

(27) Do you want to estimate the huge size of the sun with your bodily eyes as well as with the eyes of your mind? Consider the extent in which the spheres of the stars seem to cover and illuminate with lights innumerable the firma-

2 Cf. Lucretius 2.334,335.
3 *Ibid.* 4.353-363.

ment of the heavens. Yet, for all that, they do not succeed in dispersing the clouds of the sky and the darkness of night-time.[4] As soon as the sunrise has sent forth its standards, all the glowing stars vanish beneath the flashing rays of one luminary, the surroundings are unveiled, and the sky is flooded with a purple flush of light. The dawn at its inception is still breathing. In a flash the splendor of the sun's fiery rays emerge and the breeze's sweet breath is a forerunner of the rising sun. Tell me, if you please, how could the sun illuminate the great orb of the earth unless it, too, was mighty?

(28) What shall I say of the Creator's great moderation and control? He conferred such measure on the sun's operation that its fiery flame to all appearances has not by its pervading heat burned up the veins of the earth and the entire structure of matter?[5] Again, in such an extensive world the sun has not by becoming cool ceased from the act of infusing the 'seed of heat'[6] into the earth. Rather, thrusting aside infecundity and want, it has effectively bestowed on the earth the blessing of warmth with its accompanying fertility.

Chapter 7

(29) What we have stated in regard to her consort and brother applies in similar fashion to the moon, since the latter assumes the same offices as her brother, namely that of illuminating the darkness, cherishing the seeds, and increasing the produce of the soil. She has functions, also, which are different from her brother's. The moisture which throughout the day the heat has absorbed from the earth is

4 Cf. Horace, *Odes* 1.7.15.
5 Cf. Lucretius 2.61 (*species rerum*).
6 Lucretius 1.902; 6.200,201.

replaced in the short space of night in the form of dew,[1] of which the moon is said to be a generous dispenser. Hence, when the night is clear and the moon shines the whole night long, a larger amount of dew is then said to fall. Many reclining in the open air have experienced the phenomenon of collecting more dew on their heads, the longer they rested in the moonlight. Wherefore, in the Canticles, Christ speaks to the Church: 'For my head is full of dew and my locks of the drops of the night.'[2]

Then, again, the moon goes through a process of waxing and waning. It becomes smaller when as a new moon it rises, at which point it gradually approaches a fuller form. In this we can see a great mystery. The elements are affected by the waning of the moon. After a period of exhaustion, strength is regained at the time of the moon's waxing. We may note this process in two instances: in the brains of living things and in the amount of water in shellfish. In fact, oysters and many other kinds of shellfish are said to be more developed at the time when the moon is becoming fuller. The same phenomenon is related by those who have made special investigation into the internal structure of trees. We see, therefore, that the waxing and waning of the moon is not the result of weakness, but of plan and purpose. If it were not that the Creator had thought fit to bestow unusual excellence and beauty on such significant changes, these changes would not have been allotted to matter.

(30) Some learned men, including some who are Christians, have claimed that the air usually changes at the rising of the moon. Yet, if these lunar changes should result in some unusual upheaval, then clouds would conceal the sky and rain would fall at every rising of the moon. So, when there was talk the previous day of a much desired rainfall,

1 Cf. Virgil, *Georgics,* 2.202.
2 Cant. 5.2.

some person remarked, 'See, the new moon will bring it.' Although we were all eager for rain, I had no desire to believe that such assertions are true. Hence, I was delighted when no rain fell, until it was granted as a consequence of the Church's prayers. Wherefore, it was made manifest that one should not expect rain to follow the new moon, but that is should be granted by a provident and beneficent Creator.

In fact, although channels of water during other phases of the moon rise and afterwards sink to their former level or even rush along violently without any external force, these same bodies of water remain calm at the time of the new moon before its light is observable.[3] When in the course of time the moon comes into view, then the waters return to their accustomed ebb and flow. Again, during those days when the new moon is not in evidence the ebb tide, which is reputed to exist in the ocean, is said to follow its usual course. On the occasion of the moon's rise, according to report, clear indications of change make their appearance. To be more precise, the western sea,[4] towards which the ebb tide directs itself, rises and falls with greater force, as if it were driven backward and forward by the same lunar exhalations, until it ultimately falls back into its normal and accustomed channel.

Chapter 8

(31) Hence, if you wonder at the fact that the moon can suffer a loss of light while it has in itself the power to produce change, consider that we are here in the presence of a

3 Cf. Virgil, *Eclogues* 2.26.
4 The Atlantic Ocean; see S. Giet, *Basile de Césarée* (Paris 1949) 382 nn. 2-4.

great mystery. From this let men deduce the lesson that nothing can exist in the universe, be it human or any other created thing, which shall not at some time pass away.[1] Even the moon, to which the Lord has granted the important office of illuminating the whole world, goes through the process of waxing and waning. All things, which spring from nothing, reach their perfection and again diminish in perfection, being subject to decline. Hence we are told: 'Heaven and earth shall pass away.'[2] Why, then, do we not moderate our emotions and face adversities with courage? For He who has created all things from nothing has the power to bear you aloft to the summit of perfection. In a similar manner, we should control our feelings of joy in prosperity and not take pride in our positions of wealth and power. Likewise, we should not boast of our physical strength or beauty which is liable both to corruption and to constant change. Rather, we should strive for that beauty of soul which endures into future time.

If you are afflicted with sadness at the sight of the waning of the moon 'which repairs its losses' and renews itself,[3] all the more ought you to be saddened if your soul, which has been filled with the fruit of virtue, should frequently afterward change its intent and purpose by an attitude of inconstancy and heedlessness. This is the height of stupidity and ignorance, for, as Scripture says: 'A fool is changed as the moon.'[4] Hence, a wise man does not change with the moon: 'He shall continue with the sun.'[5]

Wherefore the moon does not partake of folly, because the moon does not change like the fool, but the fool like the moon. The seed of the just remains 'as the moon, perfect for

1 Cf. Horace, *Odes* 2.11.10-12.
2 Matt. 24.35.
3 Horace, *Odes* 4.7.13.
4 Eccli. 27.12.
5 Ps. 71.5.

ever and a faithful witness in heaven.'[6] To perform one's function is one thing; to have no fixed beliefs and to be carried away by unstable whims and emotions presents a situation that is quite different. The moon toils for you[7] and by reason of the will of God is made subject: 'For creation is made subject to vanity, not by its own will but by reason of him who made it subject in hope.'[8] It is you who undergoes changes of your own volition, not the moon. The moon 'groans and travails in pain'[9] in its changes. You, without understanding, often find joy in this. The moon frequently awaits your release from sin, that it may be realeased from the servitude in which all creation shares. But you place obstacles to your release from sin and to the moon's freedom. The fact that you yourself still await that conversion which fails to come,[10] whereas the moon suffers change, is, then, the result, not of the moon's folly, but of your's.

(32) Your opinion of the moon should be based, not on the observation of your eyes, but on the insight of your mind. The moon diminishes in size so as to make an addition to the sum of physical phenomenon. This, therefore, is a great mystery. He who has allotted His gifts to all things has allotted this to the moon. He has emptied it so as to replenish it. He has even 'emptied Himself'[11] that He might replenish all, for He emptied Himself that He might come down for us. He came down for us that He might ascend for all. It is written, in fact: 'He who ascended above the heavens that he might fill all things.'[12] Hence, one of the Apostles says: 'For of his fullness we have all received.'[13] The moon, there-

6 Ps. 88.38.
7 Cf. Virgil, *Georgics* 2.478.
8 Rom. 8.20.
9 Rom. 8.22.
10 Cf. Rom. 8.19.
11 Phil. 2.7.
12 Eph. 4.12.
13 John 1.16.

fore, has made known the mysteries of Christ. It is no slight thing in which He has placed His sign. No slight thing is that which contains the type of His beloved Church, as the Prophet points out when he says: 'In his days shall justice spring up and abundance of peace till the moon be taken away.'[14] And in the Canticles the Lord says of His spouse: 'Who is she that looks forth as the morning rising, fair as the moon, excellent as the sun?'[15]

Deservedly is the moon compared to the Church, who has shone over the entire world and says as she illuminates the darkness of this world: 'The night is far advanced, the day is at hand.'[16] Fittingly does she say: 'She that looks forth,' as if looking from a higher position on one's own, in accordance with the statement: 'The Lord hath looked down from heaven upon the children of men.'[17] Looking down, then, the Church has, like the moon, her frequent risings and settings. She has grown, however, by her settings and has by their means merited expansion at a time when she is undergoing diminution through persecution and while she is being crowned by the martyrdom of her faithful. This is the real moon which from the perpetual light of her own brother has acquired the light of immortality and grace. Not from her own light does the Church gleam, but from the light of Christ. From the Sun of Justice has her brilliance been obtained, so that it is said: 'It is now no longer I that live, but Christ lives in me.'[18]

Happy, in truth, is that which merited such an honor! Wherefore I would not call you happy by reason of your renewals, but by the fact that you are a type of the Church.

14 Ps. 71.7.
15 Cant. 6.9.
16 Rom. 13.12.
17 Ps. 13.2.
18 Gal. 2.20.

In the former case you are but a servant; in the latter, our beloved!

(33) How ridiculous is the current belief that you can be brought to earth by magical charms! These are old wives' tales, the gossip of the common crowd. Who would believe that a work of God assigned to such important service could be affected by the superstitions of the Chaldeans? He who was brought down not by magical charms but by his own will, who 'disguises himself as an angel of light,'[19] may very well have fallen from heaven. To be sure, there are those who believe that the Church, too, can be moved from her place and position. There are many men who provoke the Church, but the charms of the magician can not harm her. Magical chants are of no avail there where the canticles of Christ are chanted daily. Her own chanter is Jesus, our Lord, through whom magical charms and serpents' poison were made void. She is like a serpent which placed on high devoured the snakes,[20] and, although a deadly Egyptian chant be murmured,[21] its force is lost at the utterance of the name of Christ. So, too, Paul blinded Elymas,[22] thus depriving him of his eyesight and of his futile magic powers at one and the same time. In like manner, Peter cast down to the ground Simon, who by the evil power of his charms sought to soar aloft by magic to the heights of heaven.

Chapter 9

(34) I feel sure that the fourth day has come to a close in a wonderful way. How does it happen, then, that many

---

19 2 Cor. 11.14.
20 Cf. Num. 21.8; John 3.14.
21 Cf. Exod. 7.11.
22 Cf. Acts 13.11.

people generally avoid the fourth day and think that it is useless to begin anything in association with a number with which the entire world blazoned forth in a new light? Do they believe that the sun came into being under inauspicious circumstances? And how is it possible for a person to predict good fortune for another, if he himself is unable to choose for himself the day of his own birth? How can they make known the horoscope of a person without knowing anything of his birth? What do we say of the moon which rises on the fourth day?[1] Does not the fourteenth day indicate for us the day of salvation?[2] Is the date on which is celebrated the mystery of the Redemption an occasion for our displeasure? Hence, the demons are responsible for attempts to avoid the number four, for in it their wickedness was destroyed. And so the Gentiles maintain that nothing should be initiated with it, because they know that then for the first time their schemes began to be of no avail. Moreover, the Gentile race had already come into the fold of the Church.

If the moon is at its fourth rising be 'clear and with undimmed horns,'[3] it is thought that this is an indication that the remaining days of the month will be serene up to the very end. To think that people are unwilling to start anything on those days which are destined to be followed by calm weather!

But we must in the midst of this discourse of ours be on our guard lest the fourth day should suddenly come to an end. 'Longer shadows are falling from the mountain-heights,'[4] as the light becomes dim and the shades of evening grow more dense.

---

1 Cf. Virgil, *Georgics* 1.432.

2 The Jewish Christians observed the feast of the Resurrection on the 14th day of the month Nisan.

3 Virgil, *Georgics* 1.433-435.

4 Virgil, *Eclogues* 1.84.

BOOK FIVE: THE FIFTH DAY

THE SEVENTH HOMILY

Chapter 1

THE ENTIRE EARTH was now arrayed in its verdant garb of diverse plants. The sun, too, and the moon, those twin luminaries, and the stars in their splendor shone forth in the heavens. A third element still remained, in which the blessing of life was to be bestowed by the gift of God. All things on earth are being sustained and nourished by the air above.[1] The earth opening up the seeds gives life to everything. Then under the command of God's word, it blossomed forth at the gift of creative life. Water alone seemed not yet to have been affected by the generosity of God's' gift. There still was something which waited for the hands of the Creator. With the water He saved a certain fitting and special endowment which He would set aside for the functions appropriate to it. The earth was the first element on which the boon of life was conferred, but this life has no animating soul. The water, in its turn, was bidden to produce that which would bestow the force and dignity of

1 Cf. Virgil, *Aeneid* 6.726.

something that is alive—something that is provided with a sense of self-preservation and with the instinct of shrinking from death.

(2) And God also said: 'Let the waters abound with life and above the earth let winged creatures fly below the firmament of the heavens.'[2]

At this command the waters immediately poured forth their offspring. The rivers were in labor. The lakes produced their quota of life. The sea itself began to bear all manner of reptiles and to send forth according to its kind whatever was there created. The tiny creeks and the muddy marshes were not without exercising the power of creation granted to them. Fish leaped from the rivers. Dolphins frolicked in the waves. Shell-fish clung to the rocks. Oysters adhered to the depths and the sea-urchins waxed strong.

Alas, enticement, the mother of our life of ease, existed before the creation of man! Before man there existed things to delight us! The temptation of man antedated his creation. But this was not nature's fault. Nature gave us nourishment and did not prescribe vice. These things were given for common use. Therefore, you were not to claim anything as your own personal property. For you did the earth give generously of her fruits. For you did the waters generate the *scari* and the *acipenseres* and all their produce.[3] Not satisfied with these, you have tasted food that is forbidden to you. Everything is heaped up before your envious eyes, so that the perversity of your greed may become all the more grievous.

(3) But we are unable to record the multiplicity of the names of all those species which by divine command were brought to life in a moment of time. At the same instant

---

2 Gen. 1.20.

3 A species of fish regarded as a delicacy by the Romans.

substantial form and the principle of life were brought into existence; associated was a sort of vital vigor and power. The earth was replete with plants. The sea was filled with living things. In the one, vegetative life blossomed forth; in the other, animal life prevailed. In the earth, too, water claimed its part. The earth is laved by the fish of the sea. From it comes their prey. Gnats buzz and frogs croak even around the borders of the marshes that gave them birth. They, too, have heard the command of the Lord: 'Let the waters abound with life.'

(4) We know that the serpent species is given the name of 'creeper' from the fact that it is creeps over the earth. With more assurance we can say that every creature that swims presents the natural appearance of a creature that creeps. For, when these animals sink into deep water, they seem to cleave through it. Yet, when they swim, they seem to creep with their whole body as they propel it over the surface of the water. Hence David has also said: 'This great sea which stretcheth wide its arms; there are creeping things without number.'[4] There are a great many such animals provided with feet for walking. They are amphibians, living either in the water or on land; for example, seals, crocodiles and water-horses. The latter are called hippopotamuses from the fact that they are generated in a river, in this case, the Nile. These animals do not walk, however, when they are in deep water. Rather, by using their feet they are able by swimming to propel themselves forward; not, however, as one would perform the act of walking. The animal makes progress as one would with the use of an oar, just as a boat glides along with the help of oars and 'ploughs the waters with its keel.'[5]

---

4 Ps. 103.25.
5 Virgil, *Aeneid* 5.142.

Chapter 2

(5) 'Let the waters abound with life,' said the Lord—a brief statement, but a significant one and one that is widely effective in endowing with their nature the smallest and the largest animals without distinction. The whale, as well as the frog, came into existence at the same time by the same creative power. Without effort does God produce the greatest things. He is not averse to creating the least.[1] Nature is not in pain when she gives birth to dolphins, just as she is not in pain when she produces tiny animals like snails and purple-fish.

Take note of the fact that there are far more animals in the sea than on land. Count, if you can, all the species of fish from the smallest to the greatest, for example, the cuttle-fish, the polypus, the oyster, the sea and river crab, and even the different types among these. What shall I say of the different species of serpent, of the dragon, the murena, and the eel?—not to mention the scorpions, the frogs, the tortoise, the mustela, also, and the sea-dog, the sea-calf, the monstrous shark,[2] the dolphin, the seal, and the sea-lion. What need is there to add to our list the sea-ousel, the sea-thrush, and the sea-peacock, whose colors we see in the feathers of birds as, for example, the black ousel and the peacock with its varied colored back and neck; also in the feathers of the thrush with its spotted breast and in the feathers of the rest of the birds whose names and species belong to this earth of ours? These, as a matter of fact, came into existence in the seas and in the multitudinous rivers, since the waters at the divine command were the first to produce 'creeping creatures having life.'

(6) Add to this the beneficence of God whereby what we

1 Cf. Cicero, *De natura deorum* 3.86,93.
2 Cf. Virgil, *Aeneid* 5.822.

cherish in the water is an object of fear on land. This is true, because what is harmful on land is in water without harm—even the water-snakes are bereft of poison. The lion is a terrifying animal on land; he is gentle in the water. The murena, which is said to be somewhat harmful, is a choice table food. The frog is repellent when in the marshes, is pleasing when in water, and excels all in its deliciousness as food. If you desire to know more on this subject, make enquiry of fishermen in different localities, for no one person can possibly know all there is to know.

Be on your guard, of course, against dogs; even those in the sea. These the Apostle instructs us to beware of and to avoid even in the Church: 'Beware of the dogs, beware of the evil-workers.'[3] The mustela (marten), which on land is malodorous, is sweet-smelling in the sea. As a land animal it is capable of defending itself by its odor; as a marine animal, it affords no less pleasure when caught than when it is free.

I shall not refrain from addressing by name the thymallus,[4] endowed with the name of a flower. Wherever you are found, whether in the waters of the Ticino or of the beautiful Adige, a flower you are. A more forceful testimony to the fact that you give forth a sweet odor lies in the facetious remark: You smell like a fish or a flower. According to usage, therefore, the odor of the fish is identical with that of the flower. What is more pleasing than your appearance, more delightful than your sweetness, and more fragrant than your odor? You emit from your body an odor which may well be compared to that of honey.[5]

What shall I say of the tender qualities of the ravens and wolves of the sea? These wolves do not inspire fear in lambs. Such is the charm of water that its sea-lions flee from the

---

3 Phil. 3.2.
4 Probably a species of salmon.
5 Cf. Virgil, *Georgics* 4.169.

sea-calves, as follows from the prophetic utterance on the sanctity of the Church: 'Then the wolf and the lamb shall feed together, the lion and the ox shall eat straw.'[6] This is not to be wondered at, since even in the Church the effect of water [of baptism] is such that the guilt of the wicked, once it is washed away, has become assimilated to innocence.

Why should I make mention here, also, of the purple of kings which adorn their banquet halls and give color to their garments? What is venerated in kings is a gift of water;[7] of water, too, is the brilliance of their array. Add to this fact that the sea-pig was esteemed by the Jews, because there is nothing impure which water does not make clean. For this reason, that which is not in the same status as the land animal they cannot consider to be impure.

Chapter 3

(7) Innumerable are the ways, innumerable, too, are the species of fish. Various kinds[1] of larger fish, such as trout, produce eggs. They entrust these seeds to the fostering care of the waters. The water, therefore, like a fond mother of living things, gives them breath and life and carries out the function, as if it were a perpetual one, provided by the first primal law. Others, such as the female of the mustela, produce from their bodies living offspring. This is true of the sea-dogs and the monstrous whales, the dolphins, seals, and others of that species. If, perchance, when they have brought forth their offspring, they have a presentiment of some situation of extreme danger, in order to protect their youthful progeny and to allay their panic, they have recourse to

6 Isa. 65.25.

7 Cf. Virgil, *Aeneid* 1.637-642.

1 Cf. Isidore, *Etymol.* 12.6.6; A. C. Andrews, *TAPA* 86 (1955) 314 n. 43.

the following manifestation of maternal affection. Opening their mouths, they cause their offspring to attach themselves to their teeth, which in this case cause no harm. It is related, also, that they receive and hide their offspring within their bodies, even within the womb that bore them.

What human emotion can compare with this devotion on the part of fish for their progeny? We are satisfied to offer a kiss. It is not sufficient for them to open their wombs to receive their young. They invite them back without inflicting harm and reanimate them by the fostering heat of their bodies. They restore them by their breath, so that they live as two in one body. This they do until conditions are safe for their young or while by the interposition of their bodies they are able to defend their own brood from the perils which lie in wait for them. Who on beholding this devotion would not, even though he were able to attain it, consider himself to be their inferior by far? Who would not in his wonder be astonished that nature should retain among fishes that quality which men have lost? Many men have slain their long-wanted sons because of suspicion and hate of a step-mother. Others, as we read,[2] have eaten the flesh of their own children. A mother became the tomb of her own dear ones, whereas the womb of the parent fish serves as a sort of rampart to protect the innocent fosterlings sheltered within her womb.[3]

(8) Different species of fish, therefore, follow diverse customs. Some produce eggs; others give birth to offspring alive and already formed. Those which produce eggs do not, as birds do, build a nest. They do not undergo the fatigue resulting from an extended period of brooding; they do not at great discomfort to themselves give nourishment to their young. The egg falls and is received in the womb of mother

2 Cf. Deut. 28.53; 4 Kings 6.28.
3 Cf. Cicero, *De officiis* 1.97.

nature, who welcomes it as a fond nurse would, quickly forming it into a living being by the exercise of fostering care. No sooner is the egg given life by the touch of the parent that it falls and fish issues forth.

(9) And then what pure and untarnished generations follow without intermingling one after another, so that a thymallus produces a thymallus; a sea-wolf, a sea-wolf. The sea-scorpion, too, preserves unstained its marriage bed. Thus it shares in the chastity of its species, but not in its poisonous qualities, for the sea-scorpion does not sting. On the contrary, it has curative qualities.

Fish, therefore, know nothing of union with alien species. They do not have unnatural betrothals such as are designedly brought about between animals of two different species as, for instance, the donkey and the mare, or again the female donkey and the horse, both being examples of unnatural union. Certainly there are cases in which nature suffers more in the nature of defilment rather than that of injury to the individual. Man as an abettor of hybrid barrenness is responsible for this. He considers a mongrel animal more valuable than one of a genuine species. You mix together alien species and you mingle diverse seeds. You go to the extent of frequently forcing animals to a forbidden copulation—all this in the name of 'efficiency.' And because you cannot cause in man a lack of fecundity by a mingling of species, you take from man that with which he was born—you take what is virile from man and deny him the use of his sexual organs. In this way you make a man a eunuch, so effecting by your audacity what is denied to man by nature.

(10) How good a mother water can be we can learn from the considerations that I here propose. Man has taught that parents should repudiate their sons; he has taught separations, hates, and injuries. For your benefit learn of the close ties between parents and children.

Fish cannot live without water. They cannot endure separation from the association with their parents and from the nourishment provided for them. Nature has so ordained it that they die immediately when they are separated from their element. They do not live, as other animals do, by breathing this air of ours. Nature has not furnished them with the means of respiration; otherwise, they would not be able to keep living under water without breathing in air. Our air corresponds to their water. Just as air provides for us the means of living, water for them serves a similar function. Life leaves us the instant our organs for breathing are cut off, because we cannot even for a brief moment be deprived of the breath of life. When deprived of their sustenance in water, fish, too, cease to live.

(11) The reasons for this are clear. We have lungs which receive the air as it enters through the larger passages of the thorax. Being permeated with numerous pores, the lungs are able by the infusion of air to cool the internal heat. When the thorax receives nutriment, it separates what is superfluous from the health-giving juices and the blood; so, too, the lung is accessible in order that the intake of air may all the more readily reach it. Fish are furnished with gills which sometmes fold up and close, at other times expand and open up. In the process of closing and opening, the function of respiration is carried out as water is received and transmitted within.

Fish, therefore, have their own peculiar nature, which is not shared with other animals. They have distinctive habits and find their material for sustaining life in a very special and alien substance. Wherefore they do not receive nourishment from man and do not find, as land animals do, any pleasure and delight from the touch of man's hand, not even if they are kept alive in private fish-ponds.

Chapter 5

(12) What shall I say about the closely packed arrangement of the teeth of fish? They do not have what sheep and oxen possess, partial denture on one side of their gums. Rather, they are armed with teeth on both sides, because, if they delay in the act of swallowing their food in water, their prey could easily be washed and carried away by the water's action. For that reason their teeth are closely-packed and sharp so as to be able to bite and dispatch quickly their food and swallow it easily without delay. Hence, they do not chew the cud, as the scarus is said to do, if we are to believe those who either by chance or design have come to know such matters.

(13) To be sure, not even these have been able to escape experiencing acts of violence imposed on them by their fellows. The weaker everywhere are subject to the greed of the more powerful. The weaker one is, the more is he an object of prey. Many, it is true, feed on herbs and tiny worms, but there are those, also, who devour each other and feed on their own flesh. The lesser among them is the food of the greater and the greater in his turn is attacked by one stronger than he. The one who uses another as his prey becomes the food of still another. So it comes to pass that he who has devoured one fish is devoured in turn by another. They both meet in the same belly: the devourer and the devoured. The result is that together in the same entrails there is fellowship of victor and avenger.[1]

In their case, perhaps, this violent way of living has grown from inner compulsion, whereas with us it springs from avarice, not from nature. Again, fish are given to man for

1 For the vogue of this subject, see W. Parsons, *Traditio* 3 (1945) 382.

his use. They also constitute for us a pattern of the vices to be observed in our society. They serve, too, as an example to be avoided, lest the attack of the stronger on the weaker may present an occasion for the former to be exposed in turn to the violence of one who is still more powerful than he. In this way the person who does injury to another prepares for himself a snare for his own ultimate destruction.

(14) Those of you who attack another with deadly intent and those of you who drown the weak and pursue your victim even into the depths follow the example of this sort of fish. Be on your guard, while you are in pursuit of him, against an attack of a still stronger foe. The person who escapes your trap may well lead you into another. While he is in dread of the calamity in store for himself, your misfortune may first come before his eyes.

What is the difference between a rich man driven by his wicked lusts to absorb the patrimony of the weak and the fish called silurus whose belly is filled with the blood and flesh of smaller fish? 'The rich man died'[2] and his spoils were of no use to him. Why, even the infamy of his deeds of depredation have made his name a by-word. The silurus is taken and the futility of his predatory acts is revealed. How many are the fish found here who have themselves devoured others! And you, rich man, have in your conscience the fate of one who preyed on another, who had himself come into possession of a poor man's patrimony. In ruining him you added two patrimonies to your possessions, yet you are not satisfied. You say that you are taking vengeance on others when you are performing the same deed for which you are seeking vengeance. Thus, you are more unjust than the unjust, more iniquitous than the iniquitous, more avar-

2 Luke 16.22.

icious than the avaricious! See that you do not come to the same end as the fish. Beware of the hook and the net!

But you do not anticipate any resistance to your power. The silurus did not foresee that someone would throw out a fish-hook or stretch out a net. He believed that, if he were caught in the net, he would be able to break through it. Still he did not escape the fisherman's trident. He became emeshed in bonds that were too strong to permit him to escape. Without a doubt, the more serious the iniquities which he commits, the more difficult is it for a person to escape his crimes, until one day he is forced to pay for his evil deeds the debt which is certainly difficult for him to avoid.

Chapter 6

(15) We are justified, therefore, in comparing man to a fish. Listen to the reason for that statement: 'And the kingdom of heaven is like to a net cast into the sea that gathered in fish of every kind. When it was filled, they hauled it out and sitting down on the beach, they gathered the good fish into vessels, but threw away the bad. So will it be at the end of the world. The angels will go out and separate the wicked from among the just and will cast them into the furnace of fire.'[1]

Fish, then, are either good or bad. The good are preserved for their reward; the bad are straightway burned. The good fish is not ensnared by the net, but is lifted up. He is not slain or killed by the hook, but is suffused with the blood of a precious wound. In his mouth is found the

1 Matt. 13.47-50.

good price by which the apostolic tribute and the tax due to Christ may be paid.[2] For thus is it written in the words of the Lord: 'From whom do the kings of the earth receive tribute or customs; from their own sons or from others? And Peter replied: "from others." The Lord said: "Go to the sea and cast a hook and take the first fish that comes up. And opening its mouth thou wilt find a stater; take that and give it to them for me and for thee." '[3]

(16) Do not, then, hold in fear, my good fish, the hook of Peter. It does not kill. Rather, it consecrates. Do not underestimate yourself because your body is weak. You have in your mouth something which may serve as an offering for Peter and for Christ. Do not hold in fear the nets of Peter, to whom Jesus speaks:[4] 'Put out into the deep and lower your nets for a catch.' He does not throw out his net on the left, but on the right side as was commanded by Christ. Do not have fear for his catch, because it was to him that was said: 'Henceforth thou shalt catch men alive.' He threw out his net, therefore, and caught Stephen, who in the Gospel was the first to arise having in his mouth a stater of justice. Whence he called out with sure confession of faith: 'Behold I see the heavens opened and the Son of Man standing at the right hand of God.'[5] The Lord Jesus is a true representative of this fish, for He knew that in the mouth of the fish there was the tribute of His tax. Stephen, a generous witness of his faith, fulfilled the judgment and the teaching of Peter on him as well as the grace of Christ by a glorious martyrdom.

2 Cf. Matt. 17.26.
3 Matt. 17.24-26.
4 Luke 5.4.
5 Acts 7.55.

Chapter 7

(17) Do not be troubled by the fact that I have compared the Gospel to a sea. The sea is the Gospel on which Christ walked. It is the Gospel on which Peter, with the support of Christ's right hand, discovered a defense for his faith and the grace of stability, although he swerved from the way by denying Him. And it is precisely from the Gospel that Stephen arose. The Gospel is the sea in which the Apostles fish, into which is cast the net which is like the kingdom of heaven.[1] The Gospel is the sea in which the mysteries of Christ are revealed. The Gospel is the sea by which the Hebrew made his escape and the Egyptian was overwhelmed and slain.[2] The Gospel is the sea, because the Church is the bride of Christ and is also the plenitude of divine grace, which is poured over the seas, as the Prophet said: 'He hath founded it upon the seas.'[3] Man should immerse himself in the waters, because he is in truth a fish. Let not the floods of this world overwhelm you. If there is a storm, make for the high seas and the depths. If the weather is calm, play in the waves. If a tempest should come, beware lest the seething waters drive you on the rocky shore, for it is written: 'Be therefore wise as serpents.'[4]

(18) Since the example of the cunning serpent has been offered, let us be cunning, also, in regard to entrance into the state of matrimony and to remaining therein. Let us love this mutual association which has become our lot. If those who have at the time of their births lived in entirely

1 Matt. 13.47.
2 Cf. Exod. 14.21-24.
3 Ps. 23.2.
4 Matt. 10.16.

different regions yet agree to live together, if it happens that the husband should undertake a trip to a foreign land, no distance or abstinence should diminish the cherished love of the pair. The same law binds the present and the absent; the same bond of nature cements together the rights of conjugal love between the absent as well as between the present. The necks of both parties are linked together in the same beneficent yoke, even if one of them should find himself in regions entirely remote, because both parties share in the yoke of grace which is one of the spirit, not of the body.

When the viper, the deadliest kind of animal and the most cunning of the whole species of serpents, evinces a desire for copulation, he searches for a sea-murena already known to him or he seeks for a new mate. Proceeding toward the shore, he makes his presence known by a hissing sound, whereby he invites conjugal embrace. The sea-murena does not repulse the appeal and yields to the poisonous serpent the desired enjoyment of their conjugal bond.

What is the purpose of such a discussion as this, if it does not mean that we should put up with our married partner and, if he is away from home, that we should await his return to his family? Although he may be cruel, deceitful, uncouth, wayward, and drunken, can this be more intolerable than the poison which is no obstacle to the sea-murena in dealing with her mate? When invited, she does not fail to respond and embraces the slimy serpent with great affection. The male endures your defects and your feminine levities. Can you not bear with your husband? Adam was deceived by Eve, not Eve by Adam.[5] It is right that he whom the woman enticed to do wrong should assume the office of

5 Cf. 1 Tim. 2.14.

guide, lest he fall once more because of feminine instability.

But he is repugnant and uncouth! Yes, but he pleased you at one time. Do you think that a husband should be chosen more than once? The ox and the horse look for and cherish their mates, and, if a substitution takes place, they are unable to carry the yoke together. They feel that they do not form an integral part of the team. You repudiate your yoke-mate and think that a frequent change should be made. If one day he fails you, you bring in a rival and straightway without knowing why, yet knowingly, you do violence to your sense of modesty.

The viper searches for his absent mate, calls to her with a hiss of invitation. When he feels his mate approaching, he spits forth the poison with due regard for his consort and the nuptial rite. Why do you repel your husband coming back from a far country? The viper gazes upon the sea in an endeavor to find his consort. You put obstacles in the path of your husband. You stir up the poison of litigation. You reject him and in the conjugal embrace emit dread poison, scorning your husband and putting to shame your nuptial bond.

(19) As for the man—for we can apply this example to him, also: lay aside the inordinate emotions of your heart and the rudeness of your manners when you meet your patient wife. Get rid of your obstinacy when your gentle consort offers you her love. You are not a master, but a husband. You have not acquired perchance a handmaid, but a wife. God designed you to be a guide to the weaker sex, not a dictator. Be a sharer in her activities. Be a sharer in her love. The viper pours forth his poison; can you not get rid of your hardness of heart? Although you have by nature a severity of character, you ought to temper it in consideration of your

married state and control your tendency to rudeness by holding in respect your conjugal relationship.

There are occasions for sin. Do not seek the bed that belongs to another. Do not by guile enter into another union. Adultery is a grievous offense. It does violence to nature. At the beginning God formed two creatures, Adam and Eve; that is, man and wife. He formed woman from the man; this is, from the rib of Adam. He bade them both to live in one body and in one spirit. Why, then, do you cleave one body apart? Why do you divide one spirit? That is an adulterous offense against nature. It is a lesson which is taught us by the willing union of sea-murena and viper, a union not grounded on similarity of species, but on ardent desire. Give ear, men! He who desires association with such a serpent may be likened to one who seeks occasion to have adulterous relations with another man's wife. It can be said that he has the very traits of a serpent. He hastens to the viper who embraces him in the devious ways of lubricity, not in the righteous ways of love. He hastens to one who takes up again his poison like the viper and who is said to consume again the poison, once the act of copulation has been completed. The adulterer is like a viper. Hence Solomon says that when a man is intoxicated his passions are aroused. His body is swollen as if bitten by a snake and his poison is spread abroad like a basilisk's. That you may realize that he has spoken of an adulterer, he added these words: 'Thy eyes shall behold strange women and thy mouth shall utter perverse things.'[6]

(20) Do not form the opinion that we have based our argument on contradictions, in that we have made use of the example of a viper in order to point both a good and a

6 Prov. 22.33.

bad moral. It serves the purposes of instruction to bring forward a two-fold consideration. On the one hand, we are like the serpent in being ashamed to be loyal to our beloved. Again, by severing the bonds of holy matrimony we prefer the harmful and the lubricous, as in the case of union with a serpent, to what is really and truly salutary.

Chapter 8

(21) As we have entered upon a discussion on the trait of craftiness, whereby a man strives to circumvent and deceive his brother and to contrive new ways of deception, thus trapping by guile and trickery a person whom he cannot overcome by force, it is not my intention to overlook the well-known deceitful character of the polypus. This animal, coming upon a rock on a shallow coast, fixes itself firmly on it. At the same time, it assumes by subtle art the color of the rock and conceals its back in a similar fashion. In this manner a great number of fish, unsuspecting any fraud and innocently believing that what they see is a rock, are taken into this artfully contrived trap to be waylaid by the tentacles of the polypus.

The prey thus makes its approach without external compulsion. It is captured by such methods as one would expect of those who often change their nature and stir up diverse means of ill,[1] so as to tempt the minds and hearts of all severally. Some boast of their continence when in converse with the continent. Associating with the intemperate, they show themselves to be devoid of chastity and to wallow in the troughs of intemperance. Those who see or hear them yield easily to their influence and for that reason soon fall into temptation, being unable to turn aside or avoid what

1 Cf. Virgil, *Aeneid* 7.338 *(Allecto).*

is likely to injure them. Weakness, when cloaked in the veil of benignity, can inflict harm of a more serious nature. And so we should be aware of those who extend the tentacles of their deceit far and wide or those who assume various shapes. These people are like the polypus that has manifold entanglements and many astute ways by which it can ensnare whatever falls into the rocky shores wherein we are beguiled.

(22) What tricks are displayed by the crab in its eager search for food! The oyster is a special objective in its quest for a delicious banquet. But its eagerness for food is tempered by its sense of the possibility of being involved in danger, for the chase is as difficult as it is perilous. Its difficulty lies in the fact that the flesh of its victim is enclosed in a shell of more than usual solidity. Just as in compliance with divine power the delicacy of the flesh of its prey has been stoutly defended by nature which nourishes and fosters it in the form of an encircling rampart, so all in vain are the crab's attacks, because the closed oyster cannot be opened by any display of force. There is the danger, too, that the oyster may hook it in its claws. Therefore, the crab resorts to artifice and contrives new ways of waylaying its prey.

Accordingly, since every living being is attracted by sentiments of pleasure, the crab looks for an occasion when the oyster, finding a place protected from the wind and within range of the sun's rays, opens wide its double doors and unbars the bolts of its shell in order to enjoy to the full the open air. At that moment the crab, by stealthily injecting a pebble within the shell of the oyster, prevents it from being closed. Having acquired an entrance in this manner, the crab insterts its claws without danger to itself and devours the flesh within the shell.

(23) There are men who, like the crab, exercise surreptitiously their guile on others and fortify their own weaknesses

by the use of certain inherent characteristics. Thus they weave a web of deceit around their brethren and find their sustenance in another's anxieties.

Be content with what is your own and do not let your well-being be based on doing harm to your neighbor. You may find your livelihood in the simplicity of innocence. The man in possession of his own good knows nothing of waylaying others. He is not inflamed by the desires of the avaricious man, whose every gain is at the expense of virtue and a further incentive to cupidity. Therefore, 'should he come to know his blessings,'[2] the poor man is truly happy who lives righteously in a manner which is to be preferred to all the treasures of the world, because 'better a little with the fear of the Lord than great treasures without fear.' How much under these circumstance does man need to support life? If you go beyond that little and seek that, also, which others find pleasure in possessing, that, too, has little to commend it: 'It is better to be invited to herbs with love than to a fatted calf with hatred.'[3]

Let us use our talents, therefore, for the acquisition of grace and the attainment of salvation, not for the circumvention of others who harm us not. We may well make use of examples taken from the sea, not for the purpose of exposing others to danger, but to make ourselves more perfect in the way of salvation.

Chapter 9

(2) The urchin, a tiny, common and despicable animal—I refer to the sea variety—is frequently used by navigators as a sign of a threatening storm or as a harbinger of clear

2 Virgil, *Georgics* 2.458.
3 Prov. 15.16,17.

weather. The reason for this lies in the fact that at the approach of a wind storm this little creature takes hold of a fairly large pebble and uses it as a sort of ballast or anchor so as to avoid being carried out of the water.[1] Thus it balances and directs itself by means of an alien weight, not by its innate strength. This sign gives an indication to the sailor that a storm is brewing. Accordingly, he takes precautions lest the sudden approach of a hurricane may find him unprepared.

What follower of the occult sciences, astrologer, or Chaldean can reveal in a comparable way the course of the stars, the movement of the heavens, and of the zodiacal signs? By what natural instinct has the tiny creature acquired this art? What teacher has instructed it? Who served as its interpreter of augural lore? Men behold the turmoil in the air and are often deceived, because at times the winds rush in without bringing on a tempest. The sea-urchin is not beguiled. Never at any time do its special signs fail to bring results.

(25) Whence did this tiny creature acquire such sure knowledge of the future? As there is nothing in the animal itself which can make possible such foreknowledge, be assured that it, too, has obtained the gift of prescience through the loving-kindness of the Lord of all things.

For, if God so clothes the grass of the field that we are struck with admiration; if He feeds the birds of the air;[2] 'if he provides food for the raven, when her young ones cry to God';[3] if He has given to women skill in the art of weaving; if the spider, who so artfully and delicately 'hangs on the doorway her loose-woven nets,'[4] is not left bereft of

1 Cf. Virgil, *Georgics* 4.194-196. (bees).
2 Cf. Matt. 6.26,30.
3 Job 38.41.
4 Virgil, *Georgics* 4.247.

wisdom; if He has given strength to the horse and sends forth terror from his mane, so that he exults in the field and laughs in the face of kings as he smells the battle afar off and is aroused by the sound of the trumpet[5]—if He has filled with the largesse of His wisdom these manifold irrational creatures as well as the grass and lilies of the field,[6] who can doubt but that He has distributed this gift of foreknowledge also to the sea-urchin?

He has left nothing unexplored, nothing unrevealed. He sees all who nourishes all. He fills all things with wisdom who, as it is written, 'has made all things in wisdom.'[7] And so, if He has not neglected the sea-urchin as beyond the range of His visitation; if He has care of it and moulds it so as to enable it to see signs of what is to come—if that is true, has He no care of you and yours? Surely He has, as He testifies in the words of His own holy Scripture: 'Look at the birds of the air'; if He feeds them, 'are not you of much more value than they'?[8] For, if God so clothes 'the grass of the field which flourishes today and tomorrow is thrown into the oven, how much more you, O you of little faith?'[9]

Chapter 10

(26) Are we to suppose that fish without a special gift of nature possess also that instinct whereby each species has allotted to it a definite space which no one species may leave and into which no other species may enter? What geometer has plotted the bounds of these habitations, never at any time to be broken? We have heard of one who has

5 Cf. Job 39.19-25.
6 Cf. Matt. 6.28.
7 Ps. 103.24.
8 Matt. 6.26; Luke 12.28.
9 Matt. 6.30.

measured land, never of one who has applied measurements to the sea. Yet fish know their own confines, which are not bounded by city walls, by gates, or by buildings; neither are they marked as in the boundaries of fields. But each has a terminal limit of space in accordance with its need, so that only so much is given to each as to satisfy completely its wants —not so much as its unregulated greed can claim for itself.

There is, if I may say so, a law of nature that one should seek only what suffices for nourishment and that the allotment 'which thy fathers have set'[1] should be in proportion to the need for food. One species of fish breeds and flourishes in one arm of the sea; another species, in another. Hence, you will not find different species of fish mixed together. What in one place is abundant is, contrariwise, lacking elsewhere. This bay is the haunt of the *cephali*. In another bay we find the sea-wolves. In still another live certain species of crustaceans. Each is not free to wander as it pleases, yet the passage is not impeded by intervening mountain ranges nor by river channels. Rather, by force of habit each one is by nature constrained to keep itself within the bounds of its native habitat and to consider suspect a fish that leaves the regions of its fellows.

(27) But for us, men, there are far different sentiments. We desire change for various reasons: a wish for travel, for release from daily associations. We long for the approval of strangers and to remove the age-long boundaries which our ancestors have set up, adding estate to estate, household to household.

The earth alone does not suffice. We use the sea itself for our foundations. On the other hand, in compliance with individual whims, the land is excavated and sea water is brought in so as to form islands or straits for men's use.[2] Men

1 Prov. 22.31.
2 Cf. Horace, *Odes* 2.18.17-26.

claim the sea for themselves by right of ownership and boast that they have subjected fishes like slaves to a condition of servitude. This, they say, is my bay; that one belongs to another. Like sovereigns, they divide the elements among themselves. For some people, oysters are bred in water. For others, fish are enclosed in a fish pond.

The sea does not suffice for their luxuriant living. They must have reserve stores of oysters. They keep a reckoning of the age of each oyster bed. Receptacles are built for the fish in case the rich man's table may not be replenished from the sea. How they are all ears when the word 'neighbor' is mentioned! How eagerly will they gaze on his possessions! What plans enter their minds day and night to take something away from their neighbors! 'Shall they alone dwell in the midst of the earth?' exclaims the Prophet.[3] The Lord is aware of this and waits to punish them.

(28) How alien to the fish is this monstrous greed! Men seek after what is remote in the realm of nature. They are familiar with the seas beyond the bounds of the known world. There no islands intervene, nor are there bodies of land either in that region or situated beyond that point. For that reason, in that place where the wide extent of water precludes every desire to gaze upon it and every sentiment of boldness to sail thereon for the sake of gain, there the whale is said to have his lair. There, too, live a huge species of fish, reported to be mountainous in size by those who have ventured to approach and see them. This huge fish lives tranquilly there, remote from islands and uncontaminated by the nearness of port towns. They have their separate habitats and locations all their own. They are unaffected by the presence of neighboring boundaries and do not desire frequent change of place and to flit aimlessly to

3 Isa. 5.8.

and fro.[4] Rather, they cherish their habitat as their native land and consider it a delight to dwell therein.[5] They have selected these regions in order to pass their lives in solitary fashion, remote from interference and from contact with other creatures.

(29) There is another species of fish which changes its location, not because of natural instability, but from the necessity of spawning. They formulate a plan and design to reach a certain place at a time of the year which is right and opportune. Gathering together, as if with joint purpose, from many places and from diverse inlets of the sea, they go out in search of the north wind, swimming in massed array. Impelled, as it were, by a law of nature, they hasten to their familiar haunts in the northern regions. If you were to behold this huge school of fish on the move, you would have the impression of encountering an ocean current—such is the force of their onward rush through the waters, such is their mad desire to reach the Black Sea through the straits of Propontis.

Who announces these places, who prescribes these seasons for the fish? Who has arranged their itinerary for them, their plan for mass movement, their destination, and the time of their return? Men, of course, have their commanders whose orders are waited, whose watchwords are agreed upon, whose edicts are made known to the people of the provinces for the purposes of assembly, and whose dispatches are sent to the military tribunes, fixing the day—notwithstanding all these preparations, many people find it impossible to come on the appointed days. What commanding officer has given the order? What teacher has given this this instruction, what surveyor has plotted the journey, what guide has led the way, so that no obstacle is encountered?

4 Cf. Lucretius 3.1057,1058.

5 Eccle. 3.2.

But I am aware of the identity of the Commander, who by reason of divine dispensation infuses His orders in the senses of all created things, who, without the use of words, allows mute animals to follow the directions of natural instinct. His instruction reaches even to the smallest creatures; it is not limited to the largest. Fishes follow a divine law, whereas men contravene it. Fishes duly comply with the celestial mandates, but men make void the precepts of God. Because a fish is mute and deprived of reason, is it, therefore, an object of contempt in your eyes? See to it that you do not begin to be more contemptible to yourself, if you prove yourself to be more irrational than the irrational creatures.

What is more rational than this migration of fish, a procedure which becomes less intelligible as we recount it than it is when we look at the facts themselves. They advance in summer time to the straits of the Black Sea because the water in this region is sweeter than in others. The sun does not linger in those waters as long as it does elsewhere. There is not, therefore, a loss of sweet and drinkable water. Who is not aware of the fact that marine animals often find delight in fresh water? Hence it happens that different species of fish are frequently caught while they are on the way to spawn in the upper reaches of a river.

This, therefore, may be the reason why they manifest preference for the Black Sea. It may well be, too, that the prevailing north wind tempers the summer heat there. Again, they select that region as a more suitable one for the task of bringing up their offspring. Their young, in fact, can hardly endure exposure to the vicissitudes of a different climate. The gentle clemency of the climate in that locality fosters their growth. Accordingly, when their objective is achieved, all return together to the point from which they departed.

(30) Let us reflect on the reason for this. The Black Sea

forms a body of water which is exposed to the north wind and to other winds of the most violent nature. Hence, when a severe storm rages and tempests are brewing in that region, sand is churned up from the deep, as the turbidness of the water there gives proof. This condition is intensified by the force of the wind. The water becomes more dense and presents, we can be sure, an intolerable situation not only for sailors, but even for animal life in the sea. An additional reason is offered by the condition of the Black Sea itself. Into it flow numerous and mighty rivers. Hence, this body of water is very cold in the winter season and freezes over, augmented by the continual inflow. Wherefore the fish, acting like supreme lords of the waters, seek to take advantage of the cooler air there in the summer season. When they have enjoyed this pleasant temperature, they hasten back once more in order to avoid the wintry blasts. So they flee from the bitter weather of the northern regions and take themselves into other bodies of water where the winds are kindlier and calmer or where a more temperate sun can bring spring-like weather.

The fish knows 'the time to be born.'[6] Solomon in his wisdom declared this to be a great mystery, this knowledge of the time to go and the time to return, the time for performance and the time for change. Fish are not deceived in this knowledge, because they follow an instinct of nature, the true teacher of loyal devotion, and not the deliberations of reason and rhetorical argumentation. Hence, all living creatures have a prescribed time for bringing forth offspring. By man alone are such times undetermined and ill-planned. The other creatures seek out a season of clement weather. It falls to women alone to give birth in seasons of inclemency. An unsettled and arbitrary desire to produce offspring leads to an uncertain time for childbirth.

6 Eccle. 3.2.

Fish cross over so many seas in order to bestow some benefit on their species. We, too, cross over manifold seas. But how much more commendable is a voyage which is undertaken, not for the sake of material profit, but for the love of one's offspring! Loyal devotion is the propelling motive in their case. In our case the motive is commercial gain. They bring back with them their own progeny, more precious to them than any kind of merchandise. Urged by a dire lust for gain, we bring back a cargo that is far from atoning for the dangers involved. They make an effort to reach their home, while we abandon it. They, as a result of their migration, acquire an addition to their species. We, on the other hand, in the course of navigation are subject to a decrease.

(31) When we behold this preparation made with such keenness of instinct for a ritualistic migration to the north for the production of a numerous progeny, and again when we note that other marine animals possess such power in their tiny bodies that they are able to bring to a stop mighty ships sailing along under full sail, who would then deny that such an instinct and capacity have been infused in them by a divine power? We have reference here to a little fish called *echeneis*, which is said to slow up without effort a huge ship. The vessel seems to be adrift and, as it were, rooted in the sea, for at times this fish keeps the ship motionless. Do you suppose that this marine animal has such potential power without the aid of divine intervention?

What shall I say of the sword-fish, the saw-fish, the sea-dog, the whale, or the hammer-fish? What shall I say of the turtle which inflicts a sting even when dead? Just as a person who treads on the still palpitating head of a viper is said to suffer a more serious injury—in fact, an incurable wound[7]—than he would from poison, so, too, a turtle when

7 Cf. Ovid, *Metamorphoses* 1.190; 10.189.

dead is reported to inflict a more dangerous wound from its sting than it does when alive. Again, the hare, which is a timid animal on land, is formidable as a sea animal and causes infection which spreads rapidly and is not easily cured. The Creator has so ordained it that not even at sea are you to be quite safe from lurking perils. Because of these few harmful creatures you should take your stand like a sentry on guard, armed always with the weapons of faith and the shield of devotion, awaiting the protection of your Lord.

Chapter 11

(32) We wish, now, to return to the Atlantic Ocean. What whales are found there, of huge bulk and measureless size! If they were to float on the surface of the sea, you would imagine that they were islands or extremely high mountains whose peaks reach to the sky! These animals are said to appear, not on the coast or on shore, but in the depths of the Atlantic Ocean. To catch sight of them sailors are enticed to risk navigation within those regions. But these elemental mysteries are not likely to be faced without experiencing mortal terror!

(33) Now let us rise upward from the depths of the sea. Let our discourse emerge a little therefrom and take itself to higher regions. Let us take note of matters which are pleasing in themselves and which also have come under the observation of many people. We hear of water changing into masses of salt so solid that an axe is frequently required to cut it. In fact, we do not need to marvel at what is reported of salt in Britain. This takes on the appearance and the dazzling splendor of marble itself and, in addition, is a salutary aid to bodily needs of food and drink. Note, too, how the not unpleasing coral is only a sea plant which, when

exposed to the air, becomes solid as a stone. We see how nature has inserted in the oyster a highly valuable pearl, which by the action of sea water has become a solid particle within the oyster's soft flesh. Wealth which is hardly attainable by kings lies open to common gaze along our shores. It is found in, and gathered from, rugged rock and cliff.

Water also produces a 'golden fleece' and the sea coasts are the source of a wool which is similar in appearance to the metal just mentioned. Its color has not been duplicated up to now by those who apply to woolen goods different types of dye. For that reason human ingenuity is unable to compete with the natural products of the sea. We are aware of the care and attention given to the less costly sheep's wool. No matter how perfect it is, under no circumstances do we find wool that comes naturally dyed. Here is a color that is natural—a color never yet approached by the application of dyes. And to think that this [golden] fleece is a fish! Moreover, the shell-fish that yields the purple which distinguishes a king is itself a marine animal.

(34) What delightful scenes in meadow or garden can equal the prospect of a light blue sea? Your flowers may flash forth a golden hue, but the wool of the sea has its golden refulgence, too! Whereas the colors of the flowers quickly fade, the other retains its hue for many a day! From afar we note the lily's brilliance in the garden. From afar, too, we see the flashing sails of the ships. A breath of perfume follows one; a breeze, the other. What use does a leaf supply to equal the advantage of the commerce of ships at sea? Lilies give us sweet odors for the pleasure of our senses, whereas sailing ships bring sustenance for mankind.

Add to this the picture of the flying fish and the frollicking dolphin. Moreover, there is the additional delight in the roar of the resounding billows, in the sight of ships flitting to shore or sailing out to sea. 'Even as when from the barriers the chariots stream forth'[1]—what an occasion for delight and enthusiasm on the part of the spectators! Yet, in contrast to the ships of commerce, the steed runs to no purpose. The latter, because devoid of cargo, runs in vain.[2] The other has its holds filled with sustenance for men.

What is more to be desired than what is speeded along, not by the impulse of a whip, but by a breeze, where there is nothing to hinder one's progress, where all is favorable, and where no one who reaches his goal is a loser.[3] All the boats which come to land are given a wreath. The palm is the prize for a successful voyage and victory is the reward for their homecoming. What a difference between the outgoing course and the return! One shows a cautious pace. The other is affected by the urge to make the goal. Add to this the sight of the shore with its line of boats awaiting a breeze from the skies as a signal for the start. Whereas the charioteer at the conclusion of his race is granted mere empty applause, the boatmen take part in giving thanks for their safe return.

(35) How shall I adequately speak of Jonas, whom the whale swallowed to grant him life and to return him to his activity as a prophet? The water restored to him the understanding which the earth had taken away. He who grieved when on land began to sing psalms in the belly of the whale. Again, the redemption of both elements is not lost sight of. The salvation of the earth had its forerunner in the sea, because the marvelous act of Jonas stands for that of the Son of Man. As Jesus lay 'in the heart of the earth,'[4] so was Jonas in the whale's belly. There is salvation in both elements. However, the sea furnishes a more significant example of

1 Virgil, *Georgics* 1.512.
2 Cf. Ps. 32.17.
3 Cf. Virgil, *Aeneid* 5.268,269.
4 Matt. 12.39.

piety, since a fish gave welcome to him whom men had repelled and has preserved, in the person of Jonas, Him whom men have crucified. Peter, too, weakened when on the sea,[5] but he did not fall. What he had admitted on the waters, however, he denied on land.[6] And so, in the former occasion he was accorded a hand-clap as to one who was loyal; in the latter case, because of his forgetfulness, he was met with a look of rebuke.[7]

But now let us request the Lord that our words, like those of Jonas, be cast on the land and not be suffered to float any longer on the sea. And it was well that the gourd-vine sprang up so as to shield us from misfortunes. But the earth, now parched by the advancing sun, warns us to seek rest, lest our minds begin to suffer from the earth's heat and our words, too, may fail us. Be assured that water has been given to us, more than it was to the Ninevites, as a source for the remission of sins.[8]

5 Cf. Matt. 14.30.
6 Cf. Matt. 26.69-75.
7 Cf. Luke 22.61.
8 Cf. Jonas 4.6-11.

THE EIGHTH HOMILY

Chapter 12

He remained silent for a little while and then resumed his discourse.

(36) We have shied away, beloved brethren, from the necessity of dealing with birds, and our discussion on this subject might have taken wing along with the birds! It follows, somehow, as a natural consequence that those who hold some object in view or who desire to give expression to it in words are apt to take on the qualities of that which they behold or of that which they express orally. The result is that we linger, when exposed to what is more than usually inactive, and our observation takes on speed with the swift action of the object in view. This variability extends, also, to the area of literary style. Accordingly, at the moment when I am on my guard lest objects sunk deep in the sea may escape my observation—at such a moment the entire race of winged creatures has already escaped my ken. While I was bent over in diligent examination of the lowest depths of the sea, I paid no heed to the aerial flights of birds and

not even the shadow of 'nimble wings'[2] flashing in the waters has caused me to verge from my task.

In fact, when I arrived at the point where I believed that I had exhausted my subject, and when I felt that I had completed the fifth day, this reflection came into my mind: It is customary for the birds at nesting time 'to charm the sky with song,'[3] in joy that their allotted task is done. This usually happens, following, as it were, a ritual pattern, at dawn and at sunset, when the birds sing the praises of their Creator, at the moment of transition from day to night or from night to day. By such an omission I would have lost a mighty incentive for arousing our religious devotion. For what person of natural human sensibility would not blush to terminate the day without a ritual singing of the psalms, since even the tiniest bird ushers in the approach of day and night with customary devotion of sweet song?

(37) Let us return, therefore, to a discussion of the winged flock. We have almost lost sight of them as, like eagles they have taken flight, and hidden themselves amid the clouds. We realize that our pen should be recalled to the task when our eyes, laved in the waters, reached from the sea upwards to the sky and there beheld the birds 'borne through the empty air.'[4] You who are snarers of my words will act as judges as to whether they have flown off with better purpose or whether they have fallen into your nets to add to your good fortune.

I am not disturbed in my discussion on birds by any possibility of boredom in your part—a boredom which was not in evidence when I examined the depths. Otherwise, some of us would have nodded off during my sermon, only to be awakened by the song of birds. But I surely have no

2 Virgil, *Aeneid* 6.15.
3 *Ibid.* 7.34.
4 Virgil, *Georgics* 3.109.

doubt that those who kept awake amid the mute company of fish will be unable to fall asleep when the birds sing, such is their charm to inspire wakefulness. A subject which might well have been passed over in our treatment of the third part of created living beings should not, in fact, be regarded as an indifferent one. The fact that there are three races of living creatures those of the earth, the air, and the water—is not open to doubt. Therefore it has been written: 'Let the waters bring forth reptiles, living creatures according to their kind, and winged creatures, flying over the earth along the firmament of heaven, each according to its kind.'[5]

(38) We are recalled to our previous theme like forgetful travelers who, because they have heedlessly passed their destination, are compelled to return. He, however, is a good traveler who makes up for the loss of time involved in retracing his steps by corresponding speed in the rest of his journey. I believe that I should act especially in this way now that I have come to the subject of birds, whose speedy flight often dazzles the eyes of men.[6] Why should one see fit to linger in those subjects in which swiftness generally brings pleasure? Let our discussion get on its pathless and unwonted way of literary composition. Let it resound and 'ring with the musical song of birds.'[7]

(39) But where shall I find the swan's song which gives us pleasure when sung in moments of grave danger, even to the point of imminent death? Where shall we find those strains of natural chant which emanate even from marshy regions—strains of most tuneful and delightful music? Where shall I find the voice of the parrot and the sweet song of the blackbird? Would that the nightingale were to give forth a song to arouse a sleeper from his slumber! That is the bird

5 Gen. 1.20-24.
6 A Ciceronian expression; cf. *De senectute* 12.42.
7 Virgil, *Georgics* 2.328.

accustomed to signal the rising of the sun at dawn and to spread abroad joy more penetrating than morning light. Still, if sweetness is lacking to their song, we have with us the moaning turtle-dove, the cooing pigeon,[8] and 'the raven who with deep tones calls down the rain.'[9] Wherefore let us illustrate as far as we can in our discourse the 'haunts of the birds'[10] in the countryside, relying on the knowledge which we have garnered from rustic folk.

Chapter 13

(40) Now that we have discussed creeping creatures in the water, it is a highly difficult task to transfer our discourse at a moment's notice upwards to the birds in the sky. Let us, then, first speak of these birds which frequent the seas and the rivers. With their aid we can emerge. Accordingly, let us begin our discussion with the halcyon. This is a sea bird that is to be found bringing up her young on the shore, depositing her eggs in the sand about mid-winter. This is the time allotted for the hatching, when the sea is at its stormiest and the waves make their most destructive inroads on the shore. Wherefore the graciousness of this bird should appear all the more evident because of the periodic and unexpected recurrence of calm weather, because atmospheric conditions suddenly take on a milder tinge at the moment when the eggs are laid, when the sea is still stormy. The stormy blasts and violent winds subside while the halcyon broods over her eggs, 'when the sea was at peace and still.'[1] The eggs are hatched in seven days. At the end of that period the young

8 Cf. Virgil, *Eclogues* 1.57,58.
9 Virgil, *Georgics* 1.388.
10 *Ibid.* 2.430.

1 Virgil, *Eclogues* 2.26.

brood leaves the protecting shell. At this point there is another period of seven days, during which the fledglings are nourished until they grow to maturity. Do not wonder at the fact that such a slight amount of time is needed for their growth, because very few days are necessary for the completion of the brooding stage. So much significance has been accorded by divine power to this tiny bird that sailors keep on the lookout for these fourteen days, which they call 'halycon days,' during which they expect calm weather and dread no more the tumult of the raging tempest.

(41) 'Are you not of more value than the sparrow?'[2] Thus the Lord spoke. If, therefore, at the sight of a tiny bird the sea rises suddenly and as suddenly subsides, and if in the midst of winter's cruel storms and tempests a tranquillity, permeating all the elements, 'sweeps the clouds from the sky,'[3] quickly calming the waves—if this is true, do you realize, you, a man made to the image of God, how much hope you ought to have, if only in your eagerness for a pious life you would imitate that little bird's trusting confidence. The halcyon is not turned aside from her purpose at the sight of the approaching tempest and of the winds that rage at winter's onrush—rather, she is impelled all the more. Hence she lays her eggs on the shore where the sand, still wet from the retreating waves, welcomes them. She does not dread the rising waves, which she beholds as they break on the shore with threatening sound.

(42) And that you may not conclude that the halcyon shows slight regard for her eggs, she builds her nest without delay at the very place where she laid her eggs. She broods over her offspring and, while the waves pound the shore, shows no fear for her own safety. Rather, she enstrusts herself to the winds and waves, secure in the beneficence of

2 Luke 12.7.
3 Horace, *Odes* 1.7.15.

God. That is not all. Many more days still remain to complete the period of growth. During this time she has no fear that the tranquillity of the perfidious sea will be broken. She relies on her own merits, based now on the regular pattern of nature. She does not hide her brood in some secret corner of a house or in a cave. On the contrary, she entrusts them to the bare, cold ground. She does not protect them from the cold, but considers that they will be safer with the comfort of divine warmth, by means of which she may all other things disdain.

Who is there among us who does not cover his little ones with garments and who does not protect and shield them within the walls of his home? Who is there who does not close the windows on all sides to prevent even the slighest breeze to enter? And while we so anxiously attend to clothing and warmth, we are therefore depriving them of the protecting cover of celestial clemency, whereas the halcyon, by casting her brood out naked, has thereby clothed them with vesture that is divine.

(43) I shall not overlook the diving gulls. They have acquired that name from their frequent diving operations. They are always able by their diving to gather signs of the approach of a wind storm. When they see a threatening tempest, they quickly 'fly back from mid-ocean' and withdraw 'while their screams rebound on the shore'—to safety! What shall I say of the waterfowl—a bird that finds delight in the depths of the sea? Soon he sports in the shallows, after taking refuge from the sea's upheaval which he foresaw. And the heron that is found to frequent the marshes 'quits his familiar haunts' and, fearful of the rain storms, 'soars above the clouds' to escape the storms generated in that region. Let us take note of the different varieties of sea birds, who at the coming of a wind storm take refuge in marshy regions, where they find a safer and for the

moment a more pleasant habitation. They rummage round after their familiar food in some remote corner of the world.[4]

(44) Who does not marvel at the nightly sentry watches of the geese, who give evidence of their vigilance by their constant cackling? That was the way in which they defended even the Roman Capitol from the Gauls. You, Rome, rightfully owe to them the preservation of your empire. Your gods were sleeping, but the geese were awake. And so on those festal days you perform sacrifices, not to Jupiter, but to a goose; your gods give way to the geese, who were once their defenders, as they came to realize. The gods themselves might have been taken prisoners were it not for their aid.[5]

Chapter 14

(44) After our description of the various fishes we have appropriately taken up next in order the subject of those birds that are also associated with water, in so far as they, too, in a similar fashion find pleasure in the art of swimming. Hence these birds seem to be primarily related to the fish species, since each has a certain element in common, that of being able to swim. The second elements which fishes and birds also share lies in the fact that the art of flying is an aspect of that of swimming. As a fish cuts through the water in the act of swimming, so a bird 'cuts the air'[1] in his swift flight. Both species are provided in a similar way with tails and 'with the oarage of wings.'[2] So the fish directs himself forward and advances to distant points by the aid of his wings [fins]. He uses his tail as a rudder in order to guide

4 Virgil, *Georgics* 1.361,362,364,365; cf. 383,384.
5 Cf. Servius on *Aeneid* 8.652; see *Speculum* 2 (1927) 477.

1 Virgil, *Georgics* 1.406.
2 A Virgilian expression; cf. *Aeneid* 6.19.

himself or change his route by a sudden movement from one area to another. Birds also exercise their wings in the air as if they were floating on water, using them in the way one would use one's arms. By use of their tails they are able to direct themselves upward or downward at will.

Hence, while all of these species follow the same pattern, they are but complying with the divine precept that places the origin of both in water. For God said: 'Let the waters bring forth reptiles, living creatures according to their kind, and winged creatures flying above the earth along the firmament of heaven, each according to its kind.'[3] Not without reason, therefore, do both species have the innate faculty of swimming, since both have their origin in water.

(46) While, of course, both the slimy snake and all species of serpents—who derive their name from the fact that they creep, not walk—and the dragon, too, like the general run of fish are without legs, nevertheless there is no species of bird devoid of the use of legs. They need to obtain food from the earth. For this reason they use the support that legs give as a necessary aid in acquiring their natural food. Accordingly, other birds like the hawk and the eagle, who live by plunder, are provided with claws to catch their prey. Others make fitting use of them in the acts of either walking or of searching for food.

(47) There is one name for 'bird,' but there are various species. Who can know them all or hold their names in memory? There are birds, for example, who live on flesh. Hence, they have sharp claws, a curved and sharp beak, and are swift on the wing. Thus they live by plunder, and are able to lay hold of what they pursue, and with their beaks and claws eviscerate it. There are birds, also, that search for and find their food in seeds. Others search for different kinds of food as they come upon them.

3 Gen. 1.20-23.

There is diversity, too, in the way in which they group together. Those birds that are intent on plunder are devoid of this tendency. They do not act in common, because of their rapacity and the necessity of snaring their prey. Hence they disassociate themselves from groups—for greed avoids participation—moreover, a large flock would easily betray its own purposes. For birds of this sort there is no group life except that of conjugal relationship. This is the mode of life among the eagles and hawks. On the other hand, birds such as doves, cranes, starlings, crows, ravens, and even thrushes flock together for the most part.

(48) There are also other species of birds. Some are stationary, that is, stay in one place. Others are migratory birds who fly off to other regions and return at the end of winter. Still others return to us in winter time and fare abroad in summer. In the former case they seek a warmer climate in winter. In the latter case they spend the summer each year in those places which they know to be pleasanter. Hence thrushes return at the end of autumn when winter is already beginning and summer has passed for them. We contrive snares for them, acting as cruel hosts. We catch them in different ways, either by surprising them when they land or by deceiving them by a whistling sound, or by trying 'to snare game in toils.'[4] The stork returns, holding high the standard of spring. The crane, because of his partiality for flying high, often finds delight in voyaging afar.

(49) Some birds submit themselves to be handled. They are 'accustomed to the table,'[5] and are delighted to be fondled. Other birds shrink from this through fear. Some find pleasure in frequenting man's habitations, whereas others choose to live in remote deserts, where their difficulties in procuring food find compensation in their love of liberty.

4 Virgil, *Georgics* 1.139.
5 Virgil, *Aeneid* 7.490.

Some birds utter cries, while others delight us with sweet and modulated song. Certain birds by nature, others by training, learn 'to match the measures'[6] of different tones, so much so that you would think a man, and not a bird, had spoken. How sweet is the voice of the blackbird; how distinct the words of the parrot!

There are also other birds; some guileless like the dove, or artful like the partridge. The cock is inclined to be boastful; the peacock, to be vain. There are birds, too, that display diversities in their lives and habits. Some love to consult together in groups, thus helping to form by their combined strength a state of their own under a king.[7] Other birds love to look out, each one for his own interest, avoiding a systematic rule, and, when captured, long 'to quit a slavery'[8] that is disdainful to them!

Chapter 15

(50) Let us begin, then, with those birds which have become examples for our own way of life. These birds have a natural social and military organization, whereas with us this service is compulsory and servile. How well do the cranes carry out their guard duty at night without orders and without compulsion! You may note the watchers at their appointed places. Again, while the rest of the flock is at rest, some make the rounds and make certain that no attack is attempted from any quarter. With unabated vigilance they render complete protection. When the watcher has completed his period for guard duty, he prepares for sleep, after arousing with a warning cry the sleeper who is destined to

6 *Ibid.* 6.646.
7 Cf. Virgil, *Georgics* 4.212.
8 Virgil, *Eclogues* 1.41.

take his place as the next sentry. The latter willingly accepts his lot. He does not act as is the custom with us when, under such circumstances, we are loath to give up our sleep. Rather, he rises eagerly from his resting place, performs his duty, and repays with equal care and courtesy the favors that he has received. Hence there are no deserters, because their loyalty is a natural one. Hence their guard duty furnishes real protection, because their wills are free.

(51) They also follow this procedure when in flight. In this way they alleviate fatigue as they perform in turn the function of leadership. At a certain prescribed time one takes, a position ahead of the rest, in advance of the banners, so to speak. Later, he turns back and yields to a successor the task of leading the flock. What is nobler than this, wherein toil and preferment is open to all, where power is not the privilege of the few, but is distributed in voluntary fashion equally among all?

(52) This was the functional process of the primitive community. It resembled the constitution of a free state. From the beginning men began in this manner to establish a political system based on nature, with the birds as models. Thus there was equal participation in both labor and office. Each individual in his turn learned to set up a division of responsibilities, to take his share in doing service and in supervising it. Thus no one was devoid of office and no one was without his allotment of work.[1]

Here was an ideal state where no one became accustomed to unbroken power. Again, no one was intimidated by a long period of servitude, because advancement, due to interchange of office and to the fitting measure of its duration, appeared all the more supportable in that it resulted in establishing that each one would have a share in the task of government. No one ventured to exact servitude of another

1 Cf. Virgil, *Georgics* 4.149-196 (bees).

when the latter in his term of office could retaliate with frowns of scorn. Toil was not heavy when the thought of a dignified office in the future could bring comforting relief.

But when the lust for domination began to arrogate to itself powers that were acquired, and when this same lust encouraged unwillingness to relinquish powers that were assumed, when military service began to take on the character of servitude rather than of a right shared by all, when men were more eager to seize power than to follow due process of law to attain it—when this became a fact, then the performance of hard tasks was regarded as a burden and what was not undertaken voluntarily left the way open for displays of negligence. How unwillingly do men submit to be assigned to guard duty, how difficult it is to induce anyone to accept a perilous post in camp, when the vigil is imposed by the command of a king! Penalties are set for neglect of duty. Yet, indifference often asserts itself and the sentries fail to be vigilant. That necessity which imposes obedience on the unwilling is often accompanied by a loathing, for nothing is so easy as not to seem difficult to one who acts unwillingly. Therefore, unbroken toil repels good will. Continuous and prolonged power breeds arrogance. Where can you find a man who of his own volition lays down his imperial office, gives up the insignia of his leadership, and willingly moves from the first position to take his place among the last?[2] Not only do we struggle to reach first place, we are often concerned even about a position of modest import. We lay claim to the first position at a banquet and, moreover, we desire that what has once been assigned to us should be ours in perpetuity.

On the other hand, the cranes carry out their activities with equanimity and perform their official duties with humility. They are instructed to take up in their turn the post of

---

2 Cf. Mark 9.34.

watch. No admonishment is necessary that they lay down their powers. In the former situation the tranquillity of natural sleep has to be broken; in the latter, an occasion presents itself to show their pleasure in the performance of a voluntary act of service.

Chapter 16

(53) It is related that storks proceed in orderly array in the direction in which they propose to advance and that in many places in the East they form ranks together as if they were soldiers marching under the command of an officer. You could well believe that you were witnessing an army going forward with banners displayed—such is the pageant of military precision which they show. They are under the leadership and direction of crows who accompany them, providing a stout escort and auxiliary force against any attacking army of birds. They undertake at their own risk campaigns that are planned by others. A proof of this is deduced from the fact that these crows are not found to stay any length of time in these regions. Moreover, when they return, they are covered with wounds. Clear evidence of their having undergone a severe and bitter conflict may be gathered from what may be termed their cries of blood and from other indications. Who, then, has set forth for them the penalty for desertion? Who has laid down the laws of severe punishment for deriliction of military duty? The fact is, no one attempts to steal away from the lines of these friendly escorting troops. On the contrary, each one strives to outdo his companions in carrying out his allotted task.

(54) Let men learn to preserve the rights of hospitality and from the example of birds realize what reverence is due and what courtesies accorded to one's guests—courtesies

which expose crows even to danger. Whereas birds offer even their own lives for strangers, we close our doors to them. We ban from our doors those birds who at the risk of peril to themselves serve as escort to others. Whereas the storks consider these as their defenders, we frequently treat them as enemies.

I may be in error, but this may have been the reason why the people of Sodom suffered punishment or why the fury of the Egyptians, when they attempted war on the people who had been their guests, brought its penalty for their lack of hospitality when the waters overwhelmed that perfidious race.

(55) We should dwell on the fact that while the gentleness of human beings is equal to the loyalty and wisdom of this bird [the stork], none of us have effectively imitated the virtues of irrational creatures, not even when an example has been set before our eyes. In fact, the offspring, gathering around the body of their 'father sick unto death,'[1] cherish with the movement of their wings the limbs of their parent, now, because of his advanced age, bereft of his plumage and deprived 'of the oarage of his pinions.'[2] Furthermore—need I add—the offspring offer a contribution of food, wherewith loss of natural strength is repaired, so that, lifting by the leverage of their wings their aged parent, they make him fit for flight and restore to strength their dear father's limbs, now unaccustomed to perform their primary functions.

Who is there among us who is not loath to lift up the burden of his ailing father? Who would place his 'wearied sire' on his own shoulders[3]—a fact which is scarely credible when related in history? Who would not rather, to fulfil his duty, hand this out over to servants? The birds do not refuse to provide food for their parents. This duty many men

1 Cf. Virgil, *Aeneid* 12.395.
2 A Virgilian phrase.
3 Cf. Virgil, *Aeneid* 2.596,707,708.

have refused to do even under compulsion of necessity and when driven by fear of punishment. Birds, on the other hand, are bound by a natural and not by a written code of laws.[4] By no ordinances, but rather by the prescriptions of natural grace, they carry unashamedly the body of a revered and aged parent. This act of carrying one's parent is, in fact, an expression of piety. Popular belief has borne witness to it to the extent that it has acquired, as is fitting, a merited fame. The Romans are accustomed to call this bird 'pious'—a title which these birds have without exception merited has been bestowed by decree of the Senate on scarcely a single emperor. These birds have been accorded this designation by a decree of their own elders, for it is right that sons be first declared 'pious' by virtue of what their fathers believed. They also have the approval of all mankind, for 'thankfulness' is called ἀντιπελάργησις, a word derived from πελαργός, which means a stork. Such is the derivation of the word denoting this virtue. A repayment for kindness is associated with the name of the stork.

Chapter 17

(56) We have an example of devotion to parents on the part of a bird's progeny. Let us now listen to an impressive instance of a mother's solicitude for her children. The swallow has a very small body, but gives evidence of extremely great affection and devotion. Although devoid of all goods, she constructs her nest as cunningly as if it were a thing 'more precious than gold.'[1] What wiser act is there for a bird given to wandering than that she should avail

4 Cf. Cicero, *Pro Milone* 4.10.

1 Prov. 16.16.

herself of her liberty and build for her little ones homes near the abodes of men, where no one would attack her brood? It is a commendable act to cause her nestlings from their very birth to become accustomed to human society and thus make them safer from the snares of their bird enemies. Notable, too, is the admirable way she, like a skilled artisan, builds her home without a helper. She gathers twigs in her beak and dips them in the mire so as to fasten them together. Because she is unable to lift the mire with her feet, she sprinkles the tops of her wings with waters so that what before was dry dust now becomes mud. In this way twigs and straw are collected and made compact. Thus is the entire nest built. The nestlings find no obstacles as they busy themselves on the smooth surface within their little house. At the same time, no intruder can damage the structure by planting his feet in an opening. The young ones, too, are not affected by draughts of cold air.

(57) This industrious activity is common to many birds. The extraordinary characteristics just mentioned show the high regard they have for paternal affection and are an indication of a far-seeing and instinctive knowledge. These birds give evidence of possessing a medical skill. If any of the nestlings suffers blindness as a result of an injury to an eye, its eyes are restored to their former effectiveness by the application of certain curative agents.

Let no one, therefore, complain of poverty because he has not provided money for his household. The swallow, who lacks money, is poorer—but is rich in industry. She builds and spends not. She erects a shelter without depriving a neighbor of anything. She experiences no compulsion to harm anyone, either because of indigence or poverty. She does not resign herself to despair when at times her offspring becomes helpless. We on the other hand, are affected by poverty and are made anxious by the urgency of want. Indigence drives many to evil deeds and offenses. In the pursuit of gain we turn our minds to deceit and, while fitting our sentiments to the occasion, we set our hopes in the most violent displays of passion. In the process our minds snap. We lie prone, bereft of spirit and life at a time when it would have been more satisfactory, since the protection of man has failed us, to place our hopes in the benevolence of God.

Chapter 18

(58) Men should learn to love their children. We find this to be a normal sentiment among crows, who form a constant escort to their offspring in flight. Solicitous, too, lest perchance they may become weak because of their tender age, they strive to supply them with food. They continue to perform this function for a long time. On the other hand, the females of our species quickly give up nursing even those they love or, if they belong to the wealthier class, disdain the act of nursing. Those who are very poor expose their infants and refuse to lay claim to them when they are discovered. Even the wealthy, in order that their inheritance may not be divided among several, deny in the very womb their own progeny. By the use of parricidal mixtures they snuff out the fruit of their wombs in the genital organs themselves. In this way life is taken away before it is given.

Who except man himself has taught us ways of repudiating children? Who has discovered such cruel parental customs? Who, notwithstanding the fact that nature imposes equality among brothers, has casued them to be unequal? One has a superabundance from his father's legacy. The other bewails the fact that he has been given but a miserable portion of his father's rich patrimony. Can we say that nature has thus apportioned the deserts of these sons? On everyone she has bestowed on an equal basis the possibility of possessing wherewith to be born and wherewith to live. She can teach you not to discriminate in inheritance those whom you made equal by right of consanguinity. It stands to reason that those to whom you have granted the right to be born in the same manner should not themselves be begrudged to have that in common which by nature they have inherited.

(59) Hawks are said to show harshness toward their own offspring. They eject them from their nests when they notice their first attempts at flight. If they still linger, they are immediately pushed headlong by their parents, who beat them with their wings and compel them to perform the fearful action. At no time after that do they perform their office of giving sustenance to their young. Yet why should we wonder that birds accustomed to plunder find it distasteful to nourish their progeny? Let us keep in mind the fact that fear schools birds also to be cautious, never to relax their watchful care, but to anticipate and avoid dangers from birds of prey. Hence, since nature has inured these birds to a life of plunder, they appear to prepare their young from an early age to acts of pillage rather than just cut short the period of sustenance. Precaution is taken lest they become flabby in that early period, or become weak through pampering, or lest they languish in idleness. They are trained to search for food rather than expect it, so that they may not lose their innate vigor. Those activities are allowed to elapse which are connected with the nourishing of the young, who as a result of this are forced to resort to a life of pillage.

(60) It is generally stated in treatises dealing with the eagle that she, too, abandons her young. This is true, however, only of one out of two nestlings. Some have thought this situation arose from a reluctance to bring up a twin brood. But this is hardly worthy of credence, especially since

Moses has given us such convincing testimony on the devotion of this bird to her young when he said: 'As the eagle protects his nest and inspires trust in his nestlings: hovering over them, he spreads his wings and hath taken them and carried them on his shoulders. The Lord alone led them.'[1] How, then, did he spread his wings over his young if he killed one of them?

For this reason I think that this bird does not act cruelly from a desire to refrain from giving nourishment. Rather, there is a question of making a decision. For it is agreed that the eagle tests the quality of her young, lest signs of degeneracy and deformity may cause deterioration in a species which affects the role of regal dominion over all birds. And so it is asserted that the eagle exposes her nestlings to the rays of the sun and suspends with her claws her young in mid-air. If one of them stays unruffled and unmoved, fearlessly facing the light of the sun as it strikes his eyes, he is approved. He has thus demonstrated the truth of nature by the steadiness of his unaffected gaze. The one, however, who turns away his eyes, 'dazzled by the sun's rays,'[2] is rejected. He is deemed unworthy of such a parent, unfitted to be recognized as genuine offspring, and hence undeserving of support. The eagle does not therefore reject her young because of natural cruelty. This is, rather, the result of her soundness of judgment. There is no refusal of what is native, but rather a rejection of what is alien.

(61) What some consider to be a disposition toward cruelty in such a royal bird is compensated by the kindly traits of a bird of lower caste. This bird, known as the waterfowl (the Greek name is φενη), adopts the nestling of the eagle when disowned or not recognized and allows him to mingle with her own brood. She exercises over him the same

1 Deut. 32.11.
2 Cicero, *De senectute* 12.42.

maternal care as she does over her own, providing food and nourishment impartially. The φενη, therefore, supports an alien brood, whereas we show excessive cruelty when we abandon our own children. Rather, she does not acknowledge them to be such, but considers them to be base-born. Our procedure is worse. We renounce what we acknowledge to be our own.

Chapter 19

(62) Let us come now to the turtle dove, chosen as a chaste victim by the Law of God. Hence, when the Lord was circumcised, the dove was offered, because it is written in the Law that there should be a presentation of 'a pair of turtles or two young pigeons.'[1] For this is the true sacrifice of Christ: chastity of body and grace of the spirit. Chastity belongs to the turtle dove; grace, to the pigeon. It is related that the turtle dove, when widowed by the loss of her consort, was 'utterly weary of the bridal-bed' and even of the world itself, for the reason that 'her first love, turning traitor, cheated her by death.'[2] He was regarded as unfaithful from the point of view of perpetuity and as dour in respect to beauty in that he had created more pain as a result of his death than sweetness from his love. Therefore, she renounces any other marriage alliance and does not break the laws of chastity or her pledges to her beloved, reserving for him alone her love, for him alone cherishing the name of wife. Learn, women, how great are the joys of that widowhood which even birds are said to observe.

(63) Who has given these laws to the turtle dove? A search for a human law-giver will not bring results. No one has ventured to propound laws for these birds. Not even Paul

1 Luke 2.24; Lev. 12.8.
2 Virgil, *Aeneid* 4.17,18 (Dido).

has succeeded in doing so in the question as to whether a widow should remarry or not. He says: 'I desire therefore that the younger widows marry, bear children, rule their households and give the adversary no occcasion for abusing us.' And elsewhere: 'It is good for them if they so remain. But if they do not have the self-control, let them marry, for it is better to marry than to burn.'[3] Paul wishes that women should do that which is customary with the turtle doves. Also, he exhorts the younger widows to marry because our women are unable to maintain the chaste life of these birds. God has therefore infused into the turtle dove this sentiment for the virtuous practice of continency. He alone has the power to prescribe the laws which all are obliged to follow. The turtle dove is not inflamed by the flower of youth, is not tempted by occasional enticements, and cannot break her first pledge, because she knows how to preserve the chastity she promised at the time of her first marriage.

Chapter 20

(64) We have spoken of widowhood as it appears in the life of birds. We have shown how this virtue first arose among them. Now let us discuss the virtue of continency—a virtue which birds are said also to possess. This virtue can be found even among vultures. It is said that vultures 'do not indulge in conjugal embraces' or in any sort of union or nuptial tie. They are said to conceive without contact with the male seed and that without the union of sexes they generate offspring that live to a ripe old age. In fact, it is asserted that they live as long as a hundred years and that by no means does 'the limit of a natural span of life await them.'[1]

3 1 Tim. 5.14; 1 Cor. 7.8.

1 Virgil, *Georgics* 4.198, 206 (bees).

(65) What do those people say who usually ridicule our mysteries when they hear that a virgin gave birth to a child —people who consider that parturition is impossible to one who never had any relations with a man? Is that to be thought impossible for the Mother of God which is admitted to be possible in the case of vultures? A bird gives birth without contact with a male. No one has cast any doubt on that. But because Mary, though unwedded, brought forth a child, they raise doubts about her chastity. Do not our observations show that the Lord has provided many precedents in the realm of nature by which to prove the glory of His own Incarnation and assert its veracity?

Chapter 21

(66) Now I shall proceed to show what birds usually live under the control of laws in a sort of commonwealth. From this is derived the fact that the state establishes laws bearing equally on all citizens—laws which are loyally observed by all members of the community. No claim is made to a right which is clearly not permitted to all the citizens. Rather, each and every member of the group shares equally in these rights. What is not permitted to every citizen is not considered a right. All share in paying respects to their elders, by whose wise counsel the state is governed. Each one has a right to the common place of abode. Social duties are shared. They all follow a single prescribed and orderly mode of life.

(67) These facts are of great importance. In the case of bees they are even more important. Alone of all species of living creatures they share their offspring in common. All have the same abode and are confined within the limits of

one native land. They engage in the same labor. They share the same food and partake of the same activities. The same productivity is shared and—what could be more notable—the same flight on the wing. The act of generation is common to all. Their bodies are uncontaminated in the common act of parturition, since they have no part in conjugal embraces. They do not unnerve their bodies in love nor are they torn by the travail of childbirth. A mighty swarm of young suddenly appears. They gather their offspring in their mouths from the surface of leaves and from sweet herbs.[1]

(68) They appoint a king for themselves and establish their own community. Though they serve under a king, they are free. They have the privilege of selection and of extending their loyal devotion. They love him as one elected by them and they pay him honor by producing a swarming hive.

The king is not chosen by lot, because there is in a lot, not an element of discrimination, but one of chance. By virtue of the unpredictable nature of a lot, it frequently happens that what comes last is preferred to what is better. The election is not brought about by the vulgar shouts of an uninformed mob which does not hold in esteem the merits due to virtue. The mob scrutinizes, not the benefits to be bestowed by what is serviceable for all, but is swayed by the incertitude of change. This election, moreover, is not founded on hereditary privilege or in dynastic succession, since circumspection and wisdom cannot exist in one who is so inexperienced in public life. Add to this the flatteries and the inordinate pleasures which, imbibed at an early age, are apt to weaken men of the best natural endowments. Then, again, we note the custom of employing eunuchs; most of them tend to sway the king more for their own profit than for the public good.

1 Virgil, *Georgics* 4.197-201.

There are notable and natural characteristics in the king as he appears among the bees. He must be, for example, outstanding in size and beauty. Besides that, he must possess what is a conspicuous trait in a king—gentleness in character. He does not make use of his sting to inflict punishment. There are well-defined laws in nature, not set down in writing, but impressed in the mold of custom, by virtue of which those who possess the greatest power tend to be more lenient in the exercise of it. Those bees who do not obey the laws of their king are so overcome by remorse that they even kill themselves by their own stings!

This custom is observed today by the Persians. They inflict death on themselves in punishment for a transgression. But no people—neither the Persians whose subjects live under the severest laws nor the Indians or Sarmatians—hold their kings in such high esteem as do the bees.[2] So true is this that they dare not leave their abodes nor go in search of food except when the king takes the initiative by assuming for himself primacy in flight.

(69) They fly over the countryside with its fragrant gardens and sweetly smelling flowers, where a brook steals through banks of lush grass. There the young bees find occasion for spirited sport. There, too, they perform their martial exercises and find relaxation from labors. Their toil is sweet. From the flowers and the plants they erect the foundations for their camps. What is the honeycomb but a sort of camp? Hence 'they drive the drones from these folds.' Does not the square-shaped form of a camp compare favorably for beauty of construction with the art of the honeycomb in which tiny rounded cells are interlocked? What architect taught them how to arrange symmetrically the walls of these separate cells, how to hang aloft 'within

2 *Ibid.* 4.210-212.

the confines of their homes' delicate pieces of wax—to staff all this with honey and 'swell with nectar,' as it were, their granaries interwoven with flowers?[3]

You can perceive them all engaged in their tasks. Some keep guard over the food supply. Others keep anxious watch on the camp. Others are on the alert for possible rainstorms and cloudbursts. Some fashion the wax obtained from flowers, while still others gather in their mouths the dew that settles on these same flowers. Yet no one lays snares to pilfer the fruits of another's labors or aims 'to live by plunder.'[4] Would that they did not fear the cunning stratagems of thieves! However, they still can resort to their stings and, if they should be aroused, infuse poison into the honey. In the heat of attack 'they lay down their lives in the wound.'[5]

And so into the recesses of their camp abodes the moisture of the dew is poured. This in the course of time is gradually transformed into honey. What before was liquid takes on the sweetness of honey as a result of the infusion of wax together with the aroma of flowers.

(70) Scripture rightly commends the bee as a good worker: 'Behold the bee, see how busy she is, how admirable in her industry, the results of whose labors are serviceable to kings and commoners and are sought after by all men.'[6] Do you hear what the Prophet says? He enjoins on you to follow the example of that tiny bee and to imitate her work. You see how pleasing it is and what labor it entails. Her fruit is desired and sought after by all men. Its recipients do not differ in character. It supplies without distinction the same sweetness to kings and to commoners. It contributes not to our pleasures alone, but to our health as well. It

3 This entire section reflects numerous passages of *Georgics* 4.19-169.
4 Virgil, *Aeneid* 7.749; 9.613.
5 Virgil, *Georgics* 4.238.
6 Cf. Prov. 6.8 (on the ant).

soothes our throats and ministers to our wounds. Even to our organic ills it serves as a healing draught. Thus the bee, though weak in body, manifests her strength in the vigor of her wisdom and in her high regard for virtuous deeds.

(71) The bees fight, in fact, to their utmost in defense of their king. They consider it a noble act to give up their lives for his sake. While the king is safe, they stand by him with the greatest devotion. When he is lost, their enthusiasm for their work declines. They destroy their store of honey, because death has come to the prime mover of their enterprise.[7]

(72) Although other winged creatures scarcely bring forth offspring once a year, the bee is blessed with two such periods, surpassing to such a degree all other [such] creatures in fecundity.[8]

Chapter 22

(73) Let us now examine the sense of the words, 'Let the waters abound with life and above the earth let winged creatures fly below the firmament of the heavens.'[1]

It is clear that 'above the earth' is said because they search for their food on the earth. But why, 'below the firmament'? Eagles fly above all other birds, yet they do not fly 'below the firmament of the heavens.' The word for 'heaven' in Greek is οὐρανός, derived from the Greek word 'to see,' for the reason that the air is clear and transparent and so living species are said to fly through the air. One should not be disturbed by the phrase 'below the firmament of the heavens.' The word 'firmament' is used, not in its proper, but in its derivative sense. The air which we perceive

7 Cf. Virgil, *Georgics* 4.212-214.
8 *Ibid.* 4.231.

1 Gen. 1.20.

with our eyes is, in comparison with that ethereal substance, the firmament, of greater thickness and density.

(74) Now, having discussed just briefly the nature and beauty of flying creatures (we do not have time to describe every creature of the same or similar species), let us consider what diversity there is among birds themselves.

We find that the crow has talons which are divided and separated, whereas nature has formed that part differently in the raven, even in her young. Those birds that feed on flesh have hooked talons, to enable them to seize their prey. Those that are accustomed to swimming have feet which are broad, with their parts bound and joined together by a kind of membrane. Here we find examples of admirable design in nature. In one case, flight or the acquisition of food is made easier. In the other, assistance is given in the art of swimming, whereby this act, too, is made easier. They use their feet as oars in such a manner that a current of water is propelled by the broad formation of the membrane attached to their feet.

(75) We can easily comprehend why a swan has a rather long neck. With a body that is somewhat corpulent, the swan cannot easily reach the lowest depths in search for food. Hence, the neck acts as a sort of advance scout for the rest of the body when on the lookout for food in the deep waters. This long neck has the additional advantage of giving a sweeter and more modulated tone to the swan's cry, which becomes clearer the more frequently it is exercised.

(76) How sweet is the chant from the tiny throat of a cicada! In the heat of midsummer 'they rend the thickets'[2] with their songs. The greater the heat at midday, the more musical become their songs, because the purer the air they breathe at that time, the clearer does the song resound.

2 Virgil, *Georgics* 3.328.

The bees, too, have a song that is not unpleasant. In that hoarse voice of theirs is an agreeable sweetness which we appear to have first imitated 'in the broken trumpet-blasts.'[3] There is no sound more fitting than this to arouse hearts to vigorous action. Yet they have this curious gift, although they are said not to possess the function of breathing through lungs, but to breathe in the air as food. Hence they die immediately if oil is poured over them, because they are unable to take in that breath of air when their pores are closed. If one were straightway to pour vinegar over them, they quickly revive, since vinegar has the power of quickly opening those pores which had been sealed by the mass of oil.

Chapter 23

(77) Now that we are discussing flying creatures, it may not be amiss to treat here what is reported by certain eyewitnesses about the Indian worm. It is related that this horned worm is first changed into the form of a plant stalk,[1] then gradually into a chrysalis. This form is not retained, for it seems to take on wings when seen on the wide surface of a leaf. From these leaves the Chinese 'comb those soft fleeces'[2] which the wealthy appropriate for their own use. Hence the Lord says: 'What did you go out to the desert to see? A man clothed in soft garments? Behold, those who wear soft garments are in the houses of kings.'[3]

The chameleon is said also to assume new forms by a deceptive change of color. We know, in fact, from close

3 *Ibid.* 4.72.

1 St. Basil in his *Commentary on Gen.* 184D has the correct information here (caterpillar).
2 Virgil, *Georgics* 2.121.
3 Matt. 11.7,8.

observation that hares take on a white color in winter and that in summer they return to their original shade.

(78) These matters have been mentioned in order that you may be aroused by the force of such examples as these to a belief in the change which will be ours at the Resurrection. We refer to that change which the Apostle clearly indicates when he says: 'We shall all indeed rise, but we shall not all be changed.' And further on he says: 'And the dead shall rise incorruptible and we shall be changed. For this corruptible body must put on incorruption and this mortal body must put on immortality.'[4] Many, interpreting the nature and appearance of that transformation which they have not attained, are not without giving it an incongruous explanation, based on an anticipation which they do not merit.

(79) In the regions of Arabia there is reported to be a bird called the phoenix.[5] This bird is said to reach the ripe old age of 500 years. When the phoenix realizes that he is coming to the end of his life, he builds himself a casket of incense, myrrh, and other aromatic plants, into which he enters and dies when his time has come. From the moisture proceeding from his flesh he comes to life again. In the course of time this bird puts on 'the oarage of his wings'[6] until he is restored to his primitive form and appearance. By the very act of his resurrection the phoenix furnishes us a lesson by setting before us the very emblems of our own resurrection without the aid of precedent or of reason. We accept the fact that birds exist for the sake of man. The contrary is not true: that man exists for the sake of birds. We have here an example of the loving care which the Author and

4 1 Cor. 15.51-53.

5 The phoenix was considered as an example from nature of the certainty of our resurrection; see Clement of Rome, *First Epistle to the Corinthians* 25.

6 A Virgilian phrase.

Creator of the birds has for His own saints.[7] These He does not allow to perish, just as He does not permit in the case of one sole bird when He willed that the phoenix should rise again, born of his own seed. Who, then, announces to him the day of his death, so that he makes for himself a casket, fills it with goodly aromas, and then enters it to die there where pleasant perfumes succeed in crowding out the foul odor of death?

(80) You, too, man, should avail yourself of a casket: 'strip off the old man with his deeds and put on the new.'[8] Your casket, your sheath, is Christ who protects and conceals you in the day of evil. Do you wish to be convinced that it is a casket of protection? 'In my quiver he hath hidden me,'[9] Scripture declares. The casket, then, is your faith. Fill it with the goodly aroma of your virtues, that is, of chastity, compassion, and justice, and immerse yourself wholly in the inmost mysteries of faith, which are fragrant with the sweet odors of your significant deeds. May your exit from this life find you clothed with that faith, so that 'your bones may be made fat' and 'be like a watered garden,'[10] thus coming to life and flourishing. Be aware, therefore, of the day of your death, as the Apostle Paul realized when he said: 'I have fought the good fight, I have finished the course, I have kept the faith. There is laid up for me a crown of justice.'[11] Like the good phoenix, he entered his casket, filling it with the sweet aroma of martyrdom.

(81) I shall put this question before you: Why are vultures able by certain indications to foretell a man's death? Whence have they derived their knowledge? When two armies face each other in battle array to engage in

---

7 Cf. Ps. 15.10; Acts 13.35.
8 Col. 3.9,10.
9 Isa. 49.2.
10 Prov. 15.30; Isa. 58.11.
11 2 Tim. 4.7,8.

'tearful war,'[12] these particular birds follow in formation as a sign that a great number of men are destined to fall a prey to vultures. At any rate, they seem to make this observation by the exercise of an instinct analogous to human reasoning.

(82) Divine grace has penetrated even into the life of a locust. When a locust swarms over and takes possession of some extent of land, no harm at first is done to the land. Nothing is devoured by these unfriendly invaders except when a sign from heaven has been received. A passage in Exodus provides an example of this.[13] There the locust as minister of divine vengeance inflicts punishment for an offense against heaven.

(83) This animal is devoured in turn by a bird called σελευκίς—this is its Greek name—given to us as a remedy for the ills that the locust usually inflict. The Creator has given this bird an insatiable appetite wherewith the all-devouring plague, to which we have just referred, can be utterly destroyed.

Chapter 24

(84) But what is this that has happened? While we are prolonging our discourse, see how the birds of night flit around us! They admonish us by that very act to put an end to our discourse and at the same time give us a hint that they, too, should be included. Birds of different species all fly back to their accustomed nesting places. The coming of evening compels them to give way to night. Accordingly, they conceal themselves in their hiding places, saluting the close of day with a song, lest they depart without offering such thanks as a creature owes to glorify his Creator.

12 Virgil, *Aeneid* 7.604.
13 Exod. 10.12-15.

(85) Night also has its songs wherewith to soothe the hearts of men who lie awake. The night owl, too, makes a contribution of song. What shall I say of the nightingale who keeps long watch over her nest, cherishing her eggs with the warmth of her body? She solaces with the sweetness of her song the sleepless labors of a long night.[1] The highest aim of the nightingale, in my opinion, is to give life to her eggs by the sweet charm of her song no less than by the fostering warmth of her body. A woman, humble but chaste,[2] imitates this bird when she uses her arms to work 'the indented millstone,'[3] that her little ones may not lack bread for their sustenance. By her evening song she comforts herself amid the distressing realities of her poverty. In her love and attentiveness she follows the nightingale's pattern, although she fails to match the sweetness of the song.

(86) The night owl is insensible of the horrors accompanying the gloom of night because of the large yellow pupils of his eyes. Contrary to the experience of other birds—the darker the night, the freer the flight of the owl. However, when dawn with its bursts of light appears, his eyes are dazzled and he flees aimlessly as if in darkness. The owl provides us with a lesson that some there are who, although they have eyes to see, yet are unable to use them.[4] They exercise the function of sight solely in times of obscurity.

I speak of the eyes of the mind which the wise in this world have and see not.[5] They discern nothing in the light. They walk in obscurity, groping in the darkness of the demon powers, while they are convinced that they are looking at the heights of heaven. 'They trace with a rod' the

---

1 Cf. Virgil, *Georgics* 1.293.
2 Cf. Virgil, *Aeneid* 8.409-413.
3 Virgil, *Georgics* 1.274.
4 Cf. Matt. 13.13.
5 Cf. Eph. 1.18.

universe,[6] taking the measure of the air itself. Nevertheless, they become more and more involved in the darkness of eternal sightlessness. Beside them are the daylight of Christ and the light of the Church, and they see them not. They open their mouths as if in possession of all knowledge. To subjects of little value their minds are acute, but to the eternal verities they are blind. In the prolixities of prolonged disputation they reveal the obscurity of their own knowledge. Therefore, while they flit around in subtle discourse, they act like the night owl by vanishing at the approach of the light of day.

(87) The bat is an ignoble creature, whose name is taken from the word for evening.[7] They are equipped with wings, but at the same time they are quadrupeds. They are provided with teeth, in this respect differing generally from other birds. As a quadruped, too, the female brings forth her young alive and not in the oval stage. Bats fly in the air like birds but prefer to be shrouded in the dusk of evening. In flight they do not use the support of wings but rely on their webbed feet which serve as wings, both as a balance and as a means of propulsion. These common creatures have this faculty, too, of adhering one to another, assuming any position like a pendant bunch of grapes, so that, if the lowest in place gives way they all fall apart. Here we see the virtue of love in action—a virtue difficult to find among men here below.

(88) The cock's crow is pleasant at nightfall. It is not only pleasant, but useful, too. As a good domesticated fowl he arouses the sleeper, gives him warning when he is perturbed, and consoles the voyager by asserting in musical

6 Virgil, *Aeneid* 6.850.

7 The etymology here is *verpertilio* ('bat') from *vesper* ('evening').

8 Cf. *Hymnica Ambrosiana* 1 (*Aeterne rerum conditor*); cf. O. J. Kuhnmuench, *Early Christian Latin Poets* (Chicago 1929) 116; A. S. Walpole, *Early Latin Hymns* (Cambridge 1922) 27-34.

tones that night is approaching.[8] When the cock crows, the thief forsakes his schemes and the star of dawn rises to illumine the sky. When the cock crows, the sailor's gloom and trepidation disappear. Tempests and storms stirred up by gusts of wind at eveningtide subside. At his crowing the devout of heart bestir themselves for prayer and resume their reading. Finally, on this occasion 'the rock of the Church'[9] washed away his sin which he had committed before the cock crowed. At cock-crow hope returns to all, the sick find comfort, the wounded find relief, the feverish are calmed, the lapsed return to the faith. Jesus has regard for those who stumble and corrects the errant. Hence He paid heed to Peter and forthwith the sin departed. Peter revoked his denial and his confession was completed.[10] That this was God's plan and not a mere accident is revealed in the words of the Lord. It is written that Jesus said to Simon: 'Before the cock crows, thou wilt deny me three times.'[11]

In daytime Peter is quite brave, but is disturbed at nightfall. Before cock-crow he falls three times so that you may realize that his sin was not due to mere thoughtlessness, but to an emotional disturbance. The same man became braver after the cock crowed. He became worthy of Christ's regard, for 'the eyes of the Lord are upon the just.'[12] He realized that remedial action had come, following which he was unable to sin. He turned aside from the ways of error to those of virtue and wept bitterly.[13] He washed away his sins with his tears.

(89) Have regard, Lord Jesus, for us, also, that we may acknowledge our errors, efface our faults with tears of devotion and merit indulgence for our sins. And so we have

9 Peter; Matt. 16.18.
10 Cf. Luke 22.61,62.
11 Matt. 26.34.
12 Ps. 33.16.
13 Matt. 26.75.

purposely prolonged our discussion in order that the cock may come also to us as we speak. Wherefore, if any error has obtruded itself in our speech, we pray that Christ forgive our sin. Grant us the tears of Peter. Deliver us from the sinner's exultation.

The Hebrews wept and were liberated when the waters of the sea divided. Pharao was glad because he had surrounded the Hebrews, but he was swallowed up in the sea along with his people. Judas, too, rejoiced in the price of betrayal, but by reason of the same price 'he hanged himself with a halter.'[14] Peter wept for his sins and deserved to be able to forgive the sins of others.

(90) But now it is fitting time[15] that this discourse be brought to an end—a time for silence or for tears, a time in which is celebrated the forgiveness of sins. For us, too, in our holy rites that mystical cock crows, as the cock of Peter did in our discourse. May Peter, who wept so well for himself, weep also for us and may the benign countenance of Christ turn toward us. Let there come upon us the Passion of the Lord Jesus which daily forgives us our sins and effects the office of remission.

(91) The good Lord does not desire to send you away fasting lest some faint on the way. He said: 'I have compassion on the crowd for they have now been with me three days and have nothing to eat and I am unwilling to send them away fasting lest they faint on the way'[16]—Mary took note of these words on the occasion when she declined to make preparations for a meal.[17] We, too, should realize the fact that those who live on the word of God[18] are not numerous and that refreshment for the body is what is more

14 Matt. 26.14; 27.5.
15 Holy Thursday.
16 Matt. 15.32.
17 Cf. Luke 10.39,40.
18 Cf. Matt. 4.4.

generally desired. In fact, more exacting than the triduum (which we have celebrated) is that which we propose for the day that approaches.

(92) And so, now that we have enjoyed ourselves with birds and have crowed with the cock, let us sing the mysteries of the Lord. Let the eagles,[19] when they have been rejuvenated,[20] gather by the body of Jesus, for now the mighty whale has really restored Jonas to us.[21] Let us congratulate ourselves that evening has come. The morning shall become —the sixth day![22]

19 Cf. Luke 17.37; Matt. 24.28.
20 Cf. Ps. 102.5.
21 Jonas 2.11.
22 Cf. Gen. 1.31.

BOOK VI: THE SIXTH DAY

THE NINTH HOMILY

Chapter 1

THIS IS THE SIXTH DAY, which brings to a close the account of the origin of created things and at the same time terminates the discourse which we have undertaken on the genesis of matter.[1] This day calls for even greater expenditure of toil, because we have reached a critical point: the culmination of the whole debate. We must realize that during the preliminary stages of contests in music, song, or sport, however numerous and important they may be, there is no award of a wreath of victory. This presentation of a wreath for victory is assigned to the last day. On that occasion the expectant decision is reached, together with the shame or the reward which either defeat or victory brings. In such a mighty contest of wisdom as this in which every man, not just a few, acts as judge, how much more is there occasion for anxiety lest we fritter away the toils of the preceding days and suffer mortification in the present. The praetor does not face the same conditions as the singer or the athlete. In the

1 Cf. Lucretius 2.31,383 (*exordia rerum*).

latter case there is a sporting chance of misadventure,[2] in the former, an error may have serious results. If, in one instance, you make an error the spectators are censorious; in the other, the audience.

(2) Stand by me, therefore, as judges of the prize of victory. Enter with me into this mighty and wonderful theater of the whole visible creation. Not slight is the service rendered to strangers by one who watches for their arrival with the intent to conduct them on a tour around the city and to point out to them the more notable monuments. How much more ought you to welcome one who, as I do, conducts you in this assembly by the guiding hand of my discourse through your own native land and who points out to you each and every species and genus, with the desire to show you from all these examples how the Creator of the universe has conferred more abundant benefits on you than on all the rest of His creatures. It is for you, therefore, that the wreath is designed. It is my wish, with your express consent, to award to you today the crown of victory. We do not demand merely the garlands that athletes win which are destined at length to fade, but the lasting judgment of your probity, by which you are able to discern the truth that Divine Providence permeates all creatures. While you share with the rest of creatures your corporeal weakness, you possess above and beyond all other creatures a faculty of the soul which in itself has nothing in common with the rest of created things.

Chapter 2

(3) Now let us turn our discussion to the origin of beasts and to the generation of men. I already hear some who murmur and say: how much time are we to spend discussing

2 Cf. Virgil, *Aeneid* 5.328-330.

matters alien to us, while knowing nothing of what really concerns us? How long are we to learn of other living creatures while we do not know ourselves? Let him tell me what is to be for my benefit, that I may know myself. That is a just complaint. The order which Scripture laid down must, however, be retained. We cannot fully know ourselves without first knowing the nature of all living creatures.

(4) 'Let the earth,' says Scripture, 'bring forth all kinds of living creatures, quadrupeds and crawling creatures and beasts of the earth and cattle and all manner of reptiles according to their kind. And God made the beasts of the earth and every kind of cattle and every kind of creature that crawls on the ground. And God saw that it was good and God said: let us make man.'[1] I am not unaware of the fact that certain men treat of the race of beasts and cattle and crawling creatures as symbolical of the heinousness of sin, the stupidity of sinners, and the wickedness of their designs. I adhere, however, to the belief that each and every species is uncompounded by nature.

(5) I am not afraid that someone may in his mind compare me to a presumptious but poor host who, in his eagerness to be kind, invites many people to dinner. He sets before them nothing but the most common and ordinary food, so that he provokes criticism from his guests for the meanness of his service instead of being the recipient of gratitude for his generosity.

The friends of Eliseus did not accuse him of being a poor host when he placed wild herbs before them.[2] There exists that luxurious and delicately prepared banquet, hardly worthy of our notice, in which pheasants and a species of turtle are placed on the table, while chicken is actually what is served. A chicken is offered, stuffed with oysters or shell-fish. Wine

1 Gen.. 1.20-24.
2 4 Kings 4.39-43.

is drunk which from its bouquet seems to be of one kind, but from its taste seems to be of another. Food derived from the sea is stuffed with products of the land and those of the land with what is derived from the sea. We call into question in this way the providence of the Creator who has granted all these things for our sustenance without, however, mingling them one with another. At first sight, such a mixture seems pleasing. Afterward, it turns out to be bitter, for the more luxurious is our mode of living, the more ruinous and intemperate it becomes. Eliseus served bitter herbs which afterwards became sweet. Hence, those who thought that the food was of a deadly nature found it later to be sweet and life-giving.

(6) Again, there is no occasion for concern that I might have invited more people than I can possibly provide with food and that the bread of my discourse may not be sufficient for you all. We cannot attain to the perfection of faith exemplified in the case of Eliseus, who was not disturbed by the small amount of bread in his possession. It was his wish and intention to distribute it among all in sufficient amount. Accordingly, he instructed his servant to divide among the people the ten barley loaves. And his servant said: 'How much is this to set before a hundred men?' Eliseus replied: 'Give that they may eat for thus said the Lord; they shall eat and there shall be left.'[3] And I do not fear that your situation may make you ravenous. You have had your fill, yet you are returning home both hungry and empty, for it is written: 'The Lord strengtheneth the just and in the days of famine they shall be filled.'[4]

To be unashamed to offer loaves of barley and to give what you have rather than to withhold hospitality is a much more commendable act. While he gave to the people in abundance, Eliseus left nothing for himself. Eliseus, therefore, was not

---

3 *Ibid.*
4 Ps. 36.17,19.

ashamed to serve barley bread, whereas we find it shameful to have understanding of simple created things, which are called by their simple and customary names. When we read of 'heaven,' we should understand this to mean what it says. When we read of 'earth,' we should understand the fruit-bearing earth.

(7) What concern has the measurement of the circumference of the earth for me? Geometers estimate it to be 180 stadia. I gladly admit that I do not know that of which I am ignorant or, rather, that I am aware knowledge of this sort would not be of profit to me. Better than knowledge about the extent of the earth is knowledge about the concrete things in it. How can we grasp the dimensions of that which is surrounded by a sea, which is broken up by regions inhabited by barbarans, and by the many areas where the soil is marshy and impossible to traverse?

Scripture points out what is impossible for men, for God declares: 'Who hath measured the waters in the hollow of his hand and weighed the heavens with his palm and the bulk of the earth in his hand? Who hath weighed the mountains in scales and the rocks and the groves in a balance?' And further on: 'Who sitteth upon the globe of the earth, and the inhabitants thereof are as locusts, who stretcheth out the heavens as an arch?'[5] Who, then, ventures to put his knowledge in the same plane with that of God? Does man presume to offer that in the way of knowledge what God has sealed with his own oracular and majestic pronouncements?

(8) Surely, Moses was skilled in all the wisdom of the Egyptians. Yet he welcomed the Spirit of God. As His minister he preferred the way of truth to that vain and self-styled philosophical system. He laid down for us what he considered suited to our hopes, namely, that God made the earth, that the earth, produced plant life and all kinds of animal life

---

5 Isa. 40.12,22.

at the command of almighty God and by the operation of the Lord Jesus.

But he did not think that he should discuss how much atmospheric space is occupied by the shadow of the earth, when the sun recedes from us and takes away the light of day that illuminates the lower regions of the world. He did not discuss how the lunar orb is brought into eclipse in this part of the world, since in his account these phenomena were passed over as of no significance to us. Moses saw that there was no place in the words of the Holy Spirit for the vanity of this perishable knowledge which deceives and deludes us in our attempt to explain the unexplainable. He believed that only those things should be recorded which tend to our salvation.

Chapter 3

(9) Let us keep close to the meaning of the prophetical words. Let us not hold in disdain as unworthy of our consideration the language of the Holy Spirit, who says: 'Let the earth bring forth alive cattle, beasts and crawling creatures.' What is the need of further argument, since it is evident that the natural origin of terrestrial creatures is in question? The Word of God permeates every creature in the constitution of the world. Hence, as God had ordained, all kinds of living creatures were quickly produced from the earth. In compliance with a fixed law they all succeed each other from age to age according to their aspect and kind. The lion generates a lion; the tiger, a tiger; the ox, an ox; the swan, a swan; and the eagle, an eagle. What was once enjoined became in nature a habit for all time. Hence the earth has not ceased to offer the homage of her service. The original species of living creatures is reproduced for future ages by successive generations of its kind.

(10) Do you wish to turn the creatures that have been generated to the profit of man? You will all the more accomodate creatures to man's pleasure if you will not deny to all creatures what is appropriate to their natures. In the first place, nature has designed that every species of cattle, beast, and fish has its belly extended, so that some crawl on their stomachs. You may observe that even those animals that need the support of legs are, by reason of their four-footed motion, part and parcel of the earth and thus lack freedom of action. They have, in fact, no ability to stand erect. They therefore seek their sustenance in the earth, solely pursuing the pleasures of the stomach toward which they incline.

Take care not to be bent over like cattle. See that you do not incline—not so much physically as they do, but morally. Have regard for the conformation of your body and assume in accordance with it the appearance of loftiness and strength. Leave to animals the sole privilege of feeding in a prone position. Why, contrary to your nature, do you bend over unduly in the act of eating? Why do you find delight in what is a violation of nature? Why do you feed on the things of the earth like cattle, intent on food both day and night? Why do you dishonor yourself by surrendering to the allurements of the body, a slave to the whims of appetite? Why do you deprive yourself of the intelligence with which the Creator has endowed you? Why do you put yourself on the level of the beasts? To dissociate yourself from these was the will of God, when He said: 'Do not become like the horse and the mule who have no understanding.'[1]

If the voracity and intemperance of the horse and his whinny of pleasure directed toward the mare give you delight, you should also find pleasure 'with bit and bridle to bind fast your jaws.'[2] If you revel in ferocity, the dominant trait of

1 Ps. 31.9.
2 *Ibid.*

savage beasts for which reason they are slain, see that you, too, may not become a victim of your own atrocious cruelty.

(11) The donkey is a slothful and stupid animal, an easy prey to all mischance. What is the lesson that this animal conveys? Is it not that we should become more alert and not grow dull from physical and mental inactivity? Why not, rather, take refuge in a faith which tends to lighten our heavy burdens?

(12) The wily fox hides away in pits and caves. Is not this proof that the animal has no purpose? Because of his habit of plundering he deserves our hatred and warrants our aversion for his total lack of caution while laying snares for his victims.

(13) The partridge is cunning in that she steals the eggs of another partridge and fosters them with her own body. But she is unable to profit from this, because she loses the brood as soon as she has hatched it. When these hear the voice of the partridge who has laid the eggs, they leave their adopted nest and, following a natural instinct, go to her whom they recognize as their true and natural mother. In this way they indicate that the function of a nurse is totally different from that of a mother. Thus, she performs her own proper labors in vain and pays the penalty of her own deceit. Hence Jeremias says: 'The partridge uttered a cry and gathered what she did not lay,'[3] that is, she gathered the eggs and gave forth a cry as if rejoicing at the effect of her own deceit. But she spends her labor in vain. Her prolonged period of brooding benefits another and not herself.

The Devil imitates this bird in his endeavor to lay claim to the generations of the eternal Creator. If he succeeds in bringing together a group lacking in wisdom and devoid of sound sense, he allures them with corporeal enticements. As soon as the voice of Christ reaches the hearts of the little

---

3 Jer. 17.11.

ones, they depart and take themselves to their mother, who embraces her young with an endearing mother's love.[4] The Devil did not create the Gentiles, but he gathered them in. When Christ in His Gospel sent forth His message, they eagerly fled so as to be under the protection of the shadow of His wings. He consigned them to the fostering care of Mother Church.[5]

(14) The lion, proud in the fierceness of his nature, will not brook mingling with other wild animals. Like a king, he disdains association with them. He scorns the food of the previous day. He turns away even from the fragmentary remains of his meal. What wild beast would venture to associate with him whose roar of itself inspires such terror that many animals who could outrun him will quail on hearing it, as if struck dumb by some strange force.

(15) Scripture is also not silent about the nature of the leopard. By the varied character of his coat he betrays the variety of his emotions. Jeremias says: 'If the Ethiopean can change his skin or the leopard his spots.'[6] This is not said merely of what is external. It refers, also, to changes in the fierce nature of the animal. The Jewish people, whose characters were spoiled because of the gloomy and uneasy fluctuations of their hearts and minds, could not attain the grace of good purpose. Once they had acquired the fierce character of a wild beast, they were unable to return to a better and improved mode of life.

Chapter 4

(16) There is in the nature of quadrupeds something which the language of the prophetical books exhorts us to imitate.

4 Cf. Matt. 23.37.
5 Cf. Ps. 16.8.
6 Jer. 13.23.

We should follow their example and avoid slothfulness. Neither because of size nor bodily weakness should we desist from our eagerness to carry into effect the lofty aims of a virtuous life.

The ant is a tiny animal, yet she ventures to achieve things beyond her strength. She is not driven to labor as a slave is. Rather, without compulsion and with freedom of foresight, she lays up provision for a future day. Scripture admonishes us to imitate the industry of the ant: 'Go to the ant, thou sluggard, and consider her ways and be wiser than she.'[1] She has no land under cultivation. Yet, without a taskmaster to urge her on as she looks after her stock of food, what a harvest has she in store for herself—a harvest gathered from the results of your labors! While you may frequently be in need, she wants for nothing. There are no granaries closed to the ant, no guards impassable, no stores of grain untouchable! The guard sees and dares not prohibit the theft. The owner gazes on his loss and exacts no punishment! Over the plain moves the dark column. The paths are aglow with the concourse of voyagers and particles of grain which cannot be seized by their narrow jaws are heaved along by their shoulders![2] The owner of the crop beholds all this and blushes to refuse such trifles to co-operative industry such as this!

(17) What shall I say about dogs who have a natural instinct to show gratitude and to serve as watchful guardians of their masters' safety? Hence Scripture cries out to the ungrateful, the slothful, and the craven: 'Dumb dogs, not able to bark.'[3] To dogs, therefore, is given the ability to bark in defense of their masters and their homes. Thus you should learn to use your voice for the sake of Christ, when ravening wolves attack His sheepfold. Have the word ready on your lips, lest, like a silent watch-dog, you may appear because of

1 Prov. 6.6.
2 Cf. Virgil, *Aeneid* 4.402-407.
3 Isa. 56.10.

your unfaithfulness to abandon the post entrusted to you. Such a dog was the friend and companion of an angel. Not without reason did Raphael in the prophetic book cause this dog to accompany the son of Tobias when he went on a journey, in order to drive out Asmodeus and thereby confirm the marriage. The demon is driven out as the result of a grateful recognition and the union is stabilized.[4]

And so, under the symbolism of a dumb animal, the angel Raphael, as director of the young man Tobias whom he had agreed to protect, was able to arouse sentiments of gratitude in him. Who would not feel shame if he did not return thanks to those who are well deserving of it, when he sees that even beasts shun the sin of ingratitude? These animals hold in grateful memory the sustenance they have acquired. Are you not mindful of the salvation you have received?

(18) Although 'a bear lies in wait,' as Scripture says[5]—for she is a wild beast full of deceit—when she finds her young at the moment of birth to be formless, she immediately proceeds to lick them with her tongue until they become like her in form and shape. Do you not marvel that a wild animal should show such devotion with her tongue, an animal whose inherent nature is manifested by love for her young? The bear, therefore, forms her young into the likeness of herself. Are you not competent to train your sons, so that they, too, may become like yourselves?

(19) What shall we say about the bear and the art of medicine? She knows, in fact, how to heal herself when suffering from the effects of a serious wound. She lies under a plant called by the Greeks '*flomus*'[6] and touches it with her open sores, which are thereby healed.

Serpents, too, are able to rid themselves of blindness by

4 Cf. Tob. 6.1; 3.8; 8.3; 11.8.
5 Lam. 3.10.
6 Mullein.

eating the fennel plant. Accordingly, when they feel their eyesight becoming weaker, they search for their familiar remedy and are not disappointed in its results.

When tortoises, after eating the entrails of a serpent, feel the poison circulating through their bodies, they have recourse to a plant called marjoram in an effort to find a cure. Even when they lie concealed in their lairs in the marshes, they instinctively seek for a curative antidote. By this assured cure they attest that they know the efficacy of plants. You may observe that foxes, too, heal themselves with resin from a pine tree. By making use of such a remedy they postpone the time of imminent death.

(20) The Lord gave utterance to these words in the book of Jeremias: 'The turtle and the swallow and the sparrows of the field observed the time of their coming, but my people have not known the judgments of the Lord.'[7] Swallows know the time of their coming and of their return. These dutiful birds know how to announce the signs of spring by the testimony of their arrival.

Ants also keep watch for the coming of sunny weather. When they notice that their store of food remains soggy because of rain storms, a careful exploration is made of atmospheric conditions to determine when a series of warm days should arrive. Then they release the food supply, which is carried out of their hiding places to be dried by prolonged exposure to the sun. For that reason you will never experience stormy weather during that whole period of time, except when it should, in the interval, happen that the ants have changed their minds and decided to restore their supply of food to their granaries.

Sheep, at the approach of winter, browse on grass with an appetite that is insatiable. They have a presentiment of the coming of inclement weather. For this reason they proceed to

---

7 Jer. 8.9.

fill themselves to satiety before vegetation dies from the effects of bitter frost.

Hedgehogs, commonly called *iricei,* on sensing the approach of danger, 'gather themselves behind their shields'[8] so that anyone who has in mind to harm them may be wounded by their prickly armor. In anticipation of eventualities, these animals are provided with two organs of respiration. For example, then they sense the coming of northerly winds, they close the aperture open to the north. When they note that 'the clouds have been cleared away by the south wind,'[9] they turn toward the north so as to avoid the harmful breezes coming from the opposite direction.

(21) Hence, the Prophet rendered praise worthy of the Lord when he said: 'How great are thy works, O Lord. Thou hast made all things in wisdom.'[10] The divine wisdom penetrates and fills all things. Far more conviction is gained form the observation of irrational creatures than from the arguments of rational beings. Of more value is the testimony given by nature than is the proof presented by doctrine. What animal does not know how to look after his own safety —by offering resistance where force is necessary, by flight or by watchfulness where speed or cunning is called for? Who has instructed them on the curative powers of herbs? Human beings are often deceived by the appearance of herbs. Frequently, we discover those to be noxious which we had considered to be salutary. How often has death crept into repasts that were delicious! How frequently has death-dealing food penetrated even past the watchers and servants of the palace halls to bring death to kings! Wild beasts, merely by the sense of smell, are able to discern what is beneficial and what is harmful. They feed on the plant without the intervention

8 Virgil, *Aeneid* 10.412.
9 Horace, *Odes* 1.7.15,16.
10 Ps. 103.24.

of lackeys or food-tasters and receive no harm! Nature is a better guide and teacher of what is actual and true. She inspires into our senses the perception of what is sweet and health-giving and needs no director. She, too, instructs us how to avoid the bitterness of that which brings ultimate pain. The sweetness of life is set against the harshness of death.

Nature entrusts to the lioness the care of her whelps. Maternal affection makes gentle the savagery of the beast. Nature checks for the moment the ferocity of the tigress and turns her aside as she is on the point of seizing her prey. The minute she discovers that her young have been taken, she sets out on the track of the despoiler. Although he may have the advantage of a fast horse, he is aware that he may be outdone in speed by the wild beast. In a situation where there is available no means of escape he has to resort to the following stratagem. When he perceives that he is being overtaken, he lets fall a glass ball. The lioness is deceived by her reflection, thinking that she sees there her young. After being retarded by the deceitful image, she once more expends all her strength in her effort to seize the horseman. Spurred on by rage, she comes closer and closer to her fleeing victim. Again he throws out the glass ball, thus slowing down his pursuer. Yet her remembrance of past deceits does not prevent her from complying with her maternal instincts. She keeps turning over the reflected image that deludes her and settles down on it as if to nurse her young. Thus, deceived by her own maternal solicitude, she suffers at once the forfeiture of her vengeance and the loss of her offspring.[11]

(22) We have here the message of the Scriptures which declares: 'Children, love your fathers; parents, do not provoke your children to anger.'[12] Nature has implanted in beasts the instinct to love their own brood and hold dear their own

11 Cf. Claudian, *De raptu Proserpinae* 3.263ff.
12 Col. 2.20,21.

progeny. They know nothing of relations-in-law. Here, parents do not become estranged from their offspring by the act of changing their consorts. They know nothing of preferences given to children of a later union to the neglect of those of a former marriage. They are conscious of the value of their pledges and are unaquainted with distinctions in respect to love, to incentives due to hate, and to discriminations in acts that involve wrong-doing. Wild creatures have a nature that is simple and one which has no concern in the perversion of truth. And so the Lord has ordained that those creatures to whom He has bestowed a minimum of reason are endowed with the maximum of feeling.

What wild animal would not willingly face death in defense of her young? What wild beast, although exposed to countless armed men advancing 'in wedge formation,'[13] would not protect with her own life's blood her own progeny? With her body she sets up a wall of stout defense around her little ones, so that they are immune from peril in the midst of 'a harvest of spears'?[14] What has man to offer—he who pays no heed to what is enjoined on him and is oblivious to the dictates of nature? A son despises his father; a father disinherits his son. An occasion when a man's own progeny is condemned to death is regarded as an act of justice. A father actually passes judgment on himself by treating his own child as something without real substance. An act in which nature is punished with sterility is considered to have the sanction of authority.

(23) That dogs are devoid of reason is beyond all doubt. Nevertheless, if you consider the keenness of their senses, you can well believe that their sagacity of sense perception has taken on the trappings of reason. Hence, one can easily perceive that they are able to understand, by the training given

13 Virgil, *Aeneid* 12.575.
14 *Ibid.* 3.46.

by nature, what it has taken a few individuals a long period of time to achieve with the aid of the refinements of syllogistic argumentation acquired in the advanced schools of rhetoric. When they discover the tracks of a hare or of a stag at a point where there is a side path or a crossroad leading in several directions, they proceed to make note of the starting point of each of these trails. In silence, they weigh the problems one with the other. By applying their keenness of scent they seem to make the following observation: 'Our quarry has gone either in this direction or in that,' they say, 'or surely he has fled into this clearing. Yet he has not taken this route or that. One direction remains. There is no reason, therefore, to doubt that he has taken this route.' What men, with the aid of prolonged discussion and meditation, achieve with difficulty nature readily supplies to dogs, who weigh first the false hypothesis and when that is repudiated finally discover what is true.

Is it not true that philosophers spend whole days setting forth problems on sand, 'tracing with a rod'[15] each proposition one by one? Since it must be that of three propositions only one is true, these men first eliminate two of these as not in conformity with truth. And so they conclude that the essence of truth is found in the proposition that remains.

Who is as mindful of benefits and as grateful for kindness as the dog? For their masters' sake they go so far as to leap on robbers and to keep off strangers prowling at night. They are prepared, too, to die in defense of their masters and even to die with them! Dogs have often been the means of convicting people accused of homicide by showing clear evidence of the crime committed. Reliance is made in many cases on their testimony.

(24) It is related that in the early morning in a remote part of the city of Antioch a man who had a dog as a com-

15 *Ibid.* 6.850.

panion was found slain. The killer was a certain soldier bent on robbery. In the dusk of the morning hours he was able to find refuge in another region. The body lay unburied and attracted a crowd of bystanders. The dog bewailed with mournful cries the loss of his master. It happened that the man who committed the murder, in order to assure his innocence and make himself secure by his presence—such is human astuteness—joined the circle of people and with the air of displaying sympathy approached the corpse. At that moment the dog relinquished his whine of distress and assumed the role of avenger. He attacked him and held him prisoner. Raising a pitiful cry after the manner of an epilogue in a speech, the dog brought tears in the eyes of everyone present and inspired trust in his testimony. This man alone of all the men present was seized and held fast. The man thereupon became alarmed. He was unable any longer to deny his guilt. Such a clear indication of his offense could not be made void by pleas of hate, enmity, ill-will, or of injury inflicted. Since he had not succeeded in his master's defense, the dog in this case undertook a more difficult role, that of avenging him.

What meritorious act do we do for our Creator, on whose bounty we live? We close our eyes to insults against God Himself. Often, too, we set before the enemies of God food which we have received from His very hands.

(25) What animal is more innocent than the lamb? We are accustomed to make an analogy between lambs and our own little children. It often happens that in a large flock a lamb decides to wander over the whole sheepfold, roaming in search of his mother. When she on her part is unable to find her lamb, she attempts to discover his whereabouts by bleating frequently. By this means she hopes to cause him to give an answering cry whereby he could direct back 'his truant footsteps.'[16] Although he has wound his way among thousands of

16 Virgil, *Eclogues* 6.58.

sheep, he still recognizes the voice of his parent. He hastens to his mother and finds his way to the familiar sources of his mother's milk. Notwithstanding the lamb's eager desire for milk, he passes by other udders heavy with milk. These udders, in fact, may overflow with milk, yet he persists in searching for his mother. The depleted store of his mother's udders means just full abundance. She, too, can distinguish her offspring among the many thousands of lambs. In outward appearance they are the same. One can find no differences in the sound of their bleating. The mother picks out her own progeny from the rest of the flock. She recognizes her brood by the sole testimony of parental love. Whereas the shepherd may err in making his selection, the lamb cannot make a mistake in recognizing his mother. The shepherd is deceived by appearances, but a sheep is guided by natural affection. To all appearances, each one has the same odor, yet nature provides for them the power of distinguishing a scent which their own progeny, by I know not what peculiar potency, alone gives forth.

(26) Nature has her own customs and her own innate instincts. Scarcely has the infant got his first teeth when he is able to test his own arms. The puppy does not yet have his teeth, yet in defense he acts as if he had. The deer is not yet provided with horns, yet he practices and butts with his head, threatening with weapons with which he is not furnished. A wolf takes away a man's power of speech by first staring at him. The wolf despises this man over whom he is victorious by reason of his loss of speech. On the other hand, if a wolf perceives that he has been seen first, he loses his fierce character and is unable to run away. A lion is in dread of a cock, especially of one white in color. A she-goat when wounded searches for a plant called *dittany* and by this means rids herself of arrows. Wild animals, too, have instinctive knowledge of suitable remedies. A sick lion searches for an ape which,

when devoured, restores him to health. To a leopard the blood of a wild she-goat serves as an antidote against physical weakness. A sick bear devours ants. A deer chews the branches of an olive tree.[17]

(27) Wild animals know, therefore, what is beneficial to them, whereas you, man, have no knowledge of your remedies. You do not know how to snatch power away from your adversary, so that he, like a wolf taken by surprise, is unable to escape. You are unable by the eye of your mind to outwit his treacherous designs, to obstruct his flow of speech, and dull the edge of his impudent display of rhetoric. If he comes on you by surprise, he will deprive you of your power of speech. If dumbness comes upon you, loosen your foot-gear in order to loosen your tongue. If a wolf should attack you, pick up a rock—and he turns in flight! Christ is your rock. If you find refuge with Christ, the wolf will take flight and not terrify you. This is the rock which Peter, when he hesitated on the water, sought for and found, because he held on to the right hand of Christ.[18]

(28) Why do I need to mention the fact that men are fond of garlic and use as a food a substance which the leopard avoids? Hence, as soon as a person gets ready to prepare garlic, a leopard, who is unable to tolerate it, is apt to leap forth from that region. To think that you use for food and infuse into your vitals a substance[19] whose very odor a ferocious wild beast cannot endure! But it serves as medicine for those in pain. Let it be used as medicine, then, for invalids and not as food for banqueters. You have in mind to procure a drug, but you shun fasting as a restorative, as if you could find another remedy as efficacious as that! A serpent suffers death after tasting the sputum of a man who is fasting. You see,

17 Much of this lore is found in Pliny, *Historia naturalis* 8 and 10.
18 Cf. Matt. 14.30,31.
19 Cf. Horace, *Epodes* 3.5.

then, what potency there is in fasting, when a man can kill a serpent with his own sputum. If this is true of an earthly being, how much more true is it of the realm of spirit!

(29) How great is the wisdom which the Lord has infused even into little creatures! The turtle-dove covers her nest with onion sprouts to prevent wolves from attacking her fledglings. She knows that wolves usually shun these sprouts. The fox knows how to protect her own young, whereas you are ignorant of the means to do so. Why are you heedless in not making provision against the onslaughts of the iniquitous wolves of the spirit by providing greater security for the life which will follow this?

Chapter 5

(30) But let us return to the creation of different species and reflect on the reason why the Lord formed some beasts, such as lions, tigers, and bears, with shorter necks, whereas other animals, such as elephants and camels, were created with longer necks. Do we not find clear reason for this in the fact that animals which are carnivorous do not need long necks? They bend down their necks and jaws to the earth in the act of feeding. They use them for waylaying a deer or for dismembering an ox or a sheep. On the other hand, the camel, a taller animal, would be unable to feed on the smallest plants unless in the process of feeding he was able to extend his long neck to the ground. Accordingly, to the camel there has been allotted a neck that is longer in proportion to his stature. This is true, also, in the case of such herbivorous animals as the horse and the ox.

(31) The elephant, too, has a prominent trunk; otherwise he would be unable, because of his surpassing size, to reach the ground in order to find pasturage. He therefore makes use of this trunk in his search for food. Through it this monstrous

beast imbibes huge quantities of water. This trunk is hollow and capacious. In the effort to satisfy his thirst this huge beast empties entire troughs. Thus he inundates himself within with rivers of water. In fact, his neck is smaller than the massive size of his body demands, so that it may serve a useful function and not be an encumbrance.[1] For the same reason the animal does not bend his knees. In order that such a mighty contrivance be held in balance, there is need that his legs be like columns of a more than ordinary rigid character. The extremities of his feet are slightly curved, but the remaining parts of his legs are rigid throughout from top to bottom. Such a huge beast cannot bend his knees as we do. Naturally, therefore, he does not share with the rest of animals the ability to bend over or lie down. In order that without danger to himself he may sway a little in his sleep, he is supported on both sides by what may be called huge beams, inasmuch as he has no articulated joints in his limbs. For elephants that are tame a type of support has been contrived by men who are expert in this work. For the wild and untamed there is certainly an element of danger in the fact that no provision has been made for such supports.

(32) Elephants actually make use of trees either for scratching their sides or for relaxation in sleep. These trees are sometimes bent or broken by the weight of such a body, which causes the animals to fall headlong. Being unable to raise himself up, he lies there and dies. He may be discovered by his cries of pain, as he exposes the softer parts of his body to wounds and death. Weapons cannot easily penetrate his back and the other harder parts of his body. Hunters in search for ivory prepare the following scheme to trap these animals. From the trees which the elephant makes use of they cut away a small section on the sides opposite those which generally

1 Cf. Sallust, *Bellum Jug.* 14.4

served his purpose. The trees subjected to this pressure cannot sustain the weight of the elephant's limbs and become the immediate cause of his downfall.

(33) To find fault with these facts is like finding fault with the height of buildings which often threaten to fall headlong and are with difficulty restored. But if we frequently raise these aloft for the sake of artistic beauty or to serve as watch-towers, we ought to approve of this, too, in the case of elephants, because they perform a useful service in time of war. The Persians, for example, a race of fierce warriors, are noted for their expertness in archery and in similar arts. They advance in battle array surrounded by what appear to be moving towers, from which they shoot their weapons. When shot from a higher position these do more execution against the enemy below. In the center of the battlefield the combat seems to be concentrated around a rampart, citadel, or watch-tower, where the entrenched warriors appear to be spectators of the war rather than participants in it. They seem to be so remote from danger behind the protective bastion of the beasts. Who would venture to approach them, when he could be hit by a weapon from above or be annihilated by the onrush of the elephants from below? As a result, the battle line with its battalions drawn up in wedge formation gives way before them. The camping grounds which were laid out in blocks of squares have completely vanished. The elephants attack the enemy with a force that is irresistible. They cannot be held back by any embattled array of soldiers with massed shields. They take on the appearance of mountains moving in the midst of the battle. Conspicuous with their high crests and emitting a loud trumpet sound, they inspire fear in everyone.

What avail are feet or strength of muscles or manual dexterity to those who have to face a moving battlement packed with armed men? What use is his steed to the horseman? Driven by fear at the hugeness of this beast, his horse flees in panic! What can the bowman do against such an onslaught, although the armored soldier may not be affected by a rain of arrows directed from above? Moreover, the beasts' hides, even when unprotected, are not easily penetrated by a weapon. Protected by this armor, they cut their way through and overwhelm the opposing masses of men without any risk of danger to themselves.

(34) As in the case of huge buildings, we see that elephants, too, are supported by foundations of unusual strength. Otherwise, they would totter in a brief space of time because of lack of comparable sustaining power in their extremities. We are told nowadays that elephants live 300 years or more—a fact that corresponds to the hugeness of their bodies. And so their limbs are all the more sturdy because they are compact, not disjointed as ours are. How frequently it happens that our knees and feet cause us suffering, if we have been standing a long time or have been running at too high speed or after prolonged walking. Limbs that are jointed and articulated are more subject to pain than those which are compact and solid.

(35) And no wonder that elephants, when equipped with arms, are an object of fear. Actually, they always present an armored front, with their tusks acting as a natural spear! Whatever they take hold of they break into pieces with their trunks and whatever they trample on they annihilate—such is the force of their onrush! To provide themselves with food they take possession of whole groves. Like huge dragons they involve with their serpentine folds whatever they waylay. Often, their trunks take on a circular form when in the act of eating or drinking. We have here a proof that nothing created is superfluous. Yet this huge beast is subject to us and complies with our commands.

Chapter 6

(36) Inasmuch as we propose to discuss the nature of man, it is fitting that, by way of preface, something be said that reflects credit on him.

There appears to be no creature which has more physical strength or by its size inspires more terror than an elephant. No animals are as fierce as the lion and the tiger. Yet these beasts serve the interests of man and as the result of man's training lay aside their natural instincts. They forget their innate propensities and assume those which are imposed on them by command. Why need I say more? They are taught as if they were children. They cringe like weaklings and are lashed like timid creatures. They are corrected as are those subject to us and assume our habits since they have lost their own peculiar impulses.

(37) Wonderful, therefore, is the work of nature in both great and little things, for 'wonderful is the Lord on high.'[1] Just as we admire the level plains no less than we do the high moutains, so we marvel no more at the height of the cedar than we do at the fruitfulness of the vine or of the modest olive tree. In like manner, I admire the elephant for his hugeness no less than the mouse for the fact that he inspires the same elephant with terror.

Nature, therefore, has the power of causing fear in certain aspects and of being fearful in others. Each and every creature is endowed with certain characteristics which are their special mainstay. The elephant is a formidable object to a bull, but is fearful of a mouse. The lion, king of beasts, is disturbed by the slight sting of a scorpion and dies from the bite of poisonous serpent. The lion has extraordinary beauty as he shakes his mighty mane and raises his head on high. Yet, who does not marvel at the fact that huge bodies are subject to

1 Ps. 42.4.

death from a scorpion's slight sting—so slight as to be without substance?

(38) Let no one impugn the work of the Creator of serpents. He has, in fact, exposed His creatures to all other kinds of poisons, either animal or vegetable. These have come into being for our correction, not for our destruction. As a matter of fact, that which is an object of terror either to the cowardly, the weak, or the godless is a source of usefulness for others. A tutor, for example, seems severe, harsh, and unyielding toward his charges. He is unsparing with the whip, tames their boisterousness, and exacts their obedience. He surrounds them with fear, so that he may curb their boyish spirits. As a result of this severe treatment they turn out to be virtuous, temperate, and restrained, more eager for commendation than for sport. Do you not see how these fear-inspiring whippings are able to serve a good purpose?

Thus, serpents act as scourges for those whose pronounced character is immature and infantile, whereas no harm can come to the robust. The following words were meant for him who trusted in the Lord: 'You shall tread upon the asp and the viper; you shall trample down the lion and the dragon.'[2] Paul was bitten by a viper. It was believed that he, being a sinful man scarce rescued from shipwreck, would soon die of poison. Because he shook off the viper from the fire and still suffered no harm, the onlookers regarded him with more veneration.[3] Addressing all men, the Lord says:[4] 'He who believes and is baptized shall be saved, but he who does not believe shall be condemned.' And He said these signs shall attend those who believe: they shall fondle serpents, yet cannot suffer harm from these nor from the drinking of any deadly thing. A man's lack of faith is more to be feared

2 Ps. 90.13.
3 Cf. Acts 28.3-6.
4 Mark 16.16; cf. 17,18.

than poisonous serpents. Have fear of these, therefore, so that the occasion of your dread may at least lead you to faith. But, if you have no fear of God, then beware of the avenging poison of perfidy.

(39) Now, since you behold both lions and elephants subject to you, recall to mind, man, that the saying 'know thyself' is not something emanating from Pythian Apollo, but from Solomon, who says: 'If thou know not thyself, fairest among women.' Furthermore, long before this time Moses wrote in Deuteronomy: 'Keep thyself.'[5] The Law says: 'Man, keep thyself.' And the Prophet says: 'If you know not thyself.' To whom does he say these words? He adds: 'Fairest among women.'

What constitutes the beautiful among women if not the soul, an outstanding attribute in both sexes? Not without reason is the soul comely, since it longs, not for the things of earth, but for those of heaven; not for the corruptible, but for the incorruptible, the beauty of which is not liable to perish. All corporeal things, on the other hand, suffer decay either in the march of time or because of the inroads of disease. 'Keep thyself,' says Moses, in that in which you form a totality—that in which the better part of you consists. Hence, the Lord explained your nature when He said: 'Beware of false prophets,'[6] for they cause your soul to weaken and your mind to totter. Thus, you are not flesh alone. What is flesh without the guidance of the soul and the vigor of the mind? We put on the garment of flesh today and tomorrow it is laid aside. The flesh is temporal, whereas the soul is lasting. Like a garment for the body, such is flesh for the soul. You are not, therefore, a garment, but one who puts on a garment for use. And so you are told to 'strip off the old man with

5 Cant. 1.7; Deut. 4.9.
6 Matt. 7.15.

his deeds and put on the new'[7]—you who are renewed not in the quality of the body, but in the spirit and affirmation of the mind.

Flesh you are not, I repeat. It is not said of the flesh: 'For holy is the temple of God and this temple you are.' And elsewhere: 'You are the temple of God and the Spirit of God dwells in you,'[8] that is to say, in those who have had a new birth and in the faithful in whom the Spirit of God dwells. It does not dwell among the carnal, for it is written: 'My spirit shall not remain in these men forever, because they are flesh.'[9]

Chapter 7

(40) But let us consider the precise order of our creation: 'Let us make mankind,' He said, 'in our image and likeness.'[1]

Who says this? Was it not God who made you? What is God: flesh or spirit? Surely not flesh, but spirit, which has no similarity to flesh. This is material, whereas the spirit is incorporeal and invisible.

To whom does He speak? Surely not to Himself, because He does not say: 'I shall make,' but 'let us make.' He does not speak to the angels, because they are servers, and servants cannot have a part in a work along with their Master and Creator. He speaks, rather, to the Son, although the Jews are unwilling to accept this and the Arians object to it. But let the Jews preserve silence and let the Arians with their progenitors be mute, who, while they exclude One from sharing in the divine work, introduce more participants and grant to underlings a privilege which they deny to the Son.

7 Col. 3.9,10.
8 1 Cor. 3.17,16.
9 Gen. 6.3.

1 Gen. 1.26.

(41) But suppose that God appears to you to have need of the assistance of servants in His work. If God operates in conjunction with the angels, have God and the angels a common 'image'? Would He say to the angels: 'Let us make mankind in our image and likeness'? Listen to the Apostle who tells us who is the image of God: 'Who has rescued us from the power of darkness and transferred us into the kingdom of the Son of His majesty in whom we have our redemption and the redemption of our sins, who is the image of the invisible God and the first-born of every creature.'[2] He is the 'image' of His Father who always is and was from the beginning. Hence it is the 'image' who says: 'Philip, he who sees me sees also the Father.' And again, although you behold the living 'image' of the living Father: 'How canst thou say, show us the Father? Dost thou not believe that I am in the Father and the Father in me?'[3]

The 'image' of God is virtue, not infirmity. The 'image' of God is wisdom. The 'image' of God is He alone who has said: 'I and the Father are one,'[4] thus possessing the likenesss of the Father so as to have a unity of divinity and of plenitude.

When He says 'let us make,' how can there be inequality? When, again, He says 'to our likeness,' where is the dissimilitude? So, when He says in the Gospel: 'I and the Father.' there is no reference to one sole person. But when He says: 'We are one,' there is no distinction either in divinity or in operation. Both, therefore, do not have one person, but one substance. Well did He add: 'We are,' because the divine essence is eternal. So, then, He whom you would consider unlike the Father is co-eternal with Him! He is eternal of whom Moses spoke: 'I AM WHO AM.'[5] Fittingly, too, there preceded

2 Col. 1.13-15.
3 John 14.8-10.
4 John 10.30.
5 Exod. 3.14.

the words: 'I and the Father.'[6] If He had mentioned the Father first, you would consider the Son to be lesser. But He mentioned the Son first, then—as it is not fitting that the Son be above the Father—He added the Father, so that you may note that between the Father and Son there is no precedence of rank.

(42) 'Attend to thyself alone,'[7] says Scripture. In fact, we must distinguish between 'ourselves,' 'ours,' and 'what surrounds us.' 'Ourselves' refers to body and soul. 'Ours' are the members of our bodies and our senses. 'What surrounds us' consists of our money, our slaves, and all that belongs to this life. 'Attend to thyself,' therefore, 'know thyself,' that is to say—not what muscular arms you have, not how strong you are physically, or how many possessions or power you have. Attend, rather, to your soul and mind, whence all our deliberations emanate and to which the profit of your works is referred. Here only is the fullness of wisdom, the plenitude of piety and justice of which God speaks—for all virtue comes from God: 'Behold, Jerusalem, I have painted thy walls.'[8] That soul of yours is painted by God, who holds in Himself the flashing beauty of virtue and the splendor of piety. That soul is well painted in which shines the imprint of divine operation. That soul is well painted in which resides the splendor of grace and the reflection of its paternal nature. Precious is that picture which in its brilliance is in accord with that divine reflection.

Adam before he sinned conformed to this image. But after his fall he lost that celestial image and took on one that is terrestial. Let us flee from this image which cannot enter the city of God, for it is written: 'In thy city, O Lord, thou shall

6 John 10.30.
7 Deut. 4.9.
8 Isa. 49.16.
9 Ps. 72.20.

bring their image to nothing.'[9] An unworthy image does not enter there; no sooner does it enter than it is excluded, because we read: 'There shall not enter into it anything common nor he who practices abomination and falsehood.'[10] He in whose forehead is written the name of the Lamb will find entrance there.

(43) Our soul, therefore, is made to the image of God. In this is man's entire essence, because without it man is nothing but earth and into earth he shall return.[11] Hence, in order to convince you that without the soul the flesh is nothing, Scripture says: 'Do not be afraid of those who kill the body but cannot kill the soul.'[12]

Why, then, do you presume in the flesh, you who lose nothing when you lose the flesh? Rather, be fearful lest you be deprived of the aid of your soul. 'What will a man give in exchange for his own soul?'[13] In this is no slight part of himself—in fact, it is the substantial part of the entire human race. This is the means by which men lord it over other living things, wild beasts, and birds. Your soul is made to the image of God, whereas your body is related to the beasts. In one there is the holy seal of imitation of the divine. In the other there is found base association with beasts and wild animals.

Chapter 8

(44) But let us define more accurately the meaning of the phrase, 'to the image of God.' Is it true that the flesh is made 'to the image of God'? In that case, is there earth in God, since flesh is of earth? Is God corporeal, that is to say, weak and subject like the flesh to the passions? Perhaps the

10 Apoc. 21.27.
11 Cf. Gen. 3.19.
12 Matt. 10.28.
13 Matt. 16.26.

head may seem to you to be made in the likeness of God because it stands aloft, or the eyes because they observe, or the ears because they hear? As to the question of height, are we to consider ourselves to be tall just because we tower a little over the earth? Are we not ashamed to be thought of as like to God merely because we are taller than serpents or other creeping creatures or even than deer, sheep, or wolves? In that respect, how much taller are elephants and camels in comparison with us! Sight is important to us in order to enable us to behold the things of the world and to have knowledge of what is not reported by any person, but is grasped by our sense of sight. How significant, in fact, is this power of sight! Because of it we may be said to have the likeness of God, who sees all, observes all, comprehends our hidden emotions, and searches into the secrets of our hearts!'[1]

Am I not ashamed to admit that it is not in my power to see parts of my body? What is in front of me I can see, but I am unable to see what is behind me. I have no view of my neck or of the back of my head and I cannot see my loins. In like manner, what avail is our sense of hearing if we cannot either see or hear what is only a short distance away? If walls should intervene, both sight and hearing are impeded. Furthermore, our bodies are fixed and enclosed in a narrow space, whereas all wild animals have a wider range and are also swifter than men.

(45) The flesh, therefore, cannot be made to the image of God. This is true, however, of our souls, which are free to wander far and wide in acts of reflection and of counsel. Our souls are able to envisage and reflect on all things. We who are now in Italy have in mind what seems to pertain to affairs in the East or in the West. We seem to have dealings with men who dwell in Persia. We envision those who have their homes in Africa, if there happen to be acquaintances of

1 Cf. Rom. 8.27; 1 Cor. 14.25.

ours who enjoy the hospitality of that land. We accompany these people on their departure and draw near to them in their voyage abroad. We are one with them in their absence. Those who are separated far from us engage us in conversation. We arouse the dead even to mutual interchange of thoughts and embrace them as if they were still living. We even go to the point of conferring on these people the usages and customs of our daily life.

That, therefore, is made to the image of God which is perceived, not by the power of the body, but by that of the mind. It is that power which beholds the absent and embraces in its vision countries beyond the horizon. Its vision crosses boundaries and gazes intently on what is hidden.[2] In one moment the utmost bounds of the world and its remote secret places are under its ken. God is attained and Christ is approached. There is a descent into hell, and aloft in the sky there is an ascent into heaven. Hear, then, what Scripture says: 'But our citizenship is in heaven.'[3] Is not that, therefore, in which God is ever-present made to the likeness of God? Listen to what the Apostle says in that regard: 'We all, therefore, with faces unveiled, reflecting as in a mirror the glory of God, are being transformed into his very image from glory to glory, as through the Spirit of the Lord.'[4]

(46) Now that we are convinced that the soul is made to the likeness of God, let us take up the question as to whether the statement 'let us make man' can be said of the soul. Give ear to the words of Scripture, where in Genesis the word 'soul' is used for man: 'And the sons of Joseph that were born to him in the land of Egypt, two souls. All the souls of the house of Jacob that entered into Egypt were seventy.'[5]

---

2 Cf. Sallust, *Bellum Jug.* 12.5.
3 Phil. 3.20.
4 2 Cor. 3.18.
5 Gen. 46.27.

Appropriately enough, the soul is called *homo* in Latin and ἄνθρωπος in Greek, the former being derived from 'humanity' and the latter from a word associated with the lively faculty of 'seeing,'[6] a faculty which has more kinship with the soul than with the body. This agrees well with what is said in the Lamentations of Jeremias: 'The Lord is good to them that support him, to the soul that seeketh him.'[7] He made reference to men and thought it necessary to add 'soul.' God preferably seeks after the soul when it is alone, thus dissociating Himself from the slime of the body and from the cupidity of the flesh.

The soul, then, is made to the image of God, in form like the Lord Jesus. Those men are saints who are conformed to the Son of God. So we read in the Apostle Paul: 'Now we know that for those who love God all things work together unto good, for those who, according to His purpose, are saints through his call. For those whom he has foreknown he has also predestined to become conformed to the image of his Son, that he should be the first-born among many brethren. And those whom he has predestined, them has he also called and those whom he has called, them he has also justified, and those whom he has justified, them he has also glorified.'[8] I request a reply to the question: Is justification bestowed on you in terms of the body or of the soul? But there can be no doubt about the answer, since justice, from which justification is derived, is naturally a mental, not a physical, quality.

(47) Man has been depicted by the Lord God, his artist. He is fortunate in having a craftsman and a painter of distinction. He should not erase that painting, one that is the product of truth, not of semblance, a picture, expressed not in

6 From the supposed connection between *ops* and the last two syllables in anthr*opos*.
7 Lam. 3.25.
8 Rom. 8.28-30.

mere wax, but in the grace of God. I speak, also, of women. They erase that painting by smearing on their complexion a color of material whiteness or by applying an artificial rouge. The result is a work not of beauty, but of ugliness; not of simplicity, but of deceit. It is a temporal creation, a prey to perspiration or to rain. It is a snare and a deception which displeases the person you aim to please, for he realizes that all this is an alien thing and not your own. This is also displeasing to your Creator, who sees His own work obliterated. Tell me, if you were to invite an artist of inferior ability to work over a painting of another of superior talent, would not the latter be grieved to see his own work falsified? Do not displace the artistic creation of God by one of meretricious worth, for it is written: 'Shall I take the members of Christ and make them members of a harlot?'[9] By no means!

He commits a serious offense who adulterates the work of God. It is a serious charge to suppose that man is to be preferred to God as an artist! It is serious, indeed, when God has to say this about you: 'I do not recognize My colors or My image, not even the countenance which I have made. What is not Mine I reject. Take up your abode with him who has painted you. Seek your favors from him to whom you have given payment.' What will be your reply?

(48) If it is a serious matter to adulterate the work of God, what shall we say of those who slay the work of God, who shed human blood and take away the life that God has granted? They say: 'Let us take away the just because he is useless to us.'[10] Hence we read today in the Gospel: 'The foxes have dens and the birds of the air have nests wherein to rest; but the Son of Man has nowhere to lay his head.'[11] So the fox hides himself in a den and the birds protect

9 1 Cor. 6.15.
10 Wisd. 2.12.
11 Matt. 8.20.

themselves in their nests. Man, however, does not hide himself in a den—rather, he is beguiled. The mouth of man is a den, and a deep den, too, is the heart of man where injurious and deceptive counsels and thoughts of evil reside.

You make preparations to take a walk while another man is setting a trap for you. 'You are going in the midst of snares'[12] which your enemies have planted secretly in your way. Make careful observations, therefore, so as not to be trapped in a net like a deer or in a snare like a bird. The deer avoids the net by the keenness of his vision. The bird escapes the snares by surveying the territory from a point aloft. No one plants his net or conceals his snare up there. And so, one whose 'citizenship is in heaven'[13] is not likely to be captured like a bird of prey.

And why do you wonder at man's deception of man when the Son of Man has nowhere to lay His head? In fact, He has purposedly made man to be such that He could find therein a place to rest His head. But when our neighbors find no repose in our hearts, but traps and snares therein for our fellow men, to whom we ought to give help, then Christ turns His head away from us—this head which He was so willing to offer on our behalf even to the point of death! Do not expose yourself, therefore, to deceitfulness, cruelty and unkindness, so that there may be occasion for Christ to rest His head on you.

(49) Moreover, He did not find rest when He had created such irrational creatures as fish and the various species of wild beasts. He found rest, however, after He had made man to His own image. Give ear to Him as He states on whom He finds rest: 'Or on whom shall I rest but on him that is humble and gentle and that trembleth at my words?'[14] There-

12 Eccli. 9.20.
13 Phil. 3.20.
14 Isa. 66.2 (Septuagint).

fore, be humble and gentle, so that God may find rest in your affection.

He who does not find his rest in the beasts of the field will much less find repose in his bestial heart. There exist minds of bestial nature and wild beasts, too, in the form of men, concerning whom the Lord says: 'Beware of false prophets who come to you in sheep's clothing but inwardly are ravening wolves.'[15] God does not find repose in these, but in the actions of man whom He has made to His image and likeness and who ought not to veil his head, since 'he is the image and glory of God.'[16]

To the soul of such a man He says: 'Behold, Jerusalem, I have painted thy walls.'[17] He did not say 'I have painted thy belly' or 'thy lower parts,' but 'I have painted thy walls,' thus proclaiming that the strong protection of walls was granted to man. In this way, by keeping careful watch on the walls, man can ward off the dangers involved in a siege. He says, therefore: 'I have given you neither delights nor the allurements of desire, neither incentives to luxurious living nor eagerness to possess another's dignities. You have been granted a substantial basis for erecting walls and lofty turrets by means of which you can banish fear of an enemy's assault and the dread of terrifying raids from legions of soldiers.'

In fact, you have in Isaias the speech made by the soul of a just man or of the Church: 'I am a fortified city, I am a city besieged,'[18] defended by Christ and besieged by the Devil. But he whom Christ aids ought not to be fearful of a siege. He is defended by spiritual grace and is besieged by the perils of this world. Hence, also, it is said in the Canticles: 'I am a wall and my breasts are as a tower.'[19] The wall is the

---

15 Matt. 7.15.
16 1 Cor. 11.7.
17 Isa. 49.16.
18 Isa. 27.10; Ps. 30.22.
19 Cant. 8.10.

Church and the towers are her priests, who have full power to teach both the natural and the moral sciences.

(50) Be fully aware, O beautiful soul, of the fact that you are the image of God. And, man, be aware that you are the glory of God. Hear the words of the Prophet on the question of glory: 'Thy knowledge is become wonderful to me.'[20] That is to say, in my work your majesty, O God, has become more wonderful; in the counsels of men Your wisdom is exalted. When I contemplate myself such as I am known to You in my secret thoughts and deepest emotions, the mysteries of Your knowledge are disclosed to me.

Know then, man, your greatness and see to it that you never on any occasion become entrapped in the snares of the Devil, so as not to fall, perchance, into the jaws of that dread beast 'who as a roaring lion goes about seeking someone to devour.'[21] Take heed of what goes into you and what comes out. I do not refer to food which is absorbed and ejected,[22] but to words and thoughts. Do not allow yourself to be led into concupiscence in regard to a neighbor's wife or let your eye be captivated by the beauty of a woman who passes by. Your mind and your conversation should shun being involved in the crafty ways of seduction. Deceit should be far from your thoughts and you should not indulge in slander against your neighbor.

God has made you a hunter, not a harrier, for He says: 'Behold I will send you many hunters'[23]—hunters, not of crime, but of absolution therefrom; hunters, certainly not of sin, but of grace. You are a fisher of Christ, for whom it is said: 'Henceforth thou shalt make men live.'[24] Spread your nets, direct your eyes, and control your tongue in such a man-

20 Ps. 138.6.
21 1 Peter 5.8.
22 Cf. Matt. 5.11,17-19.
23 Jer. 16.16.
24 Luke 5.10.

ner that you destroy no one, but bring rescue to those who struggle in the waters. He has declared: 'Let him so stand so as to take heed lest he fall' and 'So run as to obtain the prize.'[25] So struggle that you may often discover that the crown is awarded only to him who has competed according to the rules.[26]

You are a soldier. Then take stock of the enemy, lest at night he may creep upon you. You are an athlete. Come to grips with your enemy, not with your head, but with your arms, lest he strike you in the eye. Let your vision be unobstructed and your offense be cautious so as to parry the attack; take advantage of his weaknesses, 'shunning blows on the body with watchful eyes'[27] and repelling the assault by aggressive action.

If you should suffer a wound, take heed and run to a physician, to seek a remedy in repentance. Take heed, because you are made of weak and stumbling flesh. May the good physician of souls, the Divine Word, come to your assistance. May the oracles of the Lord be to you like health-giving medicines. Take heed that no unrighteous word lie hidden in your heart, for it creeps through your body like poison, bringing with it deadly infection. Take heed, lest you forget the God who made you, and do not take His name in vain.

(51) When you have eaten your fill, build a home for your habitation, abounding in flocks and in gold and silver, together with all that you possess in plentiful abundance. Then 'take heed that thine heart be lifted up and thou remember not the Lord,'[28] as the Law states.

For 'what hast thou that thou hast not received?'[29] Do not

---

25 1 Cor. 9.24.
26 Cf. 2 Tim. 2.5.
27 Virgil, *Aeneid* 5.438.
28 Deut. 8.14.
29 1 Cor. 4.7.

these things pass like a shadow?[30] Is not this home of yours but dust and desolation? Are not all these things false? Are not the treasures of the world mere vanities? Are you not yourself just ashes? Look into the sepulchers of men and take note that nothing will remain of you but bones and ashes. Look inside, I repeat, and tell me who in there is rich and who is poor? Distinguish now between the needy and the powerful. Naked we come into this world and naked we leave it. There are no distinctions discoverable among the bodies of the dead, unless, perchance, it may well be that those of the wealthy give forth a stronger odor because they were bloated with luxurious living. Who ever heard of a poor man dying of indigestion? His impoverished condition is beneficial to him. He exercises his body and does not overload it. 'I have not heard of the just man forsaken nor his descendants begging bread,'[31] because the man who labors well in his own land has a plentiful supply of food. Take heed, therefore, man of wealth, because you, like the poor man, bear your burden of flesh.

(52) Because your soul is a priceless thing, poor man, be on your guard. The soul is everlasting, although the flesh is mortal. Although you may lack money, you are not therefore devoid of grace. Although your house is not commodious, your possessions are not scattered. The sky is open and the expanse of the world is free. The elements have been granted to all for their common use. Rich and poor alike enjoy the splendid ornaments of the universe.

Are the paneled ceilings decked with gold[32] in the homes of the very wealthy more beautiful than the face of the heavens decorated with glistening stars? Are the estates of the rich more extensive than the surface of the world? Hence it was said of those who join house to house and estate to

30 Cf. Eccle. 7.1.
31 Ps. 36.25.
32 Cf. Horace, *Odes* 2.18.1.

estate: 'Shall you alone dwell in the midst of the earth?'[33] You have actually a larger house, you man of low estate—a house wherein your call is heard and heeded. 'O Israel,' said the Prophet, 'how great is the house of God and how vast is the place of his possession! It is great and hath no end: it is high and immense.'[34] The house of God is common to rich and poor. However, 'with difficulty will a rich man enter the kingdom of heaven.'[35]

Perhaps you resent the fact that 'the light of golden lamps'[36] do not shine in your home. But how much more brilliant is the suffused light of the moon! In winter you find a cause for complaint that you do not possess a room-heater with its 'breathing vapors.'[37] But you possess the heat of the sun, which tempers the surface of the earth and protects you from the cold of winter. Do you really consider those people happy 'who are attended by a mighty throng'[38] of obsequious servants? But those who rely on the feet of others lose by disuse the power of using their own. Hence, only a few of the servitors act as outriders; most of them are needed as bearers.

You may gaze in admiration on their abundance of money: gold and silver. You see how much they have in abundance, but you not see how much they need. To be able to recline in litters in ivory is, to your mind, the height of luxury. But you do not realize how luxurious a possession is the earth, which spreads its couch of grass for the humble man. Here are sweet repose and gentle sleep—such sleep as the restless owner of a golden bed seeks in vain to attain. How much happier does he consider you to be as you lie there so peacefully! So hard is it for him to invite sleep.

---

33 Isa. 5.8.
34 Bar. 3.24,25.
35 Matt. 19.23.
36 Virgil, *Aeneid* 1.726.
37 *Ibid.* 8.421.
38 *Ibid.* 4.136.

Besides, there is, of course, another aspect which is much more important. I refer to the fact that the just man who is in want here will find abundance yonder and that he who has endured toil here will find elsewhere his consolation. Moreover, whoever has acquired goods here cannot hope to receive there a return for his investment. The poor man saves up his interest, whereas the rich man squanders it.

(53) The poor man and the rich man should therefore take heed, because there are temptations for the man of poverty as well as for the man of wealth. And so the wise man says:[39] 'Give me neither beggary nor riches.' He tells you how this can be attained. Man has enough when he has a sufficiency, because a wealthy man tends to distend his mind with cares and anxieties, just as he gorges his stomach with rich food. For that reason the wise man prays that he may have what is necessary and adequate, saying: 'Lest perhaps being filled I should be tempted to deny and say, who sees me? Or being compelled by poverty I should steal and forswear the name of the Lord.'

Shun and avoid, therefore, the temptations of the world, so that the poor may not despair and the rich may not grow proud. For it is written, when you have expelled the heathen and have begun to make use of their land: 'Lest thou shouldst say, my own might and the strength of my own hand have achieved all these things for me.'[40] Such a one is he who ascribes all his success to his own merits, and hence, feeling self-assured, does not recognize his own errors which drag him with their .extended rope afar.[14] For, if he believes that his acquisition of property is due either to mere chance or to shrewd cunning, there is no occasion for him to feel undue pride in matters to which there is no glory attached,

39 Prov. 30.8,9.
40 Deut. 8.17.
41 Cf. Horace, *Epistles* 1.10.47,48.

or where the labor results in naught, or where there is evidence of shameless cupidity, which prescribes no limits in its pursuit of pleasure.

Chapter 9

(54) But something must be said on the subject of the human body. Who can deny that it excels all things in grace and beauty? Although it seems in substance to be one and the same with all earthly things, certain wild animals have superiority in strength and size. Yet the form of the human body, by reason of its erectness and stature, is such that it lacks massive hugeness as well as abject lowliness. Moreover, the very appearance of the body is gentle and pleasing without those extremes of size and of insignificance which might lead either to dread or to indifference.

(55) First, let us make note of the fact that the body of man is constructed like the world itself. As the sky is preeminent over air, earth, and sea, which serve as members of the world, so we observe that the head has a position above the other members of our body. In the same way, the sky stands supreme among the other elements, just as a citadel amid the other outposts in a city's defense. In this citadel dwells what might be called regal Wisdom, as stated in the words of the Prophet: 'The eyes of a wise man are in his head.'[1] That is to say, this position is better protected than the others and from it strength and prevision are brought to bear on all the rest.

What avail are the strength and vigor of our muscles or the swiftness of our feet without the direction and assistance of the head, its commander-in-chief? From this source comes

1 Eccle. 2.14.

real support for all the members or their complete abandonment.

To what avail is courage in combat without the aid of the eyes? To what avail is flight, if sight be lacking? The body as a whole may be likened to a dark and filthy prison unless it is illuminated by the visual power of the eye. The eyes in man correspond to the sun and moon in the heavens. The sun and moon are the 'twin lights of the firmament.'[2] Our eyes are in our heads like stars which shine aloft and with their bright lights illuminate objects below, thus permitting us to avoid being involved, as it were, in nocturnal darkness. They are our sentries which keep watch day and night. They are aroused from slumber quicker than our other members and on awakening take stock of everything. They are nearer to the brain, the seat of our ability to see.

In answer to those who think that I have made a too hasty descent from the rest of the head in order to praise the eyes, I maintain that it is not unfitting to commend in part that which is most significant in itself. It is clear that the eyes constute a part of the head. And so with the aid of the eyes the head examines all things. With the ears it lays bare what is secret, obtains knowledge of what is hidden, and hears of events that occur in remote lands.

(56) How gentle and pleasing is the sight of the top of the head, how attractive are its locks of hair, an object of regard for our elders, of reverence for our priests! For warriors, how fear-inspiring, for the young, how pleasing can these locks be, whether arranged becomingly as in the case of women or with the soft sheen of youth! Long hair is unbecoming to one sex; shorn locks do not become the other.

One can learn from trees how charming a human head can be. In the treetop everything stands for fruit, for beauty. The tree's hair-like foliage shields us from rain storms or

---

2 Cf. Virgil, *Georgics* 1.5.

protects us from the sun. Take away the tree's leafy locks and the tree is wholly devoid of beauty. How precious, therefore, is this adornment for the human head! It protects and invests with hair the very center and source of all our senses, the brain, so that it may not be unduly affected by cold or heat! Therein is found the primary source of all our feelings. It is natural that beauty should be the attribute of that which is most sensitive to ill.

(57) What is man without his head, since the totality of man is in his head? When you see a head you recognize a man. If the head is lacking, no recognition is possible. He lies an ignoble trunk, without honor, 'a nameless corpse.'[3] Men pay reverence merely to the heads of princes cast in bronze or to their features carved in bronze or marble.[4]

Not without reason, therefore, do the other members pay their respects to the head as to their director. They surround it like servants bearing a litter and carry it aloft as something divine. Hence, it has the power of a censor, whereby directions and orders are given to the servants and special instructions are relayed to each individual. You have there a picture of each man willingly and without pay serving his commander-in-chief. Some serve as porters; others take care of the provisions. Some act as bodyguards; others as orderlies. They obey his orders as chief and minister to him as their master. Before him there seems to precede what may be termed the countersign or standing order, whereby the feet are directed to approach a certain region, enjoining what military service the hands should initiate and complete, and what disciplinary orders should be imposed on the stomach in the way of indulgence or abstention from food.

(58) A forehead free, open and with bare temples, adorns the head. According to its appearance one may judge a

3 Virgil, *Aeneid* 2.558.
4 Cf. Virgil, *Aeneid* 6.848.

person's state of mind, now joyful or sad, now frowning in moments of seriousness or smooth in moments of relaxation, answering in forensic fashion to one's inmost wish or will. Here we have a image of a mind giving, as it were, expression to words. Here is a foundation for belief, on which daily the name of the Lord is inscribed and preserved.

A two-fold hedge, the eyebrows, are next in order. These serve as a line of defense for the eyes and have a charm to lighten a beautiful smile and at the same time are attentive to their protective function. If any speck of sand or dirt, drops of misty vapor or of streaming sweat should fall down, the eyebrow serves to check it, so that no obstruction can disturb the delicately formed organs of vision.[5]

(59) Close to these mountain-like eyebrows are arranged the eyes, which are made safer by this bulwark of protection. From their high position they are enabled to perceive all things as if from a loftier stage. A position of less eminence, such as that of the ears, mouth, or cavernous nose, would ill befit the eyes. Watch towers are always placed on high, so that the approach of hostile bands can be detected—bands which are ready to take by surprise a city in the midst of a celebration, together with its people and its proud imperial army.

In this way, too, attacks from robbers may be anticipated, if scouts are placed on walls, towers, or on the brows of a high mountain. From these points the level regions below can be observed where raiding parties can find no hiding place. It happens also at sea that, when the nearness of land is suspected, a lookout eagerly climbs the topmost mast or the high yard arms and announces the sight of a distant land still invisible to the rest of the navigators.

(60) Perhaps you may say that if a watch must necessarily be placed in a high position, why are not the eyes not set in the very top of the head, as in the case of crabs and

5 Cf. Cicero, *De natura deorum* 2.143 (on the eyelids).

beetles who have no apparent head, but whose necks and backs are higher than the rest of the body? But these have a tough shell, whereas human beings have a tender covering of skin which can easily be cut and torn by briers and brambles. Moreover, other animals are so constituted that they either can guard their eyes by bending their heads toward their shoulders, as in the case of horses, oxen, and nearly all wild beasts, or turn them, as birds do, toward their wings for complete repose and protection.

It is right that the eyes should be set in the highest part of the body in a sort of citadel, there to defend themselves from all, even from the slightest attacking force.[6] Here we are faced with what appears to be a contradiction. If the eyes were placed in a lower position for reasons of safety, they would be unable to function; if in a higher, they would be exposed to injury. Wherefore, lest anything detract from their usefulness or lest any precaution against injury be not available, God has placed the eyes in a position where the eyebrows above provide no little defense and where the cheeks below contribute their mite of protecting embankment. In addition, the nose offers a covering for the interior position, while the exterior seems to be surrounded by a bulwark of defense in the protuberant masses of forehead and jaw—a structure, notwithstanding its connecting joints, arranged with due evenness and balance.

In the midst of these are found the orbs of the eyes. They are in a secure position for defense. They are free to make observation and, crystal-like, give forth beauty. In their midst are the pupils, which are the organs of sight. To provide for any possible injury, they are encircled with a rampart composed of an orderly arrangement of filaments of hair.

Hence, in requesting help and safety for himself the

---

6 *Ibid.* 2.140.

Prophet says: 'Keep me, O Lord, as the apple of your eye.'[7] He asks for the necessary custody and the protection of Him who has deigned to fortify the pupil of the eye with natural palisades. Because innocence and purity may be violated by the intrusion of a slight speck of dust and thus be deprived of the gift of grace, we must for that reason be on our guard lest the dust of error may cloud it or that any speck of sin cause it pain. It is written: 'First cast out the beam from thy own eye and then wilt thou see clearly to cast out the speck from thy brother's eye.'[8]

(61) Those skilled in the art of medicine maintain, in fact, that the brain is placed in a man's head for the sake of the eyes and that the other senses of our bodies are housed close together on account of the brain. The brain is the source of our nervous system and of all the sensations of voluntary movement. From it emanates the cause of all that we have discussed. It is the starting point of the arteries and of that natural heat which gives life and warmth to the vital parts. Many are of the opinion that this starting point is the heart. The nerves serve as organs of each of the senses. These proceed from the brain like cords and musical strings. They fulfill their individual functions throughout the various parts of the body.

Hence, the brain, because it is the gathering point of all the senses, is softer than the other organs. From it emanate the nerves which report everything; for example, what the eye sees and what the ear hears, what odor has been perceived, and what sound the tongue has given forth or what taste the mouth has experienced. That which is softer is more susceptible to impressions. The harder quality of the nervous system, which results in a certain tautness, makes for more efficacy in action.

---

7 Ps. 16.8.
8 Matt. 7.5.

(62) The sense of hearing has also a highly important function, nearly on a par with that of sight. The ears are rather prominent for this and for several other reasons. They serve a decorative purpose and, secondly, are in the way of anything, moist or otherwise, which may fall from the top of the head. Again, their commodiousness makes it possible for them to receive in their recesses repercussions of sound without the danger of injuring the interior structure. If this were not the case how astonished we would be at the instrusion of any sound or of a voice stronger than usual! Even with our present organs of hearing are we not often benumbed by an unexpected burst of sound? You may note the fact however that they present a bulwark against bitter cold and burning heat. The open passage ways are impenetrable to these same attacks, whether from severity of cold or excess of heat.

The sinuous quality of the interior part of the ear furnishes a basis for training in modulation, since a certain rhythmic movement follows from the natural windings of the ear. The entry of a sound of a voice results, too, in specific tonal modifications. Again, our own experience tells us that such a sinuous character of the ear tends to better receptivity of the spoken word. We see that the voice is rendered gentler and sweeter in situations where we hear an echo in the mountain hollows, in rocky caves, or along winding streams.[9] Not without its usefulness, too, is the wax in the ear. It helps to keep the voice intact, a result which at one and the same time aids the memory and is a source of pleasure.

(63) What shall I say of the form of the nose, which offers for the perception of odors a cave-like structure with its two distended openings? The odor does not pass through in indifferent fashion, but stays long within, so that by this procedure it is able to satisfy fully the brain and the senses.

---

9 Cf. Virgil, *Georgics,* 4.49,50.

It frequently happens that a transient aroma may continue to stay with you for an entire day. Through the nose, too, flow purgaments issuing from the head in such a way that the body is not adversely affected in the process.

(64) The sense of touch is not without its significance. It represents the keenest sort of pleasure and gives as well an honest report of facts. Frequently, we are able to prove by touch what we cannot do with the aid of the eyes.

(65) Finally, there remain the functions of the mouth and tongue, which furnish strength to all the others. The eyes would not have the power of vision without the substantial basis of physical force provided by food and drink. The ears, nose, and hands would not be capable of hearing, smelling and touching, if the whole body were not sustained by nourishment. Our strength declines unless it is restored by continued absorption of adequate food. For that reason, those exhausted by hunger have no sensation of pleasure in the use of the senses. Not being, as it were, participants,[10] they have no part in the predelictions of these senses.

(66) What shall I say of the rampart of teeth built for the mastication of food and for the full expression of the human voice? Without teeth, what pleasure would our daily sustenance give us? Hence we note that in this respect there is often a clear indication that old age has been reached. Because of the loss of teeth, really nourishing food cannot be assimilated.

(67) The tongue, too, fulfills a most important function in eating as well as in speaking. It acts like a plectrum or quill[11] in the production of speech. It might be compared to a hand in the process of bringing to the action of the teeth the food particles that otherwise would tend to fall. Speech has its special function. It is carried through the void on the

10 Cf. Virgil, *Aeneid* 6.428.
11 Cf. Cicero, *De natura deorum* 2.149.

wings of the air which is affected by this impulsive force, at once stirring and calming the emotions of the hearer, pacifying the angry, lifting up the down-hearted, and consoling the grief-stricken. Granted that man shares his vocal powers with the birds,[12] there is, nevertheless, nothing in the irrational animals which can be equated with the sound of the human voice, provided, as it is, with rational powers.

We share, in fact, with the rest of living beings the ordinary sense channels, but they do not make use of them in the same way we do. The heifer raises her eyes to the sky, but she is unaware of what she sees. This is true, also, of wild animals and birds. All living things have the same liberty to see, but man alone has the will to interpret what he perceives. He gazes at the rising and the setting of the celestial signs. He sees the glory of the sky and marvels at the starry orbs. He is aware of the diverse aspect of each star. He knows when the evening and the morning star arise and why they appear at these times. The movements of Orion, as well as the phases of the moon, are well known to him. He understands how 'the sun knows the hour of its setting'[13] and how it preserves its allotted course with due regularity.

Other living beings also have the power of hearing, but who other than man acquires knowledge by the sense of hearing? Man alone of all terrestial beings is able by listening, reflection, and wisdom to gather the secrets of knowledge. He is able to say: 'I will hear what the Lord God will speak to me.'[14] The most important of all things is this: Man becomes the organ of the voice of God and gives utterance with his corporeal lips to the oracular words from

12 Cf. the Epicurean doctrine in Lucretius 5.1379.
13 Ps. 103.19.
14 Ps. 84.9.

heaven, such as: 'Cry. What shall I cry? All flesh is grass.'[15] He heard what he ought to say and he cried aloud.

Let those who mark out with a compass the regions of the sky and of the earth keep their wisdom for themselves. Let them have that knowledge of which the Lord speaks: 'The wisdom of the prudent I will reject.'[16] Neither the rhythm of a speech nor the tones and notes of musical science will enter into my discussion at this point. I shall confine myself to that wisdom of which the Prophet speaks: 'The uncertain and hidden things of thy wisdom thou hast made manifest to me.'[17]

(68) What shall I say of the kiss which is a symbol of affection and love? Doves exchange kisses, but what is this compared to the charm of a kiss of a human being in which the note of friendliness and kindliness is conspicuous, and where is expressed the indubitable sense of our sincerest affection?

Hence the Lord, condemning His betrayer as a species of monstrosity, says: 'Judas, dost thou betray the Son of Man with a kiss?'[18] That is to say, changing the emblem of love into a sign of betrayal and to a revelation of unfaithfulness, are you employing this pledge of peace for the purpose of cruelty? And thus by the oracular voice of God reproof is given to him who by the bestial conjunction of lips bestows a sentence of death rather than a covenant of love.

It is worthy of note, too, that it is given to men alone to express with their lips what they feel in their hearts. Hence we make evident our tacit mental reflections with the speech that flows from our lips. What is the mouth of man but an

15 Isa. 40.6.
16 1 Cor. 1.19; Isa. 29.14.
17 Ps. 50.8.
18 Luke 22.48.

avenue for discourse, a fount of disputation, a reception hall for words, a repository of the will?

We have now completed our general discussion of the human body. It can be compared to a royal palace, which, though it has a number of adjoining halls, still preserves the appearance of a unified whole.

(69) To come down to particulars, there is the throat or neck through which vital contacts are made with the whole body and through which, too, the coursing flow of this breath of ours is poured.

Next we have the arms, and the strong fore-arm muscles, together with the hands strong for action and adaptable for holding objects by reason of their prolonged fingers. Hence that greater aptitude for work, that elegance in writing, and that 'pen of the scrivener that writeth swiftly,'[19] whereby the oracles of God are set down in writing. It is the hand that serves the mouth with food. Great are the deeds for which the hand is eminent. The hand is placed on the holy altars as conciliator of divine grace. Through it we offer as well as partake in the celestial sacraments. It is the hand which performs and at the same time dispenses the divine mysteries. The Son of God did not disdain to declare by the mouth of David: 'The right hand of the Lord hath wrought strength: the right hand of the Lord hath exalteth me.'[20] It is the hand which has created all things, as the omnipotent God has said: 'Did not my hand make all these things?'[21] The hand is the outpost of the entire body, as well as the defender of the head. Although it is lower in position, the hand serves to decorate and beautify the top of the head with becoming adornments.

(70) Who can worthily describe the wicker-work of the

19 Ps. 44.2.
20 Ps. 117.16.
21 Isa. 66.2.

chest[22] or the tenderness of the stomach? If it were not for these, the more delicate internal organs could not be protected and the folds of the intestines would undoubtedly be injured by the hard structure of bone. What is more conducive to health than that the lungs should hold a position contiguous to the heart? When the heart flares up with anger and indignation, it can soon be moderated by the action of the blood and vapor in the lungs. Again, the lungs are tender because they are ever filled with moisture so as to offset immediately the rigidity induced by indignation.

We have set forth these matters in a fashion so brief and succinct that we seem, in the manner of the unskilled, just to touch on the merely obvious. Our purpose is not to probe deeply like a physician nor is it our design to search into what is hidden far in the haunts of nature.

(71) The close association of the spleen and the liver leads to good results. The spleen absorbs what it feeds on, eliminates whatever refuse is found there. The result is that whatever food is left is able in its liquified condition to pass through the very fine fibers of the liver and is then transformed into blood. This serves to produce vital strength and is not evacuated with the excrements of the body.

The construction of the intestines with their involved folds, woven without entanglement one with the other, indicates nothing else but the divine providence of the Creator, inasmuch as food particles neither pass quickly through the stomach nor are they immediately evacuated. If this were to happen, men would have an incessant hunger and continuous craving for food. For, when the interior is emptied and drained at the moment when the food is being immediately evacuated, an inordinate and insatiable desire for food and drink must necessarily follow—a result which without question may lead to an early death.

22 Cf. Virgil, *Aeneid* 12.508.

It is providentially designed, therefore, that the food be first digested in the upper ventricle and next be liquified in the exhalation of the liver. The resulting fluid is then transfused into the rest of the body. Our limbs are nourished by this substance, providing growth for the young and endurance for the old. The superfluous residue is carried through the intestines and finds its exit by the customary 'door in the side.'[23]

(72) In Genesis it is fittingly stated that the ark of Noe, was formed in the fashion of the human body. Of the ark God said: 'Make thee an ark of timber planks. Thou shalt make little rooms and thou shalt pitch it within and without.' The outward appearance was as follows: 'The door in the ark thou shalt set in the side with lower, middle chambers and third stories shalt thou make it.'[24] By this the Lord meant that 'the door set in the side' was to be the place through which superfluous food was to be ejected. It is fitting, also, that the channel for refuse was placed by the Creator remote from man's countenance, so that, when we bend over, our countenance may not be contaminated. At the same time, take note of the fact that the shameful parts of the body are placed there where they cannot cause us shame when they are suitably covered with clothing.

(73) The pulsation of the veins is a messenger either of infirmity or of health. Although the veins are spread throughout the entire body, they are neither exposed nor uncovered. They are sheathed in such a slight coating of flesh that one can easily find then and as readily feel them. There is no thick covering of flesh which can conceal them from view. The bones, too, are all covered with a thin coating of flesh and are bound with the tendons. Those on the top of the

23 Gen. 6.16.
24 Gen. 14.1.

head have the advantage of being covered with a thin skin. They are clothed, also, with a thick growth of hair, the better to provide protection against rain and cold.

What shall I say of the genitals, which from the veins in the region of the neck through the reins and loins receive the generating seed destined for the function and satisfaction of procreation?

(74) What shall I say of the purpose of the legs, which, without suffering any ill effects, are sufficient to sustain the weight of the whole body? The knee has a certain flexibility, by reason of which the offended master is especially appeased, his ire softened, and his favors induced. This is the gift of the most high Father to His Son: 'That in the name of the Lord every knee should bend of those in heaven, on earth and under the earth and every tongue should confess that the Lord Jesus is in the glory of God the Father.'[25]

There are two things which above all others give delight to God: humility and faith. The leg expresses the emotion of humility and the submission of constant service. Faith makes the Son equal to the Father and makes evident that the same glory belongs to each.

That man should have two legs and not more is altogether fitting. Wild animals and beasts have four legs, while birds possess two. Hence man has kinship with the winged flock in that with his vision he aims at what is high. He flies as if 'on the oarage of wings'[26] by reason of the sagacity of his sublime senses. Hence it was said of him: 'Your youth is renewed like the eagle's,'[27] because he is near what is celestial and is higher than the eagle, as one who can say: 'But our citizenship is in heaven.'[28]

---

25 Phil. 2.10.
26 A Virgilian expression often repeated.
27 Ps. 102.5.
28 Phil. 3.20.

Chapter 10

(75) But now we seem to have reached the end of our discourse, since the sixth day is completed and the sum total of the work of the world has been concluded. There has taken place, in fact, the creation of man himself, who holds the principate over every living thing and is what might be called the summation of the universe and the delight of every creature in the world.

Surely we should now make our contribution of silence, since God has rested from the work of the world.[1] He found repose in the deep recesses of man, in man's mind and purpose, for He had made man with the power of reasoning, an imitator of Himself, a striver after virtue, and one eager for heavenly grace. God finds comfort in these traits, as His own testimony declares: 'Or on whom shall I find repose but on him who is humble and peaceful and who trembles at my words?'[2]

(76) I give thanks to our Lord God, who made a work of such a nature that He could find rest therein. He made the heavens. I do not read that He rested. He made the earth. I do not read that He rested. He made the sun, moon, and stars. I do not read that He found rest there. But I do read that He made man and then found rest in one whose sins He would remit.

It may well be that He had given a symbolic picture then of the future Passion of the Lord, thus revealing that in man one day Christ would find repose. He anticipated for Himself repose [of death] in the body for the redemption of mankind, as He declares is His own words: 'I have slept and taken my rest and I have risen up, because the Lord

1 Cf. Gen. 2.2.
2 Isa. 66.2 (Septuagint).

hath protected me.'[3] He, the Creator, rested. To Him be honor, praise, and glory everlasting from the beginning of time, now, always, and for ever. Amen.

---

3 Ps. 3.6.

PARADISE

PARADISE

Chapter 1

On approaching this subject I seem to be possessed by an unusual eagerness in my quest to clarify the facts about Paradise, its place, and its nature to those who are desirous of this knowledge. This is all the more remarkable since the Apostle did not know whether he was in the body or out of the body, yet he says that he 'was caught up to the third heaven.'[1] And again he says: 'I know such a man—whether in the body or out of the body I do not know, God knows—that he was caught up into paradise and heard secret words that man may not repeat. Of such a man I will boast; but of myself I will glory in nothing save in my infirmities. For if I do wish to boast, I shall not be foolish; for I am speaking the truth.'[2] If Paradise, then, is of such a nature that Paul alone, or one like Paul, could scarcely see it while alive, and still was unable to remember whether he saw it in the body or out of the body, and, moreover, heard words that he was forbidden

1 2 Cor. 12.2.
2 2 Cor. 12.3-6.

to reveal—if this be true, how will be it possible for us to declare the position of Paradise which we have not been able to see and, even if we had succeeded in seeing it, we would be forbidden to share this information with others? And, again, since Paul shrank from exalting himself by reason of the sublimity of the revelation, how much more ought we to strive not to be too anxious to disclose that which leads to danger by its very revelation! The subject of Paradise should not, therefore, be treated lightly. With these words let us set aside the question of what was hidden to Paul.

(2) Nevertheless, we can find out who was the Creator of this Paradise. We read in Genesis that God planted a garden to the east and he put there the man he had formed.'[3] Who had the power to create Paradise, if not almighty God, who 'spoke and they were made'[4] and who was never in want of the thing which He wished to bring into being? He planted, therefore, that Paradise of which He says in His wisdom: 'Every plant which my Father has not planted will be rooted up.'[5] This is a goodly plantation for angels and saints. The saints are said to lie beneath the fig tree and the vine.[6] In this respect they are the type of the angels[7] in that time of peace which is to come.

(3) Hence, Paradise has many trees that are fruit-bearing, with plenty of sap, and vigor. Of these it is said: 'All the trees of the woods shall rejoice.'[8] The woods flourish ever with the green shoots of merit, just like that 'tree which is planted near the running waters, whose leaf shall not fall off,'[9] because its fruit is plenteous. Here, then, is Paradise.

3 Gen. 2.8.
4 Ps. 32.9.
5 Matt. 15.13.
6 Mich. 6.6.
7 Cf. Mark 12.25.
8 Ps. 95.12.
9 Ps. 1.3.

(4) The place where it is planted is called delight; wherefore holy David says: 'Thou shalt not make them drink of the torrent of thy pleasure,'[10] for you have read that 'a river rose in Eden watering the garden.'[11] These woods, therefore, which were planted in Paradise are watered by the outpouring of the waters of that spirit concerning which He says elsewhere: 'The stream of the river maketh the city of God joyful.'[12] Here is that city of Jerusalem which above is free,[13] in which the different merits of the saints come to fruition.

(5) In this garden, therefore, God put the man He had formed. Take note that He placed man there not in respect to the image of God, but in respect to the body of man. The incorporeal does not exist in a place. He placed man in Paradise, just as He placed the sun in heaven, awaiting lordship over the heavens, just as the creature expects the revelation of the sons of God.[14]

(6) Hence, if Paradise is a place where shrubs have opportunity to blossom, then Paradise has a certain vital force which receives and multiplies seeds in which each and every virtue is planted, and where flourishes the tree of life which is called Wisdom. Of this, Solomon says that Wisdom arose not of the earth but of the Father: 'For she is the brightness of eternal light' and 'the emanation of the glory of the almighty God.'[15]

---

10 Ps. 35.9.
11 Gen. 2.10.
12 Ps. 45.5.
13 Cf. Gal. 4.26.
14 Cf. Rom. 8.9.
15 Wisd. 7.25,26.

Chapter 2

(7) There was a tree of the knowledge of good and evil in Paradise. This was so because 'God made to grow a tree pleasant to sight and good for food, the tree of life also in the midst of the garden and the tree of the knowledge of good and evil.'[1] We shall see later whether this tree, like the others, was pleasant to sight and good for food. The question will be more fittingly discussed at the point where, on tasting the fruit of this tree, we find that man was deceived. Meantime, we should now reproach ourselves for not being able to know precisely the reasons behind these facts. We should not form a hasty judgment in respect to this product of creation, if it presents to our intellect what seems to us—like the creation of serpents and certain poisonous creatures—difficult and incomprehensible. In fact, we are unable, owing to human weakness, yet to know and understand the reason for the creation of each and every object. Let us, therefore, not criticise in holy Scripture something which we cannot comprehend. There are very many things which must not be subjected to the judgment of our intellect. Rather, these should be surveyed from the lofty heights of Divine Providence and from the intentions of God Himself.

(8) Without prejudice, then, to what we shall say hereafter, set it down as a first principle that the subject of this tree of the knowledge of good and evil is to you a displeasing one. After men had tasted of this tree, they realized that they were naked.[2] Nevertheless, I will state for your benefit that as a consummation of God's creation this tree grew in Paradise and that it was permitted by God, in order that we might be able to know the pre-eminence of good. How could we learn to know that there was a difference between good

1 Gen. 2.9.
2 Cf. Gen. 3.7.

and evil, if there existed no knowledge of good and evil? We could not have come to realize that evil was evil, unless there was knowledge of good, and that there could not be knowledge of good, unless there was actual good. Again, we could not have know what in itself was good, unless there was knowledge of evil. Take an example from the nature of the human body. There exists as a matter of fact a certain bitter and poisonous substance which has been discovered to have a general salutary effect on the health of men. Hence, what we regard as evil frequently turns out to be not in every respect evil, but to be advantageous for general use. Just as poison exists in a part of the body but has a beneficial effect on the body as a whole, so God established the knowledge in part of what is good and evil, in order that the whole might be benefitted.

(9) Hence it follows that the serpent in Paradise was certainly not brought into being without the will of God. In the figure of the serpent we see the Devil. That the Devil existed even in Paradise we are informed by the Prophet Ezechiel, who in discussing the Prince of Tyre says: 'Thou wast in the pleasures of the paradise of God.'[3] We maintain that the Prince of Tyre stands for the Devil. Shall we, therefore, accuse God because we cannot comprehend the treasures—with the exception of those which He has deigned to reveal—of His majesty and wisdom which lie hidden and concealed in Christ? Yet He did reveal to us the fact that the wickedness of the Devil is fruitful for man's salvation. This would not be the Devil's intention, but the Lord makes the wickedness of him who stands in opposition to us contribute something to our salvation. The wickedness of the Devil has caused the virtue and patience of one holy man to shine in a clearer light. The justice of Job was so disciplined and

3 Ezech. 28.13.

exercised by the wickedness of his opponent that eventually he gained the crown of victory over his adversary, the Devil. No one is crowned 'unless he has competed according to the rules.'[4] Joseph's chastity, too, would never have been recorded for us, if it did not happen that a woman, the wife of his master and friend, incited and goaded by the Devil's allurements, had not played with his affections.[5] This woman finally endeavored to bring about his death. This event added more to the fame of a man who by his continence faced death in defense of chastity. Do you desire to know God's plan? Here is an instance. Through the instrumentality of the Devil there was once an occasion when a just man prepared to perpetrate manslaughter. The situation was one that involved the murder of one's own son. Yet, for all that, the Lord tempted Abraham in this wise. He demanded that Abraham sacrifice his son to Him. By reason of this temptation he was able to prove himself faithful to the Lord, since compliance to his vow and not pity for his beloved son brought about repeal of the order.[6] There was, therefore, in Paradise a tree of knowledge of good and evil which appeared to the eye to be beautiful and to the taste to be edible. It was not actually good to eat, for its fruit appeared to have a harmful effect on man. What is injurious to individuals may nevertheless have a beneficial effect on men as a whole. The Devil, for example, did harm to Judas,[7] but he bestowed the wreath of victory on all the other Apostles, inasmuch as they were able to face and overcome the force of his temptation.

(10) Accordingly, let it not be a subject of reprehension or doubt that the Devil existed in Paradise. As a matter of

4 2 Tim. 2.5.
5 Cf. Gen. 39.17.
6 Cf. Gen. 22.1.
7 Cf. Luke 22.3.

fact he was powerless to bar from the saints the way of their ascent. As one who had the right of possession, he did not evict the just from their habitation. It may be that he turned away from the occupancy of that high estate some who were in fact slothful and vicious. There is a recorded event that arouses to a much greater degree our regard and our admiration. This is the fact that the Devil was excluded from the prayers of the saints as the result of an event which was to take place: 'I was watching Satan fall as lightning from heaven.'[8] Let us, therefore, not fear one who is so weak that he is destined to fall from heaven. He actually received the power to tempt us but not the competency to subvert us, except when our weak and unassisted will falters because it is powerless to summon aid. For that reason we need to know what was the nature of the deceit inflicted on the first man. We ought to know, too, the method and manner of the Devil's procedure and what in man he thought was subject to temptation, so that we, in knowing this, may proceed to take precautions.

(11) Many people nevertheless are of the opinion that the Devil was not in Paradise, although we read that he stood with the angels in heaven.[9] These persons interpret the statement of Scripture according to their own fancy. In this way they put aside any objection which they may have to the words of Scripture. We stand by the conviction held by one who preceded us that sin was committed by man because of the pleasure of sense. We maintain that the figure of the serpent stands for enjoyment and the figure of the woman for the emotions of the mind and heart. The latter is called by the Greeks αἴσθησις. When according to this theory, the senses are deceived, the mind, which the Greeks call νοῦς, falls into error. Hence, not without reason

8 Luke 10.18.
9 Cf. Zach. 3.1.

the author to whom I refer[10] accepts the Greek word νοῦς as a figure of a man and αἴσθησις as that of a woman. Hence, some have interpreted Adam to mean an earthly νοῦς. In the Gospel the Lord sets forth the parable of the virgins who awaited the coming of the bridegroom with either lighted or extinguished lamps. Thus He exemplifies either the pure emotions of the wise or the impure senses of the unwise.[11] If Eve, that is, the emotions of the first woman, had kept her lamp lighted, she would not have enfolded us in the meshes of her sin. She would not have fallen from the height of immortality which is established as the reward of virtue.

Chapter 3

(12) Paradise is, therefore, a land of fertility—that is to say, a soul which is fertile—planted in Eden, that is, in a certain delightful or well-tilled land in which the soul finds pleasure. Adam exists there as νοῦς [mind] and Eve as 'sense.' Take note of what this soul of ours has in the nature of defense against natural and weak tendencies or against situations which might be unfavorable to us in our attempts to avoid danger.

(13) There was a fount which irrigated the land of Paradise.[1] Is not this stream our Lord Jesus Christ, the Fount as well as the Father of eternal life? It is written: 'For with thee is the fountain of life.'[2] Hence: 'From within him there shall flow living waters.'[3] We read of a fountain and a river which irrigates in Paradise the fruit-bearing tree that

10 Cf. Philo, *De opificio mundi* 59; *Legum allegoriae* I 29.
11 Cf. Matt. 25.1.

1 Cf. Gen. 2.10.
2 Ps. 35.10.
3 John 7.38; cf. Isa. 58.11.

bears fruit for life eternal. You have read, then, that a fount was there and that 'a river rose in Eden,'[4] that is, in your soul there exists a fount. This is the meaning of Solomon's words: 'Drink water out of thy own cistern and the streams of thy own well.'[5] This refers to the fount which rose out of that well-tilled soul, full of pleasant things, this fount which irrigates Paradise, that is to say, the soul's virtues that blossom because of their eminent merits.

(14) 'The river,' we are told, 'is separated into four branches. The name of one is Phison which encircles all the land of Hevila, where there is gold. And the gold of that land is good; bdellium and onyx there. The name of the second river is Gihon. This river encircles all the land of Ethiopia. The name of the third river is Tigris, which river flows by the Assyrians. And the fourth river is the Euphrates.'[6] There are, therefore, four rivers. Phison—so called by the Hebrews, but named Ganges by the Greeks—flows in the direction of India. Gihon is the river Nile, which flows around the land of Egypt or Ethiopia. The land enclosed by the Tigris and Euphrates rivers is called Mesopotamia because it lives between these two rivers. This name conveys its location even to far-distant peoples and, besides, expresses popular belief. But how is the fount called the Wisdom of God? That this is a fount the Gospel tells us in the words, 'If anyone thirst, let him come to me and drink.'[7] Wisdom is a fount according to the Prophet: 'Come and eat my bread and drink the wine which I have mingled for you.'[8] As Wisdom is the fountain of life, it is also the fountain of spiritual grace. It is also the fountain of other virtues which guide us to the course of eternal life. Therefore, the stream

4 Gen. 2.10.
5 Prov. 5.15.
6 Gen. 2.10-14.
7 John 7.37.
8 Prov. 9.15.

that irrigates Paradise rises from the soul when well-tilled, not from the soul which lies uncultivated. The results therefrom are fruit trees of diverse virtues. There are four principal trees which constitute the divisions of Wisdom. These are the well-known four principal virtues: prudence, temperance, fortitude, and justice. The wise men of this world have adopted this division from us and transferred it to their writings. Hence, Wisdom acts as the source from which these four rivers take their rise, producing streams that are composed of these virtues.

(15) Phison, therefore, stands for prudence. Hence it has pure gold, brilliant rubies, and topaz stones. We often refer to wise discoveries as gold, as the Lord says, speaking through the Prophet: 'I gave to them gold and silver.'[9] Daniel says of the wise: 'If you sleep among the midst of the lots, you shall be as the wings of the dove covered with silver and the hinder parts of her back like to gold.'[10] In this way one who puts his trust in the aid of the Old and New Testament can by resourceful inquiry attain the inmost secrets of the Wisdom of God. Here, therefore, is found pure gold, not the metal which is melted, which belongs to this earth, and is subject to corruption. In this land, we are told, there is found the brilliant ruby stone in which there exists the vital spark of our souls. Here, too, is the topaz stone which by the nature of its color reveals an effect of greenness and vitality. Plants which are alive give forth green sprouts, while those that are dead are sapless and dry. The earth grows green when it is in bloom. The seeds, too, sprout forth green shoots in their periods of growth. The river Phison is rightfully given first place. The Hebrews call it Pheoyson, which means 'change of mouth,' because it flows even through Lydia and not merely around one nation, for Wisdom, which is of

9 Osee 2.8.
10 Ps. 67.14.

benefit to all men, is productive and useful. Hence, if a person were to leave Paradise, this river of Wisdom would be the first object he would meet. Thus he may not become inert and arid and his return to Paradise may be facilitated. Many men resort to this river, which is considered to have marvelous beauty and fecundity. Accordingly, it is regarded as a figure of Widsom, which confers manifold fruits in the coming of the Lord of Salvation. It flows, too, to the very ends of the earth, because, by Wisdom all men have been redeemed. Wherefore it is written: 'Their sound hath gone forth into all the earth and their words unto the end of the world.'[11]

(16) The second river is Gihon, by which, when they were sojourning in Egypt, was laid down the law of the Israelites that they should depart from Egypt,[12] and having girded their loins they should as a sign of temperance partake of a lamb. It is fitting that the chaste and the sanctified should celebrate the Pasch of the Lord. For that reason, the observance of the Law was first carried out beside that river, the name of which signifies an opening of the earth. Therefore, just as an opening absorbs the earth and whatever defilements and refuse there may be in it, in like manner chastity tends to consume all the passions of the body. Appropriately, then, the observance of the established Law first took place there, because carnal sin is absorbed by the Law. And so Gihon, which is a figure of chastity, is said to surround the land of Ethiopia in order to wash away our lowly bodies and quench the fires of our vile flesh. The meaning of Ethiopia in Latin is 'holy and vile.' What is more lowly, what is more like Ethiopia, than our bodies, blackened, too, by the darkness of sin?

(17) The third river is the Tigris, which flows by the

11 Ps. 18.5.
12 Exod. 12.11.

Assyrian land. To this river the deceiver Israel was dragged as a prisoner. This river is the swiftest of all rivers. The Assyrian dwell by it, guarding its course—for this is the meaning of its name. Hence, those who by their fortitude hold in check the guileful vices of the body and direct themselves to higher things are thought to have something in common with this river. For that same reason fortitude emanates from that source in Paradise. Fortitude in its rapid course tosses aside everything standing in its path and like this river is not hindered by any material obstacle.

(18) The fourth river is the Euphrates, which means in Latin 'fecundity and abundance of fruits.' It presents a symbol of Justice, the nourishment of every soul. No virtue produces more abundant benefits than Equity or Justice, which is more concerned with others than with itself, neglecting its own advantages, and preferring the common good. Many derive Euphrates from the Greek ἀπὸ τοῦ εὐφραίνεσθαι, that is, from a 'feeling of gladness,' because the human race rejoices in nothing more than it does in Justice and Equity. The question as to why, although the location itself of other rivers is reported, we have no description of the regions through which the river Euphrates flows calls for an answer. The waters of this river are considered to have a vital quality which fosters growth and increase. Wherefore, the wise men among the Hebrews and the Assyrians called this river Auxen [increase] in contradistinction to the water of other rivers. The opposition has been well established between wisdom and malice, fortitude and irascibility, temperance, and other vices. Justice, on the other hand, is the most important as it represents the concord of all the other virtues. Hence it is not known from the places from which it flows, that is to say, it is not known in part. Justice is not divisibile into parts. It is, as it were, the mother of all virtues. In these four rivers are symbolized,

therefore, the four principal virtues. It may well be said that these virtues have been the determining boundary lines for the four great ages of the world. This, in fact, is the topic of the discourse which follows.

(19) The first age, then, is the age of Wisdom. This period extends from the beginnings of the world up to the time of the Flood. The Lord has given us the names of the just men of this age. Abel was so called, and so was Enos, a man made to the image of God, who hoped to invoke the name of the Lord God. Henoch, also, whose name in Latin means 'grace of God,' was carried up to heaven,[13] and Noe, who was a just man,[14] and one who might be called a guide to tranquillity.[15]

(20) The second age of the world is that of Abraham and Isaac, Jacob, and a number of other patriarchs. This was a period in which religion flourished in its more temperate and purest form. Pure was Isaac, a son given to Abraham according to promise, not as an offering of the body, but as a gift of divine beneficence. In him there is found the figure of Him who is pure as the Apostle teaches. 'The promises were made to Abraham and to his offspring. He does not say, "And to his offsprings," but as of one, "And to thy offspring," who is Christ.'[16]

(21) The third age lies in the period of the Law of Moses and in the time of the other Apostles. 'For time will fail me if I tell of Gideon, of Barac, of Samson, of David and of Samuel, Elias and Elisaeus, who by faith conquered kingdoms, wrought justice, obtained promises, stopped the mouths of lions, quenched the violence of fire, escaped the edge of the sword, recovered strength from weakness, became

13 Cf. Gen. 5.24.
14 Cf. Gen. 6.9.
15 Cf. Isidore, *Etym.* 7.6.15.
16 Gal. 3.16.

valiant in battle and captured the camps of aliens.'[17] Not without reason, then, do these men stand as types of fortitude. Further on we are told: 'They were sawed asunder, they were tempted, they were put to death by the sword. They went about in goatskins, destitute, distressed, afflicted—of whom the world was not worthy—wandering in deserts, mountains, caves and holes in the earth.'[18] Appropriately, therefore, do we set these men down as types of Fortitude.

(22) The figure of Justice is, according to the Gospel, a meritorious one, because 'it is unto salvation to everyone who believes.'[19] Hence, the Lord Himself says: 'Permit us to fulfill all justice.'[20] She is truly the prolific parent of the other virtues. Yet, whoever possesses any of the above-mentioned principal virtues has the other virtues, also, since these virtues are so connected as to form a unit. Surely, Abel, a just and courageous man, Abraham, a man of great patience, the Prophets, men of the greatest wisdom, and Moses, a man of great learning, considered that the inglori-ousness of Christ brought far greater honor than the treasures of Egypt. Who was wiser than Daniel? Solomon, too, sought wisdom and merited it.[21] Enough has been said, therefore, on the subject of the four rivers of virtue whose waters are salutary. We have discussed, too, the reason why Phison is said to have not only the gold, but also the ruby and the topaz stone, of that goodly land. We propose now to develop the latter topic.

(23) Since Enos in his wisdom yearned to know the name of God, he seems to us to stand for gold that is good.[22] Henoch, who was borne aloft and did not see death, can be

17 Heb. 11.32-34.
18 Heb. 11.37,38.
19 Cf. Rom. 1.16.
20 Matt. 3.15.
21 Cf. 3 Kings 3.8.
22 Cf. Gen. 4.26; 5.24.

likened to a ruby stone of pleasant odor which holy Henoch by his works offered to God, thus exhaling in his active and exemplary life something akin to sweetness. Noe, on the other hand, like the green topaz stone, suggests a color which represents life, since he alone at the time of the Flood preserved in his ark the vital seed of the formation of the world to come. Paradise, a land watered by many rivers, is then appropriately situated in the East and not in the regions facing it. This reference to the East is significant, for the rising sun may be compared to Christ[23] who flashed forth a gleam of eternal light which exists in Eden, that is, in a land of delight.

Chapter 4

(24) 'And God took the man whom he has created and placed him in the garden of Eden to till it and keep it.'[1] Note, now, the person who was taken and the land where he was formed. The virtue of God, therefore, took man and breathed into him, so that man's virtue will advance and increase. God set him apart in Paradise that you may know that man was taken up, that is to say, was breathed upon by the power of God. Note the fact that man was created outside Paradise, whereas woman was made within it. This teaches us that each person acquires grace by reason of virtue, not because of locality or of race. Hence, although created outside Paradise, that is, in an inferior place, man is found to be superior, whereas woman, created in a better place, that is to say, in Paradise, is found to be inferior. She was first to be deceived and was responsible for deceiving the man. Wherefore the Apostle Paul has related that holy

23 Cf. Matt. 24.27.

1 Gen. 2.15.

women have in olden times been subject to the stronger vessel and recommends them to obey their husbands as their masters.[2] And Paul says: 'Adam was not deceived, but the woman was deceived and was in sin.'[3] This is a warning that no one ought to rely on himself, for she who was made for assistance needs the protection of a man.[4] The head of the woman is man, who, while he believed that he would have the assistance of his wife, fell because of her.[5] Wherefore, no one ought to entrust himself lightly to another unless he has first put that person's virtue to the test. Neither should he claim for himself in the role of protector one whom he believes is subservient to him. Rather, a person should share his grace with another. Especially is this true of one who is in the position of greater strength and one who plays the part of protector. We have advice of the Apostle Peter, wherein he recommends that husbands pay honor to their wives: Husbands, in like manner, dwell with your wives considerately, paying honor to the woman as to the weaker vessel and as co-heir of the grace of life that your prayers be not hindered.'[6]

(25) Therefore man was placed in Paradise, while the woman was created in Paradise. The woman, even before she was deceived by the serpent, shared grace with a man, since she was taken from a man. Yet 'this is a great mystery,'[7] as the Apostle said. Wherefore he traced the source of life from it. And so Scripture refers only to man in the words: 'He placed him in the garden of Eden to till it and keep it.'[8] The act of tilling and the act of keeping are one and the same thing. In tilling there is a certain exercise of

---

2 1 Peter 3.1.
3 1 Tim. 2.14.
4 Cf. Gen. 2.18.
5 1 Cor. 11.3.
6 1 Peter 3.7.
7 Eph. 5.32.
8 Gen. 2.15.

man's virtue, while in keeping it is understood that the work is accomplished, for protection implies something completed. These two acts are required of man. In this way, it is generally assumed, man can seek after something new and may keep what he has acquired. Philo, on the other hand, limited his interpretation of this Scriptural passage to its moral aspect, since, because of his Jewish tendencies, he did not understand its spiritual import. He maintained that the two aspects were those of tilling the fields and of protecting the home. Although, he said, Paradise did not require labor in the fields, the first man, even in Paradise, undertook a kind of toil so as to furnish a law for future ages by which to bind us to the performance and to the preservation of our bounden duty and to the function of supporting hereditary succession.[9] Both these point of view, the moral and the spiritual, are exacted of you. The prophetic psalm instructs you regarding this: 'Unless the Lord build the house, they labor in vain that build it. Unless the Lord keep the city, they watch in vain that keepeth it.'[10] It is obvious that the laborers are those who engage in the actual operation of building, while the watchers are those to whom the duty of protecting the perfected work is entrusted. Hence the Lord said to the Apostles, as if they were on the point of perfecting their work: 'Watch and pray that you may not enter into temptation.'[11] By this He meant that the function of a nature that was perfected along with the grace of abundant virtue should be preserved and that no one, even one who has attained some perfection, ought to feel really secure of himself unless he remains vigilant.

---

9 Cf. Philo, *Quaestiones in Gen.* 1.14 (found in a Latin translation from the Armenian); see Colson and Whitaker, *Philo,* suppl. vol. I.

10 Ps. 126.1.

11 Matt. 26.41.

Chapter 5

(26) 'And the Lord God commanded the man thus: 'from every tree of the garden thou shalt eat, but of the tree of the knowledge of good and evil, you shall not eat, for the day you eat of it you shall die.'[1] Why did He use the singular 'thou shalt eat' when He bade them eat of every tree, and, again, when He bade them eat of the tree of good and evil, why did He use the plural 'You shall not eat'? This is no trifling question. This problem can, in fact, be solved by the authority of the Scriptures if you study them carefully. Scripture refers to something good and something that should be done. What is good is naturally associated with what should be done. On the other hand, what is base is separate and unrelated to what should be done. And so the Lord, aiming always at oneness, gave orders in accordance with this principle. Hence He achieves oneness who 'has made both one'[2]—He not only made both one, for He bade us to be 'one body and one Spirit.'[3] 'The first-born of every creature,'[4] since He is in union with the faith, is always closely joined to the Father, because 'the Word was with God.'[5] Wherefore He says: 'I and the Father are one,'[6] in order to show His union with the Father in majesty and in dignity. But He bade us to be one and transfused into us by the adoption of grace the likeness of His own nature and His own oneness, saying: 'Father, that they may be one, even as we are one, I in them and thou in me.'[7] When He

1 Gen. 2.16.
2 Eph. 2.14.
3 Eph. 4.4.
4 Col. 1.15.
5 John 1.1.
6 John 10.30.
7 John 17.22.

prescribes a good, therefore, He does it to one person, saying, 'Thou shalt eat,' for the oneness cannot be gainsaid. Where, however, He says that the tree of the knowledge of good and evil should not be tasted, He speaks in effect to several people: 'You shall not eat.' What has been prohibited has general application to several people. But I have another opinion on this matter. I am able to discover the meaning of what we are discussing in the very words of God Himself. Adam alone was bidden to taste of every tree and it was foreseen that he would follow that injunction. In the plural sense, and not in the singular, God sees that the tree of the knowledge of good and evil should not be tasted. He knew that the woman would sin. Thus, by using the plural, God points out that they will not follow the injunction, because, where there are many, there are differences of opinion.

(27) If we look into the sense of the words as expressed in the Septuagint,[8] the meaning is clear. Symmachus, however, takes both expressions in a singular sense. This is explained by the fact that in the Law, God, addressing His people, uses the singular: 'Hear, O Israel, the Lord thy God is one Lord' and 'Thou shalt love the Lord thy God.'[9] I am not influenced by the interpretation of Symmachus, who could not see the oneness of the Father and Son, although at times both he and Asylas admitted it in their discussions. The fact that God addresses in the singular number a people who will later contravene His commands should not lead us to think that I am dissenting from my former statement, inasmuch as the Jewish people, regarded as a single person, violated the injunctions imposed upon them. We have here a law of the Spirit whereby God addresses the people in

8 The Vulgate has the singular form: *ne comedas;* the Septuagint has the plural: οὐ φάγεσθε.

9 Deut. 6.4,5.

divine language. In this case we should consider not so much the words as their prophetic import. Wherefore He says: 'Thou shalt not boil a kid in the milk of his dam.'[10]

(28) From this point on, the celestial precepts present no great difficulty. However, there has been raised by several authors a question which we ought to answer lest simple minds be led astray by erroneous interpretation. Many authors, like Apelles in his thirty-eighth volume,[11] propose the following questions. How is it, for example, that the tree of life has more power for giving life than the breath of God? Again, if man is not made perfect by God and each person acquired by his own effort a more perfect state of virtue for himself, does it not seem that man would gain for himself more than God had bestowed on him? Then they make the objection that, if man had not tasted death, he certainly could not be aware of what he had not tasted. What man had not tasted was something unknown to him. Accordingly, he could not be afraid of that of which he had no knowledge. To no purpose, therefore, did God inflict death as a punishment on men for whom it holds no fear.

(29) We should be aware of the fact, therefore, that where God has planted a tree of life He has also planted a tree of life in the midst of Paradise. It is understood that He planted it in the middle. Therefore, in the middle of Paradise there was both a tree of life and a cause for death. Keep in mind that man did not create life. By carrying out and observing the precepts of God it was possible for man to find life. This was the life mentioned by the Apostle: 'Your life is hidden with Christ in God.'[12] Man, therefore, was, figuratively speaking, either in the shadow of life—

10 Exod. 34.26.
11 Apelles; cf. Harnack, *TU* 6.3.116.
12 Col. 3.3.

because our life on earth is but a shadow—or man had life, as it were, in pledge, for he had been breathed on by God. He had, therefore, a pledge of immortality, but while in the shadow of life he was unable, by the usual channels of sense, to see and attain the hidden life of Christ with God. Although not yet a sinner, he was not possessed of an incorrupt and inviolable nature. Of course, one who afterwards lapsed into sin was far from being as yet in the category of sinner. Hence, he was in the shadow of life, whereas sinners are in the shadow of death. According to Isaias, the people who sinned sat in the shadow of death.[13] For these a light arose, not by the merits of their virtues, but by the grace of God. There is no distinction, therefore, between the breath of God and the food of the tree of life. No man can say that he can acquire more by his own efforts than what is granted him by the generosity of God. Would that we had been able to hold on to what we had received! Our toils avail only to the extent that we take back again what was once conferred on us. The third objection, that one who has not tasted death cannot fear it, finds its solution in our common experience. There is an instinct innate in all living creatures which impels them to dread even what they have not yet experienced as harmful. Why is it that doves, even at the moment of their birth, are terrorized at the sight of a hawk? Why are wolves dreaded by sheep and hawks by chickens? In irrational animals there is a certain innate fear of creatures of a different species to the extent that, even though these animals are irrational, they have a feeling that death is something to be shunned. Such being the case, how true is it that the first man, fully and indubitably endowed with reason, should be conscious of the fact that death is something to be avoided!

13 Isa. 9.2.

Chapter 6

(30) There are some, again, who suggest for solution difficulties such as the following. For example, they maintain that refusal to obey an order is not always wrong. If the order is a good one, then the act of obeying is commendable. But if the order is a wicked one, it is not feasible to obey it. Therefore, it is not always wrong to disobey an order, but it is wrong to refuse to obey an order that is good. The tree of the knowledge of good and evil is a creation that is good, since God had knowledge of good and evil. Hence He says: 'Indeed! The man has become like one of us.'[1] If, therefore, possessing the knowledge of good and evil is good and if what God has is a good, it would appear that the prohibition to prevent man from making use of it is not a righteous one. Such is their argument. But, if they were to realize the real significance and force of the word 'knowledge' as they should—'The Lord knew who belong to him,' 'that is, He knew those surely among whom He dwells and walks, who were made one out of so many—then certainly these people would know that knowledge is not to be interpreted merely as superficial comprehension, but as the carrying out of what ought to be accomplished. Man ought to obey the command. A failure to obey is a violation of duty. The man, therefore, who disobeys falls into error because violation of duty is a sin. Even if these people should agree to a modified meaning of the word 'knowledge' and consider that an imperfect comprehension of good and evil was prohibited, in that respect, too, there is a violation of duty in not complying with the command. The Lord God has made it clear that even an imperfect comprehension of good and evil should be prohibited.

---

1 Gen. 3.32.
2 Num. 16.5; 2 Tim. 2.19.

(31) Another problem: The man who does not know good and evil differs in no respect from a little child. A judge who is just does not consider a child to be guilty of crime. The just Creator of the world would never have found fault with a child for his lack of knowledge of good and evil, because a child cannot be charged with a violation of a law. In the preceding passage, however, we have said that, once you accept the fact that there is a knowledge that is imperfect, then knowledge of good and evil may be taken in two senses. It is certainly false to hold that the man who does not know good and evil is not different from a child. If it is wrong to maintain that such a man does not differ from a child, then Adam is not to be thought of as a child. If he was not a child, then surely he is liable to sin, inasmuch as he is not a child. If he is subject to sin, then punishment follows the sin, because the man who cannot avoid sin is reckoned to be liable to punishment. It can even happen that the person who has no knowledge of good and evil may not be a child: 'For before the child knew good and evil, he refused the evil.' Again we read: 'For before the child knew to call his father and mother, he will receive the strength of Damascus and the toils of Samaria.'[3] Perfect, therefore, is the man who performs a good deed even if he has not attained the knowledge of good and evil, just as 'many are a law to themselves'[4] even before they know the Law. Was the Apostle before he learned: 'Thou shalt not lust,' quite unaware that concupiscence was a sin? On this point he says: 'I did not know sin save through the Law. For I had not known lust unless the Law had said, "Thou shalt not lust."'[5] Even a child can become by the law of nature perfect in that respect before he knows that con-

3 Isa. 7.16; 8.4.
4 Rom. 2.14.
5 Exod. 20.17; Rom. 7.7.

cupiscence is a sin or admit the sin of concupiscence. Hence, God willed that man know the nature of evil in a superficial fashion lest, being imperfect, he may be unable to avoid evil. By not obeying a command we are subject to blame. We are thus led to admit our error. Again, if we are referring to a very profound knowledge of good and evil which in itself makes for perfection . . .[6] A little child is not, like a grown-up, immediately to be chastised, because he has not yet reached a capacity to understand.

(32) Again, more criticisms crop up.[7] There is the objection that a person who does not know good and evil is unaware that disobedience to a command is in itself an evil, nor is he aware that that obedience to a command is itself a good. Hence it is argued that the person who is in this respect ignorant is deserving, not of condemnation, but of pardon. What we have already maintained above presents a ready solution to this problem. Man is capable of realizing that the utmost deference should be given to his Maker because of what God had already conferred on him, namely, the fact that God had breathed on him and that he was placed in the Garden of Delight. Wherefore, if he was ignorant of the meaning of good and evil. neverthe-less, since the Creator of such mighty things had declared that one should not eat of the tree of good and evil, loyal adherence should be given to Him who gave the command. It was not a question of technical knowledge, but of fidelity. He certainly was aware that God was in a position of pre-eminence and, as such, heed should be paid to His command. Although he did not understand the precise significance of the commands, he was conscious of the fact that deference should be paid to the person of the Commander. This conviction on his part stemmed from nature. He was as yet

6 Schenkl points to a lacuna in the manuscript here.
7 From Apelles; cf. Harnack, *op. cit.*

incapable of discriminating between good and evil. Wherefore the woman answers the serpent: 'Of the fruit of all the trees in the garden we shall eat, but of the fruit in the middle of the garden, God said, you shall not eat of it.'[8] She knew, therefore, that the command must be obeyed. Hence she said: We shall eat of every fruit which the Lord ordered, but God has given an order that one should not eat of the tree in the middle of the Garden, lest he die. Wherefore, she who knew that the command should be obeyed was surely aware that it was wrong not to comply with the command and that she would be justly condemned for her refusal to obey.

(33) One more point. The circumstances connected with the tree of the knowledge of good and evil were such as to convince us that both good and evil were recognized. We are led to believe from the evidence of Scripture that such was the case: 'When they both ate, their eyes were opened and they realized that they were naked,'[9] that is, the eyes of their mind were opened and they realized the shame of being naked. For that reason, when the woman ate of the tree of the knowledge of good and evil she certainly sinned and realized that she had sinned. On realizing this, she should not have invited her husband to share in her sin. By enticing him and by giving him what she herself had tasted she did not nullify her sin; rather, she repeated it. Certainly it stands to reason that she did intend to lure the person whom she loved to share in her punishment. She should be expected to ward off from one who was unaware of it the danger of falling into a sin of which she had knowledge. Yet this woman, knowing that she could not remain in Paradise after the Fall, seems to have had a fear that she alone would be ejected from the Garden. Hence, after the

8 Gen. 3.2,3.
9 Gen. 3.6,7.

Fall, they both went into hiding. Being aware, therefore, that she would have to be separated from the man she loved, she had no desire to be deceived.

(34) Another point. Knowledge of evil does not make evil. An act is necessary to complete its conditions. There is no immediate connection between the knower of what is evil and the doer. He is guilty who does what he knows to be evil. Either anger or cupidity is the customary means of arousing a person to perform an evil act. It does not necessarily follow that one who has knowledge of evil, unless he is the victim of anger or cupidity, will do what he knows is wrong. To repeat what we have said, the incentives to sin are anger and cupidity. To these we may add extreme fear, which itself may give rise to cupidity, inasmuch as everyone is anxious to avoid what is the cause of his fear. With reason, therefore, have we established that the incentives to the other vices are anger and cupidity. Let us consider, then, whether Eve was aroused to wrong-doing by these incentives. She was not angry with her consort. She was not a victim of cupidity. Again, she merely erred in giving her husband to eat of what she had already tasted. Cupidity had been at first responsible for her error in inducing him to eat and it was the occasion for the subsequent sin. This can be explained in the following way. She was unable to desire what she had already eaten and, after eating she acquired a knowledge of evil. She ought not, therefore, have made her husband a partaker of the evil of which she was conscious; neither should she have caused her own husband to violate the divine command. She sinned, therefore, with forethought, and knowingly made her husband a participant in her own wrong-doing. If it were not so, what is related of the tree of knowledge of good and evil would be found to be in error, if it were established that, after she ate of that tree, she was without knowledge of evil. But, if what Scripture

says is true, cupidity was the motive of her act. Many, however, are of the opinion that she should be excused for the reason that, because she loved her husband, she was afraid that she would be separated from him. They offer this as grounds for her cupidity: namely, that she desired to be with her husband.

Chapter 7

(35) Still another problem arises.[1] From what source did death come to Adam? Was it from the nature of a tree of this sort or actually from God? If we ascribe this to the nature of the tree, then the fruit of this tree seems to be superior to the vivifying power of the breath of God, since its fruit had drawn into death's toils him on whom the divine breath had bestowed life. If we maintain that God is the responsible cause of death, then we can be held to accuse Him of inconsistency. We seem to accuse Him of being so devoid of beneficence as to be unwilling to pardon when He had the power to do so, or of being powerless if He was unable to forgive. Let us see, therefore, how this question can be resolved. The solution, unless I am mistaken, lies in the fact that, since disobedience was the cause of death, for that very reason, not God, but man himself, was the agent of his own death. If, for example, a physician were to prescribe to a patient what he thought should be avoided, and if the patient felt that these prohibitions were unnecessary, the physician is not responsible for the patient's death. Surely in that case the patient is guilty of causing his own death. Hence, God as a good physician forbade Adam to eat what would be injurious to him.

(36) Another point. To know what is good is better than

1 From Apelles; cf. Harnack, *op. cit.*

to be ignorant of it. It is fitting that a person who knows what is good know, also, what is evil, in order that he may know the means to avoid it and, by taking the necessary precautions, that he may act with discretion. Again, it is not sufficient to know merely what is evil, lest, although you know what is evil, you may find yourself deprived of what is good. It is best, therefore, that we know both so that, since we know what is good, we may avoid evil. Again, from the fact that we are aware of evil we may give our preference to the charm of what is good. Moreover, we ought to know both so that our knowledge may be profound and so that we may put in practice what we know, act and acknowledge to be in perfect balance. Besides, Scripture points out that more is expected of him who has general knowledge of both than of him who is ignorant of them.[2] Knowledge of what you cannot achieve or avoid is a grievous thing. Grievous, too, is knowledge which is not put into practice and into operation to its fullest extent. Without knowledge of what is harmful or beneficial to a patient and without the power of being able to utilize to the best advantage that knowledge, a physician is likely to act in such a way as to lose his reputation. Hence, knowledge is not salutary unless it is put into practice in the best possible way.

(37) Still another point. Not without reason was the tree of knowledge of good and evil grown in the middle of the Garden, and the prohibition against it was unnecessary if it was grown for each and every man. This tree was designed for the use of just one man, who received the command that he make use not only of that tree, but of the other trees besides. You can find many, even countless, instances in which a person can, because of ignorance of procedure, suffer real harm. Wealth itself will be found to be unprofitable to a rich man if he refuses to act in a

2 Cf. Luke 13.47,48.

generous fashion toward the poor. He may shut out the needy and deprive them of assistance and, because of his superior powers, he may extort for his own purpose what belongs to another. The very possession of beauty and of physical charm is more likely than deformity to lead one to vice. For that reason, therefore, does anyone desire to have children who are unsightly rather than handsome? Or desire their offspring to be poverty-stricken rather than well-to-do? There are many instances of this sort which are not to be ascribed to the lack of wisdom in the giver, but to the person who misuses the gifts. The fault lies not so much in the person who makes the gifts as in the person who makes use of them.

Chapter 8

(38) Another problem.[1] Did God know that Adam would violate His commands? Or was He unaware of it? If He did not know, we are faced with a limitation of His divine power. If He knew, yet gave a command which He was aware would be ignored, it is not God's providence to give an unnecessary order. It was in the nature of a superfluous act to give to Adam, the first created being, a command which He knew would not at all be observed. But God does nothing superfluous. Therefore, the words of Scripture do not come from God. This is the objection of those who do not, by interposing these questions, admit the authenticity of the Old Testament. But these people are to be condemned out of their own mouths. Since these same persons concede the authenticity of the New Testament, they must be convinced by evidence to believe in the Old. If they see that God is consistent in His commands and in

1 From Apelles.

His deeds, it is clear that they must concede that both Testaments are the work of one Author. The following example should convince them that a command to one who will disobey is not something superfluous or unjust. The Lord Himself close Judas, one who, He knew, would betray Him. If these men think that he was chosen unwisely, they restrict the power of God. But they cannot hold this opinion, since Scripture declares: 'For Jesus knew who it was who should betray him.'[2] These defamers of the Old Testament should therefore hold their peace.

(39) Possible objections on the part of the Gentiles who do not admit this evidence stand in need of a response. Since the Gentiles demand a rational explanation, here is the reason why the Son of God either gave a command to one who is going to disobey it or has chosen one who is going to betray Him. The Lord Jesus came to save all sinners.[3] He was bound to show concern even for the wicked. Accordingly, He was bound not to disregard one who was to betray Him. He wished that all might take note that in the choice even of His betrayer He was offering a sign for the salvation of all of us. No injury was done to Adam in that he received a command, or to Judas because he was chosen. God did not lay it down as a necessary consequence that one should disobey and the other should betray Him. Both could have abstained from sin if they had guarded what they had received. Hence, although He knew that all the Jews would not believe, He stated: 'I have not come except to the lost sheep of the house of Israel.'[4] The fault is, therefore, not in the one issuing the command; the sin is rather in the one who disobeys. God's intent was this: He wanted to show to everyone that He willed to give freedom to all

2 John 6.65.
3 Cf. Luke 19.10.
4 Matt. 15.24.

mankind. I do not mean to maintain that He did not know of the disobedience to come. Rather, I contend that He did know, but that He should not for that reason be subject to reproach for a betrayer who met death. God should not be accused of being the cause why both lapsed. In fact, both stand convicted and condemned, because one received a command not to fall into sin, and the other was enrolled among the Apostles in order that he, as the result of kindness, might change his intention to betray. At some time in the future when the other Apostles would be found wanting, he might well become a source of comfort to all. In effect, there would not exist any sin if there were no prohibition. Without the existence of sin there would be no such thing as wrong-doing or, perhaps, even virtue, which could not have any cause for existence or for pre-eminence without the aid of unrighteousness to offset it. What is sin, if not the violation of divine law and the disobedience to heavenly precepts? Not by the ear, but by the mind, do we form a judgment regarding injunction from above. But with the Word of God before us we are able to formulate opinions on what is good and what is evil. One of these we naturally understand should be, as evil, avoided, and the other we understand has been recommended to us as a good. In this respect we seem to be listening to the very voice of the Lord, whereby some things are forbidden and other things are advised. If a person does not comply with the injunctions which are believed to have been once ordained by God, he is considered to be liable to punishment. The commands of God are impressed in our hearts by the Spirit of the living God. We do not read these orders as if they were recorded in ink on a tablet of stone.[5] Hence, in our own thought we formulate a law: 'For if the Gentiles who have no law do by nature what the law prescribes, those having

---

5 2 Cor. 3.3.

no law of this kind are a law unto themselves. They show the work of the law written in their hearts.'[6] There is something, therefore, like the Law of God which exists in the hearts of men.

(40) These same people raise another objection. Instead of that command which we said was established in the mind of man, they would maintain that this very impression in our minds by God was itself the prescription of a divine law. The question is raised: Did the Creator of man know that man would fall into sin and so implanted those opinions of what is good and evil in the mind of man or was He unaware that this would happen? If you concede that He did not know of it, you attribute to God something alien to His majesty. If, on the other hand, you maintain that, although God was aware that man would sin, He impressed in man's mind a realization of what is good and evil, so that he would be unable, because of the admixture of evil, to live forever—then in one case you imply that God was not prescient and in the other that He was not beneficent. From this the conclusion is reached that man was not the creation of God. We have already stated that these men maintain that God had not imposed a command. Now they say that man was not created by God, because God did not create evil. Man, on the other hand, had a mental conception of evil, inasmuch as he was enjoined to abstain from evil. In this way they venture to assert that there were two gods: one who is good; the other, the Creator of man. We must follow the lines of their own logic in formulating our reply. If they hold that man was not made by God, because man is a sinner, and if they recoil from conceding this point, lest a good God may not seem to the creator of sinners (because they do not believe that God is good who made a sinner)—then let them declare whether this artificer

6 Rom. 2.14,15.

of man has in their opinion also been made by God? If, as they state, this artificer of man was created by God, how can it be possible that a God who is good is also the agent of evil? If the creator of a sinner is not good, then more serious implications result if we postulate the maker of him who is the artificer of a sinner. A God who is good is bound to prevent the birth of him who shall have to introduce the substance of sin. But if they maintain that this artificer was not created, than the problem arises as to whether a God who is good could or could not in any way prevent the growth of evil. If such a God cannot do this, then He is powerless. Inasmuch as such inconsistencies follow our line of argumentation and since the heretics get involved here, also, let us attempt a solution of the problem of why God allowed adversity to enter into this world through an artificer who either did or did not spring from Him, although He had the power to prevent it.

(41) Accordingly, while still holding that the God who is good and the one who is the artificer are one and the same, let us make clear what are the provinces of each. We should at the same time try to meet the objections of those who raise such a question as this: How is it possible that a God who is good has permitted not only adversity to enter this world but has allowed it, too, to be in such a state of disorder?[7] In truth, this objection would be valid only if this evil so affected the nature of our soul and the secret places of our hearts that riddance was impossible and if, again, this poison had left such deep wounds in our hearts and souls that medication was of no avail.[8] In fact, this grievance of theirs could be more aptly expressed by stating that, although God is omnipotent, He has permitted man to die. But since God in His pity has reserved for us the

7 From Apelles.

8 Cf. Ovid, *Metamorphoses* 1.190.

means of obtaining remedy for our sins and still has not rid us of all possibilities of contagion, then let us reflect on the following points. Would it be an unjust and unreasonable act if God, fearful, as it were, of man's frailty and mortality, permitted us to be tempted in such wise that, through penitence for our sins, grace compounded would return once more to our hearts? Again, would it be unjust if man, conscious and fearful of his own frailty (since he found that he could so easily deviate from the orderly path of divine commands) and fearful, too, lest he let loose these heavenly mandates which like a helm guide his soul—would it be unjust if man should finally attribute the recovery of the helm to divine pity and by his safe return acquire some grace as well?

Chapter 9

(42) Now let us investigate the reason why God considered that a command should be given concerning the two classes of trees: the one to be eaten and the other which it was forbidden to eat. Thus, He laid down to man injunctions on the ways of attaining that wonderful and happy life, following which he might not have to suffer death. There are some who think that is was totally inappropriate for the Creator of heaven and earth and of all things to lay down that command and that it was definitely unsuited to the inhabitants of Paradise, because life there was like that of the angels. And so we can conclude that the food provided for eating there was not earthly and corruptible, because those who do not drink or eat 'will be as the angels in heaven.' There is no merit, therefore, in food, because food does not commend us to God. Neither is there great danger therein, because 'what goes into the mouth does not defile a man, but it is what comes out of the mouth.'[1] Undoubtedly, then,

1 Matt. 22.30; 15.11.

it would appear that the precept [is quite unworthy] of such a great Creator unless you take this food to mean prophetic food, because as a great reward the Lord makes this promise to His saints: 'Behold my servants shall eat and you shall be hungry.'[2] This is the food that makes for eternal life. Whoever is deprived of this will suffer death, since the Lord Himself is the living and heavenly Bread which gives life to this world. Hence He speaks: 'Unless you eat my flesh and drink my blood you shall not have life eternal.'[3] The bread was, therefore, meant for a certain person. Instructions were given that it should be eaten be the inhabitants of Paradise Who is that person? We are told who that person is: 'Man ate the bread of angels.'[4] The bread is good if you do the will of God. Do you wish to know how good that bread was? The Son of God Himself eats of that bread of which He says: 'My food is to do the will of my father who is in heaven.'[5]

(43) Again, let us see why the Lord God said to Adam: 'Ye shall die the death.' What is the difference between saying 'ye shall die' and 'ye shall die the death'? We ought to point out that there is nothing superfluous in the command of God. Here is my solution. Since life and death are contradictory ideas, in unaffected language we say 'we live in life' and 'die in death.' But, if you wish, since life causes life, to double the force of the two concepts, the phrase 'he lives a life' is found in legal documents, and, since death causes death, there is the statement: 'He shall die the death.'[6] These expressions are not redundant, for life is related to death and death to life, because everyone living

2 Isa. 65.13.
3 John 6.50; cf. 6.54.
4 Ps. 77.25.
5 John 4.34.
6 Ezech. 33.14-16.

dies while he is alive and lives when he dies. We find, therefore four categories: to live in life, to die in death, to die in life, to live in death. Since such is the case, we should put aside prejudices due to use and custom, for usage prescribes that the act of dying should be said without distinction of him who dies by death and of him who does so by his life. Accordingly, the Lord selects two of these four distinctive phrases so as to say that the living live, with qualifications as to whether well or ill, and the dying die, without a seeming difference between a good death and a bad one. There is no precise difference in fact between the kind of life or death here referred to. It could include that of irrational creatures or of tiny infants.

(44) Putting aside, therefore, conceptions due to common usage, let us reflect on the meaning of 'to live in life' and 'to die in death' and also 'to live in death' and 'to die in life.' I believe that, in accord with the Scriptures, 'to live in life' signifies a wonderful life of happiness and that it seems to point toward an experience of life's natural functions joined and, by participation, mingled with the grace of a blessed life. This concept, 'to live in life,' means 'to live in virtue,' to bring about in the life of this body of ours a participation in the life of blessedness. On the other hand, what does 'to die in death' mean if not the disintegration of the body at the time of death, when the flesh is devoid of its customary function of carrying on life and the soul is unable to partake in life eternal? There is also the person who 'dies in life,' that is to say, one who is alive in body but, because of his acts, is dead. These are the people who, as the Prophet says: 'Go down alive into hell,' and she of whom the Apostle speaks: 'For she is dead while she is still alive.'[7] There remains the fourth category, for

7 Ps. 54.16; 1 Tim. 5.6.

there are those who 'live in death' like the holy martyrs who give up their lives so that they may live. The flesh dies, but what is good does survive. Far from us, therefore, be the thought of living as participants in death. On the contrary, we should face death and thus become sharers in life. The saint does not desire to be a participant in this life of ours when he states: 'To be dissolved and be with Christ.'[8] This has been much better stated by another: 'Woe to me that my sojourning has been prolonged,'[9] in grief certainly that he is limited by the fragility of this life, since he hopes for a share in life eternal. Wherefore I can, on the other hand, state that, although 'to live in life' is a good thing, 'to live for life' would be of doubtful benefit. One can speak of 'living for life,' that is, for the life of eternity with its struggle with the life of the body. One can also speak of 'living for life' in another sense. Anyone, even a pious person, can have a desire for this corporeal life of ours. We can take the example of one who thinks that he ought to live so virtuously as to arrive by his good actions at a ripe old age. Many people who are in weak health, but who still find life a pleasureable thing, are in this category.

(45) Now that we have examined the meaning of the phrase, 'to live for life,' let us now turn attention to the significance of the phrases, 'to die for death' and 'to live for death,' for it is possible to conceive of people who 'die for death' and who 'live for life.' For the person who 'dies for or to death' is one who so lives as to live for the sake of his own soul, because he is not subject to death. We mean by this one who has been loosed from the bonds of grievous death and one who is not bound by the chains of death eternal. He is dead to death, that

8 Phil. 1.23.
9 Ps. 119.5.

is, he is dead to sin. He is dead to punishment for whom living is contrary to punishment, that is, when a person lives for punishment he lives for death. Again, one who dies for punishment dies for death. There is also the case of one who, although placed in this life, dies for life. Such was the situation of the Apostle who said: It is now no longer I that live, but Christ in me.'[10] To sin he is dead, but he lives for God, that is, death in him is dead, but living in him is that life which is the Lord Jesus. Good, therefore, is the life of those who live for God and wicked the life of those who live for sin. There is also a middle course of life, as in the case of other living creatures, for which we may cite the Scriptural passage: 'Let the earth bring forth the living creature in its kind.'[11] There is also the life of the dead: 'The God of Abraham, the God of Isaac and the God of Jacob,' because 'He is not the God of the dead but of the living.'[12] There are those who partake somewhat in both lives, that of the living and of the dead, of whom the Apostle speaks: 'If ye have died with him, ye shall also live with him.'[13] The same Apostle has said: 'For if we have been united with him in the likeness of death, we shall also be in the likeness of his resurrection also. For we know that our old self has been crucified with him, in order that the body of sin may be destroyed, that we may no longer be slaves to sin, for he who is dead is aquitted of sin.'[14] Just as we have said that there are many forms of life, so, too, we may discover many forms of death. An evil death is recorded in the words, 'The soul that sinneth, the same shall die.'[15] The usual meaning of death

10 Gal. 2.20.
11 Gen. 1.24.
12 Exod. 3.6; Luke 20.37; Mark. 12.26.
13 2 Tim. 2.11.
14 Rom. 6.5-8.
15 Ezech. 18.20.

appears when we say that a person lived so many years and was laid among his fathers.[16] There is the meaning of death as we have it in the sacrament of baptism: 'For we were buried with him by means of baptism into death.' Elsewhere we read: 'For if we have died with Christ, we believe also that we shall live together with him.'[17] You see how the word 'death' is subject to manifold interpretation, but that this life here is ours to contend with.

Chapter 10

(46) Still another question arises, that concerning the saying of the Lord: 'It is not good for man to be alone.'[1] Recognize the fact, first of all, that, when God created man from the slime of the earth, He did not add: 'God saw that it was good,'[2] as He did in the case of each of His works. If He had said at that time that the creation of man was good, then the other statement that 'it is not good' would be a contradiction in terms, although He had said that the creation of what preceded the formation of man was good. That was the situation at the time of the creation of Adam. But, when He perceived that man and woman were joined together in creation, He did not treat each even then in a special manner, for He soon after states: 'God saw that all he had ever made was very good.[3] The meaning is clear. The creation of both man and woman is considered to be good.

(47) From this question another problem arises. How

16 Cf. Acts 13.36.
17 Rom. 6.4,8.

1 Gen. 2.18.
2 Gen. 1.14.
3 Gen. 1.31.

did it happen that, when Adam alone was created, it was not said that it was good, but when a woman also was made, then are we to understand that everything was good? Whereas God in one case commended the whole of creation, as well as every creature in it (including man who is held to be a part of nature), a special reference to man did not then seem necessary. Wherefore, when Adam alone was created, an assertion that this work was good was not thought to be by any means a fitting climax to a satisfactory achievement. It was said, moreover, that it was not good for man to be alone. Yet we know that Adam did not commit sin before woman was created. However, after creation, she was the first to disobey the divine command and even allured her husband to sin. If, therefore, the woman is responsible for the sin, how then can her accession be considered a good? But, if you consider that the universe is in the care of God, then you will discover this fact, namely, that the Lord must have gained more pleasure for Himself in being responsible for all creation than condemnation from us for providing the basis for sin. Accordingly, the Lord declared that is was not good for man to be alone, because the human race could not have been propagated from man alone. God preferred the existence of more than one whom He would be able to save than to have to confine this possibility to one man who was free from error. Inasmuch as He is the Author of both man and woman, He came into this world to redeem sinners. Finally, He did not permit Cain, a man accused of parricide, to perish before he brought forth sons.[4] For the sake, therefore, of the successive generations of men it followed that woman had to be joined to man. Thus we must interpret the very words of God when He said the it was not good for man to be alone. If the woman

4 Gen. 4.15-17.

was to be the first one to sin, the fact that she was the one destined to bring forth redemption must not be excluded from the operations of Divine Providence. Although 'Adam was not deceived, the woman was deceived and was in sin. Yet woman, we are told, 'will be saved by childbearing,'[5] in the course of which she generated Christ.

(48) Not without significance, too, is the fact that woman was made out of the rib of Adam. She was not made of the same earth with which he was formed, in order that we might realize that the physical nature of both man and woman is identical and that there was one source for the propagation of the human race. For that reason, neither was man created together with a woman, nor were two men and two women created at the beginning, but first a man and after that a woman. God willed it that human nature be established as one. Thus, from the very inception of the human stock He eliminated the possibility that many disparate natures should arise. He said: 'Let us make him a helper like himself.'[6] We understand that to mean a helper in the generation of the human family—a really good helper. If we take the word 'helper' in a good sense, then the woman's co-operation turns out to be something of major import in the process of generation, just as the earth by receiving, confining, and fostering the seed causes it to grow and produce fruit in time. In that respect, therefore, woman is a good helper even through in an inferior position. We find examples of this in our own experience. We see how men in high and important offices often enlist the help of men who are below them in rank and esteem.

5 1 Tim. 2.14.
6 Gen. 2.18.

Chapter 11

(49) Examine, now, the reason why God had by this time created out of the earth 'all the beasts of the field and all the birds of the air' and brought them to Adam to see what he would call them. How account for the fact that God brought merely the beasts of the field and the birds of the air to Adam? Animals were there, we know, each according to its kind. And so it is related further on: 'Adam named all the animals and all the beasts of the field, but he found no helper like himself.'[1] How can we explain this other than by saying that the untamed beasts and the birds of the air were brought to man by divine power, while man himself held power over the beasts that were tame and domesticated? The former lay within the province of God's activity. The latter were due to the diligence of man. Besides this, there is a reason why everything was brought to Adam. In this way he would be able to see that nature in every aspect is constituted of two sexes: male and female. Following these observations, he would become aware that association with a woman was a necessity of his lot.

(50) 'And God cast Adam into a deep sleep and he slept.' What does the phrase 'deep sleep' signify? Does it not mean that when we contemplate a conjugal union we seem to be turning our eyes gradually in the direction of God's kingdom? Do we not seem, as we enter into a vision of this world, to partake a little of things divine, while we find our repose in the midst of what is secular and mundane? Hence, after the statement, 'He cast Adam into a deep sleep and he slept,' there follows: 'The rib which God took from Adam he built into a woman.'[2] The word 'built' is well chosen in

1 Gen. 2.19,20.
2 Gen. 2.21,22.

speaking of the creation of a woman because a household, comprising man and wife, seems to point toward a state of full perfection. One who is without a wife is regarded as being without a home. As man is considered to be more skilful in public duties, so woman is esteemed to be more adaptable to domestic ministrations. Reflect on the fact that He did not take a part from Adam's soul but a rib from his body, that is to say, not soul from a soul, but 'bone of my bone and flesh of my flesh'[3] will this woman be called.

(51) Thus we have made clear the cause of the generation of man. But many who reflect deeply on this question are disturbed by another problem. How explain the fact that animals and beasts of the field and birds of the air were in Paradise, if at the beginning God bestowed this great gift to men, namely, the privilege of living there and of expecting afterward that, as a reward of merit, all just men should be restored to that place? Hence, many hold that by Paradise is meant the soul of man and that, while man was placed there as a worker and guardian, certain seeds of virtue sprouted forth. This may be taken to mean that the mind of man, whose virtue it is to cultivate the soul intensively, not only performs its appropriate function, but also acts as a custodian of the work accomplished. The beasts of the field and the birds of the air which were brought to Adam are our irrational senses, because beasts and animals represent the diverse emotions of the body, whether of the more violent kind or even of the more temperate. What else are we to consider the birds of the air if not as representations of our idle thoughts which, like winged creatures, flit around our souls and frequently lead us by their varied motions now in one direction, now in another? Wherefore our faculty of perception, which in Greek is represented by the word αἴσθησις,

3 Gen. 2.23.

constitutes the most congenial aid to the work of our minds. Except for our intellect [νοῦς,] the mind has been unable to find another faculty so like itself.

(52) Perhaps you may argue that God is Himself the Author of error, because He also placed in such a Paradise entities such as these—I mean the passions of the body and the vanity of thoughts that are fleeting and empty. Take note of what He says: 'Have dominion over the fish of the sea, the birds of the air and all the animals that crawl upon the earth.'[4] You see that He granted to you the power of being able to discern by the application of sober logic the species of each and every object, in order that you may be induced to form a judgment on all of them. God called them all to your attention, so that you might realize that your mind is superior to all of them. Why have you now willed to make part of yourself and to link close to you what you have discovered to be a totally alien substance? God surely has given you a sense of perception, whereby you can know things in general and can form a judgment about them. Because you were unable to observe God's commands you were deservedly ejected from that fertile Garden. God came to the realization that you were weak and could not discriminate. Hence, He spoke to men in their weakness. 'Do not judge that you may not be judged.'[5] He bade you, therefore, to be obedient to His imposed command, because He knew that your judgment was weak. If you had not disregarded this order, you would never had run the risk of wavering in your judgment. And, since you wished to form a judgment, for that reason He added: 'Indeed Adam has become like one of us, knowing good and evil.'[6] You desired to claim judgment as your right. Hence you ought not to

4 Gen. 1.25.
5 Matt. 7.1.
6 Gen. 3.22.

oppose the penalty for misguided judgment. Nevertheless, He placed you in such a position outside Paradise that the recollection of it may never leave you.

(53) Hence the just are caught up into Paradise, just as Paul 'was caught up into paradise and heard secret words that man may not repeat.'[7] And if by the vigor of your mind you are caught up from the first heaven to the second and from the second heaven to the third, we can explain it in this way. Each and every man is first of all corporeal; secondly, he is of a sensual nature; and thirdly, he is spiritual in that he is carried to the third heaven to behold the brilliance of spiritual grace. 'The sensual man does not perceive the things that are of the Spirit.'[8] For that reason the ascent into the third heaven is necessary for him in order that he may be caught up into Paradise. At this stage, without incurring danger, you will be caught up, in order that you may be able to pass judgment on all things, because 'the spiritual man judges all things and he himself is judged by no man.'[9] Perchance, although still infirm, you will hear secret words that man may not repeat. Forbear to reveal anything and keep in your heart what you shall hear. Paul the Apostle kept these words in his heart lest he fall and for a certainty lead others into sin. Or perhaps Paul used the words 'that man may not repeat'[10] because he was still in the body, that is to say, because he saw the passions of this body of ours and because he saw the law of his flesh 'warring against the law of his mind.'[11] I prefer to take the meaning in this sense, lest the question of future danger should seem to be disregarded. That would imply freedom during our lifetime from the anxiety and dread of snares which

---

7 2 Cor. 12.4,5.
8 1 Cor. 2.14.
9 1 Cor. 2.15.
10 2 Cor. 12.4.
11 Rom. 7.23.

might lead to sin in the future. Whoever, therefore, shall reach upward into Paradise by the exercise of virtue will hear those hidden and secret words of God. He shall hear, too, the Lord speaking as to the repentant thief who abandoned his life of thievery for one of faith: 'This day thou shalt be with me in paradise.'[12]

Chapter 12

(54) 'Now the serpent was more cunning than any of the beasts of the field which the Lord had made. The serpent said to the woman: Did God say, you shall not eat of any tree of the garden?'[1] In the statement 'the serpent was more cunning' you understand to whom reference is made. This is our Adversary, whose wisdom is of this world. Gratification of pleasure has been fittingly called wisdom, because it is called the wisdom of the flesh as in the statement, 'The wisdom of this flesh is hostile to God.'[2] The seekers after pleasure are shrewd in their choice of means for its gratification. If you understand, therefore, gratification of pleasure to be, in fact, an act contrary to the divine command and hostile to our senses, this is in accord with what Paul states: 'I see another law in my members warring against the law of my mind and making me prisoner in the law of sin.[3] If you ascribe this to the Devil, what other cause of enmity is there except envy? As Solomon says: 'By the envy of the devil death came into the world.'[4] The cause of envy was the happiness of man placed in Paradise, because the Devil

12 Luke 23.43.

1 Gen. 3.1.
2 Rom. 8.7.
3 Rom. 7.23.
4 Wisd. 2.24.

could not brook the favors received by man. His envy was aroused because man, though formed in slime, was chosen to be an inhabitant of Paradise. The Devil began to reflect that man was an inferior creature, yet had hopes of an eternal life, whereas he, a creature of superior nature, had fallen and had become part of this mundane existence. This is the substance of his invidious reflection: 'Will this inferior acquire what I was unable to keep? Will he leave the earth and attain heaven, whereas I have fallen to earth thrust down from heaven? I have many ways and means by which to deceive man. He was made of slime, earth is his mother, and he is involved in things corruptible. Although of superior nature, his soul is nevertheless subject to temptation, since it exists in the prison house of the body—witness my own experience in being unable to avoid sin. This, therefore, is my first approach, namely, to deceive him while he is desirous of improving his condition. In this way an attempt will be made to arouse his ambition. The next approach is by way of the flesh, promising fulfillment of all his desires. Finally, how else can I appear to be wiser than all men if not by the exercise of cunning and fraud in my warfare of entrenchment against man?' Accordingly, he contrived not to attack Adam first. Rather, he aimed to circumvent Adam by means of the woman. He did not accost the man who had in his presence received the heavenly command. He accosted her who had learned of it from her husband and who had not received from God the command which was to be observed. There is no statement that God spoke to the woman. We know that he spoke to Adam. Hence we must conclude that the command was communicated through Adam to the woman.

(55) The nature of the temptation presented on this occasion is now clear. In addition to this, there are other occasions when many other kinds of temptations are in store

for us. Some of these come from the Prince of this world, who has vomited into this world what might be called poisonous wisdom, so that men believe the false to be true and are emotionally carried away by mere appearance. The Enemy's attack is not always in the open. There are certain powers who put on the external form of what is desirable and gratifying so as to pour into our thoughts the poison of their iniquities. From this source come those sins which arise from indulgence in pleasures or from some infirmity of the mind. There are still other powers who may be said to wrestle with us, as the Apostle says: 'For our wrestling is not against flesh and blood but against the Principalities and Powers, against the world-rulers of this darkness, against the spiritual forces of wickedness on high.'[5] They wish by this belligerency of theirs to break us and, so to speak, to force out the breath of life from our bodies. Wherefore, like a good athlete, Paul knew how to parry the blows of the opposing powers and even to strike them as they advanced to the attack. Hence he says: 'I strike with my fists, not as one beating the air.'[6] And so like a good athlete he merited the crown of victory.[7] The temptations of the Devil, then, are manifold. For that reason he is believed to be a deadly, double-tongued serpent, doing the Devil's work by saying one thing with the tongue and by harboring other thoughts in his mind. There are other servants of the Devil who aim at us poisonous shafts of word and thought, such as are described by the Lord: 'You brood of vipers, how can you speak good things when you are evil?'[8]

(56) 'And the serpent said to the woman: Did God say, you shall not eat of any tree of the garden? The woman answered the serpent: Of the fruit of any tree in the garden

5 Eph. 6.12.
6 1 Cor. 9.26.
7 2 Tim. 4.8.
8 Matt. 12.34.

we shall eat, but of the tree in the middle of the garden, God said, you shall not eat of it, neither shall you touch it, lest you die.'[9] Although you are aware that the serpent is wiser that all creatures, his cunning is especially noticeable here. As he sets his snares, he pretends to give utterance to the words of God, for God had already said: 'From every tree of the garden you may eat, but from the tree of the knowledge of good and evil you must not eat, for the day you eat of it you must die.'[10] The serpent inserted a falsehood in questioning the woman thus: 'Did God say, you shall not eat of any tree?' Whereas God had actually said: 'From every tree of the garden you may eat, but from one tree you must not eat,' meaning, by that, the tree of the knowledge of good and evil which was not to be tasted. We need not wonder at the manner of deception. Deceit accompanies any effort at ensnaring an individual. The serpent's question was not without its purpose. But the woman's reply will indicate that there was nothing questionable in the command of God: 'Of the fruit of all the trees in the garden we may eat, but of the fruit of the tree in the middle of the garden, God said, you shall not eat of it neither shall you touch it, lest you die.' There was nothing inexact about the command itself. The error lay in the report of the command. The Scriptural passage under discussion is self-explanatory. We realize that we ought not to make any addition to a command even by way of instruction. Any addition or qualification of a command is in the nature of a falsification. The simple, original form of a command should be preserved or the facts should be duly set before us. It frequently happens that a witness adds something of himself to a relation of facts. In this way, by the injection of an untruth, confidence in his testimony is wholly shattered.

9 Gen. 3.1.
10 Gen. 2.16.

No addition therefore—not even a good one—is called for. What is, therefore, at first sight objectionable in the addition made by the woman: 'Neither shall you touch anything of it'? God did not say this, but, rather: 'you must not eat.' Still, we have here something which leads to error. There are two possibilities to the addition she made: Either it is superfluous or because of this personal contribution she has made God's command only partly intelligible. John in his writings has made this clear: 'If anyone shall add to them, God will add unto him the plagues that are written in this book. And if anyone shall take away from these words of the book of this prophecy, God will take away his portion from the tree of life.'[11] If this is true in this case, how much truer is it that nothing should be taken away from the commands laid down by God! From this springs the primary violation of the command. And many believe that this was Adam's fault—not the woman's. They reason that Adam in his desire to make her more cautious had said to the woman that God had given the additional instruction: 'Neither shall you touch it.' We know that it was not Eve, but Adam, who received the command from God, because the woman had not yet been created. Scripture does not reveal the exact words that Adam used when he disclosed to her the nature and content of the command. At all events, we understand that the substance of the command was given to the woman by the man. What opinions others have offered on this subject should be taken into consideration. It seems to me, however, that the initial violation and deceit was due to the woman. Although there may appear to be an element of uncertainty in deciding which of the two was guilty, we can discern the sex which was liable first to do wrong. Add to this the fact that she stands convicted in court whose previous error is afterward revealed. The woman is respon-

11 Apoc. 22.18,19.

sible for the man's error and not vice-versa. Hence Paul says: 'Adam was not deceived, but the woman was deceived and was in sin.'[12]

(57) Now let us examine another question relative to the addition which was made to the command. Does this addition in itself seem to be objectionable? If the words, 'neither shall you touch it,' are actually advantageous and tend to put one on his guard, why did not God expressly forbid this even to the point of seemingly permitting it by not forbidding it? Wherefore, both points must be examined; namely, the reasons why He neither permitted it nor forbade it. Some raise the question: Why did He not order that the object which He had made should be seen and touched? But, when you realize that there was in that tree the knowledge of good and evil, you can understand that He did not wish you to touch what is evil. Sufficient is it for us, using the words of the Lord, 'to watch Satan fall as lightning from heaven,'[13] and giving to his sons not the meat of life, but that of night and darkness, as it is written: 'He gave him to be meat for the people of the Ethiopians.'[14] Thus far on the subject of the reason why He did not command the tree to be touched. Here are the reasons, as I understand them, why God did not prohibit this act. There are many things which do us harm, if we make up our minds to touch them before we know what they are. We often learn, in fact, by experience to be resigned if we know beforehand that a certain food or drink is bitter. You learn to be tolerant if you believe that what is bitter is beneficial, lest your sudden realization of its bitterness may offend you and cause you to reject what may prove to be salutary. It is advantageous, therefore, first to have knowledge of this bitter quality, so

12 1 Tim. 2.14.
13 Luke 10.18.
14 Ps. 73.14.

that you may not be squeamish and that you may realize what is good for you. These are examples of what may harm us just to a slight degree. From the discussion which now follows, take warning of what may cause us more serious damage unless we make provision against it.

(58) Take the case of the Gentile who is eager for the faith. He becomes a catechumen and desires a greater fullness of doctrine to strengthen his faith. See to it that in his willingness to learn he is not exposed to false doctrine. Take care that he does not learn from Photinus or from Arius or from Sabellius. See that he does not hand himself over to teachers of this sort who would attract him by their airs of authority, so that his untrained mind, impressed by the weight of such august prestige, will be unable to discriminate the right from the wrong. He should first, therefore, determine with the eyes of his mind what are the logical sequences. Let him note where life exists by touching the life-giving qualities of holy Scripture, so that no interpreter will stand in his way. Sabellius reads for him: 'I am in the Father and the Father in me,'[15] and says that means one Person. Photinus reads that 'there is one Mediator between God and men, himself man, Christ Jesus.' And elsewhere: 'Why do you wish to kill me, a man?'[16] Arius, too, read the following: 'For the Father is greater than I.'[17] The reading is clear, but the catechumen first ought to reflect on the matter in his own mind, so as to discover the real meaning of these passages. He is influenced by the prestige of his teachers. It would have been more to his advantage if he had not investigated at all rather than have come upon such an instructor. But the Gentile, too, if he takes up the Scriptures, reads: 'Eye for eye, tooth for tooth.' Again: 'If

15 John 14.10.
16 1 Tim. 2.5; John 8.40.
17 John 14.28.

thy right hand is an occasion of sin to thee, cut it off.'[18] He does not understand the sense of this. He is not aware of the secret meaning of the divine words. He is worse off than if he had not read at all. Hence he has furnished a lesson to these men on how they should have investigated the meaning of the Word of God. A careful, not a superficial, examination of the context of the passage should be made. It is written: 'What was from the beginning, what we have heard, what we have seen with our eyes, what we have looked upon and our hands have investigated: of the Word of Life. And we have seen and now testify and announce to you.'[19] You see how he investigated, so to speak, with his hands the Word of God and afterward announced it. Hence, the Word would not perhaps have caused injury to Adam and Eve if they had first touched and handled it, as it were, with the hands of the mind. Those who are infirm can by careful examination and handling investigate the nature of each and every object which they do not understand. Certainly, those weak first parents of ours should have studied beforehand the problem presented to them: How were they to touch the tree in which they knew there was knowledge of evil? The knowledge of evil, in fact, can frequently be of advantage to us. Wherefore we read in the oracular words of Scripture of the wiles of the Devil, so that we learn how we can escape his arts. We should be aware of his temptations, not that we may follow his lead, but that by instruction we may avoid these pitfalls.

(59) At this point there are some who doubt whether God meant that the fruit of every tree should be eaten—this injunction to include every tree, inclusive of the tree of the knowledge of good and evil—or whether, in fact, He referred to every tree, but excluded only the tree of knowledge of

18 Lev. 24.20; Matt. 5.30.
19 John 1.1,2.

good and evil? These people are of the opinion that this matter is not without significance, because, although the fruit of this tree is harmful in itself, still, if it were combined with that of the other trees, it could not be injurious. They cite as example of this fact the belief that an antidote can be obtained from the body of a serpent which, being poisonous since it is extracted from a serpent, is harmful when taken alone, but when mixed with other drugs has medicinal properties. The knowledge of good and evil, also, if one possesses wisdom that is ever an aid toward survival and if one reaches out after the other types of virtue, is considered to be of no inconsiderable value. On that account, therefore, many hold that we can even understand the reason why God made this prohibition. He did not wish that tree of the knowledge of good and evil should be eaten alone and not in combination with the fruit of the others. He did not prohibit this if the other trees are taken into consideration at the same time. Wherefore what God said to Adam is cited: 'Who told you that you were naked? You have eaten, then, of the tree which alone I commanded you not to eat.'[20] This would seem to offer an occasion for disputation. In the preceding passage the woman might well have not made any reply to the serpent's question: 'Did God say, you shall not eat of any tree of the garden?' But she answered: 'Of the tree in the middle of the garden, God said, you shall not eat of it.' In this incident, as she was on the point of sinning, the woman's faith may appear to have been weak. Moreover, I shall not despoil Adam of all the virtues, so that he would appear to have attained no virtue in Paradise and would seem to have eaten nothing from the other trees, but had fallen into sin before he had obtained any fruit. I shall, therefore, not despoil Adam lest I may despoil the whole human race, which is innocent before it acquires the

20 Gen. 3.11.

capacity to know good and evil. Not without reason was it said: 'Unless you turn and become like this child, you shall not enter into the kingdom of heaven.'[21] The child, when he is scolded, does not retaliate. When he is struck, he does not strike back. He is not conscious of the allurements of ambition and self-seeking.

(60) The truth seems to be, then, that He commanded the tree not to be eaten, not even along with the fruit of the other trees. Knowledge of good, in fact, although of no use to a perfect man, is, on the other hand, of no value to a man who is imperfect. Paul speaks of himself as imperfect: 'Not that I have already obtained this or already have been made perfect, but I press on hoping that I may lay hold of it already.'[22] Hence the Lord says to the imperfect: 'Do not judge that you may not be judged.'[23] Knowledge is, therefore, of no use to the imperfect. Hence we read: 'I did not know sin unless the Law had said, thou thalt not lust.' And further on we read: 'For without the Law sin is dead.'[24] What advantage is it to me to know what I cannot avoid? What avails it for me to know that the law of my flesh assails me? Paul is assailed and sees 'the law of his flesh warring against that of his mind and making him prisoner to the law of sin.' He does not rely on himself, but by the grace of Christ is confident of his 'deliverance from the body of death.'[25] Do you think that anyone with knowledge of sin can avoid it? Paul says: 'For I do not the good that I wish, but the evil that I do not wish.'[26] Do you consider that this knowledge which adds to the reproach of sin can be of help to man? Granted, however, that the perfect man

21 Matt. 18.3.
22 Phil. 3.12.
23 Matt. 7.1.
24 Rom. 7.7,8.
25 Rom. 7.23,24.
26 Rom. 7.19.

is unable to sin. God foresaw all men in the person of Adam. Hence it was not fitting that the human race in general should have a knowledge of good and evil—a knowledge which he could not utilize because of the weakness of the flesh.

Chapter 13

(61) Let us learn, therefore, that the temptations of the Devil are full of guile. Of the things that he promised, scarcely one of them seems to be true. He contrived falsehoods, as we can see if we read elsewhere: 'And the serpent said to the woman, you shall not die.' Here we have one falsehood, for man, who followed the promises of the serpent, is subject to death. Hence he added: 'For God knows that when you eat of it, your eyes will be opened.' This alone is true, because further on we read: 'They both ate and their eyes were opened.'[1] But the truth is that as a result of this act harm followed. Hence, opening one's eyes is not to everyone's advantage, for it is written: 'They will see and will not see.'[2] But the serpent was quick to attack a falsehood to his statement, when he said: 'And you will be like gods, knowing good and evil.'[3] Hence you may note that the serpent is the author of idolatry, for his cunning seems to be responsible for man's error in introducing many gods. His deceit lay in stating that they will be like gods, for not only have men ceased to be like gods, but even those men who were like gods (to whom it was spoken, 'I have said you are gods'[4]) have fallen from His favor.

(62) 'And the woman saw that the tree was good for

1 Gen. 3.4-6.
2 Isa. 6.9.
3 Gen. 3.5.
4 Ps. 81.6.

food, pleasing to the eyes and beautiful to gaze upon.'[5] She showed her weakness in passing judgment on what she had not tasted. It is not easy under any circumstance to make such an assumption without deep reflection and a careful examination of the facts. 'She took of its fruit,' we are told, 'and ate it and also gave some to her husband and they both ate.'[6] Omission is made, and rightly so, of the deception of Adam, since he fell by his wife's fault and not because of his own.

(63) 'And their eyes were opened,' we are told, 'and they realized that they were naked.'[7] They were naked, it is true, before this time, but they were not devoid of the garments of virtue. They were naked because of the purity of their character and because nature knows nothing of the cincture of deceit. Now, on the other hand, the mind of man is veiled in many folds of deception. When, therefore, they saw that they had been despoiled of the purity and simplicity of their untainted nature, they began to look for objects made by the hand of man wherewith to cover the nakedness of their minds and hearts. They added gratification so as to increase the idle pleasures of this world, sewing, as it were, leaf upon leaf in order to conceal and cover the organ of generation. But how explain the fact that Adam had his bodily eyes closed, whereas he was able to see all living creatures and confer names upon them? Well, just as by way of an inner and deeper knowledge they were able to realize, not that they were without garments, but that the protective covering of virtue was no longer theirs.

(64) 'So they sewed fig-leaves together and made themselves coverings.'[8] We are taught by the content of holy

5 Gen. 3.6.
6 *Ibid.*
7 Gen. 3.7.
8 *Ibid.*

Scripture how we should interpret the meaning of the word 'fig' in this passage. Scripture relates that the saints are those who find rest beneath the vine and the fig.[9] Solomon has said: 'Who plants the fig tree and does not eat the fruit thereof?'[10] Yet the owner may come to the fig tree and may be offended by finding there merely leaves and no fruit. I have information from Adam himself, in fact, about the significance of the leaves. He proceeded to make a covering for himself out of the leaves of the fig tree after he had sinned, whereas he should have had its fruit instead. The just man chooses the fruit; the sinner, the leaves. What is the fruit? We read: 'The fruit of the spirit is charity, joy, peace, patience, kindness, modesty, continency, love.'[11] He who possessed no fruit possessed no joy. The person who violated the command of God did not have faith, and he who ate of the forbidden tree did not have the virtue of continency.

(65) Whoever, therefore, violates the command of God has become naked and despoiled, a reproach to himself. He wants to cover himself and hide his genitals with fig leaves, making use, as it were of empty and idle talk which the sinner interweaves word after word with fallacies for the purpose of shielding himself from his awareness of his guilty deed. Desiring to conceal his fault, he throws leaves over himself, at the same time indicating that the Devil is responsible for his crime. He offers allurements of the flesh or the recommendations of another individual as excuses for his wrongdoing. He frequently produces examples from holy Scripture, citing them as instances of how a just man may fall into sin, the sin of adultery: 'And Abraham lay with his handmaid and David loved a strange woman whom

9 Mich. 4.4.
10 Prov. 27.18.
11 Gal. 5.22.

he made his wife.'[12] He patches together examples for his purposes from the list of prophetical books of Scripture. He sees the leaves and ignores the fruit.

(66) Do not the Jews seem to you to be patchers of leaves when they interpret in a material manner the words of the spiritual Law? Their interpretation, condemned to eternal aridity, loses all the characteristic greenness of the fruit. There is a correct interpretation, therefore, which points to a fruitful and spiritual fig tree beneath which just men and saints find their rest.[13] Whoever plants this tree in the souls of every man will eat the fruit thereof, as Paul says: 'I have planted, Apollos watered.'[14] But the wrong interpretation will not confer the fruit nor conserve its viridity.

(67) It was a serious matter, therefore, when, following this interpretation, Adam girded himself in that place where it would have been better that he had girded himself with the fruit of chastity. Seeds of generation are said to exist in our loins around which we bind our garments. Hence, Adam did wrong on that occasion when he girded himself with leaves that have no utility, inasmuch as by this act he implied, not the fruit of a future generation, but certain sins which remained until the coming of our Lord and Saviour. But, when the master came, He found the fig tree uncultivated. Elsewhere, when requested that he should order it to be cut down, the owner of the fig tree allowed it to be cultivated.[15] And so we gird ourselves, not with leaves, but with the divine Word, as the Lord Himself says: 'Let your loins be girt about and your lamps burning.'[16] Where-

12 Gen. 16.13; 2 Kings 11.4.

13 Mich. 4.4.

14 1 Cor. 3.6.

15 Cf. Matt. 21.19; Luke 13.6-9.

16 Luke 12.35.

fore He prohibits us to carry money even in our girdles.[17] Our girdles ought not to store up worldly objects, but things of eternal nature.

Chapter 14

(68) 'And they heard the voice of the Lord walking in the garden towards evening.'[1] What does 'walking' mean in reference to God, who is everywhere ? In my opinion God may be said to walk wherever throughout Scripture the presence of God is implied, when we hear that He sees all things and 'the eyes of the Lord are upon the just.'[2] We read, too, that Jesus knew their thoughts and we read: 'Why do you harbor evil throughts in your hearts?'[3] When we reflect, therefore, on these statements, we have a knowledge of God in the act of walking. The sinner, in fact, had tried to hide away from the sight of God. He wished to conceal himself in his thoughts and was unwilling that his works appear in the light of day.'[4] The just man saw Him face to face,[5] because the mind of the just man is in the presence of God and even converses with Him, as it is written: 'Judge for the fatherless and defend the widow, said the Lord.'[6] When a sinner, therefore, reads these passages from Scripture, he hears the voice of God walking towards evening, so to speak. What does the phrase 'towards evening' mean? Does it not mean that the sinner realizes his sin too late and that the shame which should have for-

17 Cf. Matt. 10.9.

1 Gen. 3.8.
2 Ps. 33.16.
3 Luke 6.8; Matt. 9.4.
4 Matt. 5.16.
5 Deut.. 34.10; 1 Cor. 13.12.
6 Isa. 1.17,18.

stalled the fault before it occurred was itself too late? While the sinner is physically overcome by passions that affect the soul, he in his errant fashion does not heed, that is to say, does not hear, God, as He in holy Scripture walks in the hearts and minds of each and every one of us. God says: 'For I will dwell in their midst and I will walk among them and will be their God.'[7] Therefore, the dread of divine power returns to the soul when we are eager to hide ourselves. Then, placed as we are by the thought of our sins in the midst of the trees of Paradise where we committed sin, we are discovered to be desirous of concealing ourselves and to be thinking of hidden things which God does not demand of us. But He who is 'the discerner of our thoughts and intentions of our hearts, extending to the division of soul and spirit,' says: 'Adam, where are you?'[8]

(69) How does God speak? Is it with the voice of the body? Not at all. He utters oracular words with a voice that is far more significant than is the voice of the body. The prophets heard this voice. It is heard by the faithful, but the wicked do not comprehend it. Wherefore we find the Evangelist in the Gospel listening to the voice of the Father speaking: 'I have glorified it and will glorify it again.' But the Jews did not listen. Hence they said: 'I had thundered.'[9] We have given an instance above wherein God was thought to be walking when He was not. Here is an occasion when He was heard speaking, whereas to some people He spoke not.

(70) But let us take note of what He speaks: 'Adam, where, are you?' Even now these words have the healing power of salvation for those who hear the Word of God. Hence it is that the Jews who closed their eyes lest they hear do not deserve to hear even today. It follows that those who

7 Lev. 26.12
8 Heb. 4.12; Gen. 3.9.
9 John 12.28,29.

conceal themselves have a remedy, for he who hides himself is ashamed and he who is ashamed is converted, as it is written: 'Let them be much troubled and let them all be turned back speedily.'[10] The very fact of His calling a person is a testimony of salvation to him who comes, because the Lord calls those for whom He feels pity. When He says, therefore, 'where are you?' it is not a question of a locality to one who knows what is hidden. God did not have His eyes closed, so that a man in hiding was able to escape His notice. For that reason He said: 'Adam has become like one of us,'[11] because his eyes were opened. He, in fact, opened his eyes, so that he saw his own sin which he was unable to avoid. It happens that after we have sinned, we become, somehow or other, more aware of our crimes. We are then aware of the sin which we did not consider to be such before we actually fell into sin. Certainly we did not then believe that a sin was subject to our disapproval, for, if we had felt guilty, we would not have committed it. God sees the faults of all men and knows their offenses. His eyes penetrate into the secrets of the souls of each and every one of us. What, then, does He mean by 'Adam, where are you?' Does He not mean 'in what circumstances' are you; not, 'in what place'? It is, therefore, not a question, but a reproof. From what condition of goodness, beatitude, and grace, He means to say, have you fallen into this state of misery? You have forsaken eternal life. You have entombed yourself in the ways of sin and death. Where is that noble confidence and trust of yours? That fear that you show is evidence of your wrongdoing and that hiding place of yours betrays your dereliction. 'Where are you?' does not mean 'in what place,' but 'in what condition.' Where have your sins led you, so that you fled the God whom before you sought

10 Ps. 6.11.
11 Gen. 3.22.

after? Perhaps you are disturbed by the fact that Adam is the first to be rebuked, although the woman was the first to eat the fruit. But the weaker sex begins by an act of disobedience, whereas the stronger sex is more liable to feelings of shame and forgiveness. The female furnished the occasion for wrongdoing; the male, the opportunity to feel ashamed.

(71) And the woman said: 'The serpent deceived me and I ate.'[12] That fault is pardonable which is followed by an admission of guilt. The woman, therefore, is not to be despaired of, who did not keep silent before God, but who preferred to admit her sin—the woman on whom was passed a sentence that was salutary. It is good to suffer condemnation for our sins and to be scourged for our crimes, provided we are scourged along with other men. Hence, Cain, because he wanted to deny his guilt, was judged unworthy to be punished in his sin. He was forgiven without a prescribed penalty, not, perhaps, for having committed such a serious crime as parricide—he was responsible for his brother's death—as one of sacrilege, in that he thought he had deceived God when he said: 'I do not know. Am I my brother's keeper?'[13] And so the accusation is reserved for his accuser, the Devil, prescribing that he be scourged along with his angels, since he did not wish to be scourged with men. Of such, therefore, has it been said: 'There is no regard for their death and they shall not be scourged like other men.'[14] The woman's case is, accordingly, of a different character. Although she incurred the sin of disobedience, she still possessed in the tree of Paradise food for virtue. And so she admitted her sin and was considered worthy of pardon. 'The just is first accuser of himself in the

12 Gen. 3.13.
13 Gen. 4.9.
14 Ps. 72.4,5.

beginning of his speech.'[15] No one can be justified from sin unless he has first made confession of his sin. Wherefore the Lord says: 'Tell if thou hast anything to justify thyself.'[16]

(72) Because Eve has admitted her crime, she is given a milder and more salutary sentence, which condemned her wrong-doing and did not refuse pardon.[17] She was to serve under her husband's power, first, that she might not be inclined to do wrong, and, secondly, that, being in a position subject to a stronger vessel, she might not dishonor her husband, but on the contrary, might be governed by his counsel.[18] I see clearly here the mystery of Christ and His Church. The Church's turning toward Christ in times to come and a religious servitude submissive to the Word of God—these are conditions far better than the liberty of this world. Hence it is written: 'Thou shalt fear the Lord thy God and shall serve him only.'[19] Servitude, therefore, of this sort is a gift of God. Wherefore, compliance with this servitude is to be reckoned among blessings. We have the example of Isaac granting it as a blessing to his son Esau that he should serve his brothers. Hence he asked for his father's blessing. Although he knew that one blessing had been taken from him, he asked for another: 'Have you only one blessing, father?'[20] By this servitude, therefore, Esau, who had before he sold birthright to satisfy his appetite and who in his zeal for hunting in the field had not the benefits derived from a blessing,[21] had now come to believe that he would fare better in the future if he would pay reverence to his brother as a type of Christ. By this kind of

15 Prov. 18.17.
16 Isa. 43.26.
17 Cf. Gen. 3.16.
18 Cf. 1 Peter 3.7.
19 Deut. 6.13; Luke 4.8.
20 Cf. Gen. 27.40,38.
21 Cf. Gen. 25.27.

servitude Christian folk grow strong, as we have it expressed in the words of the Lord to His disciples: 'Whoever wishes to be first among you, let him be the slave of all of you.'[22] Hence charity, which is greater than hope and faith, brings this servitude to pass, for it is written: 'By charity serve one another.'[23] This, then, is the mystery mentioned by the Apostle in reference to Christ and the Church.[24] The servitude existed formerly, in fact, but in a condition of disobedience which was to be later made salutary by the generation of children 'in faith and love and holiness with modesty.'[25] What was certainly among the fathers a generation brought into existence in sin shall become salutary in the children, so that what was a stumbling block to the Jews shall in the society of Christians undergo improvement.

Chapter 15

(73) 'The serpent urged me,' she said. This seemed to God to be pardonable, inasmuch as He knew that the serpent found numerous ways to deceive people. 'Satan disguises himself as an angel of light' and 'his ministers as ministers of justice,'[1] imposing false names on individual things, so as to call 'rashness' a virtue and avarice 'industry.' The serpent, in fact, deceived the woman and the woman led the man away from truth to a violation of duty. The serpent is a type of the pleasures of the body. The woman stands for our senses and the man, for our minds. Pleasure stirs the senses, which, in turn, have their effect on the mind. Pleasure,

---

22 Matt. 20.27.
23 Gal. 5.13.
24 Cf. Eph. 5.32.
25 1 Tim. 2.15.

---

1 2 Cor. 11.14,15.

therefore, is the primary source of sin. For this reason, do not wonder at the fact that by God's judgment the serpent was first condemned, then the woman, and finally the man. The order of condemnation, too, corresponded to that of the crimes committed, for pleasure usually captivates the senses and the senses, the mind. To convince you that the serpent is the type of pleasure, take note of his condemnation.

(74) 'On your breast and on your belly shall you crawl,' we read. Only those who live for the pleasures of the stomach can be said to walk on their bellies, 'whose god is their belly and their glory is their shame,'[2] who eat of what is earthy, and who, weighed down with food, are bent over towards what is of earth. The serpent is well called the symbol of pleasure in that, intent on food, he seems to feed on the earth: 'On your breast and on your belly shall you crawl, dust shall you eat all the days of your life.'[3] We should not tolerate any of the excuses the Devil may make. By so doing we may, perchance, offer him an occasion to display his wickedness. We do this when we say that his iniquity resulted from his condemnation and hence that he aimed constantly to injure mankind because he was condemned for the very purpose of doing us harm. This seems to be pretty fanciful. If we regard the sentence passed on him to be in the nature of a condemnation, God did not condemn the serpent in order to cause injury to man. He pointed out what was to happen in the future. Furthermore, we have demonstrated above how that temptation can be of great service to mankind. What we are to expect can in some measure be gathered from our knowledge of what has been written: 'Whoever shall glorify me, him will I glorify and he that despises me shall be despised.'[4] God brings to pass

2 Phil. 3.19.
3 Gen. 3.14.
4 1 Kings 2.30.

what is good, not what is evil, as His words can teach you that He confers glory and disregards punishment. 'Whosoever shall glorify me,' He says, 'him will I glorify,' thus declaring that the glory of the good is the purpose of His work. And concerning 'him that despises me,' He did not say I shall deprive of glory, but that he shall be deprived of glory. He did not avow that injury to them would be the result of His action, but pointed out what was to come. He did not say, therefore, I shall make you crawl on your breast and belly and feed on earth all the days of your life. What He actually said was: 'You shall crawl and you shall eat,' in this way showing that He predicted what the serpent would do in the future rather than prescribe what he was to do. The earth, not the soul, He said, is your food, and this, in fact, can be of profit to sinners. Hence the Apostle 'delivered such a one for the destruction of the flesh, that his spirit may be saved in the day of our Lord Jesus Christ.'[5] He says that the serpent crawls on his breast and belly. This is due not so much to the shape of his body as to the fact that he has fallen from celestial happiness because of his thoughts of earth. The breast, in fact, is frequently referred to as the seat of wisdom. And so the Apostle leans his head, not on the ground, but on Christ's breast.[6] If, therefore, the wisdom of the Devil is compared to that of the most cruel of animals whose breast is between its legs, if men, too, who, 'minding the things of the earth'[7] and without the inner urge to rise towards heaven, have the appearance of crawling on their bellies—then we surely ought to fill the belly of our souls with the Word of God rather than with the corruptible things of this world. Fittingly, therefore, does David, assuming the character of Adam, say: 'My soul is humbled down to

5 1 Cor. 5.5.
6 Cf. John 13.25; 21.20.
7 Phil. 3.20.

the dust, my belly cleaveth to the earth.'[8] He used the word 'cleaveth' in reference to the serpent who feeds on earthly iniquities. Thus the Apostle says that we should take on the pattern of Christ, so that the virtue of Christ may extend to you.[9] The sentence imposed on the serpent is not considered a heavy one, since even Adam, whose offense was less serious, was accorded a like sentence.

(75) For it is written: 'Cursed is the earth in thy works; in sadness shall you eat thereof all the days of your life.' The two sentences seem to have a certain similarity, yet in that similarity there is a great difference. There is a difference in the way a person eats of the earth, as the serpent is related to have done and the manner in which this is recorded of the man: 'In sadness shall you eat.' That very phrase 'in sadness' makes the precise difference. Note how important this difference is. It is for my benefit that I should eat the earth in sadness rather than with delight, that is to say, that I should appear to feel a certain sadness in my bodily acts and senses rather than experience pleasure in sin. Many, in fact, because of their manifold iniquities have no awareness of sin. But he who says: 'I chastise my body and bring it into subjection,'[10] feels sadness because of regret for the sins to which we are subject. He himself did not have such serious faults for which he ought to feel sorrow. Hence he teaches us that that kind of sorrow is of value which has, not this world, but God, as its end. It is right, he says, that you become sorrowful, so as to feel repentance in the face of God: 'For the sorrow that is according to God produces salvation, whereas the sorrow that is according to the world produces death.'[11] Take note of those who in

8 Ps. 43.25.
9 Phil. 3.17.
10 1 Cor. 9.27.
11 2 Cor. 7.9,10.

the Old Testament were sorrowful in the midst of their bodily labors and who attained grace, while those who found delight in such pleasures continued to be punished. Hence the Hebrews, who groaned in the works of Egypt,[12] attained the grace of the just and those 'who ate bread with mourning and fear,' were supplied with spiritual good.[13] The Egyptians, on the other hand, who, in their service to a detestable king, carried out such works with joy, received no favor.[14]

(76) There, too, is that distinction between the serpent who is said to eat the earth and Adam, to whom God said: 'You shall eat in sadness the herbs of the field.'[15] We may note here a certain gradation. When we eat the earth, it seems that we are in a sort of warfare. When we eat the herbs, there is a certain advance. When finally, we eat bread, then our life of trial has reached its terminus. Let us experience a series of advancements in this life as Paul did: 'It is now no longer I that live,'[16] that is, not I who before this ate the earth, not I who ate grass, for 'all flesh is grass,'[17] but 'Christ lives in me.'[18] This signifies that living bread which comes from heaven,[19] and that wisdom, too, is living, together with grace, justice, and resurrection.

(77) Again, consider the fact that it is the serpent and not man who is cursed. And the earth is not cursed in itself but is 'cursed in your work.'[20] This is said in reference to the soul. The earth is cursed if your works are earthly, that is, of this world. It is not cursed as a whole. It will merely bring forth thorns and thistles, if it is not diligently cared

12 Cf. Exod. 2.23.
13 Tob. 2.5; cf. 1 Cor. 10.3.
14 Exod. 16.14-18.
15 Gen. 3.18.
16 Gal. 2.20.
17 Isa. 40.6.
18 Gal. 2.20.
19 John 6.50.
20 Gen. 3.17.

for by the labor of human hands. If we do not toil over it in labor and sweat we shall not eat bread. The law of the flesh wars against the law of the mind.[21] We must labor and sweat so as to chastise the body and bring it into subjection and sow the seeds of spiritual things. If we sow what is carnal, we shall reap fruit that is carnal. If, however, we sow what is spiritual, we shall reap the fruit of the spirit.[22]

21 Cf. Rom. 7.23.
22 Cf. 1 Cor. 9.27,11,12.

CAIN AND ABEL

CAIN AND ABEL

BOOK ONE

Chapter 1

IN THE PRECEDING PAGES we have discussed the subject of Paradise, including the account of the fall of Adam and Eve. We have recorded these facts to the best of our ability, just as the Lord has inspired us to interpret their meaning. Now, we have it on record that this sin did not stop at that point, but, to make matters worse, lived on and had a successor in the person of one who was still more debased. Let us take note, then, of what happened subsequently, as we follow in due order the events related in the pages of holy Scripture.

(2) Adam knew his wife and she conceived and bore Cain, saying: "I have begotten a man-child through God."[1] In using the expression 'giving birth to,' it is usual for us to consider the categories 'by what,' 'from what,' and 'through what.' The phrase 'by what' refers to the material; 'from

1 Gen. 4.1.

what,' to the author; 'through what,' to some instrument. Can the expression, 'I have begotten a man-child through God,' induce us to think of God as an instrument? Certainly not. We are to understand here that God is the Author and Creator. Hence, Eve ascribed the work to God when she said: 'I have begotten a man-child through God,' so that we, too, in a similar situation, ought not to claim our succession to ourselves, but attribute it entirely to God.

(3) 'In addition she bore his brother Abel.'[2] When anything is added, that which comes before it is eliminated. This we can see in an arithmetical calculation or by simple reflection. When one number is added to another, something new arises. The original number disappears and mentally we proceed to exclude the figure with which we started. When, therefore, Abel is born in addition, Cain is eliminated. This can be understood better if we examine the signification of their names. Cain means 'getting,' because he got everything for himself. Abel, on the other hand, did not, like his brother before him, refer everything to himself. Devotedly and piously, he attributed everything to God, ascribing to his Creator everything that he had received from Him.

(4) There are two schools of thought, therefore, totally in opposition one to the other, implied in the story of the two brothers. One of these schools attributes to the mind itself the original creative source of all our thoughts, sensations, and emotions. In a word, it ascribes all our productions to man's own mind. The other school is that which recognizes God to be the Artificer and Creator of all things and submits everything to His guidance and direction. Cain is a pattern for the first school and Abel of the second. One living being gave birth to these two schools of thought. Hence, they are related as brothers because they come from

2 Gen. 4.2.

one and the same womb. At the same time, they are opposites and should be divided and separated, once they have been animated with the life of the spirit. Those who are by nature contraries cannot abide for long in one and the same habitation. Hence, Rebecca, when she gave birth to two individuals of dissimilar nature, the one good and the other evil, and when she felt them leap in her womb (Esau was the type of wickedness, Jacob the pattern of what is good), marveled at the reason for the discord which she perceived within her. She appealed to God to make known the reason for her suffering and to grant a remedy. This was the response given to her prayer: 'Two nations are in your womb; two peoples shall stem from your body.'[3] Interpreted spiritually, this can mean the same generation of good and evil, both of which emanate from the same source in the soul. The former is likely to be the fruit of sound judgment whereby evil is repudiated and goodness is fostered and strengthened. Prior to giving birth to what is good, that is to say, to giving complete reverence and deference owed to God Himself the soul shows preference to its own creation. When, moreover, the soul is generated with faith and trust in God, relief comes at the time of parturition. Thus God, in applying the beneficial lesson of Abel to the soul of man, makes ineffective the impious lesson of Cain.

Chapter 2

(5) Following the Scriptures, I am inclined to hold that in this place we have a reference to two classes of peoples. In disposing for the Church's use the faith of His devoted flock, God has made ineffective the perfidy of the people who fell away from Him. The very words of God seem to

3 Gen. 25.23.

establish this meaning: 'Two nations are in your womb; two peoples stem form your body.' These two brothers, Cain and Abel, have furnished us with the prototype of the Synagogue and the Church. In Cain we perceive the parricidal people of the Jews, who were stained with the blood of their Lord, their Creator, and, as a result of the child-bearing of the Virgin Mary, their Brother, also. By Abel we understand the Christian who cleaves to God, as David says: 'It is good for me to adhere to my God,'[1] that is, to attach oneself to heavenly things and to shun the earthly. Elsewhere he says: 'My soul hath fainted in thy word,' thus indicating his rule of life was directed toward reflections on the Word and not on the pleasures of this world. Wherefore we realize that what we read concerning David in the Book of King is not an idle statement, but is said with due weight and reflection: 'And he was laid with his fathers.'[3] We are given to understand that his faith was like that of his father's. It is clear, then, that there is reference here to participation in life and not to the burial of a body.

(6) Hence the words of Scripture here are considered to have more than casual meaning. Leaving the appearance of this weak body which was attached to his soul as an appendage, Isaac 'was gathered to his kin'[4] because he adhered to the customs of his father. Fittingly does he say 'to his kin'—not 'to his people,' as elsewhere.[5] We read in other places that men were gathered to their people, but these men were not so prominent. A person is more prominent who is matched, not by the many, but by the few—for there are more individuals implied in 'people' than in 'kin.' It is considered, too, that similarity to a few people has more

1 Ps. 72.28.
2 Ps. 108.81.
3 3 Kings 2.10.
4 Gen. 35.29.
5 Deut. 32.50.

merit than likeness to a large number. Those, therefore, who were born in this world with God's help, who were chosen to offer with devotion approved sacrifices, who were content with one consort, that is, with the sole society of that highest of kinship, wisdom, which is ever one and harmonious—these persons, according to the testimony of holy Scripture, ought not to be put in the category of the average man. In the one case, we have an active life which included study and meditation; in the other, association with the crowd and a mingling with the populace. Those who collectively are called 'people' are for the most part swayed by hearsay. Uncorrupted purity and lofty lineage are found, not where men are subject to popular appeal, but wherever an intelligent group is gathered together solely for the task of learning. Wherefore Isaac, we are told, with the help of God was gathered to his kin rather than to his people. Thus you can come to understand that he was a man who paid more attention to what is divine than to what is merely human.

(7) Blessed is the mind of that man who, overstepping the bounds of species and race, deserves to hear what was said to Moses when he stood apart from his people: 'Stand thou here with me.'[6] Just as Isaac, the type of the Incarnation of the Lord, overstepping the custom of human generation, surpassed his predecessors, so that he acquired special distinction and veered from participation in the common and vulgar, in a similar way we learn from Scripture that 'promises were made to Abraham and to his offspring. He does not say, "and to his offsprings"—as of many, but as of one, "and to thy offspring," who is Christ.'[7] In Moses, also, there is a figure of one who was to teach the Law, preach the Gospel, fulfill the Old Testament,[8] found the New, give

6 Deut. 5.31.
7 Gal. 3.16.
8 Matt. 5.17.

heavenly nourishment to the people. He so far exceeded the dignity of his human state that he was given the title of 'God' as we read in the Scriptures, where the Lord speaks: 'I have appointed thee the God of Pharao.'[9] He was, in fact, victorious over all his passions and was not allured by the enticements of the world. He enveloped this our habitation here in the body with a purity that savored of a 'citizenship that is in heaven.'[10] By directing his mind and by subduing and castigating his flesh with an authority that was almost regal, he was given the name of 'God,' in whom he had modeled his life by numerous acts of perfect virtue.

(8) Accordingly, we do not read of him, as we do of others, that he fell sick and died. We read that 'he died by the word of God'—for a God does not grow weak or undergo diminution or addition. Hence Scripture added: 'No man hath known of his sepulture until this present day'[11]—by which we are to understand that he was taken up into heaven rather than buried, for death may be called a separation of the soul from the body. He died, therefore, as the Scripture states: 'by the word of God'—not 'in accordance with the word'—so as to make known that this was not an announcement of his death, but was more in the nature of a gracious gift to one who was translated rather than left here, and whose sepulture was known to no man. Who could ever find the remains on earth of one who has been shown in the Gospel to be with the Son of God.[12] Hence there appeared with him Elias, who was carried away in a chariot and who did not die nor was buried according to Scripture,[13] for he still lives, being with the Son of God. We read, indeed, that Moses did die, but he died by the Word of God, by which

9 Exod. 7.1.
10 Phil. 3.20.
11 Deut. 34.5,6.
12 Cf. Matt. 17.3.
13 Cf. 4 Kings 2.11.

all things are made: 'By the word of God the heavens were established.'[14] By the Word of God, therefore, there is no cessation of work, but, rather, a foundation. We are not to understand that here with the dissolution of the body we have a return to earth. A special favor was bestowed on him by the operation of the Word of God, so that to his body was granted repose rather than a monumental sepulcher.

(9) There is a clear distinction between servant and master. What is a privilege in a master is in a servant a favor. We read that no one knows the sepulcher of Moses and that Christ died and was taken up from earth to heaven.[15] Christ, in accordance with the mystery of the Law,[16] looked forward to the Redemption, so that He would rise again. Moses did not, in accordance with the favors granted in the Gospel, look forward to Redemption; rather, he himself was the bestower of it. Hence his sepulcher is not really known, but the sepulcher which the creature could not any longer endure has been set free, since of himself every creature makes haste to be delivered from 'its slavery to corruption.'[17] No one, therefore, knows the burial place of Moses, because all men have knowledge of his life. We have seen the sepulcher of Christ, but now no longer know it, since we have come to know His Resurrection. His tomb, in fact, ought to be recognized, so that His Resurrection be made manifest. Hence in the Gospel[18] His tomb is described in all detail. There is no account of this in the Law, because, although the Law announced His Resurrection,[19] it was left to the Gospels in their very detailed account to give us confirmation of this fact.

14 Ps. 32.6.
15 Cf. Mark 16.19.
16 Cf. Isa. 53.8.
17 Rom. 8.21.
18 Cf. Matt. 27.60.
19 Cf. Isa. 11.10.

Chapter 3

(10) Let us complete now our discussion of the theme: 'In addition she bore Abel.' This means that Eve, who had grievously erred before, had generated designedly something superior, so as to transcend the mistake she had previously made. Unless I am mistaken, this event is made generally evident in our own experiences. When we are born we have the physical sensibility of an infant. Then follows the period of childhood, which is devoted merely to the care of our bodies with no regard for the rites or observance of divine worship. Wherefore, in order to show that Jesus Christ, clearly revolutionizing the law of nature, was born of a virgin, the Prophet states: 'Behold a virgin shall conceive and bear a son and his name shall be called Emmanuel. He shall eat butter and honey, that he may know to refuse the evil and choose the good. For before the child know to refuse the evil and choose the good, he does not put his trust in wickedness that he may choose what is good.'[1] And further on: 'For before a child know to call his father and his mother, he shall receive the strength of Damascus and the spoils of Samaria against the king of the Assyrians.'[2] For He alone was not overcome by the vanity and emptiness of this world as one who 'humbled himself, becoming obedient even to death'[3] —one who was most unlike each and every one of us who trust in vain and are swollen with the pride of the flesh. Hence no one is without sin, not even an infant one day old, although he never committed a sin.[4] And so Cain is first to assert himself when we are born. Abel, in whom there is reverence for divinity, is born after him. Evil, therefore, is

1 Isa. 7.14-16.
2 Isa. 8.4.
3 Phil. 2.8.
4 Job 14.4; 1 Peter 2.22; 1 John 3.5.

the first to make its appearance and next the recognition of what is good. Where there is good, there is justice. Where there is justice, there is holiness, that is to say, Abel who cleaves to God.

(11) 'And Abel,' we are told, 'became a keeper of flocks and Cain a tiller of the soil.'[5] Not without reason, as Scripture teaches us, is Abel mentioned first in this passage, although Cain was the first born. The order of nature differs from the order given to the names themselves. What is the significance of this change of order in first mentioning the younger of the two, when there is reference to employment and vocation? In order to understand the reason for this preference we should take note of the differences in their tasks. Tilling the soil comes first in our experience. This activity is lower in prestige than that of sheep-herding. This is like the case of a teacher or leader who, rightfully as elders do, begins with principles that are older and better established. The younger man, on the other hand, is likely to prefer land which is not so old, which does not 'bring forth thorns and thistles,'[6] and which is generally acceptable. Accordingly, Adam, being guilty of sin, is expelled from the Garden of Delight that he might till the soil.[7] The order of nature is correctly preserved at the time of the coming of these brothers into this world. When it is a question of instruction in the art of living, the younger is preferred to the older because, although junior in age, he is superior in virtue. Innocence is later in time than wickedness. Although nearly equal in age, it is far superior in the high quality of its merits: 'For venerable old age is not counted by years nor by grey hairs but by morals, and a spotless life is old age.'[8] When, therefore, there is

5 Gen. 4.2.
6 Gen. 3.18.
7 Cf. Gen. 3.17.
8 Wisd. 4.8,9.

question of birth, Cain should take the first place. When there is question of instruction, Abel should stand first. Who can deny, then, that adolescence and the early years of manhood are subject to the temptations of the passions? Who can deny, too, that, when a more mature age is reached, peace returns after the tempestuous yearnings of youth are passed and the wearied soul finds at last a mooring place in some secluded harbor of life?

Chapter 4

(12) From such examples as these there can be no doubt, therefore, that, although wickedness has precedence in time, yet it has the infirmity which belongs to youthfulness. Wickedness has the contributory advantage of age, whereas virtue has the privilege of that sort of prestige which a man given to unjust judgments often concedes to the just. Holy Scripture is a trusted witness of this fact in the episode where Esau, whose name is linked with those who are stupid,[1] went so far as to surrender his own birthright to his brother Jacob, saying: 'Of what use to me is my birthright?'[2] But the birthright which he disregarded, a man endowed with competence (as his name[3] implies) made an effort to deserve. Does not Esau seem to you to be like one who was defeated in a contest? Does he not appear to you to be like a man who, believing on account of his inherent weakness that he was outclassed, yielded up the crown to the victor who, he perceived, was not affected by any temptations of the senses, which, like the dust of an arena, he himself was unable to endure? 'Of what use to me,' he said, 'is my birthright?' Among the craven there are no evidences of virtue. These

1 Cf. Isidore, *Etymol.* 7.6.33.
2 Gen. 25.32.
3 Cf. Isidore, *Etymol.* 7.7.5.

indications are first observable among men of wisdom, for mental activity serves as a means toward the attainment of virtue. As a warrior cannot exist without arms, so virtue is not attained without the practice of it. Hence the Lord says in the Gospel: 'From the days of John the Baptist the kingdom of heaven has been enduring assault and the violent have been seizing it.' And elsewhere: 'Seek the kingdom of God and behold all things are yours.'[4] Rewards are promised not to those who sleep or who idle away their time, but to those who strive. Toil has its recompense. Although it may not be pleasant or sweet, labor provides a wealth of compensation.

(13) This is the lesson given in the Law, as we find it recorded: 'If a man have two wives, one beloved and the other hated, and both the beloved and the hated have had children by him, and the son of the hated be the first born, and he meaneth to divide his substance among his sons. He may not make the son of the beloved the first born and prefer him before the son of the hated. But he shall acknowledge the son of the hated for the first born and shall give him a legacy of all he hath, for this is the first of his children and to him are due the first birthrights.'[5] What profound secrets lie in what we read, veiled in the language of mystery! Pay heed, soul, to your two-fold birth and examine the mystery found in the story of the hated wife. You will find the answer within you, if you stop and reflect. Look into your thoughts and into your emotions and you will recognize that to which you owe your birthright. Two women, in fact, cohabit in each one of us: women who live in discord and disagreement and who fill the house of our soul with their bickerings and contentiousness. One of these is called

4 Matt. 11.12; 6.33.
5 Deut. 21.15-17.

Pleasure. She is so pleasant, ingratiating, and agreeable that we have in mind to make her our associate and consort. The other one is harsh, bitter, and cruel. Her name is Virtue.

(14) Pleasure, then, is an impudent prostitute with mincing, alluring gait. She beckons with her eyes, winking playfully so as to trap in her snares the precious souls of young men. The eyes of a sinful libertine are used as a lure. Whomsoever she sees—'a foolish young man who passeth by the corner and goeth nigh the way of her house'[6]—she approaches with wheedling words. She endeavors to steal the hearts of young men—a woman restless at home, a wanderer in the public squares, prodigal of kisses, indifferent to shame, gaudy in her dress and countenance.[7] Since she is unable, indeed, to assume a beauty that is true to nature, she affects what is the opposite to truth—an external show of meretricious arts. Accompanied by a crowd of vicious characters and surrounded by a band of wicked men, she acts as a leader in their sinful acts. She attacks the citadels of men's hearts while uttering such words as these as a war-cry: 'I have vowed victims for peace, this day I have paid my vows. Therefore I am come out to meet thee, desirous to see thee, and I have found thee. I have woven my bed with cords. I have covered it with tapestry from Egypt. I have perfumed my bed with saffron and my home with cinnamon. Come and let us wrestle with desire.'[8] Here in the words of Solomon we behold the very picture of a wanton. What other than worldly pleasure is more characteristic of a prostitute who make her entrance stealthily into the house, first making tentative explorations with her eyes and then entering quickly, while you concentrate the gaze of your soul outward on

6 Prov. 7.8.
7 Prov. 7.12,13.
8 Prov. 7.14-18.

the public square, that is, on the streets frequented by passersby and not inward on the mysteries of the Law? She has contrived to trap us in a room devoted to the associations of common life by such solid chains that a person, although held in bondage, finds himself at ease there. As she reclines there she covers her body with coverlets of fraud and deceit so as to allure the souls of young men, alleging the absence of a husband, that is to say, her disregard for the Law. The Law does not exist for sinners, for, if it were present, it would not have been ignored. Hence we read: 'For my husband is not at home, he is gone a very long journey. He took with him a bag of money.'[9] What is the meaning of this, if not that the rich believe that there is nothing that money cannot control and that the Law is something that can be sold for profit? Pleasure scatters its fragrance because it has not the fragrance of Christ.[10] Pleasure looks for treasures, it promises kingdoms, it assures lasting loves, it pledges undreamed of intimacies, instruction without a guardian and conversation without hindrance. Pleasure promises a life bereft of anxiety, a sleep devoid of disturbance and wants that cannot be satiated. We read: Entangling him with many words and alluring him with the snares of her lips, she led him even to her home. He was beguiled and followed her.[11] The hall had all the splendor of a royal palace with walls in relief work. The floor reeked of spilled wine and emitted the odor of unguents. It was covered with the remains of fish. The flowers, now faded, made walking hazardous. Everything there was confused and contrary to the order of nature: the uproar of the banqueters, the noise of contenders, the clash of wranglers, the chorus of singers, the hubbub of

9 Prov. 7.19,20.
10 2 Cor. 2.15.
11 Cf. Prov. 7.21,22.

dancers, the laughter of the merry, and the applause of the revelers. There you find dancing girls with shorn locks and boys with curly hair, mingled with disgusting evidences of repletion and overindulgence, yesterday's intoxication and today's inebriation. Repeated bouts of intemperance, saturated with the odor of stale wine, made a stronger impression on the senses than fresh liquor would. Pleasure, standing in the midst of this disorder, said: 'Drink ye and be drunken and fall and rise no more.' With me the most wicked holds the first place in my estimation. The man who is not himself is mine and, the more evil he is, the more is he acceptable to me. 'Babylon hath been a golden cup in my hand that made all the earth drunk. All the nations have drunk of my wine.'[12] Who, therefore, is devoid of wisdom, let him turn toward me. My advice to those who are foolish is this: 'Enjoy the bread that is hidden and drink of the stolen waters that are sweeter.' 'Let us eat and drink, for tomorrow we shall die.' 'Our life shall pass away as the trace of a cloud and shall be dispersed as a mist.' 'Come, therefore, and let us enjoy the good things that are present and let us speedily use the creatures as in youth. Let us fill ourselves with costly wine and with ointments and let not the flower of our time pass by us. Let us crown ourselves with roses before they be withered. Let no meadow escape our riot. Let us everywhere leave tokens of joy.'[13] All things are left behind here and we bring with us nothing but what bodily pleasures we have experienced. I have set myself up, therefore, as a teacher of this philosophy. Nothing is true unless it brings some good, something sweet, and something pleasant. Put your trust in this philosophy, which is the very wisdom of Solomon.

---

12 Jer 25.27; 51.7.
13 Prov. 9.17; Isa. 22.13; Wisd. 2.3,6-9.

Chapter 5

(15) On hearing these words, the young man is wounded like a stag when 'the arrow pierces his liver.'[1] Virtue, having pity on him and seeing him on the point of falling, rushes to his aid. She is fearful that he, being human, may be intrigued, if there should be any delay, by such sweet allurements. 'Although you have not sought my aid,' she says, 'I have come openly before you lest this intemperate woman, who knows no shame, may outwit you in your ignorance. She sits at the door of her house upon a seat in the public squares calling them that pass by.' 'Now therefore, my son, hear me and attend to the words of my mouth. Let not thy mind be drawn away in her ways. For she has cast down many wounded and countless are those she has slain. Her house is the way to hell, reaching even to the inner chamber of death.' 'Remove from thee a forward mouth and let distracting lips be far from thee. Let thy eyes look straight on.' 'Mind not the deceit of a woman, for the lips of a harlot are like a honeycomb dropping.'[2] This for a time you may find intriguing, but soon you will discover that this is more bitter than poison. Time will not permit me to relate in detail her vices. I refer you to the Book of Proverbs where these are described. Do not let her outward appearance dazzle you. It is fraudulent and full of deceit, entirely lacking in genuineness and in truth. Do not be tricked by the artifices of her eyes. Rather, be a follower of him 'who cometh leaping upon the mountains, skipping over the hills, looking through the windows,'[3] beyond the reach of snares. The bonds of Pleasure, which give delight to the eye, charm to the ear, but pollution to the mind, are evil. What Pleasure

1 Prov. 7.23.
2 Cf. Prov. 9.14,15; 7.24-27; 4,24.25; 5.2,3.
3 Cant. 2.8,9.

offers is often spurious. Truth is obscured and instruction ignored by promises of gold to come. However, 'choose knowledge rather than gold and wisdom above precious gold. It is better than all the most precious things.'[4] I will not conceal from you the sum total of the effects of Pleasure. I should not want to conceal her ugliness or dissemble her enticements, for she lifts up and excites the mind by the eloquence of her speech. In effect, she shows all the kingdoms of the world and says: 'All these things I will give to thee, if thou wilt fall down and worship me.'[5] At that point be on your guard lest you be deceived by the impermanent and the passing which tempt us mightily.

(16) The Lord Jesus has pointed out to you[6] how you may resist temptations of this sort. The Devil first tried to snare Him with an appeal to the satisfaction of hunger: 'If thou art the Son of God, command that this stone become a loaf of bread. But he answered and said, "Not by bread alone does man live, but by every word of God".'[6] Thus was the snare broken. Again the Devil laid another snare, this time, one of vainglory, a vice that often leads men to destruction in their hour of prosperity. 'And he led him to Jerusalem and set him on the pinnacle of a temple and said to him. "If thou art the Son of God, throw thyself down from here, for it is written, he has given his angels charge concerning thee, to preserve thee, because upon their hands they shall bear thee up, lest thou dash thy foot against a stone." ' And so, although the Lord Jesus might have cast himself down without danger because of His command over the elements, yet, lest He be subject to pride, He gave this reply to the Devil: 'Thou shalt not tempt the Lord thy God.' In this way He taught us how to ward off the temp-

4 Prov. 8.10,12.
5 Matt. 4.9,10; cf. Luke 4.7.
6 Luke 4.4-12.

tations of the Devil. If a real opportunity for vainglory should thus be passed by, how much greater occasion do we have to exercise humility when we are presented with a situation that is entirely different! We should not neglect to mention the third time when the Devil attempted to snare the Lord by appealing, on this occasion, to avarice and ambition. 'He took him to a mountain and showed him all the kingdoms of the world in a moment of time.' Since these things cannot endure, the expression 'in a moment of time' is quite appropriate. Wait a little while and these things pass away. Wherefore, those who follow such pursuits seem to themselves to be on a mountain top. But their position is temporary, for it is written: 'I have seen the wicked highly exalted and lifted up over the cedars of Libanus and I passed by, and lo, he was not.'[7] Those who consider temporary things to be of prime importance seem, in fact, to worship the Devil: 'Their god is the belly, their glory is their shame.'[8] Set your glory in God's hands who says to you: 'The Lord thy God shalt thou worship and him only shalt thou serve,'[9] from whom you will attain not what is temporal but what is everlasting.

(17) Those, indeed, who find delight in things that endure should make their petitions in due course to Him who is the true source of all things. Those things which the Devil seems to claim as his property are not really his, as he maintains: 'To thee will I give all this power and their glory, for to me they have been delivered.'[10] Put your hope in Him, therefore, who is the Creator of each and every creature, although the brevity of this life does not call for provision for a long journey. God has ordained that the Devil be given

7 Ps. 36.35,36.
8 Phil. 3.19.
9 Luke 4.8; Matt. 4.10.
10 Luke 4.6.

power to tempt man for a while, but not to possess him. The crown of victory cannot be attained without a contest.[11] The unstable must be put to the test, so that they may become just and thus merit the reward.

(18) God, therefore, assigned this office to the Devil because thereby the person involved is subject to punishment if he misuses his opportunity. Where does the man given to pleasure find his treasure if not in luxurious living? But the thrifty man, not the spendthrift, is held in esteem. Hence, follow the example of the frugal man when you sit at table. Do not by overindulgence become an object of hate: 'Watching and choler are with the intemperate man,' and again: 'If thou hast been forced to eat much, arise, go out and vomit; and it shall refresh thee and thou shalt not bring sickness upon thy body.'[12] Many are the victims of gluttony, whereas temperance claims none. Frugality in the use of wine is beneficial, but countless individuals harm themselves by overindulgence. Many are the victims of excess at the banqueting table—an excess which deprives them of the use of speech. These who are harmed by gluttony are the victims of intoxication, which, while in itself a sin, drives some men to commit sin and reduces others to poverty. Take note of the type of person whom Christ would finally exclude from heaven: 'When the master of the house has entered and shut the door, you will begin to stand outside and knock at the door, saying, "Open for us!" And he shall say to you in answer, "I do not know where you are from." Then you shall begin to say, "We ate and drank in thy presence and thou didst teach in our streets." And he shall say to you, "I do not know where you are from." ' You have heard what He said about those who in eating were epicures. Now pay heed to what He says about those who fast: 'Blessed are

---

11 Cf. 2 Tim. 2.5.
12 Eccli. 31.23-25.

they who hunger and are thirsty now, for they shall be satisfied.' And again: 'Woe to those who are filled! For you shall hunger.'[13]

(19) But do you wish to eat and drink? Enter into the banquet hall of Wisdom, who invites all men, proclaiming with a loud voice: 'Come, eat my bread and drink my wine which I have mingled for you.'[14] Do you find delight in songs which charm the banqueter? Listen to the voice of the Church, who exhorts us not only in canticles, but in the Canticle of Canticles: 'Eat, O friends, and drink and be inebriated, my brethren.'[15] But this inebriation makes men sober.[16] This inebriation is one of grace, not of intoxication. It leads to joy, not to befuddlement. It the banquet hall of the Church there will be pleasant odors, delightful food, and drink in variety. There will be noble guests and attendants who grace the occasion. It will not be othérwise! What is there that is nobler than to have Christ at the Church's banquet, as one who ministers and is ministered unto? Attach yourself closely to Him who reclines as a guest at that banquet. Unite yourself to God. Do not disdain the banquet table which Christ chose, saying: 'I am come into my garden, O my sister, my spouse. I have gathered myrrh with my aromatic spices. I have eaten my bread with my honey and I have drunk wine with my milk.'[17] The garden is the Garden of Paradise, that is to say, the place of the Church's banquet, where Adam was before he committed sin and where Eve sat before she become responsible for a deed of wrong. There you will gather myrrh, that is to say, perform the burial of Christ, so that as 'you are buried with him by

13 Luke 13.25-27; 6.21,25.
14 Prov. 9.5.
15 Cant. 5.1.
16 Cf. St. Ambrose, Hymns 2.23,24 (*bibamus sobriam ebrietatem*).
17 Cant. 5.1.

means of baptism into death,'[18] and as He has risen from the dead, you, too, may rise. There you will eat bread which 'strengthens man's heart.'[19] You will taste of honey which is a delight to the tongue. You will drink wine along with milk, that is to say, with splendor and purity. This refers to the purity of simplicity or to grace which is untainted and is applied to the remission of sins. Its effects are comforting as milk is to infants at breast, who thereby grow with delight into the plenitude of perfect age. Approach, therefore, this banquet. Are you afraid that the house is too narrow and that the banquet hall may restrict you because of its smallness? 'O Israel, how great is the house of God and how vast is the place of his possession! It is great and hath no end: it is high and immense. There were the giants, those renowned men that were from the beginning, of great stature, expert in war. The Lord chose not them.'[20] They did not deserve to be chosen, for they had knowledge of war, not of peace. Learn, therefore, the ways of peace, that you may be chosen by God. But that you may perhaps be aware that the hugeness of His house is not without adornment and that you may find delight in serried rows of columns, 'Wisdom hath built herself a house, she hath hewn her out seven pillars.'[21] Our Lord Jesus, too, states that 'in my Father's house there are many mansions.'[22] In this house, then, you will enjoy food for the soul and drink for the mind, so that you may never after hunger or thirst, for he who eats here eats to satiety and he who drinks here drinks to the point of inebriation.

(20) But this inebriation serves as a guard over modesty, whereas the inebriation due to wine is a stimulus to lust,

---

18 Rom. 6.4.
19 Ps. 103.15.
20 Bar. 3.24-27.
21 Prov. 9.1.
22 Job 14.2.

by which the fleshly organs within us are heated, our minds are inflamed, and our souls enkindled. Lust serves as an uncontrolled stimulus to wickedness. It never allows our emotions to find rest. Night and day, asleep or awake, we are disturbed by its inroads. Our minds cannot function and unreason displaces reason. Lovers are made uneasy and sinners incline to more sin. Even the chaste feel its effects. The victim is overcome and kept subdued by the application of fire. Sinfulness and wickedness become uncontrollable and the devotee of sin can have his fervor extinguished only by death. Hence the Apostle says: 'Flee fornication.'[23] By a swift flight we can shun the savagery of such a rabid mistress and escape from such vile servitude.

(21) What shall I say concerning avarice, that insatiable longing, that very lust for gold which is ever desirous of more—no matter what accumulated treasure is stored away. An object of envy to all, but to himself despicable, the avaricious man is poor in the midst of riches, slighting the fact that his bank balance is large. His desire for gain is as limitless as are his opportunities for making a profit. He is so consumed with passion that the only difference between him and an adulterer is that one has an inordinate love for physical form, the other, a desire for a farm, a rich estate. The avaricious man does violence to the elements by ploughing the earth and cleaving the sea. He importunes the very heavens with his vows. He ever gives expression to displeasure whether the skies are serene or cloudy, and is censorious no matter what his annual returns are from land or sea. Here is clear evidence of his sickness of soul. Wherefore Ecclesiastes says: 'There is a grievous illness which I have seen under the sun: riches kept to the hurt of the owner.' And again he says: 'A covetous man shall not be satisfied with

23 1 Cor. 6.18.

money.' 'There is no end to their getting.'[24] If you are desirous of treasure, take the invisible and the intangible which is to be found in the heavens on high, not that which is in the deepest veins of the earth. Be poor in spirit and you will be rich, no matter what your worldy goods are.[25] 'A man's life does not consist in the abundance of his possessions,' but in his virtue and in his faith. This richness will enrich you if you are rich in your relations to God.[26]

Chapter 6

(22) You have heard the secret rites of Pleasure. You have heard, too, what we offer from our store. I considered it proper that these last be not concealed by outward trappings. I wished that they be arrayed in the unadorned words of Scripture in order that they may gleam in their own light and that in due order they may speak out plainly for themselves. The sun and the moon need no interpreter. The brilliance of their light is all-sufficient—a light that fills the entire world. Faith serves as an illumination for the inspired Word. It is, if I may say so, an intestate witness having no need of another's testimony, yet it dazzles the eyes of all mankind. Our works are not announced, therefore, to the world. They speak aloud for themselves. Lest I seem to omit what is required in the way of effort, certain essentials are in this regard quite necessary. We need to have faith and zeal, together with deeds. The three elements requisite for the expression of man's religious duties are defined by our Lord Jesus: 'Ask and it shall be given you. Seek and you

24 Eccle. 5.12,9; 3.12.
25 Matt. 5.3.
26 Luke 12.15; cf. 12.21. Here ends the discourse given by Virtue which began in (15).

shall find. Knock and it shall be opened to you.' And again: 'Everyone therefore who hears these my words and acts upon them is like a wise man.'[1]

(23) The person who zealously pursues these objectives will receive an unusual blessing. He will be like the patriarch Jacob, who eliminates all vestiges of human passion by his faith and continence. He states: 'God has been good to me and I have all I need.'[2] We should merit, therefore, this goodness by the exercise of our faith, our zeal, and our accomplishments. By this means the people of Israel found the grace of God which itself provided them with everything. They rejoiced in the attainment, not of the things of this world, but in their training in virtuous deeds. Let us make as our heirs those virtues which holy Abraham adopted for himself in respect to his son Isaac. He handed over his entire inheritance to one who was wise and just. He did not grant the right of inheritance to his maid-servants or to their children. He presented them merely with a gift.[3] Those who are perfect in virtue receive the entire patrimony of glory, whereas a mere trifle is bestowed on the mediocre and commonplace. Accordingly, Agar, whose name in Latin means 'dwelling near' and Chettura, signifying 'fragrant,' are not heirs of Abraham. Those whose training is mediocre are neighbors of the home of Wisdom, not dwellers therein. That which has a modicum of fragrance has not reached its fulfillment in fruit. Food, not mere fragrance, is conducive to health. Fragrance is just the herald of fruit to come. We conclude, therefore, that those who are leaders in virtue are to be preferred to those who are slackers and that native dwellers have preference over those who are merely neighbors in the land of Virtue.

---

1 Matt. 7.7,24.
2 Gen. 33.11.
3 Cf. Gen. 21.10-13.

(24) This is a rational interpretation. But there is another, a mystical one, according to which Abraham, the father of the race, confers the entire legacy of his faith to his lawful seed which is Christ,[4] who, like a stranger on earth, strove to restore the fragrance of this life rather than the fruit. When the mind gives heed to this meaning, it turns away from Pleasure and links itself to Virtue in admiration of what is truly beautiful, what is pure in feeling, what is simple in thought, and what is seemly in external appearance. This means that Virtue is not arrayed 'in the persuasive words of wisdom but in the demonstration of the Spirit.'[5] Such is the nature of the apostolic message, in appearance clothed in all manner of wisdom and piety, shining forth more brilliantly, and more precious, too, than gold of any sort. Moreover, this message inculcates the grace that proceeds from that choral band of virtues: namely, Prudence, Temperance, Fortitude, and Justice. Stirred in such wise, the soul strives after those virtues to which Jacob, a man of wide experience, had applied himself. Wherefore he is depicted as a shepherd herding sheep.[6] This signifies that he was considered to have surpassingly good qualities to be able to lord it over his body and his senses, and to be able to control his tongue, lest it wander like a lost sheep—qualities which are of greater import than the power of dominion over cities and peoples. It is more difficult for a person to rule over himself than over others. To exercise control over one's mind, to restrain one's wrath, and to integrate the conflicting ordinances of soul and body are characteristics of a man who is immortal by nature, a man whom the infernal portals shall not enclose. Hence the lawgiver himself claimed this as his right: to pasture the flocks of Jethro (whose name means 'superflu-

4 Cf. Gal. 3.16.
5 1 Cor. 2.4.
6 Cf. Gen. 30.31.

ous') and to drive them into the desert.[7] This means that he compelled the irrational loquacity of one whose language was common and superfluous to enter into the mysteries of sound doctrine, for 'shepherds were repugnant to the Egyptians.'[8] All who surrender themselves to the passions of this body of ours and indulge in its pleasures are sworn enemies of those who stand for virtue. And so in a parable Moses has informed us that those virtuous principles and deeds which foolish men avoid are offerings suitable for God. Hence Abel was a shepherd and Cain a tiller of the soil,[9] who in foolish fashion could not brook the bright lineaments of virtue that adorned his own brother.

Chapter 7

(25) 'In the course of time Cain brought to the Lord an offering of the fruit of the ground'[1]—a twofold error: first, that his offering came after a period of time, and second, that it was composed of fruits of the ground. Again, the offering was not of the first fruits. This would have been commendable from the point of view of speed and of desirability. Wherefore we have the precept: 'When thou hast made a vow, thou shalt not delay to pay it,' and 'It is much better not to make a vow than after a vow not to perform the things promised,'[2] for, although you make a vow, you do not carry it out. A vow is a request for a benefit from God with a promise to give something in return. Hence, when you have obtained what you sought, it would be an

7 Cf. Exod. 3.1.
8 Cf. Gen. 46.34.
9 Cf. Gen. 4.4.

1 Gen. 4.3.
2 Deut. 23.21; Eccle. 5.4.

ungrateful act to delay what you have promised. But, at times, men are apt to be heedless and forgetful of the blessings they have obtained or to become proud and haughty and claim the resulting favors as their own. They tend to refer the results to their own peculiar virtues and to consider that they, and not the Author of the favors, are responsible for their success. There is a third category of error which is of lesser import, but comparable because of its arrogance. We have reference to those who actually do not deny that God is the giver of good things, yet are of the opinion that they have obtained them as a result of their adherence to prudence and to the other virtues. Wherefore they believe that they are deserving of divine grace, inasmuch as it appear that they are by no means unworthy of such merits from God's beneficence.

(26) To avoid the eventuality of causing your whole approach to prayer to be imperfect, there is a law laid down by God, the Lawgiver, for your instruction and guidance: 'Take heed and beware lest you forget the Lord thy God and neglect his commandments and judgments and justice which I command thee this day, lest after thou hast eaten and art filled, hast built houses and dwelt in them, and when your sheep and oxen are filled, and you have plenty of bronze, of gold and of silver and of all things, and when thy granaries are full, thy heart be lifted up and thou remember not the Lord thy God.'[3] When you are forgetful of yourself, then, also, will you forget the Lord. If you realize how weak you are, then you will discover that God is supreme over all things and you will not be unmindful of the fact that you owe a debt of reverence to Him.

(27) Now learn how each and every one of us may be warned against thinking of himself as the originator of his

3 Deut. 8.11-14.

own good: 'Lest thou shouldst say,' we are told, 'in thy heart: my own might and the strength of my own hand achieved this virtue for me. But remember the Lord thy God that hath given thee strength that thou mightest attain virtue.'[4] Wherefore that Apostle is to be commended who, in not boasting of his own virtue, followed the Law and said that he was the last of the Apostles and that we owe what we have, not to our own merits, but to divine grace.[5] He said: 'What hast thou that thou hast not received? If thou hast received it, why dost thou boast as if thou hadst not received it?'[6] Here is the lesson of humility rather than of arrogance. You should strive, therefore, to be industrious rather than be powerful. Here is advice that is salutary. Do not, then, make light of the experience of a surgeon who makes a deep incision so as to rid a wound of all infection.

(28) The man who justifies himself, lest he be puffed up with the swelling of his heart, has hearkened also to the salutary mandate of the oracle: 'Say not in thy heart, when the Lord thy God shall bring to destruction those nations in thy sight: Because of my justice hath the Lord brought me in to possess this land, whereas the Lord will destroy these nations before thy face for their wickedness. It is not for thy justices nor the uprightness of thy heart that thou hast gone in to possess that land, but because of the wickedness of the nations, the Lord will destroy them from thy sight and will accomplish his testament which he promised by oath to thy fathers.'[7] The testament referred to is the perfect grace of God. God gives nothing that is imperfect. Perfect is virtue and perfect, too, the works of virtue. This testament is one which brings with it a legacy of what is good. Rightly,

4 Deut. 8.17,18.
5 Cf. 1 Cor. 15.9,10.
6 1 Cor. 15.4,7.
7 Deut. 9.4,5.

too, is this testament called divine, because what is really and truly good is bestowed on us and granted to us by celestial mandate. And the testament referred to is one that is old in type but new in truth, because it is sealed in blood. By this testament we hold the pledge of divine grace: 'For God so loved this world that he delivered his only Son for us all.'[8] Wherefore the words of the Apostle points to the perfection of grace: 'How can he fail to grant us also all things with him?'[9]

Chapter 8

(29) Swiftness of fulfillment is the primary characteristic of a vow. Hence Abraham, when he was commanded to offer his own son as a sacrifice, did not, like Cain, fulfill the command after a period of time, but, 'arising early in the morning he harnessed his ass, took with him two of his servants and his son Isaac and cut wood for a holocaust. Then he set out on his journey and on the third day came to a place which God had indicated to him.'[1] Take note first of the speed, haste, and eagerness of the expectant sacrificer. He was delayed only by the time it took to listen to the oracle, to harness his ass, so as to comply with God's commands and make the necessary preparations for the sacrifice. He was able, also, to lead away his victim to the accompaniment of the two virtues of faith, namely, certainty in the power of God and confidence in His goodness.

(30) Something can be said in reference to the time element, that is, 'the third day.' Abraham's purpose needed the quality of continuity and perpetuity, for time is tripartite, taking in, as it does, the past, the present, and the future.

8 John 3.16.
9 Rom. 8.32.

1 Gen. 22.3,4.

By this we are admonished that there should not be any trace of forgetfulness of the beneficence of God whether in the past, present, or future. We should, rather, be steadfast in the recollection of His grace and in our compliance with His command. Another reason for this reference to time lies in the fact that the person who performs a sacrifice ought to put his trust in the brilliant light of the Trinity. For him whose sacrifice is grounded in faith has ever around him the light of day. For him there is no night. So in Exodus Moses says: 'We will go three days' journey to sacrifice unto the Lord our God.'[2] Elsewhere, too, when God appeared to Abraham by the oak of Mamre, we are told that 'Abraham raised his eyes and saw three men standing at a distance from him. As soon as he saw them he ran to the entrance of the tent door to meet them and bowed down to the earth and said: My Lord, if I have found favor with you.'[3] He beholds three and one he adores. He offers three measures of fine flour.[4] Although God is immeasurable, He nevertheless holds the measure of all things, as it is written: 'Who hath measured the waters in his hand and weighed the heavens with his palm and the bulk of the earth in the hollow of his hand?'[5] The holy patriarch, therefore, offered sacrifice in the secret recesses of his heart to the Trinity made perfect in each of the Persons. This is the spiritual meaning of the measures of fine flour. This is the measure of fine flour mentioned in the Gospel which was ground by the woman who 'will be taken.' 'One will be taken; the other will be left.'[6] The Church 'will be taken'; the Synagogue 'will be left,' or the man of good conscience will be taken and the man of bad conscience, left. That you may know that Abraham believed

2 Exod. 3.18.
3 Gen. 18.2,3.
4 Cf. Gen. 18.6.
5 Isa. 40.12.
6 Matt. 24.41.

in Christ, we read: 'Abraham saw my day and was glad.'[7] He who believes in Christ believes, too, in the Father, and who believes in the Father believes, too, in the Son and Holy Spirit. There were three measures, therefore, and one substance of fine flour. This means that there was one sacrifice which was offered to the Blessed Trinity with an equal measure of devotion and a corresponding plenitude of piety.

(31) There is still another example of speedy and zealous devotion. We read: 'He ran and picked out a good tender bullock and gave it to the servant who hastened to prepare it.'[8] Everywhere we find devotion that is ready and eager and, hence, an acceptable gift to God. In another passage we are recommended to anticipate the sunrise with a prayer: 'Run to meet the rising of the sun.'[9] There is the incident[10] in the Gospel of the Lord Jesus, saying: 'Zacchaeus, make haste and come down.' And he who attained his wish to see Christ and who further succeeded in being seen and addressed by Christ made haste to descend and welcomed Him with joy. And so the Lord approved of this display of his emotions and was quick to reward him in return, saying: 'Today salvation has come to this house.' The Lord hastened to perform His act of kindness. He did not wait and promise to fulfill it later, but first acted and then spoke of it, for He said: 'Salvation has come,' which was, of course, the act of one who anticipates, not of one who promises. The just man gives an added force to his vow by acting quickly. Accordingly, our fathers ate the paschal lamb in haste, girding up their reins, and with shoes in their feet, and standing ready equipped for departure.[11] The Pasch is the passage of the Lord from passion to the exercise of virtue. It is called the

7 John 8.56.
8 Gen. 18.7.
9 Wisd. 16.28.
10 Luke 19.5,9.
11 Cf. Exod. 12.11.

Pasch of the Lord because the truth of the Passion of the Lord was then indicated in the type of the lamb, and its benefits are now being observed.

(32) Go quickly, then, my soul, in search of this, in order that you may quickly hearken unto it as did Jacob: 'How did you find it so quickly, my son?'[12] To which Jacob, following instructions, replied: 'The Lord your God let me come upon it.' God gives quickly: 'For he spoke and they were made; he commanded and they were created.'[13] The Word of God is not, as a certain writer maintains,[14] something achieved, but rather being achieved, as it is written: 'My father works even until now and I work.'[15] The Word of God came before all things. It exists before all things like the Father and is in every respect like the Father, penetrating all things. It is strong, and keen, keener than any sword, extending even to the division of the soul and spirit, of joints, also, and of marrow, a discerner of the thoughts of all.[16] Apropos of this, God the Father says: 'Thou shalt presently see whether my word shall come to pass or not.'[17] Wherever God is, there is the Word, as He said: 'We will come to him and make our abode with him.'[18] You may read elsewhere concerning God: 'I stood here before thee.'[19] And so the Word said: 'Before thou wast under the fig tree I saw thee.' It was said of the Word, that is, of the Son of God, that 'in the midst of you there stands one whom you do not know.'[20] Wherever there are holy men, there stands the Word of God in their midst, penetrating their inmost hearts and filling

---

12 Gen. 27.20.
13 Ps. 32.9.
14 Cf. Philo, *De sacrificiis Abelis et Caini* 18.
11 John 5.17.
16 Cf. Heb. 4.12.
17 Num. 11.23.
18 John 14.23.
19 Exod. 17.6.
20 John 1.48,26.

the sea and the land. When the Word is here, it is elsewhere, also, without a change of place. Every place is surcharged with the presence of the Word. That which penetrates everything and is in everything leaving no place vacant—that exists everywhere. Where now the Word is present had before been possessed by the Word, and contrariwise. Hence, when a man is aware of the celerity of the Word of God, he is quick to make a petition and as quickly attains his wish.

Chapter 9

(33) Take the example of Pharao, a man given to vain empty thoughts. His land of Egypt was afflicted with a plague of frogs. They gave forth a surfeit of sound, meaningless and senseless. Moses said to Pharao: 'Set me a time when I shall pray for thee and for thy servants and for thy people that the Lord may exterminate the frogs.' Pharao, who because of his plight should have besought him to offer prayer, replied: 'Tomorrow,'[1] thus showing himself indifferent to the punishment that the delay would bring, although he was still intent on saving Egypt from the plague. And so, when his prayer was finally granted, he was unmindful of gratitude. Being puffed up in his heart, he forgot God.

(34) Prayer is made effective by humility. We have the parable of the Pharisee, who in his prayer enumerated his fasts as acts of commendation and who seemed to reproach God as he boasted of his virtuous life. The publican, on the other hand, 'standing far off, would not so much as lift his eyes to heaven but kept striking his breast, saying: O God, be merciful to me the sinner!' Hence, in the words of holy Scripture, he was preferred before the other: 'This man went

1 Exod. 8.9,10.

back justified rather than the Pharisee.'[2] He is justified who confesses his own sin, as the Lord Himself has said: 'Tell if thou hast anything to justify thyself.'[3] And David said: 'A sacrifice to God is an afflicted spirit.' Again: 'A contrite and humble heart God does not despise.'[4] Jeremias also says: 'The soul in anguish and the troubled spirit cries to thee.'[5] The Assyrian, like Pharao, said: 'Who are they among the gods of the nations that have delivered the country out of my hand, that your God will deliver Jerusalem out of my hand?'[6] They were cast down from their exaltation. The just man, like Jacob, acknowledges that all good things of whatever sort which he has obtained come from God the Creator, saying that all he saw was for his benefit: 'The Lord thy God has given these into my hands.'[7] This is an example of how one should accept the fulfillment of a prayer. David says: 'Offer to God the sacrifice of praise and pay thy vows to the most high.'[8] To praise God is to offer Him a prayer and to give thanks for its fulfillment. Wherefore preference above all the other lepers is to be given to the Samaritan, who alone of the ten cured of leprosy returned, according to the Lord's injunction, to give thanks and glorify Christ. Of him did Jesus say: 'Has no one been found to return and give thanks to God except this foreigner?' And He said to him: 'Arise and go thy way, for thy faith has saved thee.'[9]

(35) Furthermore, a vow or a prayer is commendable to the extent that its substance is not divulged. We should keep intact the hidden mysteries just as Abraham did when he

2 Luke 18.10-14.
3 Isa. 43.26.
4 Ps. 50.19.
5 Bar. 3.1.
6 4 Kings 18.35.
7 Gen. 27.20.
8 Ps. 49.14.
9 Luke 17.14-19.

caused loaves to be baked under the ashes.[10] This our fathers did, too, when they made into loaves, like those which in Greek are called 'covered,' the dough that was brought out of Egypt.[11] They covered this dough with ashes, an act like that which the woman in the Gospel performed when she buried leaven in three measures of wheat until the whole was leavened.[12] Therein is a profound lesson. Our Lord's teaching on prayer is revealed to us more clearly in the Gospel: 'But when thou prayest, go into thy room and closing the door, pray to the Lord in secret and thy Father, who sees in secret, will reward thee. But in praying do not multiply words.' And He adds: 'For your Father knows what you need before you ask him.'[13] Your room is the secret place of your heart and soul. Enter into this room, that is, enter into the depths of your soul, remove yourself entirely from the exterior vestibule, and close your door.

(36) What is meant by the phrase 'your door'? 'Set a watch, O Lord, before my mouth and a door around my lips.'[14] Paul makes a prayer for himself when he says: 'That God may open the door of his Word for me to announce the mystery of Christ.'[15] Appropriate for the occasion was the substance of his prayer. In preaching the Gospel he was clearly chosen to be the one who opened the door of the Word, from which issued the salvation of the Gentiles and life itself for all people. We should, however, close this door lest sin enter in and that from our tongue should issue no unseemly word. Sin enters in when we open our mouths to utter what is unrighteous. How does sin find entrance? We

10 Cf. Gen. 18.6.
11 Cf. Exod. 12.34.
12 Cf. Luke 13.21.
13 Matt. 6.6-8.
14 Ps. 140.3.
15 Col. 4.3.

read: 'In the multitude of words you shall not escape sin.'[16] When a multiplicity of words has come forth, sin has found an entrance, for in this very multiplicity of words what we utter is not in the slightest degree subject to measure. Because of lack of prudence we fall into error. In fact, to give expression to our thoughts without duly weighing our words is in itself a grave sin.

(37) For that reason be not imprudent in your speech. The lips of the imprudent man furnish an occasion for evil. Do not be given to self-praise: 'The prayer of him that humbleth himself has pierced the clouds.'[17] Do not be incautious and reveal the mysterious import of the Lord's prayer. Do you not know how serious it is to commit sin in the act of saying a prayer at the very moment when you are looking for a favor? The Lord has assured us that we are subject to sins of speech when He says: 'And may his prayer be turned to sin,'[18] unless you regard this to be of slight concern to you. To believe that your prayer is not heard unless you cry out aloud is to distrust the power of God. Your deeds, your loyalty, your affections, your passions, all cry out. Your blood, too, cries out as in the case of Abel, a man gives to goodness, concerning whom God spoke these words to Cain: 'The voice of your brother's blood cries to me.'[19] He who cleanses you from your secret sins hears you in secret.[20] We cannot hear a person unless he speaks. Our thoughts, not our words, reach God. To realize this you have only to read what the Lord Jesus said to the Jews: 'Why do you harbor evil thoughts in your hearts?' These are the words, not of one who raises a question, but of one who

16 Prov. 16.19.
17 Cf. Eccle. 10.12; 35.21.
18 Ps. 108.7.
19 Gen. 4.10.
20 Cf. Ps. 18.13.

knows. The Evangelist makes this clearer when he says: 'Jesus knew their thoughts.'[21] What the Son knows, therefore, is known also by the Father. In this case you are aware that the Son knew. We have testimony elsewhere of the Son's participation in the Father's counsel: 'For your Father knows what you need before you ask him.'[22] Let the Holy Spirit furnish heat to cook the loaves under the ashes. Do in like manner to the passions of your soul, using the heat of the Word. Although your passions, because you have come lately, perhaps, from the land of Egypt, are somewhat intemperate, cover them up and cook them, as it were, under slow heat, lest they be unable to endure a greater heat and thus be half-burned rather than cooked. There are many examples which illustrate the point that what is ill-cooked is displeasing and that what is well-cooked is pleasing. Cherish in your hearts the profound mysteries, lest you entrust to weak and unrealiable ears sentiments which are rudely conceived or not well matured. In this way your hearers are likely to take warning and to recoil with horror. But, if they find that these sentiments have a certain maturity, they can derive an element of sweetness from this food of the spirit.

(38) The Lord Jesus has shown you the goodness of a father who knows how to bestow good gifts, in order that you may find it opportune to ask what is good of Him who is good.[23] He has urged us to pray frequently, not in a series of outbursts, but by praying persistently and frequently.[24] It often happens that a long petition is packed with empty phrases and that one which is intermittent is fraught with infelicities. Hence He warns us that, when we plead for

21 Matt. 9.4; Luke 6.8.
22 Matt. 6.8.
23 Cf. Luke 11.13.
24 Cf. Matt. 26.41.48.

leniency for ourselves, we should be conscious that this is the moment especially when we should be generous to others, thus commending our prayer by actual deeds.[25] The Apostle also teaches us that men should pray without wrath or contention,[26] so that our petition may not be characterized by emotional disturbance. He teaches us that we should pray everywhere, although the Saviour says: 'Go into thy room.'[27] But we must understand that the reference here is not to a room surrounded by walls for the shelter of our person. We are, rather, to understand a room within us in which to house our thoughts and our perceptions. This habitation for our prayers is everywhere with us—a secret place known only to God.

(39) You are instructed above all to pray for the people, that is, for all men,[28] for all members of your family, which is a conspicuous sign of mutual love. If you make a petition for yourself, then you pray merely for your own satisfaction. If everyone were thus to make a petition just for himself, he would become, not a petitioner, but an intercessor for favors. We conclude, therefore, that a petition for oneself is restricted to the person petitioning, whereas a petition for all men includes oneself, as you are a part of that number. Hence, great is the recompense wherein all men are accorded the benefits acquired by the prayers of each individual of the group. In this there is no question of presumption. Rather, it is much more the reflection of a humble heart, bestowing benefits more abundantly.

---

25 Cf. Matt. 18.33-35.
26 Cf. 1 Tim. 2.8.
27 Matt. 6.6.
28 Cf. 1 Tim. 2.1.

Chapter 10

(40) But it is now time to turn our attention to another point which we have made concerning Cain. We have noted that his delay in carrying out his vow was an indication of his negligence and presumption. The petition, in fact should be made early, lest we appear to rely on human arts, that is to say, on the skill of the art of medicine, thus hoping to obtain a remedy from the juices of plants rather than request God's assistance. We should, first of all, flee to Him who has the power to heal the passions of our souls. Men, on the contrary, invert the order of their request for aid by appealing first to men and afterward, when human assistance fails them, their next step is to make to God an appeal for favors.

(41) Having thus disposed of that charge against Cain, let as now discuss another fault in the performance of his sacrifice. He made 'an offering of the fruit of the ground,'[1] whereas he owed to God the first fruit of his crop. In this way he claimed the first fruit for himself and the remainder he left to God. Hence, inasmuch as the soul should be preferred to the body, just as the master should be placed over the servant, the soul's first fruits should take precedence over what the body offers. The first fruit of the soul are the primary emotions which are associated with all good thoughts and acts. Although these emotions come later in time than the first fruits of the body, which include nutrition, growth, sight, hearing, touch, smell, voice—both soul and body have a share in mind and sense—still, as senses, they exist prior to man's acts. To make an offering of thanksgiving to God with pure heart and tongue is in itself an expression of a primary act.

(42) These were the gifts made by Abel. God had regard

1 Gen. 4.3.

for his offerings[2] because they came from the first fruits and, moreover, from the firstlings of the sheep, those which were fat and sleek. Note the fact that the offering was composed of living beings, not inanimate things. What is living, since it is very closely related to what has a spirit, is more important than what is earthly. The significance lies in the fact that the living thing comes first and that next it is endowed with spirit. The living being breathes and has a vital spirit. This is not true of the fruits of the earth. Again, note that he offered not seconds, but firsts—not lean animals, but fat ones. These are the sort of animals recommended and commanded by the Law, as related in the Scriptures: 'And when God shall have brought thee into the land of the Chanaanite, as he swore to thy fathers and shall give it to thee. And thou shalt set apart all male animals that openeth the womb for the Lord, and all that is first brought forth of thy cattle and thy flocks. Whatsoever shall be born thee of the male sex, consecrate to the Lord. The firstborn of an ass thou shalt change for a sheep, and if thou doth not change it, thou shalt redeem it.'[3] Consider the profound mysteries and the wealth of wisdom imbedded in these words which in their simplicity convey to us an abundance of grace of the spirit! The Chanaanites are people who are restless and uneasy. When you enter into their land and notice how they are devoid of morals as a result of their levity, uneasiness, and instability, then you have an occasion to show your constancy. Do not be disturbed by any trifling argument or flightiness of speech. These are the characteristics of the Chanaanite, inconsistency in language, emotional instability and restless contention. Be calm and present to them a tranquillity and serenity of mind and soul. Be like one who escapes the storms of the sea by casting anchor in a safe harbor.

2 Cf. Gen. 4.4.
3 Exod. 13.11-13.

(43) The attainment of this goal is promised to you by the Lord. You are confirmed in your constancy by His assurance, which may be likened to an oath. But God does not solemnly swear because He has need of a believer's trust or because, deprived of the confirmation of witnesses, He requires the aid of an oath. He does not act as human beings do. We bind ourselves by a solemn oath to swear to tell the whole truth. God's very utterance inspires trust. His speech is a solemn oath. God is to be trusted, but not because of an oath. Rather, the oath is to be trusted because of God. Wherefore, then, does Moses speak of God as if He were in the act of taking an oath? Because we, as mortals, are bound by limitations. We wrap ourselves in the folds of public opinion as a sea-urchin does in his shell. We act like a snail who cannot breathe in the free air of heaven unless he is protected by his shell. We behave in a similar manner because we are cabined and confined in the earthy recesses of human custom. Wherefore, since we tend to believe that to be true which is confirmed by a solemn oath, lest we should falter in our trust, the same action is ascribed to God, who Himself does not take an oath, but is the avenging judge of those who commit acts of perjury. Hence it is written: 'The Lord has sworn and he will not repent: you are a priest for ever.'[4] He has assuredly kept His oath. He has given us a High Priest for ever, in order that you may know that there is a sanction for your oath and that an act of perjury will have its avenger in Him who does not deceive.

(44) Expelling, therefore, all uneasy and disturbing thoughts from your mind and heart, God will give you free and complete ownership, so that you may till the soil in full security. You will be able to reap a harvest therein and not permit the people of Chanaan to gain entrance, that is to say, you will

4 Ps. 109.4; Heb. 5.6; 7.17.

be able to avoid all offensive emotions. You will pluck out by root the vices of the Gentiles. You will overturn their groves by which truth is overshadowed and in which the clear vision of celestial knowledge is obscured by the dread darkness of disputation.

(45) But you cannot attain this condition without the assistance of God. Therefore He said: 'He shall give it to thee,'[5] that is to say, He will give you thoughts that are on the highest plane, counsels that lead to peacefulness, and ideas that bring tranquility. When He has granted these favors, you will set apart all that opens the womb and sacrifice it to the Lord. God, although He has given you everything, does not exact anything from you. He has bestowed much in abundance for the use and support of men. There is no question of God's participations in an act of nature such as eating, drinking, sleeping. These and other functions of the body were granted to you freely by God. They are not in the nature of favors. However, thoughts that are holy are the gifts of God and are inspired by His grace. On the other hand, ordinary natural and human acts 'do not defile a man, but it is what comes out of the mouth.'[6] Deceit, false testimony, and sacrilege are the acts which bring defilement to man.

(46) Let us make clean, therefore, the thoughts within us, so that our offering may not displease. Therein let us search for what opens the womb, that is to say, for what is just and excellent, because we owe to the Lord that which is holy. Yet we are not sanctified by carnal copulation, by conception, and by parturition, whereby the womb of a woman is opened and her virginity destroyed. Although a wife sanctifies a husband and a husband the wife,[7] it frequently happens that a woman's womb is opened without the sanctification of

5 Exod. 13.11.
6 Matt. 15.11,18.
7 Cf. 1 Cor. 7.14.

wedlock. Again, it is not a question of sanctification being confined solely to the husband. The wife, too, partakes in it. The natural functions of each sex are distinct in the act of conception. The husband and wife contribute what is right and proper to the sex of each. The wife furnishes the generation of human succession, a function which is outside the province of a husband.

(47) If such, therefore, be our experience in the flesh, let us turn to an examination of what is proper to the soul. There is no question that we have to deal here with something that is without sex, yet it fulfills all the offices of both sexes in that the soul conceives and, as in marriage, gives birth. Nature provides woman with a womb in which a living person is brought to birth in the course of time. Such, too, is that characteristic of the soul which is ready to receive in its womb-like recesses the seeds of our thoughts, to cherish them and to bring them forth as a woman gives birth to a child. This and no other is the meaning of the words of Isaias: 'We have conceived and brought forth the spirit of salvation.'[8] Some of these conceptions are associated with the female sex, such as malice of thought, petulance, sensuality, self-indulgence, immodesty, and other vices of that nature which tend to enervate the traits associated with what is distinctively masculine. These last are the virtues of chastity, patience, wisdom, temperance, fortitude, and justice, which make it possible for our minds and bodies to struggle with zeal and confidence in our pursuit of virtue. These are the conceptions to which the Prophet Isaias referred in the words, 'We have conceived and brought forth the spirit of salvation,' that is to say, the characteristic masculine traits conceived and gave birth to the spirit of salvation.

---

8 Isa. 26.18.

BOOK TWO

OUR SOULS SHOULD NOT ONLY CONCEIVE, but should bring forth, after the allotted days are fulfilled, offspring such as these, lest the judgment day find us still-born. Of these births the Lord has said: 'Woe to those who are with child or have infants at the breast in those days!'[1] This birth should come to pass early in our lives. Our thoughts should be accompanied by a series of good works, so that our last days may find nothing imperfect or leave anything incompletely moulded in the anvil of our life's work. Make haste, therefore, and let your soul put your conceptions into form, bring them forth in good time, and quickly give sustenance to the offspring.

(2) The form and importance of this offspring is demonstrated in the words of the Apostle: 'My dear children, with whom I am in labor again until Christ is formed in you.'[2] This is the form into which the whole contents of our minds should be poured and Christ should appear conspicuously in the life-giving womb of our souls. Our offspring should be faith and our sustenance, the precepts of Wisdom. With these precepts the infancy of our heart should be imbued, its boyhood be instructed, its youth be rejuvenated, and its

1 Luke 21.23.
2 Gal. 4.19.

old age grow old and grey: 'A spotless life is old age.'[3] That old age of the soul is good when no stains of perfidy have stained it. Hence Paul defends his offspring from this stain—'through the Gospel did I beget you,'[4] he says—lest a gust of wind of false doctrine may severely affect them in their infancy. The Apostle brought into being, therefore, masculine thoughts. He yearned to bring to perfect manhood in the unity of the faith the people whom he instructed how to attain, in the recognition of the Son of God, 'the mature measure of the fullness of Christ.'[5] He knew that the sacrifice was an acceptable one to God, for we read in the Scriptures: 'Thou shalt set apart all that openeth the womb for the Lord.' To this he added: 'All that opens the womb of thy castle and of thy herds whatsoever thou shalt have of the male sex, thou shalt consecrate to the Lord,'[6] so that no detail be missing and everything be made clear.

(3) The Apostle had spoken of the offspring of the better sort, that is, all that is associated with and is capable of reasoning. To this category he now added those of the common crowd whose concern is with what might be callad perceptions of a lowlier kind. These are compared to cattle, devoid of reasoning power. However, these last, when directed by a righteous ruler, are easily tamed to follow his commands. They are trained to endure the yoke and to quicken their pace, to stop and turn aside at the words of their master. They become accustomed to perform and undertake any task which they are bidden to do as part of their daily routine of service. In this way, nature is overcome by the power of discipline. Those animals which do not have a share in our substance nevertheless recognize the words of command we

3 Wisd. 4.9; cf. Cicero, *Pro Archia* 7.16.
4 1 Cor. 4..15.
5 Eph. 4.13.
6 Exod. 13.12.

give. While they are not themselves possessed of reason by nature, they assume by a sort of transfer the reasoning powers that we have in our own nature. We see horses which are aroused to action by the enthusiasm of the crowd, which rejoice in applause and pleasure in being petted by their master.[7] We perceive that fierce lions lay aside their natural ferocity and at command assume an air of submission. They throw off their wild natures and adopt our manners and, although they are themselves objects of terror, they learn even to have fear. A dog is slain to inspire fear in a lion. The animal who is aroused to anger because of injury to himself is curbed by beholding one inflicted on another, whereby his will is broken. How often it happens that they learn to endure hunger even at the sight of their favorite food! How often through fear of their master do they under quick and unexpected orders refrain from food even when their jaws are ready to devour it! Thus they become oblivious of their own wills while complying with ours. How different from those wild animals or those herds of horses or flocks of any kind which run wild without anyone to control them! Deprived of any guidance or direction, they give free vent to their wild nature. This is the reason for placing herdsmen, shepherds, and guard of all sorts in charge of animals. Each one performs his individual duty, directing his charges in accordance with the type of animal committed to his care.

(4) We see, therefore, that man is governed by two sorts of emotion, one that is under control and the other uncontrollable. In the latter case man rushes headlong, carried away by his animal nature, which itself lacks stability and co-ordination, into physical pleasures which are devoid of reason. In the former instance man's emotions are disciplined, subject, as it were, to the guidance and moderating

7 Cf. Virgil, *Georgics* 3.185,186.

influence of a leader. Whenever man's nature is under control, there it shows itself to be masculine and perfect. When, however, man's nature acts without a ruling force, there we find evidence of what might be called a domination exercised and imposed on man by the meaner sort. Thus we have a situation wherein a community which is deprived of the counsels of its king and chief citizens is subject to weakness in its body politics and wastes away its strength in effeminate action. Hence the apostolic injunction regarding the law in the members warring against the law of the mind, making a person a prisoner to the law of sin. Wherefore, in order to deliver himself from the body of this death, Paul placed his hopes, not in his own virtue, but in the grace of Christ.[8] It is clear, therefore, that those emotions which are in accordance with the law of the mind emanate from God's goodness, whereas all other emotions are dominated by the body.

(5) Those emotions, therefore, which are morally good are the first-fruits of our senses, whereas the others are of common and indifferent stock. This classification was used by Moses, following in that respect the language of the Jews, in his reference to the threshing floor of the Law: 'The tithes of your threshing floor and of your wine-vat thou shalt not delay to pay: thou shalt give the first born of thy sons to me.'[9] All the morally good emotions of your senses are the first fruits of the threshing floor of the soul in such a manner as grain is separated in an actual barn floor.[10] On this barn floor the wheat and the barley are separated by a winnowing process from the chaff and from other impurities, while the solid parts, now rid of their lighter coating, settle on the floor. In a similar fashion our thoughts,

8 Cf. Rom. 7.23-25.
9 Exod. 22.29.
10 Cf. Num. 15.20.

when sifted, provide a solid food and pure nourishment for the exercise of virtue, as we read in the Scriptures: 'Not by bread alone does man live, but by every word of God.'[11] What is of no real value is dispersed like smoke or like a mist, which presents opportunities for the exercise of wickedness, while at the same time it is deleterious to one's eyes. Wickedness is rightfully compared to smoke which obscures one's vision with the darkness of this world.[12]

(6) On this subject the Lord says: 'When you are come into the land to which I bring you and shall eat of the bread of that country, you shall separate first-fruits of the Lord of the thing you eat. As you separate first-fruits of your barn-floors, so also shall you give first-fruits of your dough to the Lord.'[13] We are a composite of diverse elements mixed together, cold with hot, and moist with dry. This admixture is the source of many pleasures and manifold delights of the flesh. But these are not the first-fruits of this body of ours. Since we are composed of soul and body and spirit, the first place is held by that admixture in which the Apostle desires that we find sanctification: 'And may the God of peace himself sanctify you completely and may your spirit and soul and body be preserved sound, blameless at the coming of our Lord Jesus Christ.'[14] The first-fruit of this admixture are those of the spirit, that is to say, the creative and generating thoughts that emanate from the soul in its vigor. Only those thoughts are first-fruits which are devoid of malice and wickedness and all kinds of wrong-doing. There are, of course, certain bodily pleasures which are necessary. These are the pleasures of eating, sleeping, drinking, walking, and like functional processes. These, however, are not in the cate-

11 Luke 4.4.
12 Cf. Prov. 10.26.
13 Num. 15.18-21.
14 1 Thess. 5.23.

gory of first-fruits. The Lord has put His stamp of approval, not on these, but on the others which we have mentioned, those thoughts and actions which imply chastity, piety, faith, and devotion. A clear example of this sort of thing is the offering of the patriarch Isaac. Here a father, totally immune to human emotion, proceeded to an act of sacrifice. He offered to God a clean victim and one devoid of fear and of cupidity of the flesh, although one might expect that his eagerness to offer would give way to his very real devotion as a father.

Chapter 2

(7) Let us consider the implications of the word 'first-fruits.' Should they be measured from the point of view of time or of sanctity, in other words, does everything that is first-born have the sanctity of first-fruit? First-fruits are sanctified according to the Law,[1] because therein we find the best kind of sacrifice, one which presents evidence of speedy fulfilment of a vow. Again, first-fruits become sanctified, not by time, but by devotion. The produce does not itself alone constitute sanctity. Hence, if the produce of the soil comes forth speedily without an accompanying fulfilment of a vow, an offence is committed. Not all first-born are therefore sanctified, but everything sanctified is also first-born. Hence, Cain was first-born, but not sanctified. Sanctified, too, was Israel, God's people, but they were not first in time. Yet Israel is called first-born, as it is written in the books of the Prophets: 'Israel is my first-born.'[2] And Levi was sanctified, but he was not first-born, for we hear that he was Lia's third son.[3] Furthermore, the Levites were called first-born. Their name is derived from

1 Cf. Num. 18.8,10.
2 Exod. 4.22.
3 Cf. Gen. 29.34.

that fact, as it is written in Numbers: 'Behold, I have taken the Levites from the children of Israel, for every first-born that openeth the womb among the children of Israel and the Levites shall be mine, for every first-born in mine. Since I struck every first-born in the land of Egypt, I have sanctified whatever is first born in Israel.'[4] Therefore, the Levites were called first-born who were preferred by reason of their sanctification far beyond the rest of the children of Israel. Wherefore, listen to what the Apostle says in regard to the first-born: 'But you have come to Mount Sion and to the city of the living God, the heavenly Jerusalem and to the company of tens of thousands of angels and to the first-born of the churches which were enrolled in heaven.'[5] He has set down in order here four things: Mt. Sion, the city of Jerusalem, the company of the angels, and the churches of the first-born. The Lord took, therefore, the Levites from the midst of the people of Israel because He did not wish that they be involved in human cares. Rather, He wished to make them ministers of religion, and He set aside for Himself the first-born who open the womb of the Spirit. Hence they were not from the womb of nature like sinners given over to wrong-doing of all sorts, but are chosen for their avoidance of worldly things. Wherefore they have no part in what belongs to the crown and are not reckoned as part of the populace. They possess the Word of God in their own hearts, as we read in the Gospel: 'Where two or three are gathered together for my sake, there I am in the midst of them.' And elsewhere: 'In the midst of you there stands one whom you do not know.'[6]

(8) We realize, therefore, that above all things our trust in God should commend us to Him. Once we have this trust,

4 Num. 3.12,13.

5 Heb. 12.20,23. The manuscripts here have the plural *ecclesiarum;* Schenkl would read *ecclesiae.*

6 Matt. 18.20; John 1.26.

let us put all our efforts into making our works perfect. This is indeed a full and perfect sacrifice, as the Lord tells us Himself in speaking of gifts and contributions that are His: 'You will offer to me my oblation in my festal days,'[7] sparing nothing, setting nothing aside, but offering a full, complete, and perfect sacrifice. By 'festal day' is meant the Lord's Day, a time appropriate to acts of perfect virtue. These acts are made perfect if our souls quell the anxieties of this world and the enticements of the flesh in a victorious struggle over pleasure and its attractions. Thus the soul is free from the world and dedicated to God, departing not even in the slightest way from the path of good intentions and casting aside all distractions, whether of pleasure or of toil. The wise man, and no one else, celebrates with due solemnity this festal day. How difficult it is for one to be completely immune from distractions of this sort! Then you may learn to know the difference between what is a masculine and what is a feminine trait, for there is no virtue without toil and toil is a stepping stone to virtue. The very words of the Law point this out: 'The first-born of an ass thou shalt change for a sheep.'[8] The Law has established that an unclean animal shall not be part of a sacrifice, but in its place a clean animal be offered. The Law orders that the offspring of an ass which is unclean should be changed for a sheep, which is a clean animal and suitable for sacrifice. This is the literal meaning. If one were to pursue this matter further and seek for the spiritual sense of this passage, he will discover that the ass is a laborious animal, whereas the sheep is productive. This may be interpreted to mean that labor should be exchanged for produce, since the final results of work is the produce thereof. Or we may interpret the passage

---

7 Num. 28.2.
8 Exod. 13.13.

in this manner: Every action or labor of yours you can make commendable by the pure and simple manner in which you perform it.

(9) 'And if thou do not redeem it,' we are told, 'thou shalt kill it.'[9] The order literally states that another animal be offered for the unclean one or be redeemed by a price, lest there be something inferior or something unclean in the tithe offering. If we examine more deeply into the meaning of this, we perceive that we should refrain from anything which is destined to bear no fruit. He who redeems does, in fact, free himself and in doing so pays off a certain amount of indebtedness. Those works should be avoided which do not lead to real fruitfulness and to good results. I refer to those works of a wordly sort which cannot long endure. These works are barren, and devoid of truth and, though they are pursued with the greatest diligence, provide nothing for the soul. All of those works that impose servitude on our souls are of no avail, even if they are not entirely lacking in effectiveness. A mighty victory can, for example, take place and the accompanying glory of a triumphal march. But we discover frequently that these same people see their previous victory now changed to defeat. The tables are turned when the issue of war finds them in the hands of their enemies. Those who were victorious before now taste the misery of defeat. It is imperative, therefore, that you direct all your labors towards God and obtain His approval. The athlete, for example, relies on his own powers, not on those of another, in order to win a victory. But then, when the spectacle begins, he inclines to doubt his chances. When he has attained the crown of victory, then he becomes aware that this worldly glory fades away more quickly than the very leaves of his wreath of victory. When a pilot brings his ship

9 *Ibid.*

to shore, he gives no thought to putting an end to his labors. He searches immediately for still another opportunity to work. When the soul is released from the body and has reached a terminus of this life, there is still the dubious problem of the judgment to come. What is thought to be a terminus turns out to none at all. Wherefore let us by our prayers, our purity of conscience, and our spirit of charity cling closely to our God. Let us gain His favor by beseeching Him to rescue and free us from the cares of this world as from some cruel and boorish master.[10] Let the substance of our prayers be that we be released from slavery[11] to this world, so that we may obtain the liberty of celestial knowledge, wherein alone is true freedom.

Chapter 3

(10) What is related in the Law may be cited in support of our argument. When the Egyptians oppressed the Jewish people by condemning them to various labors, to toils in rocky or in muddy soil, the children of Israel groaned and caused the Lord to have pity on them. And He said to Moses: 'I have heard the groaning of the people of Israel, wherewith the Egyptians have oppressed them into slavery, and I have remembered my covenant. Therefore say to the children of Israel: I am the Lord who will bring you out of the power of the Egyptians and will deliver you from bondage to them and redeem you with a high arm and great judgments. And I will take you to myself for my people. I will be your God. And you shall know that I am the Lord your God who will bring you out of the power of the Egyptians and will bring you into the land, concerning which I lifted up

10 Cf. Cicero, *De senectute* 14.47.
11 Cf. Virgil, *Eclogues* 1.40.

my hand.'[1] See how the Hebrew people enjoyed the fruits of their labor. They toiled in the mire with the hope of an eternal kingdom. Wherefore in the Scriptures the Lord took pity even on the empty toil of the Gentiles in the brickyards, a prey to filthy superstition and the pleasures of the flesh. A solid wall of faith, however, they were unable to build. Christ addresses the people as if speaking to the offspring of a beast of burden: 'Come to me, all ye who labor, and I will give you rest. Take my yoke upon you and learn from me, for I am meek and humble of heart and you will find rest for your souls.'[2] I seem to be more fully aware of the words and the secret meaning of the Law when I read that call of Christ. He has taught us that an ass should be exchanged for a sheep or redeemed for a price. In this way we not only can exchange an ass for a sheep, that is, an animal that is unclean for one that is clean, but we can even redeem it. A deeper meaning seems to be implied in this statement. If by a sacrifice of purification and by the rite of baptism we first cleanse ourselves of the stains of our offenses, then we are prepared to redeem those very sins of ours by the exercise of good works and by the price of faith and by contrition.

(11) Our price is the blood of Christ. Hence the Apostle Peter says: 'Not with gold or silver you were redeemed, but with the precious blood.' And Paul says: 'You have been bought with a price. Do not become the slaves of men.'[3] Therefore, not without reason did they marvel in the Gospel on seeing the Lord Jesus sitting on a colt, because the race of the Gentiles is to Christ like a victim which, according to the Law, is considered to be unclean. Hence we read in the Scriptures that the Levites redeemed them.[4] In this way they

1 Exod. 6.5-8, cf. 2.23,24.
3 Matt. 11.28,29.
3 1 Peter 1.18; 1 Cor. 7.23.
4 Cf. Exod. 13.13.

would be able by the sanctity of their lives and by their prayers to take away the sins of their people. Here in the figure of the Lamb we have the true Levite who was to come and preside over the mysteries. By His own Passion He would take away the sins of the world.[5] The word 'Levite' means 'raised up for me' or 'on me he is light.' The word 'Levite' bears witness to a perfection in virtue by which the people attain holiness. He, therefore, is the expected who was born of a virgin and who came for my salvation and for the salvation of the entire world. For me He was sacrificed; for me He tasted death; and for me, too, He rose from the dead. In Him has the redemption of all men been undertaken; in Him is their resurrection. He is the true Levite. We, His Levites, He would bring closer to God so that we might pray to Him unceasingly, hope for salvation from Him, shun all worldly affairs, and finally be numbered among the elect, as it is written: 'O Lord, possess us.'[6] Then alone is found true possession when we are not subject to the temptations of life and when we bring forth perfect fruit for all time. The Levite is one who redeems, because a man of wisdom redeems the man who is weak and foolish. He is like a physician who revives the spirit of his helpless patient. In imitation of that Physician who came down from heaven, he assuages the convalescent with healing words of wisdom, in order to point out to men the ways of wisdom and to reveal the paths of wisdom to little ones.[7] He perceived that those who suffer cannot be healed without a remedy. For this reason He bestowed medicine on the sick and by His assistance made health available to all, so that whoever died could ascribe to himself the real causes of his death. That man was unwilling to be cured, although he had a remedy

5 Cf. John 1.29.
6 Exod. 34.9.
7 Cf. Ps. 18.8; Matt. 11.25.

at hand which could effect his escape from death. The mercy of God has been made manifest to all. Those who perish, therefore, perish through their own negligence, whereas those who are saved are freed by the judgment of God, who wishes all men to be saved and to come to the recognition of truth.[8] Hence, if Sodom had fifty just men, it would not have been destroyed. If it had ten just men, Sodom would have been saved,[9] because a declaration of the remission of sin would have rescued their souls from servitude, and the plenitude of perfect knowledge would not have allowed their hearts to be consumed in the devouring flames of lust.

(12) The reference just noted to people in large numbers has a special significance. Groups of people of like character have a tendency to lift the moral tone and to contribute to society as a whole something of their own selves, which is a contributory factor to the group's preservation. Numbers blunt the force of envy, confound wickedness, arouse men to virtue, and enhance gracious acts. No one ought to begrudge praise to another person who benefits him. The man given to wickedness often imitates the character of the person who attempts to aid him. At any rate, he reveres him and often even loves him. The same man, too, if he knows how to benefit other men, is made better by this exercise of his zeal. In that way he binds people together and increases the tolerance of citizens for each other, thereby bringing fame to their communities. How happy is that city which has many just men! How celebrated does it become in the lips of all men! How unqualifiedly blessed for ever is that city reckoned to be! How happy I am to see so many gentle and wise people live long lives, when I behold chaste maidens and dignified and elderly widows living virtuous lives! The latter constitute

8 Cf. John 3.16-21; Luke 19.10.
9 Cf. Gen. 18.24-32.

in a way a venerable senate of the Church to be revered and imitated because of their conspicuous air of gravity—a fact which is conducive in itself to greater charm of manners! My joy is not for these people themselves who are subject to the manifold ills of this world while they are alive. I rejoice, rather, that many are benefited by the lives of such people. Again, when a person like this passes away, although he has by his prolonged age deferred death,[10] I am greatly afflicted for the reason that a host of younger men have been deprived of the stout defence of old age. Wherefore the demise of citizens of dignity and wisdom, both men and women, gives us the first indication that a city is destined to perish or that ruin is imminent. When this takes place, the gates are open for a flood of misfortunes. A city, therefore, in its entirety is strengthened by the presence of men of wisdom in its midst and is weakened at their departure. If their physical presence is important, their discourse, also, when it is in a high plane of serious counsel, tends to put courage in the heart and soul of each and every individual. If we add to this the practice of wide reading,[11] then we have a group of senators whose wise precepts and counsel constantly have their effects in that interior city which is in the heart of each one of us.

Chapter 4

(13) We see, then, why Moses called the Levites first-born and redeemers of others, since they offer to one man the mentality of old age, corresponding to his own mature judgment and usefulness, and to another grant redemption. Hence Moses indicated that the cities of the Levites in the

10 Cf. Virgil, *Aeneid* 12.395.
11 Cf. Cicero, *De senectute* 11.38.

Old Testament served as a refuge,[1] because he who fled to where the living Word of God resides,[2] a place like a city well-protected and defended, that person attained for himself the kind of liberty which endures. If a man was guilty of involuntary homicide and if he took refuge in the cities of the Levites, no one was permitted to slay that person, provided he had his residence in those cities. In a similar way, if a person feels sorrow for a sin which was the result of an imprudent or involuntary act, the Law releases him from every penalty due to his crime, provided he remains in residence among the Levites and has no intention of leaving those instructors who dispense the commands of God.

(14) Do not think it unreasonable that men given to evil reside together with men of good will and that those stained with guilt live side by side with the godly. Those men who have been polluted with the contagion of sin have need of purification. Thus there is a certain agreement of contraries. The Levite who has relinquished the pleasures of this world is an exile from guilt. In the same way, the person who is guilty of homicide is a fugitive from his native land. There is this difference, however, that the latter abandons his people because of fear of the Law, whereas God's minister renounces all contacts with human passions and frees himself from the exigencies of concupiscence by his pursuit of virtue. This statement is not an exaggeration. In a sense, the Levite does violence to himself, so as to rid himself of bodily pleasures with consequent annihilation of his own flesh. For example, Moses slew an Egyptian and become a fugitive from the land of Egypt so as to avoid the king of that land.[3] But he would not have slain the Egyptian if he had not first destroyed in himself the Egyptian of spiritual wickedness and had not relinquished the luxuries and honors of the king's palace.

1 Cf. Num. 3.12; 35.6-8.
2 Cf. John 1.14.
3 Cf. Exod. 2.11.

He considered that the reproach of Christ was a far better patrimony than the treasures of Egypt. To the foolish this indeed seeems to be a reproach, but the reproach of the Cross of Christ is in reality God's power and wisdom.[4]

(15) There are, in fact, two main types of power in God. There is the power which forgives and the power which punishes. Sins are forgiven by the Word of God of which the Levite is the interpreter and, indeed, the executor. Sins are forgiven by the priest in his sacred office and ministry. They are punished, too, by men who exercise power temporarily, that is to say, by judges. The Apostle says: 'Dost thou wish then not to fear the authority? Do what is good and thou wilt have praise from it. For it is God's minister to thee for good. But if thou dost what is evil, fear, for not without reason does it carry the sword. For it is God's minister, an avenger to execute wrath on him who does evil.'[5] Sins are punished even by people, as we read in the Scriptures,[6] because the Jewish people were often waylaid by men of other races. Because of some offense against God's majesty these men were frequently aroused by His command. Even the person who unwittingly committed a murder was still within the ministry of God, since the Law makes this statement regarding him: 'God delivered him into his hands.'[7] His hands, therefore, served as an instrument of divine punishment. The Levite is, then, the minister who remits, whereas the man who in the example just cited unwittingly and unwillingly struck another in a homicidal act became in fact an administrator of divine punishment. See to it that Christ is infused into the act of slaying an impious man and that sanctification accompany and be part of your attempt to abolish what is abominable.

4 Cf. 1 Cor. 1.23-25.
5 Rom. 13.3,4.
6 Cf. Isa. 13.17.
7 Exod. 21.13.

(16) The Lord has said: 'On that day in which I shall slay every first-born in the land of Egypt, I shall sanctify to myself whatsoever is first-born in Israel.'[8] This does not refer to one occasion or to one crisis, but to all time. Once wickedness is renounced, virtue finds immediate entrance. The departure of evil brings about the introduction of virtue and the same effort that banishes crime leads to an adherence to innocence. You have an example of that in the Gospel. At the moment when Satan entered into the heart of Judas, Christ departed from him. At the very instant that Judas received one, he lost the other: 'And after the morsel Satan entered into him. Jesus therefore said to him, "What thou dost, do quickly."'[9] Why is this? Because, once Satan found entrance into Judas, at that moment there came about his departure from Christ. He is ejected, then, and banished, since the person who trafficked with the Devil could have no fellowship with Christ. There is no harmony between Christ and Belial.[10] Wherefore, on receiving the command to leave, Judas immediately departed, as we read in the words of the Evangelist: 'When he had received the morsel, he went out quickly. Now it was night.'[11] It was not merely a question of departure, but it was one which was immediate and at night. The fact that one who deserted Christ should be connected with the darkness of night should excite no wonder. Just as the person who is received by the Devil is excluded from Christ, so on the other hand Zacchaeus, at the moment when he forsook gain, proceeded to welcome Christ. Marveling at the way Zacchaeus climbed a tree to see Him, the Lord was moved to say: 'Zacchaeus, make haste and come down, for I must stay in your house today. And he made haste and came down, and welcomed him

8 Num. 3.13.
9 Cf. John 13.2,27.
10 Cf. 2 Cor. 6.15.
11 John 13.13.

joyfully.'[12] By receiving Christ he got rid of avarice. He sent perfidy into exile and renounced deceit. Otherwise, there is no reason for the entrance of Christ unless vice is excluded, because He has no barter with wrong-doing. Hence He ejected the money-changers from the temple, because He did not wish to associate with them.[13] Wherefore, being aware that he could not receive Christ if he followed his old way of life, Zacchaeus ordered his former vices to leave his home in order that Christ might find an entrance therein. While people murmured that Jesus had gone to be a guest of a man who was a sinner, Zacchaeus was right in inviting the Lord to stay: 'Behold, Lord, I give one-half of my possessions to the poor and if I have defrauded anyone of anything, I restore it twofold.'[14] In this way he replied to those who said that a sinner ought not to offer hospitality to Christ. He said, in effect: 'I am no longer a publican, no longer the Zacchaeus of old, the thief and the cheat. I restore what I have taken. I, who used to take, am now the giver. I, who formerly despoiled the poor, now make restitution. I, who plundered what belonged to others, now give of my own.' Error took to flight, once Christ made entrance. Where the light of eternal light shone, there no longer existed that blindness caused by pleasures of the flesh.

Chapter 5

(17) We have discussed the problems connected with the first-born. Now let us turn our attention to the characteristic of fatness or richness of which David speaks intelligibly when he says: 'Let my soul be filled as with marrow and fatness.' Before that he had said: 'And may thy whole burnt offering

12 Luke 19.5,6.
13 Cf. Matt. 21.12,13.
14 Luke 19.7-9.

be made fat.'[1] By this he means that the requirements for a sacrifice are that it be fat or rich, that it be glistening and that it be weighted with the sustenance inspired by faith and devotion and by the rich nourishment of the Word of God. Frequently we use the word 'fat' or 'rich' when we refer to something that is heavily and elaborately adorned, and to the finest victim as one that is not thin and scrawny. Wherefore we denominate as 'rich' a sacrifice which we desire to be regarded as the 'finest.' We also have proof of this when we consult the prophetic passage in the Scriptures where fine cows are compared to years of fertility.[2]

Chapter 6

(18) Now let us reflect on the meaning of the Lord's words, 'If you offer rightly and you do not divine rightly, thou hast sinned. Hold thy peace.'[1] This signifies that God is not appeased by the gifts that are offered, but by the disposition of the giver. Hence Cain, who offered a gift which was denounced, was conscious of the fact that his offering was fraudulent, that his sacrifice was not acceptable to God, and he was downcast. When 'the mind is conscious of right,'[2] then there is occasion for veritable joy—a joy of the spirit—when one's purpose and deeds are commendable to God. Cain's sadness, therefore, bears testimony to his consciousness of right and is an indication of his failure. Again, because he offered a gift and did not in addition make a just and righteous division of it, for that reason he fell into error.

(19) There are four ways by which a sacrifice may be

1 Ps. 62.6; 19.4.
2 Cf. Gen. 41.26.

1 Cf. Gen. 4.7.
2 Virgil, *Aeneid* 1.604.

made acceptable. The sacrifice should consist of a gift, the newest of the new, or it should be dried or broken into pieces, or it should be unbroken.[3] The 'newest of the new' belongs to the early season of the year and is consistent with the nature of first-fruits. Now, it has been made clear to us that this refers to those who are renewed by the sacrament of baptism. That, in fact, is the real sacrifice of first-fruits when a person offers himself as a victim and begins of himself to act so as to ensure in the future an offering of a gift that is his very own.[4] The new faith of those who have been made new is strong and vigorous, seeking for itself an increase of virtue. The faith which is weak and slack—the faith which has the sluggish and slothful character of old age—is not one that is fit for sacrifice. We need a faith which blossoms with the lush growth of wisdom and with the youthful vigor of divine knowledge, a faith, moreover, which has the sap of ancient doctrine. There ought to be a concurrence of the old and the new, as in the case of the Old and the New Testament. It is written: 'Eat the oldest of the old store and, new coming on, cast away the old.'[5] Let our food be a knowledge of the patriarchs. Let our minds banquet in the prophetic books of the Prophets. Such nourishment should our minds partake of, the truth of the body of Christ, and not just the external appearance of a lamb. Our eyes should not be affected by the shadow cast by the Law. Rather, the clear grace of the Lord's Passion and the splendor of His Resurrection should illuminate our vision.

(20) If you offer a sacrifice of the first-born of a sheep, a rich burned offering, then you should make an offering of those first-fruits as they are specified in Scripture, according

3 Cf. Lev. 2.14.
4 Cf. Rom. 12.1,6.
5 Lev. 26.10.

to which your faith ought to be tested as if by fire and ought to glow with the Holy Spirit. Hence Jacob cooked a mess of pottage and thus took the benefits from his own brother, who would surely have attained them by the exercise of a robust faith. One, therefore, increased in strength and vigor, while the other, who was unable to cook his own food, became weak and feeble.[6] Let your soul acquire virtue by being burnt, as with fire, by the Word of God. See the example of Joseph: 'The word of the Lord inflamed him.'[7] Let your faith be roasted like the ears of corn gathered by the harvesters, who choose to gather in the crop soon after it has been browned in the heat of the sun. Frequent reading of the Scriptures, therefore, strengthens the mind and ripens it by the warmth of spiritual grace. In this way our powers of reasoninng are strengthened and the influence of our irrational passions brought to naught. Wherefore Esau was weakened when the bonds of virtue were loosed, while those who girded up their loins and were bidden not to eat 'anything raw nor boiled in water,' but who were ordered to eat the head of a lamb roasted in the fire, as it is written in Exodus—these men with stout and trusting hearts crossed the sea on dry ground.[8] In the Gospel, too, the Lord ate 'a piece of broiled fish,'[9] whereby the plenitude of His Spirit was renewed. Perhaps Esau was weak because he desired food that was cooked in water. Food which was unsuitable for himself Jacob gave to one who was infirm.

(21) Our offerings and our prayers ought not to be lacking in order. On the contrary, they should follow a precise pattern. In every case where there is disorder there is room for precision. Especially is this true of prayers and sacrifices which

6 Cf. Gen. 25.29,30.
7 Ps. 104.19.
8 Cf. Exod. 12.9-11.
9 Luke 24.42.

lack clarity unless they have clear divisions. Hence the Law commands that the limbs of a victim be cut up, for the most part.[10] The Law also commands that holocausts be offered, so that the sacrifice be pure without admixture or covering. The reason is that our faith, pure and devoid of all externals, may thus become fervent. In that way our faith may not be enshrouded in dubious and false opinion, but appear in its pure and unadorned simplicity. Again, faith may be divided into suitable parts. Virtue, in fact, is such that is can be divided into several species, the chief of which are four: Prudence, Temperance, Fortitude, and Justice. Let your prayer, therefore, give forth a fragrance of Prudence, aiming at knowledge of God and the truth of faith. Let it have the fragrance of Temperance, a virtue which the Apostle believed should be required of married people: 'Do not deprive each other, except perhaps by consent, for a time, that you may give yourselves to prayer.' The Law commands that these who intend to perform a sacrifice be chaste for one or two days previous.[11] Let your prayer show fortitude, so as not to be interrupted by fear nor be affected by weariness. Pressure of adversity should make us all the more strenuous in prayer. Our supplications should retain an element of Justice. If Judas had adhered to that virtue, his prayer would not have become sinful. At what time ought we to refrain from unjust thoughts and deeds if not when we call upon the justice of God? And so the Lord recommends us to seek justice, saying: 'Blessed are they who suffer persecution for justice' sake, for theirs is the kingdom of heaven.'[12] Judas did not have this justice; otherwise, he would not have betrayed his Lord and Master. Cain, too, did not possess this virtue; otherwise, he would have offered to the Lord

10 Cf. Lev. 24.42.
11 1 Cor. 7.5; cf. Exod. 19.10-15.
12 Matt. 6.33; 5.10.

first-fruits of the soil, not those of inferior quality. So, too, he failed to divide his gifts into parts. Hence the reply: 'If you offer rightly and you do not divide equally, thou hast sinned. Hold thy peace.'[13] You see the seriousness of the offense. Where is no division into parts, then the whole sacrifice comes to naught.

(22) One question remains for us to discuss. How much time should we spend in prayer? The Lord spent a night in prayer.[14] He did this not for His own benefit, but that He might teach us a lesson. Frequent prayer tends to strengthen our wills, so that we become more amenable to God's purposes through practice, just as we may become less amenable through indifference. Exercise of this sort, therefore, is salutary. The body's strength is increased by frequent exercise. Lack of exercise tends to diminish or weaken our bodies. In fact, persons who refrain from exercise lose even that strength which is natural to them. In like manner, fortitude of the soul is enhanced by a course of exercises. The very toil expended in such practice will, in the end, turn out to be advantageous rather than useless. Let us give our souls this nourishment, which, like the bread of God from heaven,[15] will, if it is sifted and refined by long meditation, produce real strength in our hearts. Not without reason is the bread described as sifted and refined, because we ought with our whole heart and soul to sift and polish for a long period of time the teachings of holy Scripture in order that the essence of that spiritual food may suffuse the very depths of our souls. Wherefore, if our faith blossoms forth in the spirit of youth, relinquishing the enfeeblement of age—if our faith should glow within, adhering to the principle of due division according to the Law, and if we acquire grace by constancy—then

13 Gen. 4.7.
14 Cf. Luke 6.12.
15 Cf. John 6..32.

we attain to that rich and, so to speak, unctious type of prayer of which the Prophet speaks: 'Thou hast anointed my head with oil.'[16] Just as lambs become fat from a plenteous store of milk and as sheep become sleek from rich pasture land, so, too, the prayers of the faithful profit much from drinking in the health-giving words of the Apostles.

(23) If any of the conditions which we have named is not fulfilled, a sacrifice is not approved. Wherefore Cain was warned: 'If you make a righteous sacrifice, you should divide in no unrighteous way,' because the world itself, we are told, was separated into parts. Its previous condition was chaotic, for 'the earth was waste and void.' First of all, light was created and God called it by name and 'God divided the light from the darkness and He called the darkness night.'[17] We read of each of the world's objects created in due order, of the firmament, the earth, the fruit-bearing trees, and the various species of animals. Lighter elements, such as air and fire, were given a higher position, while the heavier elements, such as water and earth, were placed below them. God could, of course, have commanded all to be created at the same time, but He preferred to keep them separate. This procedure we now follow in all our business affairs and especially in our social amenities. It is not sufficient to return what you actually received. You must make the return an acceptable one. To slight in any way a person to whom you feel indebted is much more vexatious than not to pay a debt at all. Therefore, it is the spirit in which you act and the very way in which you make your acknowledgment that count, rather than the material itself of your presentation. In this way, it is true, a person makes an offering which follows the pattern of correctness sufficient to indicate his

16 Ps. 22.5.
17 Gen. 1.2,3.

devotion and his gratitude. Still, such a person has not yet made a due distinction. He ought, first of all, to give first-fruits to God so as to attain God's favor. In fact, the division should proceed in the following way: What is primary should precede what is secondary, rather than contrariwise. What belongs to heaven should take precedence over what is of the earth—not the earthly over what belongs to the heavens.

Chapter 7

(24) Because Cain disturbed this order, he was told: 'Thou hast sinned. Hold thy peace!' All this is the teaching of God: first, that you should not sin, as He had warned Adam; and, second, that, if you have fallen into sin, you should hold your peace, as Cain was instructed to do. We ought to condemn sin and be ashamed of it. We should not apologize for it, because by our shame our fault is diminished, whereas sin is increased by our attempts to justify it. We undergo correction by keeping silent, whereas we stumble into error by our contentions. Let there be at least a feeling of humiliation where there is no occasion for forgiveness. Hence we have the statement: 'The just is first accuser of himself.' Elsewhere we read the words of the Lord Himself: 'Tell if thou hast anything to justify thyself.'[2] How great is the power of shamefacedness, which obtains that justice which the accusation of guilt has taken away! And so He says: 'Hold thy peace,' since you have no excuse to offer. You have it in your power to be weaned away from sin. The blame is not to be laid on one's brother, but the wrong-doing is to be attributed to the one who is really to blame. 'The sin returns to you,' we are told—the sin which began with you.

1 Gen. 4.7.
2 Prov. 18.17; Isa. 43.26.

You cannot plead necessity rather than intent. Your wickedness has come back on you like a boomerang. 'Thou hast dominion over it.'[3]

(25) This statement ('Thou hast dominion over it') is well expressed, for impiety is the mother of error and a person who has once sinned grievously is likely to fall easily into other sins. How is it possible for man to exercise control over human things when he has done violence to what is divine? How can a man who has done injury to God be good in the eyes of men? It follows, then, that other vices are found in the wake of serious implications of immorality, since derelictions, once entered upon, lead to others. You have dominion, therefore, over your own acts; you are master of your own transgressions. You cannot enter a plea of ignorance or of compulsion. You are subject to trial as a voluntary defendant. It was not by accident or by guile that you put yourself in the category of one accused of inflicting injury on God.

Chapter 8

(26) When you are admonished, then, to hold your peace, your conscience is aroused and your crimes become flagrant. What, therefore, is the meaning of the words, 'Let us go into the field?'[1] Does it mean that a place devoid of plant life[2] is chosen by Cain for the murder of his brother? What place was more fitting for this murder than one that was barren? Nature, it seems, had purposely denied germinating powers to a place destined for such a crime, because it was not fitting that, contrary to nature, this soil should on the one hand

3 Gen. 4.7.

1 Gen. 4.8.
2 Cf. Sallust, *Bellum Jug.* 79.6.

share in the contagion of parricidal blood and at the same time bring forth fruit in accordance with the laws of nature. When Cain said: 'Let us go forth into the field,' his words had meaning. He did not say: 'Let us go forth into the Garden where fruit grows plentifully, into a cultivated and productive place.' As a matter of fact, we know that parricides cannot obtain for themselves the fruit of their crimes. They expend time and eflort in a frightful act af impiety, yet they cannot attain their objective. They shun places that have been blest by nature's benignity. We have the example of Cain, who seems to have been afraid that a land productive of such goodly crops might be an impediment to his ghastly crime. He seems to have feared that the lushness of vegetable life with its variety of germinating fruits might by its mute appeal, even in the act of perpetating his crime, bring back to him his affection for his own brother. The highwayman shuns daylight, a witness of his crime. The adulterer blushes to see the light of day discover him. In like manner the parricide avoids land that is fertile. How could he bear to behold the common association of plants for productivity who was face to face with one who was bound to him by relationship of blood? Joseph was thrown into a dry pit. Amnon was slain in his own house.[3] Nature, therefore, by withholding her gifts from those places which were to be witnesses of a parricidal act and by her condemnation of innocent soil, makes clear to us the severity of the future punishments of the guilty. The very elements are, therefore, condemned because of the crime of men. Hence David condemned the mountains, in which Jonathan and his father were slain, to be punished with perpetual sterility, saying: 'Ye mountains of Gelboe, let neither dew nor rain come upon you, mountains of death.'[4]

---

3 Cf. Gen. 37.24; 3 Kings 13.28.
4 2 Kings 1.21.

Chapter 9

(27) Now let us examine the reason why God, as if He were unaware that Abel was slain, asked Cain: 'Where is your brother?' But we are shown God's knowledge, when Cain's attempt to deny his guilt is offset by the statement: 'The voice of your brother's blood cries out to me from the ground.'[1] A profounder meaning may be seen here in God's exhortation that sinners do penance, for confession of guilt leads to a lessening of punishment. Hence, in the civil courts, those who deny their guilt are put on the rack, whereas an admission of guilt tends to mercy on the part of the judge. To confess his guilt—not to evade his guilt, but to admit it—indicates that the sinner humbly awaits his sentence. Admission of guilt placates thc judge, whereas denial rouses his opposition. God wishes to stir you up to seek pardon. He wants you to look for indulgence from Himself. He wishes to have it made clear by your admission that He is not responsible for your wrong-doing. Those who, like the Gentiles, place the responsibility for their sins on some external force, inherent in God's decree or in His work, seem to bring God to court as one who is responsible for their sins. According to this theory, a person does not of his own will commit a murder if his actions are the result of some external force. However, we cannot condone those acts which emanate from ourselves, whereas we tend to excuse those that are beyond our own control. That the Author, not of your guilt, but of your innocence, should be made a partaker of the shame of your crime is a conception of a much more serious nature than the sin itself.

(28) Consider the parricide's reply: 'I do not know. Am I my brother's keeper?' Although this reply savors of insolence,

1 Gen. 4.10.

there is still the implication that, considering the goodness of his brother, Cain should by his actions make known his loyalty to him. Who is there to whom he is more bound by necessity to offer protection? But how could that person who did not recognize the influence of family bonds have been expected to observe what is expedient in relations of brotherly love? Or how was it possible for him to comply with the laws of nature when he did not show reverence even to God? The existence of God is denied, as if He were unaware of Cain's act. Cain shirks his duty to be his brother's keeper, as if this were beyond the bounds of nature's laws. He steers away from judgment, as if he were above judgment. Why do you feel astonishment at the fact that he did not acknowledge his loyalty to his brother, if he did not even recognize his own Creator? From these incidents in Scripture we learn the lesson that faith is the root of all virtues. Wherefore the Apostle says: 'Our foundation is Christ' and whatever you build on this foundation is uniquely profitable and conducive to reward for virtuous acts.[2]

(29) A fitting reply, therefore, was given by the Lord to one who so foolishly denied committing the crime: 'The voice of your brother's blood cries to me from the ground.'[3] This means: 'why are you ignorant of your brother's whereabouts? You were alone with him along with your parents. Among so few people, the presence of your brother should not have escaped your notice. Or are you relying on the fact that your parents are unable to play the part of accuser? I am unwilling to concede that a relationship founded on protection should become based on hazard and that in your case alone nature should revoke her laws. Do you think, then, that your crime would pass unnoticed just because your parents feel it their duty not to accuse you? Rather, you

2 Cf. 1 Cor. 3.11,12.
3 Gen. 4.10.

should be condemned all the more severely for taking that stand. Granted that those dear relatives of yours ought not to accuse you or even think of slaying you. But if you do not recognize Me as a witness of the act, there still is the voice of your brother's blood which cries out to Me to bear witness. That voice carries more conviction that if your brother was still living. You were alone. Who else could have slain him? If you accuse your parents, you charge them with the crime of parricide. The person who has no mercy on his parents is capable of killing his own brother. A person who proposes to show that his parents are parricides could well be a parricide himself. It was well said that "the voice of blood cries out," not "the voice of your brother." In the very throes of death your brother preserves his innocence and his brotherly devotion. Your brother does not bring an accusation, lest it should appear to be one of parricide. It is not his voice that accuses nor is it his mind. Rather, is it the voice of that very blood which you shed. Your brother, therefore, is not your accuser. Your accuser is your own deed of wickedness.' At this point the accused person is unable to defend himself, because one who admits that he is guilty cannot rely on the evidence of witnesses. The deed speaks for itself. Moreover, the earth which received the blood also stands as a witness of the deed.

(30) It was well said: 'The voice of your brother's blood cries from the ground.' He did not say 'cries from your brother's body,' but 'cries from the earth.' Although his brother refrains, the earth does not. If his brother is silent, the earth condemns. The earth acts as both witness and judge against you. The earth, still wet with the blood of your slain brother, is a hostile witness. As a judge, the earth, befouled by such a crime, is even more antagonistic, inasmuch as she opened her mouth and received your brother's blood shed

by your own hand. When she opened her mouth, she expected indeed to receive words of brotherly love. She had no fears when she saw the two brothers. She was aware that the relation of consanguinity was an incentive to love, not to hate. How could the earth have a suspicion of parricide, when she had not yet seen a homicide? But you shed blood for which the earth in retaliation 'will not give her fruit to you.'[4] How guileless was that act of revenge! She who was so seriously outraged limited herself to the act of withholding. She refrained from inflicting injury.

(31) No mean doctrine is expressed in the words, 'The voice of your brother's blood cries out to me.'[5] God gives ear to the just even in death, since they live unto God. And rightly are they considered to be alive, because, even if they have tasted the death of the body, they still enjoy a bodiless life and are illuminated with the splendor of their merits and are basking in light eternal.[6] God beholds, therefore, the blood of the just. He turns aside from the prayers of the impious, since, even if they appear to be alive, they are more miserable than all of the dead. They surround themselves with flesh as with a sepulcher in which they have entombed their unhappy souls. What other comparison can be made? The soul is shrouded in earth and is bound by the inordinate desires of avarice and of other vices, so that it cannot breathe the air of heavenly grace. A sinner of this sort has been cursed by earth, which is the lowest and meanest constituent in this world of ours. The higher parts are, of course, the heavens and what exists in heaven, the sun, the moon, the stars, Thrones, Dominations, Principalities and Powers,[7] Cherubim and Seraphim. There is no doubt, there-

4 Gen. 4..12.
5 Gen. 4.10.
6 Cf. Rom. 6.10-13.
7 Cf. Col. 1.16.

fore, that the person condemned by the inferior parts of the world is condemned, too, by the superior. How can Cain, when he is not absolved by the earth, be absolved by the righteous decisions made there above? Hence he is commanded to be 'a fugitive on the earth, groaning and trembling.'[8]

(32) There is no disputing the fact that the wicked are confronted with evil and always will be. Present evils cause sadness; future evils, dread; but the wicked are more perturbed by present evils than by those in the future. Wherefore Cain said the Lord: 'My punishment is too great to bear. If you abandon me today, I shall hide myself from your face.'[9] There is nothing more grievous than to be a wanderer and to be irrevocably bereft of God. With a sinner's death there comes an end of sinning, whereas his life, deprived of God, his Pilot, suffers shipwreck and disaster. If the shepherd abandons his flock, the wild beasts make their inroads. In like manner, when God deserts man, the Devil makes his entrance. To be deprived of a guide is a matter of serious consequence for the foolish. When no physician is at hand, there is occasion for diseases to creep in and inflict more injury. The man who desires to hide his faults and cover up his sins goes into concealment. The man who does wrong hates the light of day and waits for darkness to serve his iniquities. The just man, however, is apt not to conceal himself from his Lord and God. Rather, he desires to offer himself to God, saying: 'Behold, I am here as one whose conscience is clear and who fears no detection.'

(33) With reason, therefore, does the man who is conscious of evil hide himself and say: 'Whoever finds me will kill me.'[10] The man of limited vision is afraid when death has

8 Gen. 4.12.
9 Gen. 4.13.
10 Gen. 4.14.

come upon him. He pays no heed to the continuous presence of death. The judgment of God is ignored and his sole concern is his body's decease. But from what source did he fear death whose parents were the only living beings on earth? There was the possibility that one who broke the ordinances of the Law of God could have had fears of an attack from wild beasts. A person who taught man how to kill could not have assumptions regarding the rest of the animal kingdom. A person who showed how the crime of parricide could be committed might well fear a parricidal act on the part of his own parents. The parents could learn that lesson from their son which later generations learned from their parents.

(34) Now let us consider the reason for God's statement, 'Whoever kills Cain shall be punished sevenfold,'[11] and why a token was placed upon him so that no one should kill him, a parricide. A provision was made to protect a person against the slaying of an innocent man. Besides the five bodily senses, man has the power of speech and the ability to propagate. He also has an eighth power, the power of reason.[12] The other powers are subject to death unless they are subject to the control of reason. Wherefore, the man who is without reason in exercising these faculties incurs danger to himself. A loss of reason, therefore, bring with it an ineffectual use of these seven bodily gifts. They have no efficacy without the saving bonds of reason. The number seven of which we speak has better uses. It conveys ideas of rest and remission.[13] The person, therefore, who has not spared the life of a sinner has begrudged him the opportunity for the remission of his sins and at the same time deprived him of all hopes of remission.

---

11 Gen. 4.15.
12 Cf. St. Ambrose, Letter to Horontianus, in *Letters*, trans. Sister Mary Beyenka. O. P., Fathers of the Church 26 (New York 1954) 264-265.
13 Cf. Gen. 2.3.

He will, in fact, be subject in equal measure to divine justice.

(35) As regards the token God placed on Cain with the purpose of protecting him from death at the hands of another, this may be said. He wanted the wanderer to have time for reflection and by such kindness inspire him to change his ways. It generally happens that we entrust ourselves more readily to those persons to whom we are indebted. The favor granted to him was not great. Yet it was enough to scotch the foolish actions of a stupid man. This man, although liable to eternal punishment, did not demand that the punishment be remitted. He believed that he should plead for his life on this earth where there is more anxiety than pleasure. Death consists in the severance of the body from the soul and is at the same time the termination of our life here. With the coming of death, man's bodily sufferings are ready to cease, not to increase. The fears, in fact, which frequently haunt us in this present life—the griefs, pains, lamentations, and tortures of varied sort, the mutilations provoked by exposure to illness and disease—all these for mankind are more often the equivalent of death. Death under such circumstances truly appears to be a mercy, not a penalty which has the character of finality. By a sentence such as this our life is not taken away. We experience a life that is far better. When the wicked who are unwilling to quit the paths of sin leave this life, they reach, without their knowing it, not a goal set by nature, but a terminus for their wrongdoing. Those men who are indentured to sin are thus prevented from doing other deeds of wickedness. If, again, men are seen to have fulfilled life's expectations, they are believed to have migrated to another world and not to have foundered here below.

(36) This is an opportune time to discuss the question of the spirituality of the soul. Truly happy is that life when

every man who is conscious of having lived well has cast aside the trapping of his flesh and has freed himself from this prison of the body.[14] Then we are free to fly to that place above, where our souls once groaned in the act of commingling with the bodily passions of this flesh of ours. Our souls were destined there to complete the task appointed by our Pilot, namely, by the use of reason to bring under subjection the irrational emotions of our bodies. This is why the Prophets were late in accompanying the Jewish people into captivity. Otherwise, the rest of the people would have been deprived of the guidance and counsel of holy men and would thus have undergone more serious calamities. With their presence the people would be likely to be stirred on hearing words of encouragement and thus be induced to pay homage to the Lord, their God. The people, overwhelmed by the adversities of captivity, could thus avoid the sin of perfidy and not despair of their eternal salvation.

(37) At this point it is opportune to refute the arguments of those who believe that this life here is the only one—a life subject to calamity and to grief. Our refutation rests on a simple alignment of facts. We have in Cain and Abel two contrasting characters. One was just, innocent and loyal. Because of the acceptability of his offerings to God he incurred the hatred of his brother and, while still a youth, become a victim of the sin of parricide. The other brother was unjust, evil, and disloyal. Polluted even with a brother's blood, he lived to a ripe old age, married, left a family and founded cities—all this under the providence of God. Is not this a clear case for divine intervention? You are wrong in assuming that we have here an example of a life of pleasure. You do not take into account a prolonged old age, steeped in misery—an old age that experienced those anxieties that time inevitably

14 Cf. Cicero, *De republica* 6.14.

brings in its wake. Add to this the fact that we are subject to disasters every moment of our lives. Surrounded by monsters like Scylla, are we not continually exposed to the poundings of a thunderous sea and compelled to dwell as best we can in habitations of sheer rock in the manner of that monstrous animal—a monster, not merely of immemorial time, but of immemorial wickedness?[15] Hence, Cain's old age is not to be considered as something desirable. It was, rather, an occasion for punishment, inasmuch as he lived in the midst of fears and spent his extended period of time in fruitless labors. There is no penalty more grievous than that which conscious guilt imposes. Behold, then, the perpetuity of life which the just enjoy—an enjoyment in which the wicked have no share! The blood of the just man who has suffered death cries out to God, whereas the sinner's life is like that of a fugitive from justice.[16]

(38) Once the crime is admitted at the very inception of this sinful act of parricide, then the divine Law of God's mercy should be immediately extended. If punishment is forthwith inflicted on the accused, then men in the exercise of justice would in no way observe patience and moderation, but would straightway condemn the defendant to punishment. God in His providence gives this sort of verdict so that magistrates might learn the virtues of magnanimity and patience, that they may not be unduly hasty in their eagerness to punish or, because of immature deliberation, condemn a man in his innocence. This would serve as a precedent not to impose a harsh penalty on some troublesome defendant and at the same time not permit a person to go unpunished who has shown no indications that he is sorry for his crime. God drove Cain out of His presence[17] and sent him into

15 Scylla betrayed her own father.
16 Cf. Gen. 4.10-12.
17 Cf. Gen. 4.16.

exile far away from his native land, so that he passed from a life of human kindness to one which was more akin to the rude existence of a wild beast. God, who preferred the correction rather than the death of a sinner,[18] did not desire that a homicide be punished by the exaction of another act of homicide. Wherefore, punishment is meeted out seventy times sevenfold on Lamech,[19] because a person who does not reform even after a conviction has taken place commits a more serious fault. Cain had sinned at a time previous to Lamech's crime. Lamech surely should have taken precautions to avoid what he notes as reprehensible in another person. Lamech's statement was in accordance with the decree of his Judge that no one should on any occasion consider it right to strike a guilty man. From the point of view of our faith, no one ought to slay a person who in the course of nature still would have time for repentance up to the very moment of his death. A guilty man—provided a premature punishment had not deprived him of life—could well procure forgiveness by redeeming himself by an act of repentance, however belated.

18 Cf. Ezech. 33.11.
19 Cf. Gen. 4.24.; 'Sevenfold vengeance shall be taken for Cain.'

INDEX

INDEX